THE STORYTELLER

MAP OF NEWTOWNARDS CIRCA 1850

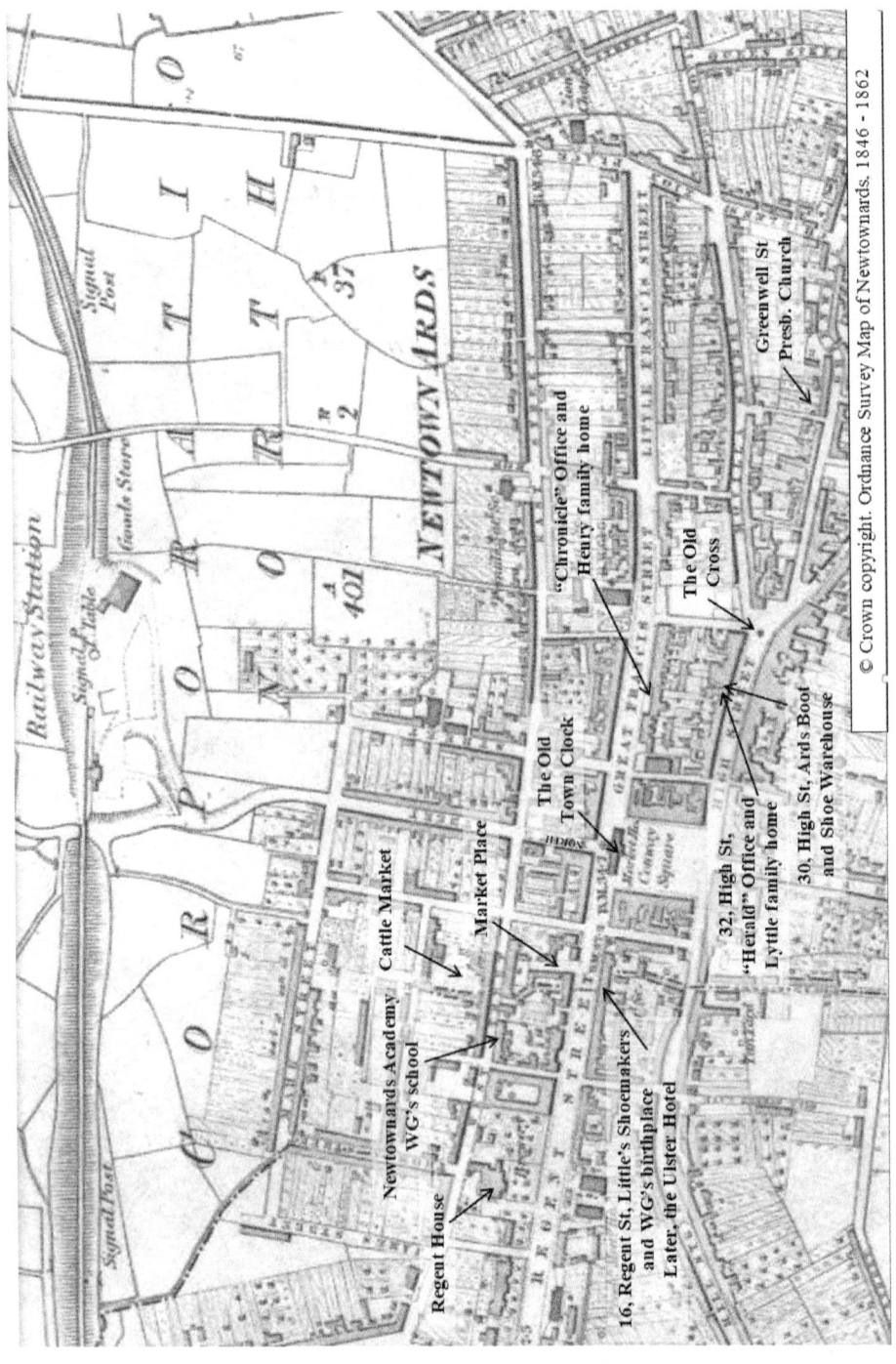

MAP OF BELFAST CIRCA 1860

MAP OF BANGOR CIRCA 1900

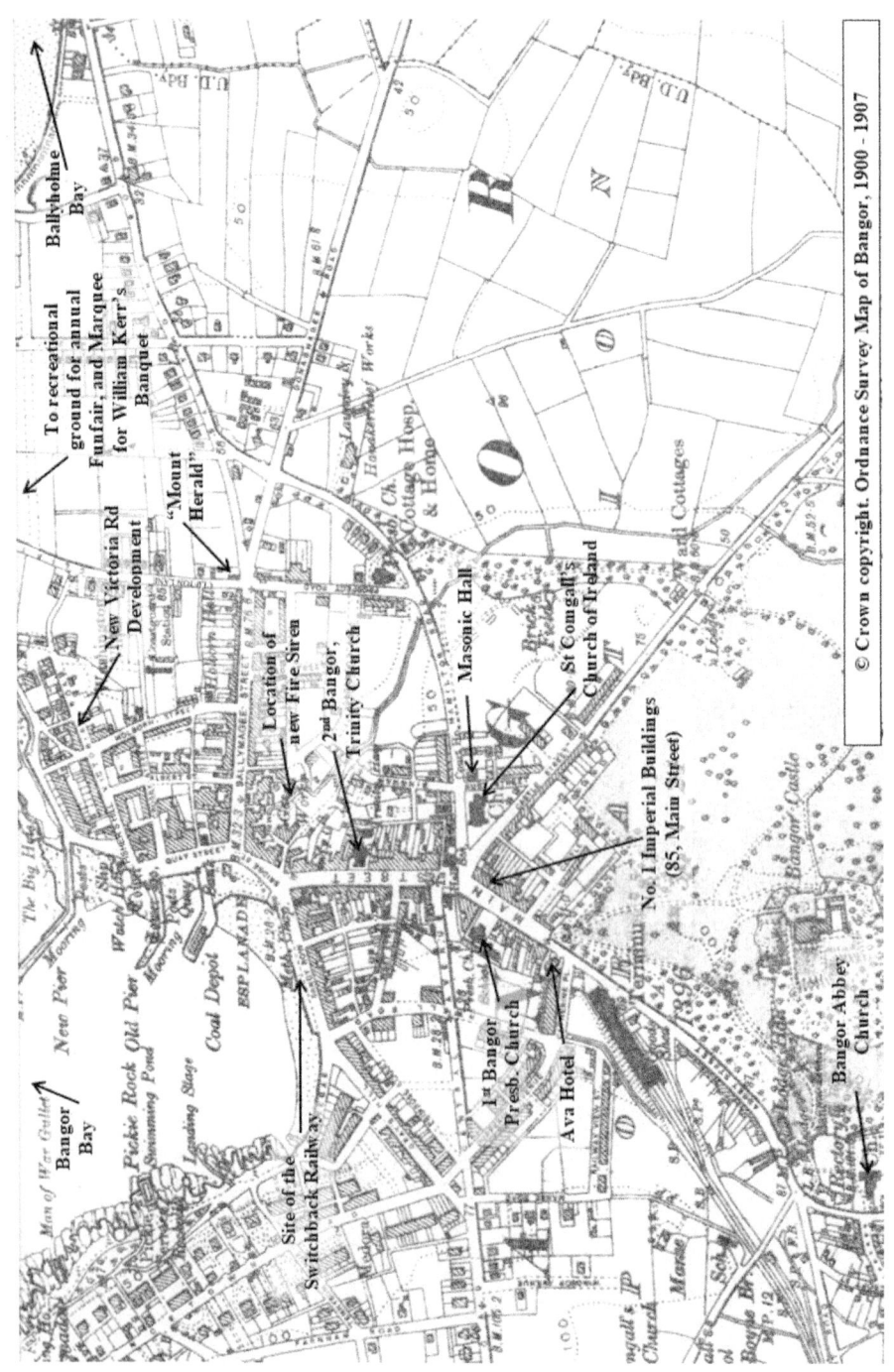

THE STORYTELLER

the improbable life of
provocative Ulster newspaper editor,
celebrated author and
hugely popular stage comedian

WG LYTTLE

by his great-grandson
AG LYTTLE

THE STORYTELLER

Published by AG Lyttle
Woking, Surrey

© 2021 AG Lyttle

All rights reserved. No part of this publication may be reproduced, stored in a retrieval system, or transmitted, in any form or by any means, including audio (apart from short quotations embodied in critical articles and reviews) without the prior written permission of the publisher.

November 2021
Book production and cover design by AG Lyttle
Printed by Kindle Direct Publishing
ISBN: 9798484888801
Imprint: Independently published

Front cover: "Robbin," WG Lyttle's stage persona.
Back cover: Stained glass window memorial to WG Lyttle in First Bangor Presbyterian Church. County Down. (See chapter 34, "Probate" and Appendix F, figures 26 to 28.)

Dedicated to my late father, GR Lyttle, who inspired in me, as a young boy, an admiration for my great-grandfather, WG Lyttle, and who faithfully passed on all the family anecdotes that have finally achieved a degree of permanence in these pages that record the improbable life of that inimitable Ulster Storyteller.

CONTENTS

Chptr.	Title	Page
	Maps	ii
	Acknowledgements	xi
	Foreword	xiii
	Prologue	1
1	A Storyteller Unveiled	5
2	The Great Hunger	10
3	Strange Pastimes	19
4	Speed Writing and a Punch Ball	30
5	A Move to Belfast and a Moving Picture Show	36
6	Temperance and Teaching	50
7	Keeping Books and Lending Books	60
8	A Parting and a Promotion	68
9	"Robin" Appears in the Papers…	79
10	…And on Stage…	91
11	…And in a Book	110
12	Live and Let Live	134
13	Universal Acclaim, Almost	158
14	Adversaries	169
15	Moving On	182
16	Toasted	191
17	The Duel	203
18	The Black Ghost of Ballygarvan	219

Chptr.	Title	Page
19	The Litigant	231
20	Demoted	244
21	Archibald Thompson	249
22	Hot off the Press	266
23	First Editions *Sons of the Sod* and *Betsy Gray*	277
24	The Battle of the Editors	288
25	Relationships—Broken and Forged	299
26	A Setback	313
27	The Strangling Angel	323
28	Retribution	334
29	Bankrupt	348
30	Sir Wesley?	357
31	The Banquet	375
32	The Herald under Fire but "Robin" Excels on Page and Stage	393
33	On the Move Again	410
34	Legacy	428
35	Lives Taken	448
36	Passing the Baton	461
	Epilogue	468

Apndx.	Title	Page
A	Lyttle Family Tree	472
B	The Works of WG Lyttle	473
C1	Humorous Readings by Robin. Volume I	481

Apndx.	Title	Page
C2	Humorous Readings by Robin, Volume II	482
C3	Readings by Robin, Volume III	483
C4	Robin's Readings, Volume I—The Adventures of Paddy M'Quilan	484
C5	Robin's Readings, Volume II—The Adventures of Robin Gordon	485
C6	Robin's Readings, Volume III—Life in Ballycuddy	486
C7	Robin's Readings, Volume I, II and III—Omnibus Edition	487
C8	Sons of the Sod—a Tale of County Down	488
C9	Betsy Gray, or Hearts of Down—a Tale of Ninety-eight	489
C10	Daft Eddie, or Smugglers of Strangford Lough	490
C11	The Bangor Season—What's to be Seen and How to See It	491
C12	Robin's Further Readings and Robin's Rhymes	492
C13	Lyttle's North Down Directory and Almanac	493
D	Robin as a Stage Performer—a Few Opinions of the Press	494
E	Images of WG Lyttle and Family	497
F	Photos of Locations Associated with WG Lyttle	503
G	Prominent Bangorians in 1891	514
H	Who Really Wrote Daft Eddie?	515
Bibliography		522
Companion Volumes		526
Author's note		527

ACKNOWLEDGEMENTS

I am most grateful to the many people who have assisted me in the production of this biography without whom I should never have managed the task. Terence Bowman provided invaluable help in the early stages with genealogical research. Michael Edgar helped me establish the site of the Ulster Hotel in Newtownards, where WG Lyttle is believed to have been born. And Sandra Milsop discovered clues to where WG's widow, Annie, was buried. Philip Robinson kindly proofread and suggested improvements to a few passages that I have written in Ulster-Scots. I owe an enormous debt of gratitude to Horace Reid who read the whole manuscript in draft and made many excellent and helpful suggestions for its enhancement.

I am grateful to Heather McGuicken and Leanne Briggs of the North Down Museum in Bangor for giving me access to three ledgers of historical newspaper clippings; to Elspeth Healey of Kansas University, to the Linen Hall Library in Belfast and the British Library in London, to Archiseek.com, the Victoria Web, Flickriver.com and the County Down Spectator, all of whom, when approached, kindly raised no objections to my using a number of images from their archives; also to Derek Rowlinson and Mark Thompson who allowed me to include photos of their copies of some early editions of WG Lyttle's books. I would like to thank Hugh Warden, who very kindly allowed me to view Betsy Gray's cottage on his land and took a picture of me beside it for this biography.

Although most of the other photographs illustrating *The Storyteller* are taken through my own lens, I must also thank, Colin Dickson, Ben Forde and his cousin, Mildred Sergeant and Gaynor Kane for generously supplying some family portraits. I am especially grateful to Michael Edgar, Trevor Low and Laura Spence, who most kindly agreed to venture out and take some specific photographs for me.

Also, an enormous thank you to my wife, Anita, and daughter, Suzy Baldwyn, for their labours of love in painstakingly proofreading the text. Inevitably, a few errors will have managed to escape all our diligence for which I can only apologise and accept full responsibility.

Finally, my thanks to all those who have urged me to write this long-awaited biography and encouraged me to complete it—not least to the many fans of my first historical thriller, *Dillon's Rising,* who kept asking when *The Storyteller* would be finished so I could start working on the next Dillon novel!

AG Lyttle, 2021

FOREWORD

By BBC NI TV's "Hame" presenter, Mark Thompson

"A jist write fur my freens aboot hame, an' if ony weel lerned buddy happens fur til see this, a hope they'll beer that in min'. They hae plenty till write gran books fur them, but there's no mony fowk bother their heids writin' ocht fur plain country workin' men..."[1]
—Humourous Readings by Robin, Volume II, Second Edition
by WG Lyttle (1886)

Right at the start of his publishing career, this is WG's manifesto of intent. My own love of his writings came through the influence of two aunts, both sides of my family deeply rooted for centuries in Lyttle country—the real location for his fictional Ballycuddy. My mother's folk are all from around Carrowdore and her sister Betty passed on to me a family heirloom copy of *Sons of the Sod*, a story set in the village. My father's folk are all from near Portavogie and his sister, Doris, gave me a copy of the *Mourne Observer* reprint of *Daft Eddie and the Smugglers of Strangford Lough* (some of its story takes place around Ballyeasborough, just down the road), and she often talked of *Betsy Gray and the Hearts of Down*. Unashamedly local and of the people, WG challenged established norms, lampooning local authority in *The Bangor Season*. He was a voice for the often marginalised and voiceless. I was, and remain, smitten.

In the first story in the famous green hardback edition of *Robin's Readings* our rustic hero travels to 1880s Belfast on "Yin Christmas

---

[1] *"I just write for my friends about home, and if any well-learned person happens to see this, I hope they'll bear that in mind. They have plenty to write grand books for them, but there's not many folk bother their heads writing anything for plain country working men..."*

Day" where those very same "weel learned buddys" mock his rural ways and speech. Reading it in my early 20s, so much of this particular story resonated with my own life experience, almost exactly a century later, of my first going to the 'big school' in Newtownards.

Once hugely popular, and with his work being reprinted in steady streams in the hundred years since they first appeared, those early copies are now hard to find. The Ullans Press and others have done a fine job in keeping the stories in print. In 30+ years of seeking and collecting rare Lyttle editions I still have relatively few originals, so it was a joy when AG (Tony) Lyttle made contact with me some years ago and he brought some of his archive for me to see. I have been delighted to share from my gatherings with Tony over the years.

But who was WG Lyttle? What can be known of his life and times, the context in which he lived, and the Ulster-Scots speaking community that he loved? There is no better person than Tony to bring the man to life once again.

Today, despite generations of exclusion—and a more recent generation of mis-handling by politics, the current affairs media and the public sector—thanks to the work of community-minded people like Tony, there is an energy around the Ulster-Scots language and traditions. It refuses to go away.

It is the right time to give WG his place in the pantheon. Not just his wonderful, renowned stories, or the communities and people that he loved, but the Storyteller, himself.

Mark Thompson, 2021

Prologue

1896

Who was the full-bearded, elderly gentleman lingering at the rear of the small crowd of soberly-dressed friends and acquaintances? Why was he wearing a blue swallowtail coat and loud, checked trousers? And why was no one remarking upon his inappropriate attire?

A fourth peal from the 15th century bell tower of the Abbey drifted off into the chill of the late autumn air.

The dying reverberations faded.

Silence returned.

Low in the west, weak rays from a lacklustre sun added a ruddy glow to the solemn faces gathered around the open grave. The clergyman shivered and drew his robes tighter across his chest. He glanced up at the clock tower. They ought to be leaving.

He knew the tall spire over the ancient timepiece had been added in more recent times but that the history of the Abbey grounds in Bangor, County Down stretched back to the 6th century; that the original Abbey had been one of the most important seats of learning in the whole of Ireland. Now Church of Ireland, it had finally been closed 14 years previously in favour of the much

THE STORYTELLER

newer, and more central, St Comgall's on Hamilton Street.

The churchyard of the Abbey was still, however, the town's favoured burial ground. Its gravestones named United Irishmen and Scottish planters, customs officers and buccaneers, diplomats and mill owners, clergymen and criminals. It was to this disparate company of the departed that the sombre gathering of mourners had committed their friend on a cold Tuesday afternoon in November, 1896.

The hands of the Abbey clock clicked on to one minute after the hour of four o'clock.

'A tragic loss to the community.'

'Indeed it is. Very sad.'

'Very sad. He'll be sorely missed.'

'Och, he will. Though a few Town Commissioners will be none too sorry to see the last of his scathing comments in the columns of the *Gazette*.'

'Aha, you could be right. But sure wasn't it his write-ups about their Board meetings that was half the fun of reading his paper?'

'Oh it was, sure enough.'

'And his funny stories, of course. Life in Ballycuddy.'

'Ah... wonderful, wonderful. A great storyteller. Did you ever catch him on stage reading one of his yarns?'

'Oh, I did, ay. All dressed up as that well-to-do country farmer fellow from the Ards.'

' "Robin," ay; with his big bushy beard and blue swallowtail coat.'

'Ah, you couldn't help but laugh along with him.'

'But he was nobody's fool. A sharp wit on stage and off. Not afraid to speak his mind—though I dare say there were occasions when he might have been wiser to say a mite less.'

PROLOGUE

'Ah, we'd have all been the poorer if he had, though. He was one of a kind.'

'He was.'

'A quare clever man.'

'We've lost him far too soon.'

'We have; we have, indeed. Far too soon.'

As these comments continued amongst the crowd at the graveside, no-one appeared to give any attention to the figure of the old man in the blue swallowtail coat and loud, checked trousers. He managed to slip amongst them without attracting a glance.

'He wus aye yin gye an' guid freen tae me,' he said to a man at his side, in his Ulster-Scots vernacular.[2] The gentleman made no audible response.

Moving on, he remarked to another, 'He wud tak me till places A'd niver hae draimit o' gaun masel'. But A was aye bravelie wi the twa o' us thegither.'[3]

No one seemed to be making way for him yet he was soon right at the front of the gathering by the open grave and looking down at the wooden coffin that concealed the remains of the man who he professed had meant life itself to him.

'A'll miss him sair. Och, A hae nae doot yous aa wull, but A'm thinkin maybe nane sae muckle as masel'.'[4]

No one else spoke.

No one noticed as the old gentleman bent low and scooped up some dirt. He threw it and watched it fall soundlessly onto the lid of the coffin.

---

[2] 'He was always one very good friend to me.'

[3] 'He would take me to places I'd never have dreamt of going myself. But I was always alright with the two of us together.'

[4] 'I'll miss him sorely. Oh, I have no doubt you all will, but I'm thinking maybe none so much as myself.'

THE STORYTELLER

'It's hard tae tak it in that ye'r deid, ma oul freen. A'll ne'er forget ye. Unnerstan that, Wesley Lyttle, A winnae. Ne'er in a hunner year.' [5]

Others were drifting away now from the last resting place of their good friend and colleague, leaving only the waiting sexton behind, leaning on his shovel. The elderly, bearded gentleman in the blue swallowtail coat and loud, checked trousers, it seemed, had already departed.

---

[5] 'It's hard to take it in that you're dead, my old friend. I'll never forget you. Understand that, Wesley Lyttle, I won't. Never in a hundred years.'

Chapter 1 – A STORYTELLER UNVEILED

"A man of ability and indomitable perseverance"—the *Belfast News-Letter*;

"A brilliant and graceful writer, a true humourist and an accomplished poet"—on his tombstone;

"A warm and generous nature"—the *Irish News*;

"A troublesome intermeddler... wallowing in the gutter, raking up all the vile charges he can gather against respectable people... inventing malicious gossip"—the *Newtownards Chronicle*.

Wesley Greenhill Lyttle, or WG, as he is still often affectionately known over a century on, provoked many and varied descriptions from contemporary sources.

Who was he, really—the true Wesley Lyttle? A man of indomitable perseverance—or a troublesome meddler? A brilliant writer—or one who raked-up vile charges? A warm and generous person—or a malicious gossip?

Over the decades we have been disappointingly short of information about this celebrated, late nineteenth century, Ulster writer, journalist and acclaimed raconteur. Now, for the first time, *The Storyteller* uncovers the man behind the public face. Public faces, in fact, for there was not one but many.

Multifaceted

WG Lyttle is best remembered today as the author of one of Ireland's most popular and enduring novels—*Betsy Gray or Hearts of Down, a Tale of Ninety-Eight*. Set in his native North Down, it is a semi-

THE STORYTELLER

documentary account of the 1798 rebellion. First published in 1887[6], it was, and has remained, so popular that it has gone through 14 editions over the years since then. The most recent, from Books Ulster in 2015, is available today on Amazon in print and e-book formats. He wrote other books, too, including a number of anthologies of humorous short stories. At the height of his career, as we shall see, his books had already sold over 50,000 copies.

As well as being a writer, WG was something of a showman. As a young man he toured Ireland as the presenter of a diorama called, *Ireland, its Scenery, Music and Antiquities*, one of the first, so-called, "moving pictures" shows. In later life, he took to the stage and enjoyed enormous local fame as a comic storyteller in the guise of an elderly country farmer from "Ballycuddy, somewhere in the Ards Peninsula." The northern edition of the Daily Mail, published in Glasgow, wrote of the "force and vigour he displays as a writer. His home-spun is mirth-provoking in a high degree… The dialect in which he writes bears the strongest possible resemblance to that of the West of Scotland; yet we are assured it is a pure reproduction of the speech of the common people in County Down, where the author was brought up and still resides."

Indeed, WG regularly drew forth gales of laughter from packed audiences when performing his droll stories in the broad Ulster-Scots dialect he knew from his youth. He brought the magic touch of his humour to the preoccupations of his Presbyterian neighbours. Courtship, child-rearing, debates at the General Assembly, the local flower show, or the merits of newfangled electrical lighting—just a few of the eclectic mix of subjects with which he entertained and delighted his audiences, mainly across north-east Ulster and southern Scotland. His written legacy still provides linguistic scholars with some of the finest written examples of late 19th century Ulster-Scots as it was used in County Down.

There was, too, the face of the diligent businessman who worked first as a young legal clerk for a firm of solicitors, using his self-taught shorthand skills in the courts; then as a teacher—the first to teach

---

[6] Not 1888, as hitherto believed (see Chapter 23 – "First edition")

1 - A STORYTELLER UNVEILED

shorthand in Ulster; as a librarian, establishing a Circulating Library franchise; and later running his own accountancy business.

While WG worked to earn enough money to feed his growing family, he did not neglect his obligations to those less fortunate. He joined the Good Templars and laboured tirelessly in his spare time for this temperance fraternity in helping people with alcohol addiction and their families. He started up a new Good Templars lodge in his own part of Belfast, and eventually became Grand Worthy Secretary to the Grand Lodge of Ireland—the third highest rank in the Independent Order of Good Templars.

Apart from writing his famous novel and other books, this multifaceted gentleman is also remembered as the proprietor and editor of Bangor's first newspaper, the *North Down Herald and Bangor Gazette*. His self-taught journalistic skills and satirical sense of humour quickly won his newspaper a large circulation which he was always striving to expand. However, when goaded by a perceived injustice, or perhaps the failings of the Bangor Town Commissioners, his sometimes acerbic personality as an editor would take over—in marked contrast to his genial approach as a stage performer and storyteller. His critical editorials in the *Gazette* won him few friends on the Board of Commissioners. Indeed, at one stage, they banned his reporters from attending their meetings!

It was also through his journalism that he made a life-long enemy of the editor of the nearby *Newtownards Chronicle*. The feud between these two rival newspapermen contributed to WG's appearance on a libel charge and, ultimately in the bankruptcy court.

Background

How Wesley Lyttle managed to overcome both those major setbacks and many more, is revealed in the pages of this new biography. Readers will also find glimpses of the Victorian-era history of Belfast and, later, of his adopted Bangor—its churches, local politicians, lawyers, and property developers, the importance of its burgeoning tourist industry and the development of its infrastructure—new streets and housing, mains water and gas, and a fire service. Many of Lyttle's local contemporaries feature, too, mostly among the Presbyterian community, some of whom seemed overly fond of litigation. Although WG did not emphasise his church affiliations in his weekly newspaper columns, his "Ballycuddy" short stories clearly reflect his own Presbyterianism. It was obviously a denomination with which he was thoroughly familiar.

There is insight, too, into the newspaper industry in North Down and Belfast at the time—the titles, personalities, printing methods, sub-contracting, apprenticeships and so on, are all touched upon.

Through all of this is woven Wesley's own story: that of a man always ready to embrace modern advances such as the telephone, for example, while still delighting in bygone tales of Ulster lore; a down-to-earth pragmatist who yet experienced the terror of the supernatural; a fun-loving family man, whose nearest and dearest knew pain, estrangement—and murder!

He was a man to whom life brought much tragedy. Of his immediate family of nine, six died long before their time. In an effort to compensate, he worked hard to bring practical help or uproarious entertainment to others. His journalism was a blend of confrontational reporting, light-hearted and humorous write-ups of local events and sometimes foolhardy satire that could easily land him in trouble. Ultimately, however, it is as an author and storyteller that Wesley Greenhill Lyttle is remembered. Yet, as we shall see, he was so much more than simply, "The man who wrote Betsy Gray."

Sources

Unlike some biographers, I have not had the good fortune of being able to draw insight from a stack of personal letters or diaries written by WG; nothing of that nature exists. There are, of course, within the family, anecdotes that have been handed down which throw light upon the type of man he was, but of his own journalism only a limited amount has survived. WG's narrative, however, can be recreated by accessing what was written about him in other journals of the day.

An online trawl through the British Newspaper Archive and time spent in the reading rooms of the British Library in London, and Linen Hall Library in Belfast proved most rewarding. There is also one invaluable remaining archive of some of WG's newspaper articles. The North Down Museum in Bangor is home to three ledgers full of

1 - A STORYTELLER UNVEILED

newspaper clippings, many from WG's own newspaper, dating from late 1886 to 1892.[7]

Birth, marriage and death certificates have been checked where possible; unfortunately, in Ireland many such records do not exist prior to 1864. I have had the invaluable help of Terence Bowman[8] in researching these genealogical records.

Apart from a few short biographical pieces written by others—each very brief and not always factually accurate, I had just one other source. What is to be gleaned about my great-grandfather, himself, from what he wrote in his novels and other publications has, with a little literary detective work, proved most rewarding. In the next chapter, for example, we shall see how he left us clues about the very house that was his childhood home.

In recounting WG's story, I have, in a few instances, broken away from traditional straight reporting of facts and related a dramatized reconstruction of certain events which are worthy of such treatment. These passages are plainly signposted and indented, with a different font to differentiate them from the main text. All the important facts in the reconstructions are true.

So my sources in preparing this biography comprise WG's own books, newspaper archives, the traditional potted biographies already in the media, genealogical research and family knowledge handed down the generations, together with background historical data from the period in which he lived.

What, then, of the young Wesley's start in life? When was he born, and where? And what of the catastrophic circumstances that could easily have ended his days when they had barely begun?

---

[7] I am indebted to the curator, Heather McGuicken, for granting me access to these.

[8] Terence Bowman, retired editor of the *Mourne Observer*, is the author of a number of books of an historical and recent historical nature, including *People's Champion – the life of Alexander Bowman, Pioneer of Labour Politics in Ireland*, Ulster Historical Foundation, 1997; *Bangor in the Sixties*, 2009; *Bangor in the Seventies*, 2011; *Bangor in the Eighties*, 2012; and with Hugh Robinson, *The Ards in the Sixties*, 2013; and with Tim Johnson, *The Ards in the Seventies*, 2015 – all published by Ballyhay Books.

THE STORYTELLER

Chapter 2 – THE GREAT HUNGER

1844 – 1849

Surname

The first thing to discover about WG, is that he was born into a family surnamed "Little," with an i.

No family documents have been discovered prior to his marriage certificate, dated 23rd December 1864. But on this, his name and signature are clearly shown as Wesley Little. The same certificate shows his father's name as Wesley Little whose occupation is given as "shopkeeper".

There would come a time when circumstances decided WG to adopt the less common spelling of his surname, replacing the i with a y (see Chapter 5—"Name Change"). By the time his first child was born, in 1866, he was signing his name, "Wesley Lyttle." He, and all his children and their descendants, have been "Lyttles" ever since.

But it was little Wesley Little who was born on Monday, 15th April in 1844—the year work began on the construction of the new Queen's Bridge across the River Lagan in Belfast. Newtownards, the town of his birth, was at that time a community of some 6000 citizens.[9] It lies at the top of Strangford Lough in County Down about ten miles east of the city[10] where the new bridge was being built. On that late spring evening only the slimmest silver crescent of the old moon could be seen in the darkened sky, shining its meagre light on the dwelling where the new-born baby lay.

---

[9] Population according to *A Topographical Dictionary of Ireland, 1837*, Samuel Lewis.

[10] Belfast was not made a city until 1888 but for ease of reference and to distinguish it from the lesser towns in the region I have taken the liberty of referring to it as the city from the start of this biography.

2- THE GREAT HUNGER

Birthplace

Potted biographies of WG are vague about where he was born. Most say, unhelpfully, "near Newtownards," or similar. The granite monolith by his grave in Bangor Abbey states that he was born "*at* Newtownards," not just *near* the town. But the real clues come from his own later writings.

In a story called "A Nicht in Newton,"[11] first published in the *Newtownards Chronicle* in January, 1879, WG writes in the guise of the old country farmer, "Robin Gordon," who had by that time become his alter-ego. He says, upon entering Newtownards on one occasion, that he was pleased to be back "in his native town"—further evidence that, like "Robin," WG was, indeed, born in Newtownards. In another story, "The Newton Flower Show," as "Robin" is driving his wife, Peggy, and their grandson along Regent Street on their way to the Newtownards Flower Show, he points out a building that was then called the "Ulster Hotel".

> '*A niver pass that hoose but a think o' them that's awa tae their lang hame, an' a fancy a see a wee lad in petticoats playin' aboot the daur. That's the hoose "Rabin" was born in, Peggy.*'[12]

Here we have what must surely be a reference to Wesley's own birthplace. Why else would he bother to have "Robin" mention the building at all, especially one that had since changed use from its former purpose as a private dwelling? The "Ulster Hotel" was situated on the south side of Regent Street, shown as number 18 on a contemporary census form. An advert for the sale of the "Ulster Hotel" that appeared in the *Irish News* in September, 1901 confirms its location as "situate in what is unquestionably the best position in the town, being exactly opposite the markets" (just beyond where the Queen's Hall now stands.) This identifies the building as the premises

---

[11] "A Night in Newton [Newtownards]."

[12] 'I never pass that house but I think of those that are away to their long home [their grave], and I fancy I see a little lad in petticoats playing about the door. That's the house "Robin" was born in, Peggy.'

currently numbered 16 which is occupied (in 2021) by Ellison's Health and Wellbeing, Ards Dental Practice and Man Cave. It seems clear that this, now mid-terrace property, formerly No. 18, and now 16, Regent Street and at one time the "Ulster Hotel", was previously a shop with living accommodation above that was leased to Wesley Little Snr. This was the house where WG was born and grew up.[13]

When "The Newton Flower Show" first appeared in print in the *Newtownards Chronicle* WG describes his ("Robin's") birthplace as "Mrs M'Kee's Hotel" and, indeed, it is a Mrs Anna M'Kee who is listed as the first proprietor of the "Ulster Hotel" in June, 1876. When WG was later editing the story for inclusion in an anthology, he changed the reference to the less intimate, but more definitive, "Ulster Hotel." It would seem that he wanted to leave no doubt about the location of his childhood home.

Wesley Little Snr

Knowing WG's birthplace, allows us to deduce a little more information about his father, who, as stated above, was described on Wesley's marriage certificate simply as a "shopkeeper." The Post Office Street Directory of 1846 for Newtownards, lists a Wesley Little on Regent Street as a "boot and shoemaker." So WG was the son of a cobbler.

Some forty years later, in his 1885 travel guide, *The Bangor Season*, WG would praise "M'Kee's far-famed Scrabo[14] Shoes" that could be purchased at the Ards Boot and Shoe Warehouse on High Street in Newtownards. It would appear that, before opening their hotel, the M'Kees may have taken over Wesley Little Snr's business. No death certificates for WG's father and mother have been found, which probably means they died before 1864 when State registration of deaths began in Ireland. WG once seemed to hint that his father died in the Workhouse (see Chapter 17, "Snubbed") and, as we shall see shortly, his mother could already have passed away.

It seems entirely possible that, with his mother gone and his father's health rapidly declining, Wesley, not yet twenty, had to

---

[13] See photograph in Appendix F, Figure 1.

[14] Scrabo Hill to the south-west of the little town of Newtownards dominated the surrounding countryside.

arrange the sale of the business to the M'Kees and for his father to be admitted to the Workhouse Infirmary to be nursed through his last days. A dozen or so years later, Mr M'Kee then decided to convert the premises to an hotel setting up his wife as the proprietress, while he moved the shoemaking business to High Street.

WG was to remain firm friends with the M'Kees and his gratitude for their help over what would have been a very difficult time is reflected in the 'free' advertisement he subsequently gave the Ards Boot and Shoe Warehouse.

Greenhill

So, with just a little detective work, we know that WG was born, the son of a Newtownards cobbler, above a shop that, in 2021, is No. 16, Regent Street.

His parents decided to name him Wesley after his father, but as to why they chose to christen their son Wesley *Greenhill* Little no evidence has been found. No trace has yet been discovered of his mother's identity. Could she have been a Miss Greenhill? As to her first name, there is a tradition that the first son of a marriage is named after his maternal grandfather and the first daughter after her paternal grandmother. WG would follow that tradition in the case of his firstborn son, John; he may have also done so with his first daughter, Agnes. So his mother may have been born, Agnes and possibly, Agnes Greenhill, but this can only be conjecture.[15]

Regarding his own name, however, as Wesley junior grew to manhood, he seldom used it in full. His signature on his Marriage Certificate is just Wesley Little. Sometimes he would include his middle initial and sign, Wesley G. or just W. G. before his surname. In modern times, when he is remembered, it is often simply as WG. This soubriquet has been used habitually within his descendant family as well. As a result, his full name has not been known to many of his latter-day fans and readers. To most of them he was always W. G. Lyttle, or just WG.

---

[15] See family tree in Appendix A

THE STORYTELLER

Wesley Guard

When the *Belfast News-Letter* published his obituary in their morning edition following his death, they printed his name in full, giving it as Wesley Guard Lyttle (the reporter possibly mixing up the name with that of a prominent Methodist minister of the time, the Rev Wesley Guard). Down through the years from then, whenever newspapers mentioned him and his writings, he has invariably been referred to (until comparatively recently) as Wesley Guard Lyttle. This persisted to such an extent that even within his own family, my father, WG's grandson, was unsure whether his middle name was Guard or Greenhill, although he was inclined towards the latter.

I am indebted to Kenneth Robinson[16] who (in an essay on W. G. Lyttle included in a 2008 re-publication of one of WG's novels) was first to reveal that the probate of his will shows his name to be Wesley Greenhill Lyttle. I have since found that on the birth certificate of one of his children he also used his full name, Wesley Greenhill Lyttle.

So young Wesley Greenhill lived and grew up above his father's shop and could often be seen, when a toddler in petticoats, playing on his own around the open front door (according to "Robin", at any rate.) Although Mr and Mrs Little would have had plenty of accommodation for a larger family, no evidence has come to light that Wesley had any siblings. Could his mother have died in childbirth? Or perhaps through the terrible circumstances that came about only a few years after her son was born…

Potatoes

Beyond the town, the land around Newtownards is renowned for its fertility. Grain harvests were plentiful and flax provided the raw material for the mills that were bringing a new prosperity to the little town, although home looms were still providing much of the employment. The constant clattering of the flying shuttles hitting the wooden frames of the looms could be heard through open windows

---

[16] Kenneth Robinson is the author of *North Down and Ards in 1798*, North Down Heritage Centre, 1998 and has edited Thomas Ledlie Birch's *A Letter from an Irish Emigrant*, 2005 and *William Sampson's Memoirs*, 2007 published by Athol Books, amongst other titles.

2- THE GREAT HUNGER

and doorways wherever you wandered through the streets. Newtownards was very much a weavers' town.

It was also the market town for the surrounding farmland and, along with the flax and cereals, there was another crop that was vital to the survival of the people. The fluvial and glacial deposits over the underlying bed of sandstone to the south and west of Newtownards provided a rich loam for its cultivation. Many would say that no better potato can be found in the land than one grown in the lee of Scrabo Hill.

Potatoes had long been the staple diet of the Irish peasantry throughout the island, being one of the few crops that would also grow on the scraps of land left over to them by their absentee landlords. Fortunately, potatoes are one of the best all-round source of nutrition there is—second only to eggs for protein—and growing them is the world's most efficient way of turning earth, water and hard sweat into a nourishing product. Potatoes were fed to the cattle and chickens, too, thus also providing the tenant farmers with their meat, milk and eggs.

Around about the time of Wesley's first birthday or a little later, a clipper arrived in Ireland carrying passengers from America. Unused food from the voyage was dumped, including potatoes bearing spores that, over recent years, had been making their way up through the American eastern states all the way from the Toluca Valley in central Mexico.

Blight

As the summer of 1845 wore on, Irish farmers were concerned to notice brown freckles appearing on the leaves of their potato plants. Soon whole fields were mottled with dark patches and when the potatoes were harvested many of them were rotten and inedible. Potato blight had come to Ireland's shores, as it had to mainland Europe and Great Britain, too, on other American vessels. In Ireland, however, the poor were utterly dependant upon the potato crop, which was reduced by over a third—a third of their major source of nutrition. There were hungry bellies throughout the land that winter.

The following year the blight hit hard again. This time three-quarters of the crops were nothing but mushy, smelly tubers tending to liquefy. The first deaths were recorded due to starvation. In 1847 the stock of seed potatoes was low and, although an average yield was obtained the tonnage of potatoes harvested was far below what was needed to feed the millions whose diet depended upon them. By '48, the crop was still only two-thirds of normal.

As a direct result of the blight in Ireland more than a million people died, either from starvation or disease, which, in their weakened state, they were unable to fight. Two million more swelled the numbers deciding to leave their homeland for good—mostly to Canada and the United States, and some to England and other parts of Europe, or to Australia.

Throughout this period the absentee landlords demanded their usual rents from the peasant farmers who had little or no income with which to pay. The landowners continued to export the abundant grain harvests to the mainland. In addition, vast quantities of other food items—livestock, fish, vegetables, lard, butter and more was shipped to England and Scotland. Much of this came from the areas in the south and west of Ireland that were worst affected by the potato scarcity.

But it was not only the poorer, Catholic areas that were badly affected. Emily Mark-Fitzgerald, in her book, *Commemorating the Irish Famine: Memory and the Monument* writes that "districts and towns in eastern Ulster, many of them predominantly Protestant, suffered greatly. Quakers compared Newtownards, in Co Down, with Skibbereen"[17]

The workhouse in Newtownards, which was first opened in 1841, three years before Wesley's birth, was extended to help meet the demand. The infirmary was stretched to bursting. Sheds and sleeping galleries were built in the grounds to accommodate an additional 200 inmates.

A comparison of the 1841 and 1851 census records reveals that Down's population fell by 44,000 over the decade, due primarily to death and emigration. The *Downpatrick Recorder* reported, in April 1849:

---

[17] Skibberine in County Cork suffered one of the greatest losses of life due to the famine.

2- THE GREAT HUNGER

> *We observe, with regret, that much of the wealth of this county is going to America and other parts of the world. It is a bad sign for Ulster when the Down Peasantry are leaving these shores. Within the last few weeks 2,000 people have left Newtownards, Lecale and other parts of this county for emigration to America with their talents and money.*

Weavers

The failure of the potato crop soon began to cause a shortage of other food stuffs. This forced up prices. People were struggling and had little or no money to spend on new linen. Orders for cloth dried up leaving numerous Newtownards weavers with no work. This, in turn, meant the Ards farmers could not get a good price for their flax if they could sell it at all. No money meant no food. Kind-hearted people shared what little they had with those who had nothing. Soup kitchens were set up and desperate folk queued from seven in the morning until late at night, sometimes fighting to get to the front to have their cans filled with something to sustain their families for another day.

Such events are vividly described in a contemporary account published in the local newspaper, some 25 years later, under the title *Clatterdom*. In his introduction, the author writes:

> *Well do I remember the famine of 1847 and 1848. When I call to mind the harrowing scenes I have beheld I can almost fancy them once more at hand. They were sad, disastrous times. Over the whole country starvation staring the people in the face, and the black death following like a grizzly, grizzly shade... I was in Newtownards during those years. I saw with my own eyes all the scenes I have attempted to describe... If you, my readers, are pained by the sad recitals of my sketches, you may rest assured that he who wrote them was not less pained.*[18]

---

[18] From *Clatterdom* by "John" (full name withheld), serialised in the *Newtownards Independent* from June, 1874.

THE STORYTELLER

The Editor of the newspaper prefaced the start of the story by adding that "Our readers may rest satisfied we will not let them be too much 'pained,' for when the story takes a painful shape we will save them by cutting it short."

Clatterdom's harrowing, eye-witness account reveals how, even in the more affluent northern part of Ireland, the good people of Newtownards suffered much deprivation during the Great Hunger.

Survival

Revenue from the shoemaking business must have plummeted as the weavers and farmers struggled to afford food, never mind new shoes. The Little household would have felt the pinch along with their neighbours. But somehow they managed to keep enough food on the table—even at the inflated prices which prevailed—for young Wesley to survive those terrible years.

Undoubtedly, though, they would have known of some who succumbed to hunger or disease and probably, too, had bid farewell to old friends they were never likely to see again, as they sailed for Canada or the New England States. In these circumstances, if she survived giving birth to him, it is not impossible that Wesley's own mother may have become one more statistic in the number of lives lost to the Great Hunger.

This, then, was the world into which Wesley Greenhill Little was born. A world in which thousands of his contemporary babes and toddlers in Ireland went to bed, night after night, with empty bellies, crying themselves to sleep and breaking their mothers' hearts. A world where countless hundreds throughout the land never saw their second birthdays.

It was a world, nevertheless, in which Wesley was destined to survive. A world that was to shape the formative years of his childhood. A world where it's possible that one unpredictable outcome of the Great Hunger ignited a spark within him that would shape the course of his future many years later.

Chapter 3 – STRANGE PASTIMES

1850 – 1862

The spark that linked back to the Great Hunger would not, in fact, be kindled in Wesley until he reached the age of thirteen. We shall come to it presently.

Back when he was still a toddler, his parents may well have seen an item in a Belfast newspaper about the spotting of a pair of Great Auks on Belfast Lough on 23 September, 1845. It was a rare sighting and worthy of note. No one realised at the time, however, that it would be the very last time any of these huge birds would be seen alive by human eyes.

Although Wesley was too young to have remembered being a contemporary of the now extinct Great Auk, he would certainly cherish the memory of Monday, 6th May in 1850. He had not long turned six and it was a day when it must have seemed to him that half the town had turned out. Wesley would have trotted along holding his father's hand and joined a throng of folk all walking up beyond North Street. The occasion was the Gala Opening of the latest station on the Belfast and County Down Railway line. The route from the city went through Dundonald and Comber and now extended as far as Newtownards. The Littles were sure to have been among the crowds approaching the new, gaily painted Ticket Office and spreading out along the platform. How Wesley must have thrilled to his first sight of a locomotive as it puffed into the station, its gleaming pistons belching steam, driving the iron wheels that screeched to a halt near where the young boy stood. And how he must have jumped as the fireman let off a deafening blast on the engine's steam whistle.

THE STORYTELLER

Schooling

Apart from the excitement of the steam train and all the railway paraphernalia, it also meant time off school, always a cause for rejoicing. In the traditional mini-biographies re-produced down the years by the media, WG is described as "self-taught", which was true of his working life. As a child, however, although school attendance was not yet compulsory, Wesley's father wanted him to learn his letters and sums, at least.

Since 1831, multi-denominational "National Schools", usually small, one-room affairs, had been established across Ireland to provide free primary education. This new National education system proved popular with the public, including the Littles. From 1849 when Wesley was five—the year before the railway arrived in Newtownards—it is believed that he attended the Newtownards Academy in West Street, where he would have been schooled in writing and arithmetic, history, geography and elocution. And where he, no doubt, took the expected schoolboy ribbing about his name—probably "Little Wes".

Again, we have WG, himself to thank for leaving us a clue in his later writing about the school he attended. The following passage is from "The Newton Flower Show", from *Robin's Readings Vol II—The Adventures of Robin Gordon*. "Robin" says:

> '*A met Mister George Dickson as a wuz steppin' aboot, but he's growen that white A didnae ken him at furst. My, its nae time ava since him an' me wuz at skule thegither, in the hoose that used tae stan' whaur the merkets is noo.* '[19]

The markets ran northward from Regent Street through to West Street and there was, indeed, a school on West Street. This school, the Newtownards Academy, would have been within a couple of hundred

---

[19] 'I met Mister George Dickson as I was stepping about, but he's gone that white I didn't know him at first. My, it's no time at all since him and me were at school together, in the house that used to stand where the markets are now.'

3 - STRANGE PASSTIMES

yards of Wesley's own front door; it would have been an obvious choice for his father to send him there.

The Academy dates back at least as far as 1846. Its school governors would go on, in 1918, to purchase, from Peter Johnston, a local brewer, a regency mansion built further up Regent Street with stone quarried from the side of Scrabo Hill. They would turn their long-standing educational establishment into a grammar school for the town, accommodating its pupils in their newly-acquired building, "Regent House." So it would seem that, when he was five, Wesley commenced attending the Newtownards Academy in 1849—104 years before his great-grandson, yours truly, started at its successor, Regent House Preparatory School, in 1953.

It is interesting, too, to see from the above quote that Wesley could have been friends with George Dickson, the son of Alexander Dickson who started the famous Newtownards rose gardens, Dicksons of Hawlmark. George, however, would have been about twelve years older than Wesley so, perhaps, more a contemporary of the fictional "Robin" than of Wesley, himself. However, since he bothers to mention the school connection in his tale, it is possible that the older boy was acting as a monitor, helping Mr Douglas, the schoolmaster, when Wesley was there, and they became friends.

Dickson Roses is still flourishing in Newtownards in 2021. This photograph of a portrait of **George Dickson** was kindly provided by the current owner, Mr Colin Alexander Dickson. It shows the white hair and beard that "Robin" commented upon.

Casual work

Wesley would have attended school until 1854 when he reached the age of ten. On leaving, he would have worked in his father's shoe shop, fetching and carrying, making deliveries, gradually learning the trade. As he got a little older

THE STORYTELLER

he may have been allowed to make entries in the ledger and use his arithmetic skills to tot up columns and calculate the profits and losses.

In his spare time he probably did what many small boys enjoyed and popped into a neighbour's home when he heard the tell-tale clackity-clack to watch a weaver at work. Perhaps he earned the occasional farthing spinning thread to give the weaver's wife a brief respite from this task. But in a market town serving a farming community there was always plenty of casual work to which he may also have turned his hand as a growing lad. A weekly cattle market was held in West Street, almost opposite his school. Wesley may have spent time helping there, his keen ear picking out the accents and country expressions of the farmers up in town for the day. Then there was hay-making in summer; he could earn 4d to 6d a day (£1.80 – £2.70, in 2021) helping the womenfolk, who were paid 6d to 10d a day (£2.70 – £4.50). In September he would have further contact with the farming community when he and his pals would have joined in with everyone available to go *tatty howkin'*. After recovery from the blight years, it was always "all hands to the fore" when it came time to gather the potato harvest.

Through growing up with this background Wesley acquired his knowledge and love of the Ulster-Scots language[20] used by the country folk: the "hamely tongue" he was to put to such entertaining, not to say, profitable, use in later life.

Recreation

It wouldn't have been all work, of course. There would have been Sunday afternoon family walks out along the shores of Strangford Lough, or maybe, in summer, to view the worldwide prize-winning blooms in Alexander Dickson's magnificent rose gardens. Young Wesley would have stood, many a time, on tiptoe to peer over the fence at the wonderful blossoms the grown-ups were enthusing about as they walked along the road that bordered the Nursery Grounds,

---

[20] Although there are some who would claim that Ulster-Scots is not a language but merely a dialect of English, the definitive work on Ulster-Scots today, *The Hamely Tongue* by James Fenton describes it as a language, as does Dr Philip Robinson in his meticulous and exhaustive *Ulster-Scots—A Grammar of the Traditional Written & Spoken Language.*

3 - STRANGE PASSTIMES

always looking out to see if he could spot his older school friend, George Dickson, working among the bushes.

When he was eleven, there would have been added excitement on the first Thursday in September when the Littles would have joined the throngs entering Dickson's grounds for the Horticultural Society's first annual show in 1855; something which seemed to become a regular treat for the family, as in future years WG would enthuse about the event in his writing.[21]

Did he also, when his father allowed him, spend time with some of his young weaver pals on "Lazy Mondays"? The weaving trade picked up again once the Hunger Years were over and the weavers soon fell back into their old habits. They would be given a job and it would have to be delivered by Sunday. Early in the week there was no urgency but this often resulted in the weaver having to work late into the night on Saturday, and even into the early hours of Sunday morning, to complete the job on time. Because of this, they traditionally took Mondays off before starting a new job of work on Tuesday. It was called "Lazy Monday" and the younger lads would be off over the fields chasing butterflies and looking for birds' nests, or playing ball games.[22]

Wesley would surely have roamed the surrounding countryside with his friends. Perhaps to wander northwards, an apple in his pocket for lunch, to Tullynagardy where the Cullys Burn feeds the lakes behind the dams built in the early decades of the century to feed the new linen mills. Or further east to the old lead mines at Conlig where dangerous open shafts lay hidden by undergrowth, perhaps to discover a treasured piece of silvery galena discarded on a slag heap. Or foraging in the shallows of Strangford Lough to find sticklebacks and crabs amongst the seaweed.

---

[21] The reference to the annual Horticultural Society Show in Dickson's nursery grounds appears in WG Lyttle's, *The Bangor Season*, 1885. It is also the subject of his tale, *The Newton Flower Show,* from *Robin's Readings Vol II— The Adventures of Robin Gordon.*

[22] This is all documented in the aforementioned, eye-witness account, *Clatterdom,* serialised in the *Newtownards Independent* in 1874.

THE STORYTELLER

Strange pastimes

There were other forms of recreation open to the youthful Wesley. He might join in the team game of "shinney", whacking an old tin can about with wooden sticks. Or he would be one of the youngsters who crept with much stealth around the bushes with the eager intention of routing a hare for the older boys to shoot at. They would be ready with their horse pistols—so-called because they came in pairs with connected holsters that could be draped across the pommel of a saddle. Other lads brandished homemade firearms and together they shot at the wretched animal as it ran.[23]

A Christmas Day tradition that Wesley knew well, was "shooting at whites" for a goose. A white square of paper was attached to a five foot stake in the ground, as the target. The contestants took turns at firing shot at it from old Queen Anne flintlock pistols and the one with the most hits after three attempts won the goose. One of the best shots was a man by the name of Johnnie M'Closkey who used to take the young Wesley out shooting with him from time to time. In his novel, *Sons of the Sod* we read:

> *Johnnie M'Closkey was known as a dead shot. Many a time has the writer of this story, when a boy, accompanied him, and beheld, with a feeling of awe, how unerring was his aim.*[24]

It was likely on these trips that M'Closkey taught Wesley how to shoot. For he did learn to use a firearm, as is evidenced from the fact that in later life, when travelling around the country, he would carry one of the small modern revolvers for his personal protection, as many did in those days.

---

[23] WG describes these games in his novel, *Sons of the Sod*, published in 1886, which is set in the Ards area at the time when he would have been about ten years old.

[24] From *Sons of the Sod*, chapter XXXV

3 - STRANGE PASSTIMES

Scrabo Tower

But what about that spark that just may have shaped young Wesley's future? That unpredicted outcome of the Great Hunger? It came about in this fashion...

During the worst years of the potato famine a few of the more enlightened landlords granted some leeway to their impoverished tenants by reducing rents or allowing more time for them to be paid. They contributed to the soup kitchens and helped with other means of getting food to the starving.

Charles William Vane (formerly Stewart), 3rd Marquis of Londonderry owned much of the land around Newtownards. This included the shop premises and dwelling on Regent Street where the Littles lived, so he was their landlord. He was largely an "absentee" landlord and not particularly liked by his tenant farmers[25]. He did, however, provide some help during the famine years, perhaps influenced by his rich young wife, Frances Anne Vane, whose surname he took upon marrying. He contributed £30 (worth just over £3000 in 2021) to the suffering poor, though there were those who thought he should have done more.

Nevertheless, when Lord Londonderry passed away a few years later in 1854, at the suggestion of his son, the 4th Marquis, a decision was taken to build a monument in his memory. As this was ostensibly because of kindness shown to his tenants during the Great Hunger, a collection towards the cost was started amongst the tenant farmers as well as his well-off friends. In the event rather less than half his "grateful" tenants contributed. The bulk of the cost of the memorial—about £3,000 (£303,000 in 2021)—came from wealthy donors in

---

[25] Quite a number of them voted for a Tenants' Rights supporter, William Sharman Crawford, in the general election of 1852. Crawford, whose family gave its name to the village of Crawfordsburn, stood in County Down as a Whig against Lord Londonderry's man, a Tory. Of those who voted for Crawford, seventy happened to be behind in their rent. There was no secret ballot at that time and Londonderry chose to evict from their homes each one who had backed Crawford if they failed to pay their rent arrears in full within two months.

Antrim and Down and not least from Napoleon III of France.[26] A tower was built in the Marquis's memory where it could be seen from all over North Down—on the summit of Scrabo Hill. A plaque over the door proclaims it was "erected by his tenants and friends" without any specific reference to the famine years.

The 135 foot (41 metres) high, square tower was built in 1857 and it would be hard to believe that thirteen-year-old Wesley was not among the hundreds of townsfolk who regularly made the 540 foot (165 metre) climb to the top of the hill to watch how the construction was progressing. This was the town's most exciting development in his lifetime, and in honour of the man who had owned his family home. He would almost certainly have been amongst the hundreds of townfolk present to watch the laying of the foundation stone by Sir Robert Bateson of Deramore on Saturday, 28th February. This special occasion was heralded with great pageantry. Wesley would have seen the party of dignitaries, which included the 4th Marquis and Marchioness of Londonderry and the Bishop of Down, amongst others, being led up the road to the summit of Scrabo by the piper from Mount Stewart, the country seat of the Londonderrys. He would have enjoyed the triumphal notes, too, from the instruments of the band of the North Down Rifles, the local militia, that preceded the ceremonial laying of the foundation stone.

I believe thirteen-year-old Wesley thus witnessed the placing of a time capsule jar into the foundations. The jar, it was announced, contained a scroll inscribed to the Marquis. Wesley would have heard that it also held a sample of each coin of the realm in current use, an ordnance survey map of County Down and a list of all the subscribers to the building of the monument—and copies of national and local newspapers of the day.

Could the presence of these journals have first awakened in Wesley the importance people attached to the printed media? At that early and impressionable age, might a seed have been planted? One that might lie dormant for years until germinated and fed by other influences. Stimuli that in later life would lead to the decision to

---

[26] Napoleon III's new bride of but a year, Eugénie de Montijo, had met and taken a liking to Lord Londonderry when she visited London with her mother in 1851.

3 - STRANGE PASSTIMES

launch a newspaper of his own. And in his home town of Newtownards.

Wesley would often have shared subsequent climbs up Scrabo with visitors from further afield; certainly in years to come, as special excursion trains from Belfast made an extra stop at the foot of the hill to drop off passengers. This is the wording of an advert that appeared in the *Northern Whig* in 1862 (the railway line having been extended in June 1861 to run on to Donaghadee):

> *EXCURSION TRIP TO DONAGHADEE*
> *AND NEWTOWNARDS FOR SCRABO HILL*
> *On Monday August 4th, 11th, 18th, 25th*
> *EXCURSION TICKETS AVAILABLE, for the Day only, will be issued for the 10:35 a.m. train from Belfast at the following fares:-*
> *Donaghadee and back... First Class 1s 6d; Covered Carriages—9d*
> *Newtownards and back... First Class 1s 0d; Covered Carriages—6d*
> *The Tickets will be available for Return by any ordinary train.*
> *No luggage allowed.*
> *Parties wishing to alight at the foot of Scrabo Hill can do so by making application to the stationmaster at the Belfast Terminus before the train starts, but they cannot be taken up there when returning.*
> *THOS. C. HAINES*
> *General Manager's Office, Belfast*

The tower proved to be a popular attraction and building it provided much needed work to bring additional income for the poor of the town. So a large number of the late Marquis's tenants contributed their labour, at least, if not their meagre finances, to the construction of the "Lord Londonderry Memorial", as it was called—or, as it has ever since been known, "Scrabo Tower." It is a moot point whether farmers, glancing upward from their toil and viewing the tower watching over them, remembered any kindnesses offered by the Marquis or were merely reminded of who was still in charge.

Tenant Rights remained a vital issue in the land. It was likely a frequent topic of conversation among the onlookers during the construction of the Tower to the memory of their landlord. It was a topic that young Wesley would have heard much about and the concerns raised remained with him into adult life.

Twenty-three years after watching the burial of that time capsule, editor WG Lyttle would touch upon the subject of Tenant Rights in the lead editorial of the inaugural issue of his newspaper.

Further education

When he wasn't climbing up Scrabo Hill or playing games or helping in the shop, Wesley still seems to have found time to further his studies. For him to have "raised himself to a high position amongst the journalists of Ireland" as was subsequently inscribe on his tombstone, and as attested by his impressive vocabulary and the literary references we see in his writings, it is clear that he was well-read and highly literate. Perhaps, on leaving the national school, aged ten, he received further tuition at a hedge school where an itinerant scholar would hold classes in a barn or in the shelter of a hedge—wherever there were sufficient pupils who could pay something towards his living expenses.

As business picked up again after the Great Hunger, Wesley Little senior should have been able to afford to contribute to an itinerant teacher's stipend, or to one of a number of learned clergyman who, for a fee, gave of their time to teaching eager pupils. Because of the contribution of such pedagogues the Ulster Presbyterians have been described as the most educated peasantry in Europe. Counties Down and Antrim, at that time, had a higher percentage of literacy amongst the population than any other county in Ireland outside Dublin.[27]

Wesley must have taken advantage of whatever opportunities there were to continue his education. His father may have been able to beg, borrow or even purchase a few suitable books for him to expand his knowledge on his own, expensive though these would have been.

---

[27] According to Ireland's History in Maps, 1845.

3 - STRANGE PASSTIMES

What is certain is that, in one way or another, he continued his love of learning and reading until he felt confident enough to seek employment independent of his father.

In or around 1862, at about the age of eighteen, Wesley Greenhill Little took the decision to leave the past security of his family home and to make his own way in the world.

THE STORYTELLER

Chapter 4 – SPEED WRITING AND A PUNCH BALL

1862 – 1864

Sir Isaac Pitman first proposed his shorthand system seven years before Wesley was born. By the late 1850s its use was becoming popular in England—more so than earlier systems of phonetic writing—partly due to its being the first ever subject that students could study via a correspondence course. WG was quick to grasp the opportunity to acquire this new ability. Shorthand was a skill not widely available in Ireland at the time. [28] Having it would certainly have helped to commend him to his first employers, a firm of solicitors in Downpatrick.

Leaving home

Wesley's home town of Newtownards had been growing in size and importance, with a population of 9,561 in 1861. However, now an older teenager (not a term he would have recognised or used himself, of course) he made the decision to move to Downpatrick. The county town with its cathedral—the burial place of St Patrick—was smaller (pop. 3,685) but it was the seat of local government in County Down. It was home to both the Protestant and Catholic Bishops of Down, the Lord Lieutenant, the Grand Jury and the Crown Solicitor. The Downpatrick Assizes were held there at the county court. It was here

---

[28] Sir Isaac's brother, Jacob, emigrated to Australia and introduced Pitman's shorthand there, whilst another brother, Benjamin, settled in Ohio and brought the method of speed-writing to the United States. Benjamin used it to record, verbatim, the proceedings at the trial of the conspirators behind the assassination of Abraham Lincoln in 1865.

4 - SPEED WRITING AND A PUNCH BALL

he could expect to find clerical work that would utilise his newly-acquired skills.

He could have travelled by the recent extension of the Belfast and County Down Railway to Downpatrick, which opened just a few years previously, in 1859. This would have involved catching a train from Newtownards to Comber and changing there for the Downpatrick train. A wearisome and slow journey to undertake twice a day. By moving into digs close to his work his newfound independence would be complete.

But with independence came responsibilities and as a young man starting out, WG was probably full of ideas for career advancement. Teaching shorthand was one notion he entertained. He also studied accountancy in his spare time to add another accomplishment to his portfolio. His keen ear for the phonetics of language had served him well in learning Pitman's and in picking up on the nuances of the dialect of the country folk (which he would later use to great effect in his writing and on stage). He may have thought, too, it left him well placed to teach elocution should an opportunity arise.[29]

Early writing

We can imagine him spending his lunch breaks strolling around Downpatrick, his mind full of grandiose plans on carving out a career. Watch him in the cathedral grounds, lost in thought as he wanders amongst the gravestones, perhaps inspired by the idea that St Patrick's bones lay at rest somewhere beneath his feet.[30] Was it here he came up with the idea of amusing his friends with some of his comedic thoughts? Views on life and people that he had been keenly observing since boyhood? Certainly the possibility of becoming a humorous entertainer began to take shape in his mind at this time. During the

---

[29] Some potted biographies reproduced from earlier times list "a teacher of elocution" as one of WG's occupations. Not all of their contents, however, have proved to be accurate. While it could be true – he was always happy to turn a penny in whatever way presented itself – I have not been able to uncover any corroborating evidence that he ever gave lessons as an elocutionist.

[30] The massive slab of granite, quarried from the Mourne Mountains, that now commemorates the burial place of the saint was not, however, set in place in the cathedral grounds until 1900, four years after WG's own mortal remains had been committed to the soil.

long winter evenings, by the flickering light of a tallow candle in his room, he must have begun scribbling some first drafts of the sort of monologues that would eventually spread his fame far beyond the confines of his meagre lodgings in Downpatrick.

According to his obituary that appeared in the *Belfast News-Letter* it was at this time that WG first dabbled in journalism. He most likely filed the odd Court Report of the more juicy or amusing cases handled by his employers. He would have been able to provide a much fuller, verbatim account of what was said, using his shorthand skills, than would otherwise have been available to the press. But I expect he was looking, too, for an early outlet for his comic verse or amusing, if exaggerated, anecdotes about the legal goings on in Downpatrick. The local newspaper, the *Downpatrick Recorder*[31] would have been ideal.

The Punch Ball

To start with, in all probability, he will have penned a few humorous verses merely to amuse his companions at parties and other get-togethers. He will doubtless have performed on one such occasion—an evening of barn dancing and revelry known, rather grandiosely, as a "Punch Ball".

Some 25 years later WG would describe just such an event in his book, *Sons of the Sod,* that is set in or around the year 1852. When he was working in Downpatrick a decade or so later and old enough to attend such soirées, the scenario would have changed little. Indeed, following the old maxim, "write what you know", the description of the Punch Ball in WG's novel is most likely based on similar events he himself had attended. He would have been familiar with the large barn a mile or so from Carrowdore that he later describes as the venue for the Punch Ball in *Sons of the Sod*. He even mentions that amongst the guests from all around were "half a dozen lively spirits from Newtownards." When back visiting his home town, WG would have thought nothing of trekking the six miles or so to join in the dancing and revelry. Why don't we accompany him on one such occasion, knowing from his own future writing what might well have occurred:

---

[31] The newspaper, established in 1835, is still going strong in 2021, now called the *Down Recorder*.

4 - SPEED WRITING AND A PUNCH BALL

Wesley and his companions heard the merry strains of Bully Wright's fiddle long before they drew near to the open barn, though the music was all but drowned by peals of laughter and merry shouting from the dancers within.

One sturdy barn door had been lifted from its hinges and placed horizontally across some barrels to make a platform for the best fiddler in the district. Bully's services were called upon for every dance for miles around. He was getting on a bit now (hadn't he played this self-same venue ten years previously?) yet his feet never stopped tapping out the rhythm of the jig while his nimble fingers and bow moved with lightning speed over the strings.

Shadows of the cavorting dancers flickered around the barn in time to their gyrations and the spluttering flames of tallow candles. These were fixed to the walls in iron holders fashioned by the local smiddy. Flagons of punch were on hand and someone called out as the newcomers arrived, 'Weel, if it isnae Little Wes! Whut wye ir ye? A didnae ken ye wur fur drappin' by the nicht. Ye'll tak a moothfu o punch tae git ye gaun?'[32]

'I'd be much obliged to you. My thanks,' said Wesley, wincing that his old pals were still pulling his leg over his surname.

'Wud ye jist listen tae the soon o' thon, taakin' aa polite. Ye'd be muckle ableeged, wud ye? Whaur's the wee lad we aa grew up wi' in Newton? Whut hae ye daen wi' him?'[33]

---

[32] 'Well, if it isn't Little Wes! How are you? I didn't know you were dropping by tonight. You'll take a little mouthful of punch to get you going?'

[33] 'Would you just listen to the sound of that, talking all polite. You'd be much obliged, would you? Where's the little lad we all grew up with in Newtownards? What've you done with him?'

THE STORYTELLER

Wesley grinned. 'Ach, awa an catch yersel' on. It's the same oul me. A was forgettin whaur A wus. A hae tae talk proper aa week, ye ken. Whaur's thon punch ye menshuned?'[34]

The punch was duly supplied—and consumed—followed by some more and Wesley and the rest of the Newtownards lads were soon prancing around the earthen floor of the barn with some of the prettiest lasses from the likes of Greyabbey, Ballywalter, Millisle, and Ballyboley.

Robust as Bully Wright still was, he couldn't keep up his fiddling indefinitely; he needed a break and sometime later a temporary halt to the dancing was called.

'Gie us yin o yer recitachuns, Little Wes,' came the inevitable call.

'Ay, cum on, Wesley. Gie us a lauch.'[35]

Ignoring the 'Little' and feigning reluctance, Wesley allowed himself to be hoisted on to the platform and cleared his throat. His audience was soon in stitches as he delivered his latest verses containing personal references to many friends he knew would be there and who laughed louder than any when their names were mentioned. For, of course, he had expected to be asked to perform and had come prepared. When he concluded, he jumped down from the barn door platform to raucous cheers and applause. He was thinking, not for the first time, how much he enjoyed entertaining others and being the centre of attention of an appreciative audience.[36]

---

[34] Wesley grinned. 'Oh, away and catch yourself on. It's the same old me. I was forgetting where I was. I have to talk properly all week, you know. Where's that punch you mentioned?'

[35] 'Give us one of your recitations, Little Wes,' came the inevitable call. 'Yes, come on, Wesley. Give us a laugh.'

[36] In *Sons of the Sod* Dominie Harvey gives a similar entertainment.

4 - SPEED WRITING AND A PUNCH BALL

To pastures new

Such thoughts would never have been far from Wesley's mind when he wasn't absorbed with the work of his employer. One night, alone in his lodgings, possibly after further honing his writing skills all evening on a humorous piece that he hoped might be published in the *Downpatrick Recorder*, he reached a major decision. His dreams for the future were not to be fulfilled in this provincial county town, nor amongst the companions of his youth. Besides, with both parents now departed, there was nothing to take him back to Newtownards.[37]

Wesley was on his own. If he was to make anything of his life he had to be prepared to take a risk and go where he would have the best chance of exploiting his various skills. Where the crowds were. Where the opportunities lay. Daunting as the thought might be for a young man of just twenty years, he needed to be living in the pulsing heart of the Province—in Belfast.

After working for the solicitors in Downpatrick for two years, Wesley bade them farewell and, taking his courage in his hands, headed for the big city.

---

[37] As mentioned, it seems likely that Wesley's parents both died prior to 1864. Since no official Irish records of births, deaths and marriages exist from before then, this would explain why I have been unable to trace any death certificates for them.

Chapter 5 – A MOVE TO BELFAST AND A MOVING PICTURES SHOW

1864 – 1871

At that time, the Old Lodge Road in north-west Belfast cut up to the Crumlin Road in a north-westerly direction from North Street, making a V with Peter's Hill which continued westward into the Shankill Road. South of the Shankill, there was much open land. What few roads there were ran down to Divis Street and the Falls Road—a predominantly Catholic area of the city ever since a movement of people from West Ulster had settled there some centuries earlier. But the Shankill, itself, had been first populated by Protestants from County Antrim, and it, and the three or four little streets that cut through the open land to the north, up towards the Old Lodge Road, were all still staunchly Protestant—as they are to this day.

It was a poor area in the 1860s with small, two up and two down properties, often in multiple occupancy with one family of ten or more in the upstairs two rooms and another in the ground floor accommodation.[38] But for young Wesley Little the important thing was that a room in one of these houses was affordable. So it is into this area that he moved in 1864 and where, at a number of different addresses, most within a stone's throw of each other, he was to spend the next 16 years of his life. At the end of that time he would have a wife, a family, an established reputation as a writer and popular entertainer, and a burning ambition to own his own newspaper.

---

[38] From the history of this area as described in "The Shankill and the Falls: The Minority Experiences of Two Communities in West Belfast. Central Library, June 1, 1995," from the CAIN Web Service.

5 - A MOVE TO BELFAST AND A MOVING PICTURES SHOW

Nuptials

John Courtnay was a carter. He was the nineteenth century equivalent of a white van man, except his vehicle would have been a one horsepower cart. John lived across the River Lagan at number 80, Madrid Street. He had two daughters: Isabella, who made shirts and underclothing, and Elizabeth Eveline—Lizzie to her friends and Eve to her family, who worked as a Jersey Comber[39], teasing out the fine jersey wool ready to be spun.

According to the age entered on her marriage certificate, Lizzie would have been born in 1843 and celebrating her twenty-first birthday the year Wesley moved to town. History does not record how the two first met but meet they did and the meeting was soon to eclipse all else that took place in Lizzie's life that year. For within a few short months she had lost her heart to the young Newtownards lad with the impish sense of humour. Although he was apparently a year her junior, she accepted his proposal of marriage, in spite of his only being able to offer to share his one room with her.

I say Wesley was "apparently" a year younger than Lizzie because her age on her death certificate puts her year of birth at 1845, making her just 19 at the time of her engagement and, in fact, a year younger than her fiancé. This is more likely to be her true age, than that quoted on the marriage certificate, as we shall see.

Wesley lived within the parish of St Anne's Church of Ireland on Donegall Street. It was popular amongst Belfast's betrothed, who lacked a church of their own, as the place to solemnise their wedding vows. We do not know of Wesley's early church life, or whether, as a child, he had been taught the Presbyterian catechism. We know only that, on moving to Belfast, he chose the more anonymous Church of Ireland in which to marry Lizzie. The modern printed copy of their marriage certificate lists the venue as St Anne's Cathedral. However, that imposing edifice was only built during the years between 1899 and 1904.[40]

---

[39] Lizzie's occupation is given on her marriage certificate but the handwriting is difficult to decipher. Jersey Comber seems the most probable interpretation of the barely legible scrawl.

[40] Most interestingly, the outer cathedral walls at that time were constructed around the existing St Anne's church, which continued to be used as a place of

So it was to the old St Anne's church[41] that the happy couple repaired on the 23rd December, 1864 to be joined man and wife. On their marriage certificate, the names of the witnesses were Robert Keenan, who we must assume to be Wesley's best man, and Matilda McKnight, probably Lizzie's bridesmaid. Lizzie's age, as I have said, is given as 21. Interestingly, so is Wesley's, anticipating his birthday by four months. WG, it seems, saw no reason to over-complicate matters when the 19- and 20-year-old couple were applying for their license by admitting that they were both underage.[42]

Perhaps this is further evidence that Wesley's mother and father had already passed away. Could lack of parental advice account for Wesley's whirlwind romance and cavalier approach to officialdom?

It is their marriage certificate that establishes that Wesley's surname, at that time, was spelt, 'Little'. While this could have been put down to an error on behalf of the clergyman who completed the form, repeating the same error, not unnaturally, when recording WG's father's surname, the fact that WG used the same spelling for his signature makes the evidence compelling.

The other piece of information offered by the marriage certificate is that WG's occupation is given as "Teacher." Had he realised his plans to teach elocution? As I have said, no supporting evidence of this has come to light. It may be that he had already taken on a few private pupils who wished to learn shorthand. This was too new a discipline to have yet been on any school curriculum. Whatever the case, it was Pitman's revolutionary phonetic form of speedwriting that was to provide Wesley, one way or another, with a source of income during many of his years spent in Belfast.

Dr Corry's Diorama

For a time, however, there was another source, which arose from his association with one, Thomas Charles S Corry, who was born around

---

worship until December 1903. Then, in less than six months, the old inner church was demolished and the interior of the first stage of the Cathedral completed and officially re-opened.

[41] Appendix F – Fig 2a shows St Anne's Cathedral as it is now and Fig 2b shows a photograph of the old St Anne's Church.

[42] The age of majority in the UK was not reduced from 21 to 18 until 1970.

5 - A MOVE TO BELFAST AND A MOVING PICTURES SHOW

1824 or 5 and grew up in Belfast. This gentleman went on to study medicine in Scotland and after becoming a Licentiate of the Royal College of Physicians in Edinburgh in 1859 he returned to Ulster to set up practice in Belfast. He contributed to the British Medical Journal and became a fellow, and later vice-president, of the Obstetrical Society.[43]

Also a prolific poet, he wrote mainly about the country of his birth of which he was unashamedly proud. His verse proclaimed Ireland's beauty, its history, its diversity and some musically gifted friends provided melodies for many of his poems. He would, eventually, in 1879, publish a volume of his works entitled, *Irish Lyrics, Songs and Poems*[44]. He confessed in the preface to his book, "Many of the trifles contained in the following pages were written during intervals of relaxation from professional duties, merely to fill up leisure moments, which might possibly have been more usefully employed."

However, much of his verse was, in fact, put to excellent use in a particular form of entertainment that had been growing in popularity over the last decade or so.

The invention of the Diorama had been enthralling audiences, increasingly, in Great Britain and Ireland, since the mid-1850s. A diorama was a series of expansive paintings, each of which could fill a stage, depicting views of places of interest to the attending public and accompanied by an informative and often light-hearted lecture. Levity was not always the watchword, however; scenes of war proved particularly appealing to many audiences. According to an advertisement in the *Huddersfield and Holmfirth Examiner* on 25th August, 1855, one of the earliest dioramas comprised "Views of… the Battles of Alma, Balaclava, and Inkerman with a pictorial map of Sebastopol showing the position of the Allied Armies now engaged in Bombardment."

The *Southern Reporter and Cork Commercial Courier* carried a report in their 20th November, 1855 edition of a "splendid diorama of the Life of Napoleon the first, and illustrating the war with Russia."

---

[43] According to his obituary in the British Medical Journal of May 30th 1896.
[44] Published by D & J Allen, Belfast, 1879; 2nd edition published by J Robb and Co, Belfast, 1884.

Others were more in the nature of travelogues, showing scenes of beauty and interest from continental Europe, Asia and America. These, in particular, were accompanied by appropriate songs and music and dance at intervals, as a break from the lecture.

In 1863, Dr Corry vacationed in Canada and the United States where he met many Irish emigrants who yearned for news of "the old country." Corry, an inveterate showman, had the idea of preparing a diorama dedicated to Ireland that he could bring over to tour America. On his return he got together with a business partner, John Cramsie, and employed the celebrated artist, JH Connop, to visit every part of the country making sketches of its magnificent scenery and antiquities. These were then developed into a series of over fifty beautiful paintings. They first went on show on Boxing Day the following year, 1864—three days after the Little newlyweds had tied the knot. The show's venue was the Victoria Hall in May Street, Belfast and it was entitled, *Ireland, its Scenery, Music and Antiquities.*

Victoria Hall, May Street, Belfast
Built by the Anacreontic Society in 1840 as the Victoria Music Hall, it later became known as the Victoria Hall. It was considered at the time to have the best "music room" [concert venue] in Ireland and was surpassed by only a few such venues in Great Britain. It was eventually demolished in 1983. (photo from archieseek.com)

"Dr Corry's Diorama", as the newspapers called it, received much critical acclaim. The viewing public flocked to see the show just as audiences of the future would fill the cinemas. In fact, the vast paintings that scrolled across the stage to change from scene to scene were described as the first moving pictures show of Ireland, half a century before Movie

5 - A MOVE TO BELFAST AND A MOVING PICTURES SHOW

Theatres began to open. The show transferred to Dublin and opened in the Rotundo[45] at the end of February where it ran through to the second week in April, 1865, to very respectable audiences. The Diorama was accompanied by a band, four soloists, a chorus and a lecturer who was, at that time, a Mr R H Hunter. The music and songs were mostly Irish, including many of Dr Corry's own compositions.

It returned for another successful run in Belfast before starting a tour in May. By then Hunter wanted a break from his nightly lectures and so for the first tour venue in Armagh, Corry was looking for a replacement. Wesley Little had a friend in the medical profession, a certain Dr M'Murtry who would have known of Wesley's fondness for performing for his friends. We don't know if Dr M'Murtry, was a mutual acquaintance and colleague of Dr Corry and recommended WG. Or perhaps the Diorama showman had had occasion to witness him reading one of his early stories and realised that here was just the young man to step into the "lecturing" role. However it came about, Wesley's performing skills on stage must have already been impressive to have convinced the renowned Dr Corry to entrust the role of lecturer for the first provincial tour of his celebrated show to a young amateur.

A new job

WG had, of course, heard of the show and had quite probably been in the audience at one of the first performances in the Victoria Hall. He would have been intrigued to learn from the good doctor just what was involved.

The Diorama, Dr Corry explained, was not a one-man-show. Musicians and singers and other entertainers were employed. Backstage assistants were needed to operate the machinery that was necessary to fill the stage with the enormous and stunning paintings of Ireland's beauty spots. Each individual was part of the show's success. The linchpin of the show, however, was the Guide or Lecturer who described the views and introduced the other artists whose songs or recitations would throw further light on the scenes

---

[45] The so-called "Round Room at the Rotundo" was an integral part of the Rotunda Maternity Hospital, used as a concert venue to raise funds for the hospital.

displayed. It was the Guide's job to engage the audience and make them feel a part of the whole entertainment, to ensure their enjoyment. Corry's enthusiasm as he sought to interest WG in joining him was infectious.

Thomas Charles S Corry may well have been a born showman, but no more so than Wesley Greenhill Little. WG jumped at the opportunity of becoming part of such a popular entertainment and no doubt accepted the offer straightaway. A man always fascinated by innovation and technical wizardry, he would have immediately wanted to learn just how the diorama worked.

The medical showman was, no doubt, just as eager to demonstrate his equipment and took WG backstage to see the giant wooden rollers erected vertically at each side of the platform and hidden from view by the specially adapted proscenium. The rollers held reams upon reams of canvas upon which the scenes were painted. The system was worked with blocks and tackle that enabled the canvas to be unrolled from one side as the slack was taken up by the roller in the opposite wing. In this way the scenes, each one of which filled the stage, could be scrolled so as to change from one painting to the next.

WG was impressed by the ingenuity of the mechanism, but more so by the stunning quality of the artwork, which would have struck him straight away the first time he had seen the show. Corry had commissioned some wonderful views of Irish landmarks from the coast of Antrim in the north to the shores of Cork in the south and from Dublin Bay in the east to Galway Bay in the west. There were scenes from all 32 counties of Ireland and WG soon became familiar with them: The Giant's Causeway, Shane's Castle, Carrick-a-rede, Dunluce Castle, Belfast, Galway City, Glendalough, The Vale of Avoca, Waterford, Cork City, Blarney Castle, The Lakes of Killarney, The Gap of Dunloe, Glengarriff and many others.[46]

As the new presenter of these wonderful vistas, WG was equally intrigued by the form of lighting Corry used to illuminate them—essential, of course, in a darkened theatre. Wesley would have heard of the invention of so-called 'limelight' earlier in the century and was interested to see it being brought into practical use in the theatres of

---

[46] This list of Corry's Diorama views is taken from an account given in the book, *I Roved Out* by Cathal O'Byrne, printed by Irish News Ltd, Belfast, 1946.

5 - A MOVE TO BELFAST AND A MOVING PICTURES SHOW

the '60s. Dr Corry showed him the cylinder block of calcium oxide—the quicklime that gave the system its name—and explained that this material could withstand a heat of over 3600°F without melting. An oxyhydrogen flame is directed at the cylinder and long before reaching its melting point the quicklime produces a bright incandescent light and then an even more intense candoluminescence. All this brilliance is directed forwards by a mirror and the effect is to bathe the scene on stage in a light almost as bright as day.

WG was more than happy to assist his new friend and business associate by stepping into the limelight—an expression that persists to this day, even though such lights were only ever in use for a few decades.[47]

Name change

Before taking up the position, Wesley thought hard about this new venture onto the professional stage. It was quite a step up from the old barn door in Carrowdore that had served as his platform at the Punch Ball a few years back. He recalled his pals' ribbing, 'Come on Little Wes, gi' us a lauch.' Just turned twenty-one, he wasn't teased much now about his name but it was still a matter which concerned him. As he discussed plans with Dr Corry about his becoming something of a public figure, it struck him, that now, if ever, was the time for action.

So for WG's first appearance with Dr Corry's Diorama, which was in Armagh during the second week of May, 1865, he was billed as Mr W. Lyttle, with a 'y'; a subtle change which, along with a newly flourishing moustache on his upper lip, gave his youthfulness that extra gravitas he felt the position required. At the time, whilst there were some 225 families in the province with the surname of Little, there were only 11 called Lyttle.[48] He had made himself part of a much more select group.

---

[47] Before the end of the 19th century limelight had been replaced by electric arc lights which served well until more modern alternatives took over.

[48] According to the Ulster Historical Foundation's Distribution of Surnames/Householders, Ulster, mid-nineteenth century report.

THE STORYTELLER

Touring with the Diorama

In its Friday 12th May edition, the *Armagh Guardian*, described the opening of the Diorama presentation: "But now the curtain is withdrawn and Mr W. Lyttle, the eloquent and intelligent guide with his white wand, invites us to a view of the enterprising town of Belfast..." Perhaps the reporter was being kind as there was, no doubt, something of a learning curve to becoming fluent at the role. Because at a later appearance—in Belfast—on the tour which took in Dundalk and Dublin amongst other venues, WG's performance was described in *The Northern Whig* as "much improved".

While WG was appearing in Dublin with the show, a young republican there, known as "the Fenian Poet", John Casey, was singing his latest song all about the ill-fated rebellion of the United Irishmen back in 1798. Its haunting appeal has endured and "The Rising of the Moon" is still high up among many people's favourite rebel tunes today. Perhaps it became a song that, whenever he heard it in later life, always reminded WG of his first taste of fame in the limelight of the capital's Rotundo Music Hall.

At the end of June, 1865, the Dublin run of the Diorama was reported to be ending shortly prior to the show leaving for America. Sadly for WG, this planned trip had to be postponed indefinitely due to John Cramsie deciding to pull out of his partnership with Dr Corry. His had been a financial role and in this capacity he apparently owned all the equipment and paintings. On Saturday 2nd September a notice appeared in the *Belfast News-Letter* which read:

> *SALE THIS DAY,*
> *NATIONAL DIORAMA OF*
> *IRELAND*
>
> *In consequence of the Dissolution of Partnership of the Proprietors, MR JOHN CRAMSIE will SELL by AUCTION, at the CORN EXCHANGE, VICTORIA STREET, Belfast, on SATURDAY 2nd September, at Two o'clock*
>
> THAT MAGNIFICENT WORK OF ART, known as the "NATIONAL DIORAMA OF IRELAND" which has been exhibited with the greatest success in several leading cities in the country

5 - A MOVE TO BELFAST AND A MOVING PICTURES SHOW

> *The Diorama consists of about 50 Views, each 20 feet by 12 feet, Painted by the most celebrated Artists, the whole being fitted with the most improved Machinery, Gas Effects, and rich Damask Draperies.*
>
> *At the same time will be Sold Two extra DIORAMA FRAMES, large, Four-wheeled VAN, Two Colossal FIGURES, in Armour; Lumber, &c.*
>
> *For further particulars, and Tickets of Admission to Sale, apply to*
> *MR JOHN CRAMSIE, 8 Waring Street.*

After some lively bidding, the purchase was completed by Dr Corry, himself, who thus became the sole proprietor of the venture he had conceived and nurtured to become the success it was. He continued to present his Diorama around Ireland using other lecturers, with WG again presiding when it returned to Belfast. The following year Dr Corry took it to Liverpool and in 1867 it had an outstanding run in Glasgow. The show continued to be well received in various cities both in Ireland and Great Britain but it was not until towards the end of 1870, when WG was no longer involved, that the good doctor was finally able to achieve his original intention of presenting it on the other side of the Atlantic.

"Dr Corry's Great Diorama of Ireland" opened in Brooklyn's Athenaeum in New York on Monday 3rd October where it played until Saturday 22nd November, 1870. From there it transferred to the New York Apollo and stayed right through until Saturday 4th March, 1871. The show then moved to the Assembly Buildings in Philadelphia before the successful seven month tour concluded at the end of April.

Thus, contrary to claims in some brief accounts of his life, WG did *not* "travel widely in America" accompanying Dr Corry's Diorama. Not only did he not accompany Dr Corry, but there is no record of his ever having visited America.

Although Wesley missed out on America, his involvement with dioramas was not over but for the time being he pursued other means of making a livelihood. Back in the winter of '65/'66 his new bride was no doubt pleased enough that the proposed American tour did not take place at that time, which could have separated her from her husband of but a year. And besides, would she have wanted her Wesley going to a country that had shot its own President just the previous April. But she approved of one outcome of her husband's time with Dr Corry. It seems she had become fond of the change to his physiognomy. She, doubtless, considered the moustache made him look distinguished, and perhaps delighted, too, in how it tickled when they kissed. In any event, WG must also have been pleased with the effect for it remained in place, neatly trimmed, throughout his life. It would be joined at a later date, when his eyes began to require assistance, by a pair of pince-nez, adding further to his look of erudition.[49]

Mary Ann McCracken

That July, Wesley would have been saddened to hear of the death, at 96, of Mary Ann McCracken on the 26th of the month. Right up to the end she had been very active in such causes as the anti-slavery movement, the Belfast Charitable Society and in running the Poor House. Mary was the patriotic sister of the famous United Irishman, Henry Joy McCracken, who had so heroically led the insurgents into battle to take the town of Antrim in the opening skirmish of the rebellion of 1798. Now, 68 years later, she was to be buried alongside her brother in Clifton Street Cemetery which was only a couple of streets away from where Wesley and Lizzie were living in a house on M'Tier Street.

Perhaps Wesley saw the funeral procession; perhaps he made a point of walking along to the cemetery to pay his respects, recalling, as he went, the catchy tune and telling words of John Casey's rebel song, "The Rising of the Moon" he had heard the previous year in Dublin. With his mind turned to thoughts of the '98, did he find himself thinking about William McComb's, *A Guide to Belfast*, only recently published in 1861? It was a book he was quite likely to have read on first moving to the city and it contained much about the history of the uprising as it related to Belfast and surrounding towns.

He no doubt recalled conversations on the subject with Dr Corry, who also took a great interest in that period of Irish history. The death

---

[49] See photograph in Appendix E, Fig. 10

5 - A MOVE TO BELFAST AND A MOVING PICTURES SHOW

of Henry Joy McCracken's sister, a lady Corry had met, inspired the doctor to write an "Ode to the Memory of Mary McCracken", and nine years later he would write another poem, "The Battle of Antrim; a Reminiscence on 1798", which would be included in later showings of his Diorama.

Was WG's own interest in the events at the end of the previous century, like that of his ex-employer, Dr Corry, stimulated by Mary Ann McCracken's death? Certainly we know that, over the next two decades WG continued to amass facts and details about the United Irishmen and their famous rebellion, mostly from talking with first generation descendants of the insurgents. These would eventually provide him with the material for his most successful and enduring novel, *Betsy Gray, or Hearts of Down—A Tale of '98*. It is interesting to realise that, although his book was published 90 years after the events it recalls, WG had lived contemporaneously with one of the protagonists in his story.

A growing family

The Lyttle's home in M'Tier Street—at the time one of just two parallel side roads that ran up from the Shankill to the Old Lodge Road—was No. 54. Even if it was, indeed, just one room, as seems likely, it suited them fine and they even considered it sufficient accommodation to make a home for their firstborn who arrived just over a year later. Wesley John was born on Friday 24th August, 1866 and, maintaining the family's "Wesleyan" tradition, his forename on his birth certificate was given as Wesley (although the registrar misspelt it as "Westly"). However, as I mentioned earlier, in keeping with established practice he was also given the name of his mother's father and, within the family, it was by that name—John—that he was known as he grew up.

Wesley John's birth certificate, as mentioned, is the first document we have bearing his father's signature with Lyttle spelled with a 'y'. Recorded on that birth certificate is the information that WG was by then earning a living from his shorthand skills; his occupation is given as "phonetic writer." By the time his son was approaching his second birthday, however, WG described his profession as "clerk" on the birth certificate of John's sister, Agnes, who, much to Lizzie's delight,

THE STORYTELLER

was born on Saturday 1st August, 1868. The proud father was working once more as a solicitor's clerk, still utilising his shorthand. A couple of years later a street index has him listed as a solicitor's shorthand writer.

In anticipation of Agnes' arrival the Lyttle family had moved their possessions across the road to Number 55, M'Tier Street. A move of such a short distance almost certainly means that the opportunity had arisen for them to take over a whole floor in the new house; two rooms to give more space for the children. There they remained for another year or so before moving once again, much further this time—to the next road, in fact, Hopeton Street. There, they settled into No. 47, another two up, two down and, with Wesley in steady employment, perhaps this time they had the whole house. In any event, they moved in time to welcome new-born Robert into the world on Thursday 8th September, 1870.

This was a traumatic period for young Wesley and his wife, who, for the time being, had taken to calling herself Eliza, according to Robert's birth certificate. They were both still under thirty and now had three extra mouths to feed. John and Agnes were only four and two, respectively, and little Robert was a sickly baby, keeping his parents awake at nights with his fitful crying and always needing so much attention from Lizzie (as we'll continue to call her, to avoid confusion), and Wesley, too, when he was available.

WG would have still recalled how impressed he had been some years back by the newspaper coverage of the trial of John Wilkes Booth. Much of the American reporting was reproduced, verbatim, in the British broadsheets and, seeing the by-line, Benjamin Pitman, he realised the full accounts of what was said at the trial of Lincoln's murderer was only made possible by the use of shorthand note-taking. WG saw that this skill, one that he had himself, was going to be of immense value and become much sought after.

With a growing family and a need to increase their income, he made some tentative enquiries about the possibility of starting an evening class in shorthand if there were sufficient interest. In the meantime he would seek to boost his private pupils. On 5th September, three days before Robert's birth, an ad appeared in the *Newry*

5 - A MOVE TO BELFAST AND A MOVING PICTURES SHOW

Telegraph, a newspaper with the self-proclaimed "largest circulation of any provincial paper in the North of Ireland." It proclaimed:

> **TO THOSE DESIROUS OF LEARNING SHORTHAND**
> WANTED LADY AND GENTLEMEN
> pupila to learn shorthand (Pitman's system).
> Terms moderate. Private lessons given.

Was that WG's advertisement? Spreading his net wider in search for more pupils? As he is generally held to be the first such teacher in Ireland, certainly in the north of the island, it seems it must have been.

With this new enterprise getting under way and their latest baby's demands ruling family life in Hopeton Street, WG completely forgot about registering Robert's birth. The child's early months passed and his parents saw no sign that his health was improving. Their concern grew. By the time he reached his first birthday he was having convulsions and there seemed to be nothing they could do to alleviate his distress.

As they celebrated his birthday, WG realised they hadn't yet registered their youngest child and he felt it ought to be done, sooner rather than later. The formalities were duly carried out and the birth certificate is dated 17th September 1871. Six days later little Robert passed away. Devastated, WG had to return to the registry office to record the death. The certificate reads:

> *Twenty-third September 1871, 47 Hopeton Street., Robert Lyttle, Male, Bachelor, 13 months, Son of shorthand writer; Convulsions 18 hours; W. G. Lyttle present at death.*

Chapter 6 – TEMPERANCE AND TEACHING

1871 – 1874

On the other side of the Atlantic, back when WG was only seven, another Wesley—Wesley Bailey, with a small group of people in Utica, New York, became dedicated to alleviating poverty and improving the lives of ordinary people. They called themselves "Good Templars" and lit a candle when they met, its symbolism radiating openness, warmth, friendship and hope for a better life free from alcohol, harm, poverty and hate.

Within a year 14 more groups had formed—or lodges, as they called themselves. Unlike fraternal societies of that time, female and family members were encouraged to join as well. They recognised the advantage of a comprehensive approach to facing problems of alcohol addiction as not just personal difficulties but as matters affecting family and community. In the summer of 1852 a conference was called to establish a Grand Lodge for the Independent Order of Good Templars (the IOGT).

The Order grew from strength to strength in America and Canada and in 1868 one of the leaders, Joseph Malins, brought the IOGT to the UK and started a lodge in Birmingham. From there, the movement spread throughout the British Isles and into Europe and beyond.

Signing the Pledge

In Belfast, the principles enshrined by the movement appealed to Wesley, now a family man. Although probably brought up as a Presbyterian[50], Wesley would likely have remembered some of the

---

[50] This was the denomination he chose to join in later life.

6 - TEMPERANCE AND TEACHING

teachings of Methodism that had first come to Newtownards during his childhood—no drinking, no dancing, no swearing, no fighting. Whether or not he paid much heed at the time, its sobering effect on sections of the weaving community, who forsook the public houses in favour of Friday-night prayer meetings, may have left an impression on his young mind to be recalled in later years.

Perhaps any youthful weekend tipples at the local dances had ceased anyway under the influence of the love of his life, Lizzie. Wesley would have known about the work of the Ulster Temperance Movement that the Presbyterian minister, Dr John Edgar, founded back in the 1830s. But it was the approach of the Good Templars that attracted Wesley and he made a decision to join the organisation. He took the vow to "be obedient to all the laws and rules of this Institution, they not conflicting with your duties as a citizen, or a Christian" and pledged to "abstain forever from the use of, or giving to others as a beverage, anything that will intoxicate."

WG's friend, Dr M'Murtry, who had no doubt been a source of comfort to the Lyttles with medical advice and perhaps even some palliative treatment for poor little Robert, also joined the Good Templars about the same time. Alexander M'Murtry was a year older than Wesley, having been born in 1843 in the little village of Ballynure, County Antrim, which lay about 15 miles north of Belfast. He was educated at the Belfast Academy and then studied medicine at Queens College, Belfast and at Glasgow before returning to Belfast to become a GP. At this time he was living in Carlisle Street, just the other side of the New Lodge Road from the Lyttles in Hopeton Street.

After a while the two friends decided to apply to the Grand Lodge of Ireland to open a new lodge in their own part of the city. This they did on 7th August, 1871, naming it the IOGT, Good Samaritan Lodge No 59. At the inaugural meeting the GWCT (Grand Worthy Chief Templar) for Ireland, Brother John Pyper, duly appointed WG and Alexander M'Murtry as joint WCTs (Worthy Chief Templars) along with others to fill the usual appointed positions—Worthy Vice Templar, Worthy Secretary, Worthy Marshall and so on. The event was subsequently reported in a new Belfast paper that was still in its first year of publication, the *Belfast Evening Telegraph*.[51]

At the close of the proceedings, according to the report, the GWCT concluded thus:

> *'Brothers and Sisters, having complied with all that our laws and usages demand, it is my pleasure and duty to welcome the members of the "Good Samaritan" Lodge into union with our Temperance Fraternity.[52] It is your prerogative, if you are but faithful and energetic, to exert a healthy influence upon the community in which you dwell.*
>
> *To reform the inebriate, to assuage the woes and afflictions entailed upon our race by intemperance, and to suppress the traffic in alcoholic poisons, is one of the holiest of callings... ...*
>
> *The perpetuity and salvation of an Institution or a Society depends more upon the example and practice of its members, than upon its mere precepts or its profession. Live above reproach; live to do good; live to improve all the higher and better faculties of man's nature; and, with the blessing of Providence, you will be instrumental in accomplishing a part of the great work of regenerating the world.'*

With this mighty and awesome exhortation ringing in their ears, M'Murtry and WG, with the help of their brother officers, determined to fulfil their duties with diligence and set about organising the activities of the lodge for its growing membership.

Yet it was within only a few weeks of the opening that WG's life came to a crashing halt with the shattering loss of little Robert. M'Murtry kept things ticking over at the Lodge until the Lyttles had time to come to terms with their bereavement and Wesley felt he

---

[51] The *Belfast Evening Telegraph* was the full name used originally for the *Belfast Telegraph*.

[52] They called it a Fraternity despite membership beng open to both men and women.

6 - TEMPERANCE AND TEACHING

could resume an active role. When he did, he must have found some consolation in the distraction of Good Templars activities in helping to promote their motto of "Friendship, Hope and Charity." He knew what it was, as a family, to suffer loss. Through the Good Templars he was helping other grieving families whose loss of a loved one to the excesses of alcohol did not need to be permanent. He worked to bring hope of reconciliation and new beginnings for others in the shadow of his own loss that could never be replaced.

Social evenings

Good Templar lodges often held social evenings or concerts with members performing songs, recitations and readings to entertain an invited audience. After some months had passed following Robert's tragic death, Wesley felt able to contribute to one such event. On Thursday 16th May, 1872, IOGT, "Erin's First" No. 1 Lodge held an open meeting. The account of the event in the *Belfast Telegraph* the following Monday said that the business was

> *pushed forward to make way for an entertainment of a miscellaneous character to which friends of temperance, not connected with the order, had been invited. The attendance was very large. A paper of an amusing, but very instructive nature, was read by Br. W. G. Lyttle of "Good Samaritan" Lodge.*

This was one of the first times WG risked presenting one of his party pieces before a larger and less intimate audience. But the response he received must have made him think, Yes, I can do this, and he determined to do it again when an occasion arose.

In August, it was the anniversary of the founding of "Good Samaritan" Lodge No. 59 and the Grand Worthy Chief Templar for Ireland, Brother John Pyper "addressed their meeting at some length" according to the account in the *Belfast Telegraph*, which also reported,

> *The anniversary was made the occasion of congratulating Brs. Dr. A. H. H. M'Murtry and W. G.*

THE STORYTELLER

Lyttle on the success which had attended their efforts in conducting the "Good Samaritan" since its commencement, and also of presenting each of the above-named brothers with a life-size portrait of himself, executed in the highest style of the art.[53]

Sectarian riots

The previous month, the Lyttles and their neighbours in Hopeton street would have been apprehensive as the Twelfth of July approached. No Orange marches, nor any other sectarian parades, had been allowed since before WG moved to Belfast. All such gatherings were banned under the Party Processions Act of 1850 following severe fighting, with fatalities, on July 12th, 1849. The Act was repealed in 1872 and bands once again led their Orange Lodges along the Shankill just yards from the home of Wesley and Lizzie and their children.

In the event, the Protestant parades passed peaceably. But trouble came when a Nationalist procession in support of Home Rule coincided with the public inauguration of the Nationalist and Catholic Ancient Order of Hibernians. They were to parade on Our Lady's Day, August 15th (Assumption Day). However, police stopped them marching through Carlisle Circus following rumours that they planned to attack St Enoch's, the big new church there where firebrand Presbyterian minister, Rev Hugh Hanna, was the incumbent. The Hibernians agreed to divert their march but they were attacked by

---

[53] It seems that WG cherished his portrait and it remained with the family, travelling with them from home to home throughout his life. When, eventually, his widow sold his newspaper business and premises, she later tried to recover a number of items from the purchaser that she said were not included in the sale and among these was "a portrait of Wesley Lyttle." Sadly, the court ruled that the items were all "fixtures and fittings" and need not be returned to the seller (see Chapter 24 under "WG's books"). Presumably the new proprietor kept the portrait on display, as the founding owner and editor of the newspaper. In the fullness of time, however, the business failed; the proprietor declared bankruptcy and the newspaper finally folded. As to the whereabouts of Wesley's portrait, "executed in the highest style of the art", no trace now remains.

6 - TEMPERANCE AND TEACHING

Protestants from the shipyards and three-way battles between the Protestants, the Catholics and the police ensued.

The incident led to a week of violence around the area with rioters clashing with the police night after night and homes being ransacked and looted. It reached a peak on Saturday 17th August with a four-hour gun battle being fought out on the Brickfield just down the road from the Lyttles' home. Heavy police and militia reinforcements were brought in and they didn't manage to restore peace until some days later. 247 homes had been destroyed and 837 families were displaced. A policeman had been shot dead and 73 more wounded, with at least 117 civilians wounded, probably many more who didn't report their injuries. The weekend of the 17th/18th was described by a contemporary historian as "a time of unremitting terror." Wesley and his family were living in the middle of it all.

Entertainments

These must have been terrifying times for the Lyttles and all their neighbours. However, for those fortunate enough not to have been directly affected by the rioting, life continued much as normal. In October, WG was invited to read one of his stories at a meeting of the IOGT "Rescue" Lodge, No. 15 where "The programme was brought to a close by a very humorous paper"—the *Belfast Telegraph* again—, "entitled 'My Country Cousin's Courtship', by Br. W. G. Lyttle." This must have been the first public airing of what later came to be called *Paddy M'Quillan's Courtship*.[54] The reference to his fictitious "country cousin" shows how WG's mind was thinking. He had found that if he spoke in the language of some of the friends he grew up with in Newtownards, his audiences seemed to appreciate the simple humour of his tales all the more. At that time, WG was not tempted to draw at all, for his inspiration, upon the political and sectarian strife that surrounded him. He confined his subject matter to the innocent rural adventures of Paddy M'Quillan.

As Worthy Chief Templar for Good Samaritans No. 59, it fell to Wesley to organise the meetings and he soon started to volunteer

---

[54] *Paddy M'Quillan's Courtship* was later published in the columns of the *Newry Telegraph* in December 1878 and then in *Humorous Readings by "Robin"— (Vol.1)*, in 1879.

himself as part of the cabaret. The account, which appeared on Saturday 07 December, 1872 in the *Belfast Weekly News* began:

> *'GOOD TEMPLARISM I.O.G.T.—Good Samaritan Lodge, No. 59—The endeavours of the members of this lodge to afford instructions and amusement to their friends by holding public meetings seems to be appreciated in a remarkable degree by those for whom they are intended. On Friday evening at eight o'clock, the commodious Lancasterian[55] School-room was crowded with a large and respectable audience. The chair was taken by A. H. H. M'Murtry, Esq., M.D., but that gentleman being called away, John Pyper, Esq., G.W.C.T. presided instead. The programme included songs, duets, readings, and recitations of a high order, and a new humorous paper by Mr. W. G. Lyttle...*

Writing Shorthand

Alongside his voluntary work for the Good Templar lodge and penning new adventures for "his country cousin" with which to amuse his audiences, WG was still earning his living as a shorthand clerk. He had placed an ad in the *Belfast Telegraph* the previous February looking for a suitable position. It said, "WANTED by a Young Man of good education, a situation as SHORTHAND WRITER in a Solicitor's, Merchant's or Shipping Office, or would take a situation as Junior Reporter. Advertiser is an expert Shorthand Writer and has a good deal of experience in the above-mentioned capacities." Becoming more involved in the newspaper industry was still an attractive possibility to WG, as seen by his inclusion of Junior Reporter in his ad.

While using his shorthand for gainful employment, he was also seeking a way to broaden his opportunities for teaching the skill. He held successful discussions with the People's Literary Institute on the

---

[55] Lancasterian – this was the common spelling in Belfast from the time the school was built.

6 - TEMPERANCE AND TEACHING

corner of Donegall Street and Academy Street, and in October, 1872 started to teach a shorthand class there.

He also knew that the Grand Worthy Chief Templar of Ireland, John Pyper, had started a school called the Pyper Academy way back in 1854. It outgrew its original premises and in 1867 moved to a brand new site at the end of a recently constructed road off Clifton Street near Carlisle Circus in Belfast. Called Glenravel Street, the new road was named after the home, in the Glens of Antrim, of philanthropists George and Edward Benn, who provided two new wings to the Poor House situated next to the road and who also built two new hospitals in the vicinity.

WG was interested to note that the new school location was even closer to where he was living than the Literary Institute. When it transferred to the new Glenravel Street site, the Pyper Academy became known as Belfast Mercantile Academy and John Pyper's son, James, took over as principal. He was to remain at the helm until well into the next century when the school would have again moved, this time to the Jordanstown area where it remains to this day, now known as Belfast High School.

Once they had consolidated their move up near Carlisle Circus, the Pypers wanted to utilise their new facilities in Glenravel Street more fully. Besides offering day-school provision for young children, they decided to run evening classes too. Increasingly, children who had left school at ten or eleven, like Wesley himself, later wanted to learn more but by then they were working during the day. Providing classes in the evenings was just what was needed for these and older students. Wesley would have become aware of the Pypers' plans through his Good Templar links and when the subject of shorthand classes was broached it was soon agreed that WG would transfer to the Academy staff. In due course adverts seeking interested pupils were placed in the local papers for classes to commence the next term. Following a successful uptake, shorthand classes became a regular part of the school's curriculum.

On a Saturday in September 1874, the *Belfast Telegraph* carried an advert worded thus:

> **SHORTHAND**
> Mr Lyttle's Classes during the ensuing Winter Season will meet at the **BELFAST MERCANTILE ACADEMY**, Glenravel Street, commencing **1ˢᵗ OCTOBER** next.
> **PRIVATE CLASSES** resumed same date.
> For full particulars, apply to Jas. Pyper, Esq., M.A., at the Academy; or to W. G. Lyttle, 73 Denmark Street, Carlisle Circus.

From this we can confirm that, in addition to his employment as a night school teacher, WG was tutoring private pupils, too. He had been right in predicting a demand for the skill.

Another new arrival

The previous year, Lizzie and Wesley's friends, the M'Murtrys, had made the short move from Carlisle Street to the next road, Eglinton Place; rather like the Lyttle's had done a couple of years previously. It was probably for the same reason—to acquire larger accommodation, for the M'Murtrys' move was in time for their baby daughter to be born there at the end of January, 1874. In the midst of all the fuss and congratulations over her friends' new arrival, Lizzie must surely have had difficulty constraining her own excitement. She had to wait, though, until she was sure.

It was not too long a wait before she was able to tell Wesley and they could both share the good news with their friends that they, too, were expecting. About seven months later, the Lyttles had also moved house once again. They had found a place on Denmark Street,[56] which, at that time, was a quiet cul-de-sac running south from Carlisle Circus, and No. 73 was only a couple of streets and a couple of minutes away from the M'Murtrys' home. It was also within a five minute walk of the Academy—no doubt another point of consideration in choosing the new address. But perhaps the main reason for the move would have been Lizzie's need for a fresh start

---

[56] Today's Denmark Street houses can be seen in Appendix F – Fig 3

6 - TEMPERANCE AND TEACHING

for the new life forming within her. A fresh start, away from the bitter memories of Hopeton Street.

She and Wesley were soon settled into their new home with John, who at eight was showing quite a talent for drawing, and his sister, Agnes, just six. Lizzie's natural concern that this time her baby would be born safe and healthy would have been assuaged a little knowing that Dr Alexander M'Murtry was only round the corner. And, of course, her sister, Isabella, still lived not too far away and could provide extra care and assistance, if needed, during her confinement.

It was just bad luck that little Eva—Elizabeth Evelyne—chose to arrive on the first of October. Her proud and, no doubt, anxious father, still painfully mindful of the trauma of the arrival of their previous offspring was forced to abandon his wife and baby daughter that same evening to take the first night class of the new season at the Belfast Mercantile Academy.

Chapter 7 – KEEPING BOOKS AND LENDING BOOKS

1874 – 1875

Mother and daughter, as it turned out, were fine and 'Eliza' had reverted to using the name 'Lizzie' once more, according to the birth certificate. Perhaps this was in honour of the new baby, Elizabeth Evelyne, although, as we have said, the child grew up as Eva, after Lizzie's middle name. The certificate gives her father's profession as 'Shorthand Writer'. Wesley, the family man and Mr Lyttle, the teacher of shorthand continued to live harmoniously alongside WG, the writer and Brother Wesley, the Worthy Chief Templar and entertainer. His services in the latter capacity were being called upon ever more frequently—particularly in Good Templar circles.

Just a month before the birth of baby Eva he was asked to attend a soirée run by the Newtownards Good Templars "Arc of Refuge Lodge." This was held in their recently acquired premises in West Street, not far from his old school. Was he reminiscing of his days as a pupil there, I wonder, as he turned up at 6:30 for the event which lasted through until ten o'clock with a full programme of entertainment. WG's contribution was to read "some original humorous pieces, capitally," according to the *Belfast Telegraph's* write-up after the event.

On another occasion, at the Lancasterian Schoolroom on Belfast's Frederick Street, he helped the 'Extreme Lodge' in a fund-raising concert for the 'John Pyper Lodge' where his "original poetical address added a pleasing variety to the proceeding": the *Belfast News-Letter*, this time.

7 - KEEPING BOOKS AND LENDING BOOKS

Business ventures

During the year following little Eva's birth WG developed three further strings to his vocational bow. From his early experience of writing court reports he would still have been submitting the odd piece for the papers. More than likely these included some of the brief accounts that were printed following a Good Templar concert in which he had participated; they never had a by-line. He knew now how the printed news was gathered from correspondents, free-lance writers and other media sources. He was a writer—mostly of amusing fiction, but there was always the possibility of branching out and perhaps becoming a reporter.

For the present, though, he noticed a second field in which his early studies in book-keeping equipped him to provide a needed service. He discussed his ideas with a friend called Martin Shaw and together they decided to set up in business as accountants. The firm was already established by March of 1875 when, according to a notice in the *Belfast News-Letter,* their services were employed as executors in the bankruptcy case of one, John M'Cann of Belfast under the newly introduced Bankruptcy (Ireland) Amendment Act of 1872.

In less than eighteen months the business had prospered and expanded, occupying city-centre premises and requiring WG to place an ad in the *Belfast Telegraph* for "Two smart, educated Boys, 12 to 14 years, for office work. Progressive salary. Apply to W. G. Lyttle & Co., Mercantile Agents and Accountants, 27 Victoria Street."

The third idea developed alongside the growing realisation that perhaps their move away from Hopeton St had been too hasty. 73, Denmark St was convenient for the Academy, but it just wasn't big enough for two boisterous children and a baby—and WG's expanding business interests. His latest plans would demand yet more space.

Circulating Library

The price of books up to this time was prohibitive to all but the well-off. To buy a typical novel a working class man might have to part with half his week's wages and even the well-heeled would think twice before splashing out for the latest publications. Because of this, some groups of readers rich enough to afford it used to club together, each becoming the equivalent of a shareholder in the group. The subscriptions were used to buy books that were then lent out exclusively to the members of their so-called Subscription Library. During the 18th century, enterprising businessmen saw an opportunity and established what became known as circulating libraries. Unlike the private subscription libraries, these were open to anyone who could afford an annual membership fee. By the mid-19th century the biggest and best known of these libraries were Mudie's and those run by W. H. Smith at their railway newspaper kiosks.

The sheer capacity of Mudie's libraries in London, Birmingham and Manchester enabled him to negotiate preferential rates with the publishers and Mr Mudie was able to undercut the membership fees charged by other circulating libraries. From a typical print run of 1000, often over 500 copies would be sold to Mudie's and the other circulating libraries around Britain, giving the publisher a guaranteed return on his investment. At the same time, it opened up the increasing number of excellent stories being written to many more readers.

Back in the 1850s parliament had passed an Act that provided for free public libraries to be established and ever since his childhood Wesley would have appreciated this intention. But he waited in vain for its implementation, which was destined not to happen until early in the 20th century. It seems likely that, when he could afford it, he joined a circulating library, himself, because he knew all about them and the excellent service they provided. So in 1875, his third idea was to establish his own circulating library and run it as another business venture.

WG would have been familiar with the plethora of accomplished contemporary writers that had emerged in the 19th century. Wonderful works of fiction were being published by the likes of Sheridan, Thackeray, Dickens, Jane Austen, the Bronte Sisters, Walter Scott, Wilkie Collins... and the poets, too: Wordsworth, Tennyson, Keats, Shelly and one of WG's favourites, Robert Burns and many more. The potential reading public in Belfast would have been spoiled for choice were it not for the prohibitive price tags. As a means of softening this economic hurdle, the three-volume novel had become common. Not like a modern trilogy, but one story divided into three parts, each to be sold at the slightly more affordable price of nine shillings. In the

7 - KEEPING BOOKS AND LENDING BOOKS

second decade of the 21st century this would equate to about £38, so "slightly" is the operative word.

When accountancy work was slow, WG saw lending books as a proficient way of increasing his coffers while providing a worthwhile service to his local community. To bring his plans to fruition, however, he had to overcome two problems. How to provide sufficient books to make the library attractive to its potential members and how to house all these volumes where they could be browsed before borrowing. The cost of meeting the first must, surely, have been beyond his means and so it is likely that he took advantage of the practice of opening a franchise with one of the large circulating libraries. As to the second problem, yet again the Lyttle's found themselves house hunting.

They soon came upon the ideal solution a little way up the Old Lodge Road. Two adjacent properties, numbers 103 and 105 became vacant. They could be adapted into one unit big enough to house the growing Lyttle family and provide space for a fine collection of books where people could come in and make their selections. It is likely that Lizzie would have been involved in this new home industry, too, as it was the practice in some circulating libraries to supply coffee to the affluent ladies and gentlemen who came to browse their shelves.

An advert for a Grand Spelling Bee to be held in the Lancasterian Schoolroom on 13 August, 1875 in aid of the Temperance cause announced that tickets were available from, amongst others, "W. G. Lyttle, at the Circulating Library, 103 & 105 Old Lodge Road."

Perhaps WG bought a new book to celebrate moving into their new home; maybe even as a gift for Lizzie. He could well have bought her a novel that had just been published, called *Far from the Madding Crowd,* by a new young writer named Thomas Hardy. It was the author's fourth novel but the write-ups that the library franchise received were already hailing it as the one that would raise this promising thirty-four-year-old to prominence.

It would certainly have been on the shelves of 103/105 Old Lodge Road, along with titles such as *Adam Bede* and *Silas Marner* by Mary Ann Evans who, WG would have been amused to discover, found getting published easier by adopting the male pseudonym of George Elliot. The more adventurous stories like Scott's *Ivanhoe* or Melville's

THE STORYTELLER

Moby-Dick were always popular with the gentlemen readers, whilst for Lizzie Lyttle and others of the fairer sex, *Pride and Prejudice* and similar novels by Jane Austen and her ilk were more to their taste.

Undoubtedly, WG's collection would have included copies of all the works of the late Mr Charles Dickens who had died just five years previously. Here was a novelist who must have impressed Wesley as a young man and who surely had an influence on how his career as a writer and entertainer progressed. It is worth going back a little to trace this development.

The Dickens' factor

WG would, no doubt, have read something of Charles Dickens' history. How he was born in Portsmouth in 1812—the year of Napoleon's ignominious retreat from Moscow and of America's "second War of Independence" against Britain. How he was thus 32 years of age at the time of Wesley's birth and had already published 8 of his 20 or so major books. But also that he had started his career as a solicitor's clerk and then became a court reporter.[57] The similarity of the starts of their careers must have intrigued WG.

When Dickens turned to writing, he was a principal pioneer of the practice of serialising his novels in periodicals prior to publishing them in book form, using his own journals, *Household Words* and *All the Year Round* for the purpose. In his youth Charles, the schoolboy, developed a fondness for the theatre, even forming his own company of players. In later life his grown-up, amateur theatre group became well known, performing on two occasions before Queen Victoria and Prince Albert. His sense of the theatrical coloured his writing in many of his books and also stood him in good stead when it came to public readings from his various works. He turned those occasions into virtuoso performances, which proved exacting on his own stamina for the more dramatic scenes.

Dickens was the first famous author to tour the country with his readings. He always ensured that there were some tickets priced to be

---

[57] Prior to becoming a Court Reporter, Charles Dickens learnt Thomas Gurney's system of shorthand in his spare time. Gurney's, which was adapted from an even earlier systems developed in the 17th century, pre-dated Pitman's, the system that WG later learned.

7 - KEEPING BOOKS AND LENDING BOOKS

affordable to the working people and yet was soon earning far more from his readings than from the publication of his books.

He first visited Belfast in 1858, when Wesley was just 14, for a well-received public reading of *A Christmas Carol* in the Victoria Hall. This was the same venue where six years later Dr Corry's Irish Diorama would open to similar acclaim and where WG, himself would later become involved as its resident lecturer.

Charles Dickens returned to Belfast in 1867 when he read from *Pickwick Papers* to a packed audience in the Ulster Hall. Seated amongst them, more than likely, were young Wesley and Lizzie Lyttle, enjoying a rare evening out, no doubt safe in the knowledge that wee John was in the capable care of Lizzie's sister, Isabel. They would have been most impressed by the performance of the bearded writer, described the following day in the *Northern Whig* as "one of the very few great authors who are also great actors."

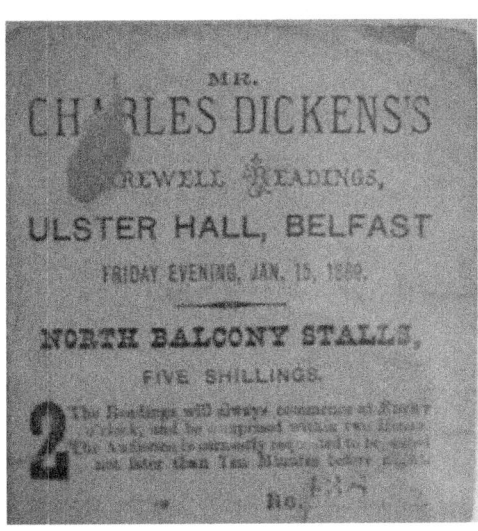

This top-priced ticket for **Dickens' Farewell Readings** (WG's may well have been in a cheaper seat) belonged to the grandfather of the late George Cash of Bangor. It is currently in the possession of George's daughter, Helen Ritchie of Bangor, who kindly allowed me to reproduce it here.

Two years later when Dickens came once more to the same venue in Belfast his health was starting to fail and the tour was billed as "Mr Charles Dickens's Farewell Readings." I feel sure WG would not have missed the opportunity of again being in the audience, perhaps, this time, without Lizzie who by then had her hands full with a five-month-old baby girl to look after as well as a toddler. So on Friday, 15th January, 1869, eagerly anticipating the appearance of the famous writer, Wesley would have been in his seat in good time, in accordance with the admonition on his ticket: "The audience is earnestly required to be

THE STORYTELLER

seated not later than Ten Minutes before Eight."

During a brilliant two-hour performance the Ulster Hall audience was enthralled by a series of readings, many light-hearted and comedic in effect but culminating in a breath-taking account of the murder of Nancy from *Oliver Twist*. Dickens delivered it with such passion and drama that many believed the energy he expended on this, night after night, hastened his early death the following year in 1870, aged just 58.

By then, WG had already had a taste of the limelight with his spell as a Diorama lecturer, but he had yet to stand up in front of an audience and read his own stories. He was surely inspired by Dickens' imposing presence that filled the stage and held his audience spellbound. He would have seen, not just a writer of wonderful tales, but a fine storyteller who, with the merest gesture or inflection of tone could portray equally the pathos of Nancy's resolute love, or the villainy of Bill Sykes, the object of her misguided affection. Or, in turn, incite the mirth and laughter of his adoring fans with an amusing account of the trial from *Pickwick Papers*.

This was surely a gentleman whom WG would wish to emulate. Or, knowing the impishness of his nature, perhaps the verb he would have employed was "parody." The vision of Dickens on stage at the Ulster Hall and the echoes of the applause he received would have stayed long with WG. He could see himself commanding a similar stage with gesture and tone as he regaled a rapt audience with his humorous tales of "Ballycuddy".

But as he walked home from the Ulster Hall on that dark, wintry night in January of 1869, by the hissing gaslight of the city's streetlamps, he could hardly have foreseen that he would one day be reading, in a parish magazine, a review of his own performance that said:

> *[WG Lyttle] was received with great enthusiasm. Those who did not see and hear him missed a treat. Some of his touches are worthy of Dickens. Tears filled the eyes, or smiles lit up the faces of the*

7 - KEEPING BOOKS AND LENDING BOOKS

audience, as the reader passed from grave to gay. The building was packed.[58]

Tired but contented, Wesley's thoughts were likely still on Charles Dickens' characters, maybe now intermingled in his mind with his own creations, when he reached home and turned his key in the latch. He would have been glad to be back with Lizzie and the children. I'm sure he wanted to tell his wife all about the great evening he had just enjoyed and about his future plans for his "country cousin."

---

[58] From the *Parish Church Magazine* of Drew Memorial Church, Grosvenor Road, Belfast.

THE STORYTELLER

Chapter 8 – A PARTING AND A PROMOTION

1875 – 1878

As WG stood in 1875, perusing the row of Charles Dickens' novels on a library shelf at 103/105, Old Lodge Road, was he recalling that last stage appearance in Belfast of the prolific author? Whether or not inspired by the great English writer, WG had now started to read his own stories in public. He continued to take opportunities to do so and they were always well received.

By the time little Eva reached her second birthday in October of '76, WG was busier than ever. Apart from entertaining his public, he had his accountancy firm, his circulating library and his evening classes teaching shorthand. In addition, his work for the Independent Order of Good Templars was taking up more and more of his spare time. There was the day-to-day running of the "Good Samaritan" Lodge but there was also time needed in relation to a rift which had developed between the British and American branches of the IOGT.

White Supremacists

The disagreement was over the American response to the white supremacist movement in the southern states. The British IOGT believed that "there are no classes or races, but one human brotherhood," while in America white Templars across the South refused to allow integrated, bi-racial lodges. On this issue, in May of 1876, the British IOGT took the decision to secede from the Right Worthy Grand Lodge at Louisville and establish what they called the Right Worthy Grand Lodge of the World.

8 - A PARTING AND A PROMOTION

It was with much concern (as we shall see subsequently) that WG learnt two months later in July that the Grand Lodge of Ireland had endorsed this decision and also broken with their American founders.

Over the next six months WG and his friend, Alexander M'Murtry worked tirelessly with other Templars seeking to reach an accommodation. In America, too, the position was being re-evaluated and many lodges, including some black lodges, came to the opinion that their Temperance objectives were too important to be compromised by segregation issues. Amid much controversy the Good Templars decided to tolerate segregated lodges to preserve their higher aims.

However distasteful it might be, WG and his like-minded brother Templars concurred with this decision to compromise, believing that the temperance work was too important to risk being side-lined by racial issues. As a result of the endeavours of such men as these, a large turnout of Good Templars attended a special session of the Grand Lodge of Ireland in Clarence Place Hall, Belfast,[59] on Thursday 25 January, 1877. The Saturday, 3 February issue of the *Belfast Weekly News* covered the event. They reported the passing of a motion proposed by Dr M'Murtry to review the resolution adopted the previous July and continued, that the meeting

> *received, amid great applause and cheering, Col. J. J. Hickman, of Kentucky, the Grand Worthy Chief Templar of the body seceded from. Col. Hickman addressed the Grand Lodge in an eloquent speech of about two hours duration after which it was moved by Br M'Murtry, seconded Mr W. P. Holmes, and enthusiastically resolved—"That the Grand Lodge, assembled in special session, having most carefully reconsidered the resolution adopted by it in July last, wherein it expressed 'its cordial approval of the action taken by the representatives of the British*

---

[59] Clarence Place Hall was a prestigious venue only recently built. Some years later in 1898 it would find itself a close neighbour to Belfast's newly-erected City Hall. See photo in Appendix F – Fig 4.

Grand Lodge and those who acted with them in reconstructing the Right Worthy Grand Lodge of the World and heartily pledged its adherence, allegiance, and support to that body as the supreme council of the Order' herby declares its conviction that that resolution was not only adopted with undue haste and without sufficient information, but was not justified by the facts of the case..."

The resolution concluded by affirming that the Grand Lodge "cordially and frankly returns to its old allegiance to the Right Worthy Grand Lodge from which it received its charter, and to whose honoured chief—Br. Colonel J. J. Hickman, GWCT*, who has just so eloquently addressed us—we offer a most hearty and fraternal welcome."

WG is the new Grand Worthy Secretary for the IOGT

The *Weekly News* then reported on the appointment of new officers to the reconstituted Grand Lodge, which is how we know of WG's approval and involvement in the affair. He now became the Grand Worthy Secretary (GWS) to the Grand Lodge of Ireland—a position of responsibility second only in importance to the Grand Chief Templar and his deputy. He placed an ad in the *Belfast Telegraph* the following day convening a meeting of the "Good Samaritan" Lodge No. 59 for that evening: "FULL MEETING of Members requested Tonight at Eight o'clock sharp to transact important business."

The nature of the "important business" will have been the same as that carried out in Lodges all around the country, re-declaring their allegiance to their American roots. One such meeting—of the I.O.G.T, The People's Lodge, No. 5—was reported in the *Belfast Telegraph* on the following Wednesday, 31 January, 1877:

> *... The lodge having been opened in due form, followed the example so worthily set them by the Grand Lodge in special session, and received, amid great applause, Colonel J. J. Hickman, of Kentucky,*

8 - A PARTING AND A PROMOTION

> *the R.W.G.T.* of the body seceded from, who addressed the lodge in an eloquent and appropriate speech, explained the present position and various phases of the now celebrated "Negro Question" and requested the careful and candid consideration of the action of the R.W.G.T.**

(* Col Hickman has variously been given the title of "Grand Worthy Chief Templar" and "Right Worthy Grand Templar" in the time-honoured tradition of imprecise journalism.)

So the Kentucky Colonel was obviously on a whistle-stop tour to win back the Irish lodges and reunite the temperance movement. The report told of the unanimous agreement to a resolution in favour of that adopted by the Grand Lodge previously, to return to their American roots:

> *... and express our sincere and hearty approval of the resolutions passed, and hail with unfeigned joy the return of the Grand Lodge of Ireland to her maternal allegiance, and beg, with fraternal greetings, to tender to Col. Hickman the right hand of fellowship, and to instruct our secretary to communicate this fact to the G. W. S., Br W. G. Lyttle, and forward to him the per capita tax for the ensuing quarter.*

An additional item of business at the Good Samaritan meeting would have been to accept the resignation of WG as their Worthy Chief Templar to enable him to take up his new role in the Grand Lodge of Ireland as the Grand Worthy Secretary—I have found no subsequent references to him as WCT with the Good Samaritan Lodge.

In his new position, his accountancy skills stood him in good stead as he kept track of the subs coming in from all the lodges around the country and his organisational ability continued to be utilised, but now on a much larger scale. That summer, he helped arrange and lead an excursion by train to Donaghadee for about a hundred members of various Good Templar lodges from the Belfast area. They met up with

THE STORYTELLER

other lodges during a stopover at Newtownards, including one from Bangor that marched from there to join them for their onward journey to the 'Dee. The event had a good write-up in the Saturday, 18th August, 1877 edition of the *Belfast Weekly News*.

Chairing at one venue; performing at another

WG's services continued to be called upon outside the sphere of the Good Templars and not only as an entertainer with his comical stories. The month following the dramatic proceedings of the Grand Lodge in Clarence Place Hall, WG was back at that venue, this time taking the chair at a "Grand Concert and Choral Union", featuring Mr. W. Gamble as conductor and Mr A. Smith as accompanist. The *Belfast Telegraph* of Thursday, 15th February, 1877 gave them this rather underwhelming build-up: "From the programme arranged, the proceedings are likely to be very interesting." We can but hope that the level of interest was only heightened by the presence of WG as chairman for the evening.

The following month William M'Murtry, the father of his old friend, Alexander, contacted WG to ask if he would do a reading on Tuesday the 27th March at the first public meeting of the Ballynure Band of Hope[60] that he was founding. His son, he explained, would also be speaking at the event. WG readily agreed to contribute and, no doubt, took the opportunity to wish Alexander success with his latest venture—launching a new Temperance monthly journal.

The first issue of a new Temperance periodical, the *Irish Templar* had just come out, edited by Dr A. H. H. M'Murtry and published by another prominent member of the Good Templars, Mr W Erskine Maine of Belfast. It would provide a voice for the leadership of the IOGT in Ireland to promote the principles and benefits of total abstinence alongside wholesome stories and other items of an

---

[60] In 1855 The United Kingdom Band of Hope Union formed to support local, Christian-based groups that held children's meetings with a variety of activities always including teaching about the dangers of alcohol. It still exists today as Hope UK, a national charity providing drug and alcohol education and training for children and young people, parents and youth workers.

8 - A PARTING AND A PROMOTION

entertaining nature. Dr M'Murtry would almost certainly have mentioned the *Templar* during his own talk at Ballynure.

The proceedings were mainly of a religious nature, opening in prayer and including the singing of a number of sacred songs and a scripted dialogue about total abstinence. WG's light-hearted contribution must have made quite a contrast. According to the *Belfast News-Letter*, Friday 30th March, 1877, "W. G. Lyttle of Belfast, then gave an original piece called 'The Christ'nin'," the local allusions being very striking." This was the first public reading of WG's latest tale about Paddy M'Quillan,

An amusing tale in itself, it is, however, not apparent to today's reader that WG mixed real people in with his fictional characters as guests at the Christening party, poking fun at some Ballynure residents who were his original audience. There is nothing else in the story, other than the guests, that could be taken as a "local allusion".

In the published version he writes, for example:

> *Efter a guid while's floosterin' an' bletherin', we a' got set doon tae oor denner, an' it wud hae din yer heart guid tae see them fowk eatin'. Dinnae let on that A tell't ye, but without ony jokin' some o' yon boys stomaks maun be made of indianrubber. Mosey Mertin had got in aside Susanna Todd; but A cud tell ye that if it's true, as the fowk sez, that they're saft aboot yin anither, it hasnae tak awa' their appetites. A set doon a hale plate o' prittas atween them, an' in less nor five minits there wuz naethin' but skins. I dae not ken what they din wi' them. 'Well' sez I, 'Dinnae forget tae leev room for the epple dumplins.' 'A'm glad ye spauk in time,' sez Jamey Menyarry; an' A saw him takin' a couple o' buttons oot o' his weskit.*[61]

---

[61] After a good while of flattering and idle chatter, we all got sat down to our dinner, and it would have done your heart good to see those folk eating. Don't reveal that I told you, but without any joking, some of those boys' stomchs must be made of India rubber. Moses Martin had got in beside Susanna Todd, but I could tell you that if it's true, as the folks say, that they are soft about one another, it hasn't taken away their appetites. I set down a whole plate of potatoes between them, and in less than five minutes there was nothing but skins. I do not

THE STORYTELLER

It would seem that, for the event, WG substituted the actual names of some of the members of the Ballynure audience for the likes of the young lovers, Moses Martin and Susanna Todd, and the portly Jamie Menary. He had learned early, when writing to amuse his friends, of the comedy to be found in these "local allusions" and he obviously continued the practice in his later stories, tailoring them to each particular venue. Perhaps not surprisingly, given the occasion of this reading, there is no mention in his story of "wetting the baby's head" (other than by the minister, with water, of course). All the festive food is washed down with tea only. Indeed, when Paddy's wife asked him who they should invite to their baby's Christening party Paddy replies, "Naebuddy but Teetotallers, for they'll get naething here tae drink stronger nor the essence o' shamrocks."[62] [63]

Family business

WG continued to travel around the country with his readings—from Newtownards to Newry and from Ballynure to Belfast, while still growing his Accountancy business. The amount of work they had continued to require the help of young apprentices and in July,'77 one of these needed to be replaced. WG put an advert in the *Belfast Telegraph*: "SMART LAD WANTED. Must write and figure neatly. Apply to W.G. Lyttle & Co., 27 Victoria Street." Their eldest child, John, at 11 was already developing a good head for figures alongside his improving artistic ability, but he would still have been a little young to take into the family business.

By mid-summer, Wesley and Lizzie knew that they were expecting yet another new arrival. At nine, Agnes would have enjoyed helping to look after her little sister, Eva, now nearly three. She must have been as delighted as the rest of the family to hear she would soon

---

know what they did with them. 'Well,' I said, 'Don't forget to leave room for the apple dumplings.' 'I'm glad you spoke in time,' said Jamie Menary, and I saw him taking a couple of buttons out of his waistcoat.

[62] Nobody but Teetotallers, for they'll get nothing here to drink stronger than the essence of shamrocks.

[63] An infusion believed to have medicinal properties—not anay blend of fine Irish whisky that today bears the shamrock name.

8 - A PARTING AND A PROMOTION

have a tiny baby to cuddle as well. And, in keeping with former practice, by the time the new baby was due, the Lyttles would have moved yet again. The new address on the birth certificate is difficult to decipher with any certainty. It says, '1 Bel???? Street' but Bel what? Although there is a Belgrave Street close to all the Lyttles' other former homes, it would be hard to interpret the illegible handwritten address as this.

More possible, however, is Belvoir Street in Ballymacarrett, East Belfast. Other evidence suggests that this was indeed where they moved, giving up the circulating library and, for the first time since Wesley came to Belfast fourteen years ago, moving away from the Shankill/Old Lodge Road district. For the first eight years of Wesley's life in Belfast this area had provided a pleasantly safe and affordable place to live. After the repeal of the Party Processions Act in 1872, however, rioting became endemic and he must have felt he was living on the edge of a war zone. After five years of that he had had enough and he moved with his family across the River Lagan to, hopefully, a safer part of town.

Built on reclaimed land that was once tidal mudflats, the newer Ballymacarrett development would have represented a step up for Wesley and Lizzie that they, no doubt, felt was more appropriate to Wesley's growing status. Confirmation that their new home was in Belvoir Street can be taken from a reference that the new child's birth place was in County Down, all their previous children having been born in County Antrim. At that time, east of the Lagan was in Down, the river forming the boundary between the two counties, although some years later the border was moved so that all of Belfast fell within the county of Antrim.[64]

No. 1 Belvoir St occupied a prime position on the corner of the Newtownards Road. It wasn't too far from the River Lagan, where the tall masts of trading ships from around the world could always be seen, even from some way off. To clinch the matter that we have, I believe, the right address, it was only five minutes' walk away from where Lizzie's sister still lived in Madrid Street.

---

[64] This explains how the Lyttle's sixth child, born later at the same address, has Antrim as the county of birth.

THE STORYTELLER

The birth of an idea—and of WG's fifth child

That year, the *Belfast Weekly News* was serialising a new novel by Mary Elizabeth Braddon, the writer of the sensational *Lady Audley's Secret* that had been published back in 1862. That novel would certainly have been amongst the books that graced the shelves of Lyttle's Circulating Library and WG will have been interested to see her latest, *An Open Verdict*, appearing in the newspaper.[65]

Ever since Charles Dickens' Farewell Readings, when WG was reminded how Dickens serialised his stories in his weekly journal, he had been noticing the books and stories he was seeing increasingly in the columns of various newspapers. He must have enjoyed the re-publication in the *Ballymena Observer* of Corbet's *The Miller of Calder*—first published in 1866—as it was written in the Ulster-Scots that he favoured himself. The final chapter, XIII, was printed in the Saturday, 15th December edition of the paper where we see that the Miller's name was Robin and he had a daughter called Peggy. Could this story, when it first came out, have been the source, perhaps unconsciously, of the names of WG's famous character, Robin Gordon and his beloved wife, Peggy?

Now, with Christmas only a week away, the Lyttles were somewhat preoccupied. The children, of course, would be excitedly anticipating their presents and hoping Father Christmas could find them alright at their new house on Belvoir Street. Lizzie must have tried to enter into the festivities as much as she could but, having grown enormous with their next baby due in a couple of weeks, she would have been grateful for any help from Wesley to keep up the family's spirits. Wesley loved his wife and children and was glad to help out, but all the time he was thinking, too, about his other great love, his as-yet-unpublished writing.

People clearly appreciated his stories. The continuous laughter as he read them and the rapturous applause he received when he finished was ample proof of that. Yet even a packed school hall or an auditorium was only a few hundred people at best. He wanted a wider audience; his work deserved it.

---

[65] For some reason, *An Open Verdict* is not included in the so-called *Complete Works of Mary Elizabeth Braddon* that is now available as an eBook.

8 - A PARTING AND A PROMOTION

He decided that 1878 would be the year he should first appear in print. Other writers were doing it; why shouldn't he? He was already becoming quite well-known and his stories popular. They would be an asset to any of the newspapers, which were always striving to boost their circulation. As mentioned, he was probably already a seasoned contributor to some of their columns with write-ups of events he had attended.

So Wesley's excitement that Christmas was as much about his publishing plans for the following year as it was for the seasonal festivities and the imminent arrival of their new baby. Seeing his tales in print would be a new departure, yet his thoughts, no doubt, kept returning to his reading engagements and comparing them with how Charles Dickens had so dramatized his stories on the stage of the Ulster Hall all those years ago. WG would have believed he managed a reasonable presentation of his own work; he must do, to judge from the audience reaction. But he'd probably have felt he could do better. What if he were to dress in the guise of one of his characters?

He would have to choose between his two main Ulster-Scots protagonists, Paddy M'Quillan and Robin Gordon, and he was likely still pondering which of these he should favour a few weeks after Christmas when Lizzie went into labour. He probably tried to keep out of the way, knowing the midwife had everything in hand. Let us imagine the scene:

> After what seemed an absolute age to WG and must have seemed a lifetime to Lizzie, with a final yell from her, the baby was delivered.
> 'What have we got? Let me see,' Lizzie cried out.
> 'Ah, now just you rest a while, Mrs Lyttle,' the midwife said, fussing over cleaning up the new-born infant.
> 'But is it a boy or a girl? I want to cuddle the wean.'
> 'Ah, it's a wee boy you have.'
> 'Well, can I see him?'
> 'I think you need to rest a bit, first; it was a difficult delivery.'
> 'I want to see my baby!'

THE STORYTELLER

The midwife held the little bundle wrapped in a towel and looked long at Lizzie. She made no move to offer up her tiny charge to his anxious mother.

Chapter 9 – "ROBIN" APPEARS IN THE PAPERS…

1878

My grandfather, Roland Alexander Lyttle, entered this world on Tuesday, 15th January, 1878. He was born with an orofacial cleft—a congenital birth defect.

> 'The child's got a harelip,' the midwife whispered urgently to Wesley before he joined his wife. The note of horror in her tone was ill-disguised.
>
> 'The medical term is a cleft lip, woman,' said Wesley as he gazed at his son, who was otherwise a fine and healthy child, 'and I'll thank you not to use that term again. There's no 17th century witchcraft involved, whatever your old wives' superstitions. Runs in my family, unfortunately. Often skips a generation or two, I'm told, but it crops up from time to time.'

Treatment

And so it was with little Roland. A setback, to be sure, but not one that couldn't be overcome with the wonderful advances in modern surgery in recent times. Wesley had heard the use of chloroform in operations was by now commonplace. He would have shuddered recalling tales his father related about some of his forbears who had had their split lips sewn together and even cleft palates operated upon in days before any anaesthetic was available. He was grateful that Roland's palate seemed intact and that, when the time came for his tiny upper lip to be joined he would, at least, be asleep throughout the painful procedure.

When the time came. That was the rub. The Belfast General Hospital in Frederick Street was so busy and overcrowded.

'The Belfast *Royal* Hospital,' Lizzie would have reminded her husband, as they discussed the way forward for their baby boy.

'Royal Hospital. Indeed. Nothing but the best for our son.' Wesley had not yet got used to the new name after the General had gained its royal charter three years previously. It would be another two decades before it changed its name again, in 1899, this time to the Royal Victoria Hospital and four years after that before it relocated to its present much larger site on the Grosvenor Road.

But, for now, it was for admission to the old cramped premises which was in so much demand that the Lyttles had to wait. Wait until such time as a space could be found for Roland to have his operation. There was the Workhouse, of course, set up under the Poor Law, which had a hundred or so hospital beds and the Lyttles had heard the rooms were even heated now, since Hugh Craig & Co, a local coal merchant, had agreed to supply them with fuel a few years back, in 1870. However, this facility, which would eventually become Belfast City Hospital, was already full to capacity and the medical officer was even trying to get permission to use part of the old men's dormitory accommodation as an overflow.[66]

The worst part of the waiting for Lizzie was not being able to suckle her little one. The wee mite knew instinctively what he had to do but try as he would, the gap in his upper lip refused to allow him to suck. The frustration made him fretful and he cried. It was just as trying for his mother who longed to cuddle him to her bosom, yet he soon gave up and wanted none of it.

Over the next weeks Lizzie had to spend many hours expressing her milk into a jug and then feeding it to the child from a teaspoon. This was a slow, laborious process. It was difficult to get him to take

---

[66] According to "Poverty and the Poor Law in Ireland, 1850–1914" by Virginia Crossman (Liverpool University Press.)

9 - "ROBIN" APPEARS IN THE PAPERS...

enough. He always seemed hungry, which made him fractious.[67] Caring for little Roland was so much more time-consuming than she had been used to with his siblings—apart from poor Robert. She would have tried hard not to neglect the other children and relied upon nine-year-old Agnes being as helpful as she could be. Even her eldest, John, at 11, probably lent a hand when he wasn't occupied with one of his paintings.

Seeking publication

Throughout this trying period, Wesley must have helped where he was able, of course, but his business commitments required much of his time and attention. In addition to his accountancy firm he was spending more time on his writing—not only with new material but editing and refining his existing stories to get them the best he could possibly make them, prior to seeking publication in the columns of a newspaper. The big question that exercised his mind as the year progressed was which paper?

I suspect the possibility that any editors might turn down his offer to contribute to their particular publications would not have occurred to the successful and confident 34-year-old; at any rate, not the provincial journals. It just might be more difficult to get accepted by one of the big city papers, which may be why he decided not to try that route.

There was another reason, however. The *Irish Templar* had proved popular in its first year, being circulated extensively among the IOGT lodges in Ireland. Probably due to pressure of other commitments, Dr M'Murtry felt he must relinquish the editorship and in March of '78 the *Londonderry Sentinel* was reporting that now the periodical "was in the hands of four able editors;" not, perhaps an ideal way of building on M'Murtry's fine start. However, whether or not at the suggestion of his friend the retiring editor, WG submitted some of his humorous sketches to the *Templar* around this time.

It was a monthly—with a decent circulation, but nothing like that of a popular weekly newspaper. But still, it would be a start. By June

---

[67] I describe Lizzie's difficulties from first-hand experience of my wife and I with one of our own children, who inherited the same condition.

THE STORYTELLER

the *Newry Telegraph*, reporting upon the latest issue of the *Irish Templar*, was saying, "Our Country Cousin is to the front as usual, and his pictures of 'Paddy M'Quillan's Wedding' is laughter-provoking. It is the best effort we have yet had of his pawky, prolific pen."

To be "to the front as usual" clearly implies that WG's stories had appeared in at least two previous issues. The press accounts showed they were being well received. WG would have taken heart from this but he still wanted the larger exposure his sketches would get in a weekly. As spring turned to summer he considered the options.

Of the provincials, some, such as the *Ballymena Observer* and the *Newry Telegraph* already ran stories, and there was the *Chronicle* in Newtownards, a fairly new paper. He had placed advertisements in the *Newry Telegraph* from time to time so had contacts there and they had reported favourably upon his stories in the *Templar*. It was an old-established tri-weekly journal and the county paper for Down with a large circulation. It was available in the principal towns of Counties Antrim, Armagh, Cavan, Derry, Down, Fermanagh, Louth and Dublin and was read, it claimed, "by the Nobility and Gentry, as well as the Professional, Commercial, and Agricultural Classes." He decided he would submit a couple of his pieces to the editor and see what response he might get.

The distant strains of a flute band drifting through his open window during a continuing warm spell in July, would have been a likely backdrop as he thumbed through his manuscripts trying to decide which tales to send. Were the Orangemen parading in the vicinity of nearby Short Strand, he maybe wondered. There had been considerable unrest in other parts of the city in the lead up to the Twelfth processions this year and if a Protestant band were to march through that Catholic area it would not improve matters. The job of the police would not be made any easier as they tried to keep the peace.

With his thoughts on the police, he turned again to a frivolous little piece he had written about an RIC[68] sub-constable from Tipperary who almost gets caught in the kitchen with Biddy, his sweetheart, when the mistress of the house returns home

---

[68] Royal Irish Constabulary

unexpectedly. It was quite short, so would be easy for an editor to fit in. Along with it, he chose another piece all about his character, Paddy M'Quillan, and some of his adventures when he decided to take a "trip tae Glesco."[69] This piece and "The Tipperary Policeman" were soon *en route* to Newry.

The Mayor's Proclamation

There was much rejoicing in the Lyttle household not long afterwards, when it was confirmed and agreed that the Newry Telegraph would be delighted to carry WG's stories—as many as he could supply. The first one would appear on Tuesday, 17th September, 1878. But an even greater cause for joy in the family was having little Roland home from hospital and recovering well from the ordeal of having the two halves of his tiny upper lip sewn together. The surgeon had done a good job. It wasn't quite even and, of course, there'd be a nasty scar, but it was so much better than before. Lizzie wouldn't have been able to stop cuddling "her darlin' wean" and giving thanks for modern hospitals. Or gazing at the babe in her arms and imagining him as a fully grown man sporting a fine moustache like his father's; one that completely hid his disfigurement. And that is exactly what Roland chose to do. In adulthood no one would have known he had had a birth defect.[70] (Cruel circumstance was later, however, to hand him an even greater cross to bear—see Chapter 34.)

While the family, safe in their home at the top of Belvoir Street, had much to be grateful for, the situation outside on the streets was a matter of concern to them, along with the rest of Belfast's inhabitants. The unrest that had accompanied the Twelfth of July parades had not lessened over the following weeks. The hot, dry spell encouraged younger or rasher elements among the citizenry to spend their evenings goading their neighbours who were of a different religious persuasion, or taunting the police who came between them. Outbreaks of violence were increasing. The 15th August was not far off when the

---

[69] Trip to Glasgow
[70] For photos of Roland with his moustache see Appendix E, Figs 12, 13

THE STORYTELLER

Catholic parades on Our Lady's Day could only be expected to worsen the situation.

Much of the rioting was around the sectarian interface between the Catholic Falls Road and the Protestant Shankill Road in West Belfast, the area Wesley and family had left behind. Where they lived now in East Belfast, however, home to the big shipyards, was not immune to strife.

Shipbuilding had become a major industry in Belfast. One company, Harland and Wolff, with shipyards on Queen's Island, had established a reputation as the world's leading constructor of ocean liners. The company's owners and their workforce of several thousands were emphatically Unionist in their politics. In a few more years the shipyard would become a bastion of opposition to Home Rule. The workers, or Islandmen as they were called, were known to intervene *en masse* in riot situations, as they had done up near Carlisle Circus in 1872 (see chapter 6.)

> It was the 7th of August, and Wesley came home from his office in Victoria Street that evening to inform Lizzie that all the talk in town was of the Mayor and his Proclamation.
>
> 'And what has he proclaimed, may I ask,' said Lizzie 'that has the town and yourself so agitated?'
>
> 'No more processions or bands to march through the streets! Banned the lot.' Wesley sounded incredulous.
>
> 'No more marching? He can't do that! Can he?'
>
> 'He's done it. There'll be ructions, mark my word.'

At the time policing in Belfast was controlled jointly by the Mayor and the Royal Irish Constabulary, often assisted by the Army. Fearing widespread disorder in August, Sir John Preston, as mayor, had decided to issue a proclamation prohibiting people from marching in procession or parading the streets with bands. While his shock tactics did seem to reduce the nightly violence on the streets somewhat, there was growing concern, not to say outrage, that the ban would mean the Islandmen's annual parade due on the 24th could no longer go ahead. This would be unthinkable. The Islandmen always started their yearly

9 - "ROBIN" APPEARS IN THE PAPERS...

summer excursion with an early morning parade through the streets behind the Ballymacarrett Brass Band. But the Mayor was adamant there could be no exceptions to his ban on such marches.

> It was in all the papers. The whole town was talking about it. And nowhere more so than among the Lyttle's neighbours around Belvoir Street. Everyone, it seemed, was either a member, or knew someone who was a member of the Ballymacarrett Brass Band. Talking to the folks round about, Wesley saw how deep their feelings ran. And, of course, it wasn't just the band but the thousands of shipyard workers, too, all equally defiant.
>
> 'I fear they'll march, ban or no ban,' he confided to Lizzie one evening as the 24th fast approached. 'I just hope your man Rea can persuade the Mayor to back down.'

John Rea was a maverick Belfast lawyer, an honorary solicitor for the shipwrights, and no mean antagonist when arguing his case in court. The mayor agreed to raise the matter before the magistrates on 23rd August—the day before the march was due to have taken place. Rea and another of the shipwrights' honorary solicitors, Mr Charles H Ward, challenged the ban, asking for it to be removed and, instead, for the Mayor to use his police to guarantee the safety of the men and their families as they paraded.

> 'What do you know? The ban's been lifted!' Wesley announced to the family when he came home that evening. From his wide grin, they might have thought that he planned to march, himself.
>
> 'Well, praise be,' said Lizzie. 'So John Rea won the day?'
>
> 'He did, though the Mayor never let on that he did. Said, since things had quietened down on the streets the ban was no longer needed.'

THE STORYTELLER

The next day, Saturday, Wesley and his family would surely have been among the thousands of onlookers that lined the streets as the procession set off for York Road railway station and their excursion train to Ballymena. They were led by a regimental figure in a three-cornered hat with feather and carrying an emblem of peace. He was followed by the flamboyant John Rea and members of the organising committee ahead of the Ballymacarrett Brass Band. Behind this came all the workers from the different branches of shipbuilding: first the caulkers, then the painters, then the riveters. They were followed by the joiners, then the shipwrights, the smiths, the drillers and the platers. The labourers marched at the back of the parade, with someone in a Prussian helmet and carrying a battle-axe bringing up the rear. It was a rousing spectacle and it all passed off without incident.

>'A victory for common sense,' Wesley remarked to his wife, as they turned for home, before lapsing into silence. He was thinking about all the fuss and palaver over the last couple of weeks since the Mayor's Proclamation. How it had gripped the town, and indeed the country. The *Newry Telegraph*, as the leading provincial newspaper reported fully upon it. An idea was forming in his mind and when he got home he sat down at once and started writing.

He sent word to the editor of the *Newry Telegraph* that he would be supplying a different story to appear on 17th September—a topical one. And in due course, once he had completed it and polished it up to his satisfaction, it was delivered to the newspaper. On Tuesday 17th September, 1878, the first story by W. G. Lyttle to appear in the *Newry Telegraph* was entitled, "The Islandmen's Procession and the Mayor's Proclamation"[71]. In it, WG recounted the whole tale in his

---

[71] I am indebted to Mark Thompson of Portavogie whose research first established that WG's stories appeared in the *Newry Telegraph,* and the dates upon which each story appeared. He notes, however, that the paper, in attributing

9 - "ROBIN" APPEARS IN THE PAPERS...

own inimitable fashion, allowing his character, "Robin Gordon" to express the indignation felt by himself and his neighbours in Ballymacarrett. This country gentleman farmer was so incensed at the Mayor's audacity that he decided to journey from his Ards home in Ballycuddy, hitching a ride on the early morning milk cart, to speak to the Mayor of Belfast, himself. This is an extract from the tale:

> *Sez Peggy tae me yin day, sez she—*
> *"What ir ye shakin' yer auld heid an' mutterin' tae yersel' aboot? A doot ye hae been daein' sumthin'."*
> *"Sorra thing A hae been daein', Peggy, but A cannae keep that proclamashun oot o' my heid, an' it maun be put a stap tae. Jamey Menyarry's gaun up tae Bilfast the morrow mornin' wi' milk an' butter, an' A'll gang up wi' him, an' if A can see that Meer A'll speak my min' gie an' freely tae him."*
> *"See what meer?" sez Peggy. "Stae at hame, an' luk efter yer ain meer, my man. Did ye gie her a feed o' corn th' day yit?"*
> *"Haud yer tongue, wi' yer havers, Peggy!" sez I. "It's a man A'm talkin' aboot, the Meer o' Bilfast, an'*

"The Islandmen's Procession and the Mayor's Proclamation" to "Robin," describes him as the author of "The Colorado Beetle" and "Paddy M'Quillan's Courtship," implying that these stories may have already appeared in print.

In *The Adventures of Paddy M'Quillan* the story of his Courtship precedes, naturally enough, the account of his Wedding. It was "Paddy M'Quillan's Wedding" that we know appeared in the June '78 issue of the *Irish Templar*. Since we also suspect that this was the third of WG's stories to be printed in the *Templar*, it seems clear from what the *Newry Telegraph* wrote that the other two must have been "The Colorado Beetle" and "Paddy M'Quillan's Courtship."

They quickly became popular items amongst elocutionists to include in local concerts. I have discovered four references in various newspapers to both these stories having been read by different entertainers earlier in 1878. This report from the *Northern Whig* of 18th April, 1878, is of particular interest: "Mr Huston will read Phil Blood's Leap, extracts from Macbeth, Pauline O'Raffetty's Sea Voyage, The Colorado Beetle, and Johnie Armstrong's Disasters." So on that occasion WG shared the billing with William Shakespeare!

no a horse; he's the man that's aboon a' the megistrates, an' sogers an' polis, an' ivery ither buddy in Bilfast, an' it's him that made that proclaymashun aboot the purcessions."

"He's a nice boy that," sez Peggy; "dae they think he's fit tae be a meer?"

"A dinnae ken, Peggy, but A'll gie him my openyin onywae."

"Ye may keep yer win' tae cool yer kail," sez she; "muckle he'll care fur what ye think. Stae at home, an' get the corn cut, an' dinnae be makin' an ass o' yersel'."

"Peggy, A'll gang if ye shud stan' on yer heid," sez I; "it's my duty tae dae sumthin' fur the guid o' my fella-men, an' noo's the time, so A'll awa an' see Jamey Menyarry. We'll be startin' aboot fower o'clock in the mornin'."[72]

---

[72] Peggy says to me one day, she says—

"What are you shaking your old head and muttering to yourself about? I doubt you have been doing something."

"Not a thing have I been doing, Peggy, but I cannot keep that proclamation out of my head, and it must be put a stop to. Jamie Menary's going up to Belfast tomorrow morning with milk and butter, and I'll go up with him, and if I can see that Mayor I'll speak my mind very freely to him."

"See what mare?" says Peggy. "Stay at home, and look after your own mare, my man. Did you give her a feed of corn today yet?"

"Hold your tongue, with your foolish talk, Peggy!" says I. "It's a man I'm talking about, the Mayor of Belfast, and not a horse; he's the man that's above all the magistrates, and soldiers and police, and every other body in Belfast, and it's him that made that proclamation about the processions."

"He's a nice boy that," says Peggy; "do they think he's fit to be a mayor?"

"I don't know, Peggy, but I'll give him my opinion anyway."

"You may keep your wind to cool your cabbage [often used for soup]," says she; "much he'll care for what you think.

9 - "ROBIN" APPEARS IN THE PAPERS...

In WG's story, of course, it's "Robin" who persuades the Mayor to see reason and go before the magistrates to rescind the ban. "Robin" saves the Islandmen's march.

A new hero

Serendipity had laid in his path this golden opportunity to present "Robin" as the hero of the hour. His story appearing just a few weeks after the papers had been full of the reporting of the actual events it was all still fresh in people's memories. It was a new departure for WG; a foray into the world of politics, something of a risk, perhaps. But the tale was received with universal acclaim by the readers of the *Newry Telegraph* and many had to be disappointed as copies of the paper ran out in the shops. By popular request, the Thursday 19th edition of the paper reprinted the story in full two days later and his tale of the hapless "Tipperary Policeman and his Sweetheart Biddy" appeared the following week on Thursday 26th September.

WG couldn't have asked for a better start for his "print debut" and, deciding to cash in on the popularity of the first tale, he wrote another story featuring "Robin" and his, by now, "old friend", the Mayor—"The Meer O' Belfast and the Fechtin' Dugs"[73]. This appeared on Tuesday 1st October and on Saturday 5th October "The Tipperary Policeman" was reprinted, such was the demand for it, too.

Just the following year an advertisement for the Newry Telegraph claimed the circulation of the paper had trebled during the last three years. WG's stories, appearing throughout the previous year, must have made a significant contribution to that success as the advert makes reference to "Robin" first appearing in the Newspaper and still being a contributor. The ad, reproduced below, appeared in WG's first

---

Stay at home, and get the corn cut, and don't be making an ass of yourself."
"Peggy, I'll go if you should stand on your head," says I; "it's my duty to do something for the good of my fellow-men, and now's the time, so I'll away and see Jamie Menary. We'll be starting about four o'clock in the morning."

[73] The Mayor of Belfast and the Fighting Dogs

anthology of short stories *Humorous Readings by "Robin,"* 1879, published by Allen and Johnston.

> ### THE "Newry Telegraph,"
> ESTABLISHED 1812.
>
> THIS Old-Established Newspaper advocates Conservative principles, and Circulates widely through the Counties of Down, Armagh, Antrim, Louth and Derry, among the Noblemen, Gentry and Farmers. It is the County Paper for Down, and contains all the Grand Jury Advertisements. The Circulation of the Paper has trebled during the last three years.
>
> "ROBIN'S" Readings first appeared in this Newspaper, and he is still a Contributor to its columns. [74]

W. G. Lyttle, the writer, was delighted with the initial reception "Robin" and his stories enjoyed on being released to a wider public. It was just what he had hoped for. Now he was convinced the time had arrived for "Robin" to make his first stage appearance before his admiring public.

---

[74] The *Telegraph's* claim to be the first newspaper to print "Robin's" stories is accurate, although their wording is misleading, as it ignores the fact that some of his stories had already appeared in the monthly journal, the *Irish Templar*.

Chapter 10 – ... AND ON STAGE...

1878 – 1879

Although sometimes preoccupied with thoughts about developing "Robin's" career, WG was not neglecting his own work including for the Good Templars. He continued to fulfil his duties as Grand Worthy Secretary to the apparent satisfaction of all. It happened about that time that the position of Secretary to the Irish Temperance League fell vacant and WG, anxious to progress his career, saw it as a natural progression and decided to apply for it. The *Freeman's Journal*, a Dublin newspaper, reported on Friday, 27th September, 1878 that "W.G. Lyttle, so well-known in Ulster as a temperance man, is a candidate for the vacant secretaryship." So his affiliation to the Templars and the good work he was doing was known beyond the confines of a few northern counties. However, in the event, the post went to a Mr J Speers Orb, and WG was left to consider other ways of increasing his income.

Another outlet for "Robin"

He had noticed a report in the *Newtownards Chronicle* on a fine banquet held by Lord Londonderry back in July. It was attended by several hundred of his tenants, invited guests and dignitaries. WG must have read it with interest round about the time he was debating as to which newspaper he should send his stories for publication. Settling upon the *Newry Telegraph*, however, did not necessarily rule out the use of other journals as additional outlets. WG had seen in the write-up of the huge banquet in Newtownards a possible opportunity for "Robin" to increase his audience in his home district of Ards.

Sometime over the next few weeks in August or early September, using the customary comprehensive account of such events that had appeared in the *Chronicle* as his source,[75] WG re-told the story of "The Londonderry Banquet" through the eyes of "Robin" who, he claimed, had been given an invitation to the banquet by none other than the editor of the *Chronicle*, William Henry, himself. Henry says to "Robin":

> *'I'll mak ye a present o' a kerd fur the supper, if ye'll cum.'*
> *'Indeed I wull,' sez I, 'an' I'll be for iver ableeged tae ye for your kindness, an' Peggy an' me'll no forget ye for it.'*[76]

WG pretty much assured his story's publication in the Newtownards paper by having "Robin" sing the praises of William Henry, who had attended the banquet and made a speech.

> *Whun it wuz near ower, they proposed the health o' the Press, and named Mr Henry's name. He got up tae mak a speech, an' dae ye know, he wuz as nice a man as I seen there.*[77]

WG's version of the event had "Robin" mention and comment, often comically, upon the doings of many individuals who were there. As usual, it was the inclusion of these names of people, familiar to many, that would have appealed to the Ards readership. That, and the fact that his story must have been a much better read than the original

---

[75] I have used the same technique, myself, on various occasions throughout this biography to give accurate and authentic background to some of WG's activities.

[76] 'I'll make you a present of a card for the supper, if you'll come.'
'Indeed I will,' says I, 'and I'll be for ever obliged to you for your kindness, and Peggy and me will not forget you for it.'

[77] When it was nearly over, they proposed the health of the Press, and named Mr Henry's name. He got up to make a speech, and do you know, he was as nice a man as I saw there.

10 - ...AND ON STAGE...

dry reportage. "The Londonderry Banquet" appeared in the *Newtownards Chronicle* probably in mid-October.[78]

It is, of course, possible that WG was, himself, a guest at the Banquet but, from the device he used to explain why he didn't quote from Henry's speech it seems more likely that his source was the newspaper article:

> *I'm vexed his speech wusnae printed, fur it wuz yin o' the best that was made that nicht, but A heered him sayin' tae Mr M'Nineth an' the tither importers, whaur they were sittin' at the table, sez he, "Lay doon yer pencils, gentlemen," sez he, "an' dinnae be importin' me."*[79]

Having thus established contact with the Newtownards editor, WG determined to look for further opportunities for Ards-related adventures for his popular character from Ballycuddy.

Becoming "Robin"

Over the past few months the image of how "Robin" should look had been becoming firmer in Wesley's mind. His original idea that the country farmer should have a full beard and moustache was necessary anyway to cover his own smart moustache. Along with it, he thought, perhaps a good head of hair—unlike his own, which was already beginning to recede and thin a little. Wesley was 35, but he envisioned "Robin" as much older—in the autumnal phase of his life, his hair turning white, and aging joints stiffening. He sought out the services of the London Hair-Dressing Rooms in Castle Place in Belfast, where

---

[78] We know this because of a reference in the *Newtownards Chronicle* of 18th January, 1879 that said "The Londonderry Banquet" had recently appeared in the *Chronicle*. It could not have been earlier than the 17th September if the *Newry Telegraph's* claim that WG's stories first appeared in that newspaper can be relied upon, and there is a two-week gap in WG's weekly appearances in the *Newry Telegraph* in mid-October.

[79] I'm vexed his speech wasn't printed, for it was one of the best that was made that night, but I heard him saying to Mr M'Nineth and the other reporters, where they were sitting at the table, says he, "Lay down your pencils, gentlemen," says he, "an' don't be reporting me."

THE STORYTELLER

H Leslie Thomas, Wig Maker and Ornamental Hair Manufacturer, fitted him out splendidly.

I have only four original studio photographs of WG and these are reproduced in Appendix E. In two of them he is dressed as "Robin", so we have always known what his stage appearance looked like, albeit in sepia. There is also a drawing of "Robin" and another of his wife, "Peggy", which appeared on the covers of some printed compilations of his stories which he produced later. Copies of these, after well over a hundred years, are of a rather poor definition but, enhanced a little by modern technology, they can also be seen in Appendix E. Rather better preserved is a portrait of WG printed as a frontispiece inside one of his books; this, too, is included in the appendix along with the one and only surviving family snap.[80]

We can imagine the fun WG must have had scouring the second-hand shops of Belfast seeking out his "costume." Something with a touch of eccentricity, a dash of flamboyance and just the right amount of aging to look dignified yet well lived in. He would have been delighted with the loud check trousers that he found—several sizes too large, but he had already determined that "Robin" should have a rather fuller figure than his own, still youthful frame. Suitable padding around the waist would ensure a good fit for the time being. In later years, as he "grew into the role", the padding would no longer be necessary!

He managed to find an old patterned waistcoat that was a good match for the trousers and then, after much thought, chose a starkly contrasting blue swallowtail coat with shiny brass buttons. On a trip to his old home town of Newtownards, he purchased a pair of sturdy brown shoes from family friend, James M'Kee, in his Boot and Shoe Warehouse on the High Street (the firm that I believe took over his father's business when he could no longer run it himself) and added spats to complete the image. For accessories he found a large, multi-coloured kerchief, which he would produce to mop his brow from

---

[80] Appendix E also includes photographs of WG's son, Roland and his family, and his daughter, Robina. There, too, is his grandson, Gerald, my father, along with a photo of myself with my son, Sean and grandson, Joseph – WG's great-great-great-grandson.

10 - ...AND ON STAGE...

time to time during his readings, some brown leather gloves and a pocket watch and chain.

We are fortunate in having a description of "Robin's" appearance on stage that was published in the *Newry Telegraph*: "His watch and chain are ponderous pieces of mechanism, made at least one hundred years ago; while his blue 'swallow-tail' with its brass buttons, his ancient vest, and his many-coloured handkerchief, made him the cynosure of all eyes." Armed with this information and a digital photo editor, a full colour version of "Robin's" photograph has been created by WG's great-great-grandson, Sean Lyttle, to whom I am indebted for his excellent workmanship.[81] This splendid adaptation of the original photograph provides *The Storyteller's* front cover.

His regalia was almost complete. Any minor fitting adjustments that were necessary were more than likely carried out by Isabella, Lizzie's sister, in Madrid Street, who sewed for a living. After all, they now lived just a few streets away. Only one thing was lacking and WG likely set off one lunchtime from his office in Victoria Street, back in the direction of his old haunts. On this occasion, however, he was just going as far as Donegall Street.

Number 39 was the premises of John S Shaw, Fashionable Hatter, Scarf and Umbrella Importer. John S Shaw was renowned when it came to headgear, so his ads inform us, for carrying "an extensive stock; every variety and shape suitable for the expression of the wearer." It was the obvious place for WG to look for a top hat for "Robin." His purchase made, he returned to work. Later that evening I expect he spent some considerable time in the bedroom at home making his preparations, before emerging to present to his family, for the first time, the authentic "Robin", gentleman farmer. I can just imagine the hoots of delight from the children and the adoring gaze from Lizzie, but above all the grin of pride on the face of Wesley Lyttle, aka "Robin Gordon of Ballycuddy".

As for John S Shaw, subsequent adverts for his business carried an additional line. Underneath the address at the bottom, it now read:

---

[81] Note: This is not the pseudo-colouring of old photographs that can now be simulated automatically online.

THE STORYTELLER

N.B.—By special appointment Hatter to "Robin".[82] And the London Hair-Dressing Rooms and the Ards Boot and Shoe Warehouse? Both added to their advertisements: PATRONISED BY "Robin".[83]

"Robin's" first appearance on stage

The big day of "Robin's" first stage appearance arrived and we are fortunate in having an "eye-witness" account of the occasion. However, we must do a little detective work to determine just when the debut occurred. One of the earliest adverts that I have been able to find relating to WG appearing as "Robin" was in the *Belfast Telegraph's* Tuesday 19th November, 1878 issue. It is not, however, referring to his first ever appearance in that guise. It said:

> **ROBIN BACK IN TOWN.**
> Robin will appear in his character of [sic] the "Fechtin' Dugs" at the People's Lodge, I.O.G.T., Soiree on TOMORROW EVENING, at Half-past Seven o'clock. A few tickets can be had at the Abercorn Rooms, 101, Victoria Street.

So his first appearance in Belfast must have been *prior* to Wednesday 20th November, when this one took place. In addition to this earlier appearance in town, he seems to have attended at least one other out of town venue for the *Belfast Telegraph* to announce him as being "Back" and, indeed, the *Freeman's Journal* announced on Monday 11th November: "WG Lyttle, of Belfast, gives his humorous recitals in Newry on Thursday evening" [the 14th]. That this was in the guise of "Robin" is confirmed by a piece in the *Newry Telegraph* about this same performance in its Tuesday edition that week which confirms that WG was due to appear as "Robin":

> *ROBIN IN NEWRY—Our readers are generally aware that Mr W. G. Lyttle of Belfast will give an entertainment in the Assembly Room, Savings Bank on Thursday evening next. Mr Lyttle's readings have*

---

[82] One such advert appears on the inside cover of *Humorous Readings by "Robin,"* 1879.

[83] Their ads appear towards the back of the same publication.

10 - ...AND ON STAGE...

> *attracted crowded audiences in other parts of Ulster. "Robin" will appear in his antiquated costume and recount his exploits anent[84] the 'Mayor's Proclamation' and the 'Fechtin' Dugs.'*
>
> *An eye witness writes :—'I have just been to see "Robin" [at his first appearance, in Belfast, we must presume] and enjoyed a rare treat. He appears to be a well-to-do farmer from County Down. He is short in stature, very stout, and the snows of some sixty winters are upon his hair and beard. His appearance was the signal for long and hearty applause, and his audience was convulsed as he rehearsed in quaint, racy language some of his latest adventures. He sat for a great part of the evening in an arm chair, and appeared thoroughly at home. I have enjoyed a perusal of his sketches in the [Newry]Telegraph, but to see and hear "Robin," himself, is something to be remembered.'*
>
> *Some local amateurs will contribute songs and readings, and altogether we expect a night's rare enjoyment.*

We can reasonably conclude that WG gave his first stage performance dressed as "Robin Gordon," the well-to-do country farmer, in Belfast during the first or second week in November of 1878. From the above account it would seem that he enjoyed an tremendous reception and carried off in style his well-rehearsed impersonation of his new alter-ego. His mannerisms and gestures, not to mention his fine mastery of the dialect of the Ulster-Scots members of his audience, obviously hit just the right note, bringing his amusing scripts to life before their eyes. As the eye-witness stated, "His listeners were convulsed as they laughed along with 'Robin', embracing him as one of their own." WG's stage debut as "Robin Gordon" was yet another resounding success.

---

[84] "opposing"

THE STORYTELLER

The *Newry Telegraph* picked up on their correspondent's description and took to including in their adverts: "The *Telegraph* publishes exclusively ROBIN'S RACY READINGS."

"Robin's" Popularity

Just how successful "Robin" became can be gauged from the fact that up until this time his public readings had always been reported as being given by "W. G. Lyttle" but such was the impact upon his adoring audiences of his appearing in his new guise that from then on the adverts and reports in the press were almost always about "Robin," not WG, and as in the case of the Hatter's advertisement, "Robin" quickly established his own persona.

> "Robin" received quite an ovation. His local points told well; he was quite at home, and at once made friends with his audience.—Larne Reporter
>
> The room was crowded to excess, and his recitals drew forth peals of laughter. The "Fechtin Dugs" was given in inimitable style.—Belfast News.
>
> His Irish Sketch, "The Tipperary Policeman," is inimitable. The applause by the audience was hearty in the extreme.—Coleraine Chronicle.
>
> "Robin" related his adventures in a manner that kept his audience in roars of laughter.—Coleraine Chronicle.
>
> The reception accorded to "Robin" by the large audience was of the most enthusiastic description, and must have been deeply gratifying to him. During his humorous recitals, he kept the house in roars of laughter. His rendering of the Northern dialect was simply perfect.—Irish Templar.
>
> "Robin" was received with great enthusiasm. Attired as a well-to-do County Down farmer, he seemed quite at home on the platform, and kept the

10 - ...AND ON STAGE...

> *house in roars during his quaint but perfectly natural recitals.—Newtownards Chronicle.*[85]

And as his popularity grew, he started to receive "fan-mail." WG was already working towards publishing some of his stories in book form. When that volume would hit the streets some six months after "Robin's" stage debut it would carry the notification: *Parties wishing to communicate with "Robin," will please address, Mr W. G. Lyttle, 27 Victoria Street, Belfast*—the business address of his accountancy firm.

That first book of his readings would also carry an advertisement for Arthur G. Massey of Abbey Street, Armagh, Portrait & Landscape Photographer, informing readers that:

> *Our good friend, "Robin," has just favoured me with a Sitting. The Pictures are pronounced to be most faithful and life-like, and I have secured the sole Copyright. As I anticipate a very large Sale, I am prepared to supply "Robin's" Photographs, Cabinet Size*[86]*, and Beautifully Finished, at Twelve Shillings for Fourteen, which is about Half the usual Price; or One Shilling Each. (About £6 in 2021.)*

Of my four Cabinet photos of my great-grandfather, the two of him dressed as "Robin" are of a later date than these first photos taken in Armagh. I should be intrigued to learn if any of Massey's anticipated "large sale" have survived.

WG—or rather, "Robin"—continued to be much in demand. The *Northern Whig* reported on a Temperance entertainment in the

---

[85] These few samples are taken from a fuller list of press quotes about "Robin" that are reproduced in Appendix D—"Robin" as a Stage Performer.

[86] Cabinet card was popular for photographic portraits from 1870 onwards. It consisted of a thin photograph mounted on stiff card, typically measuring 6.5" by 4.25"

THE STORYTELLER

Belmont Church schoolroom on Tuesday evening, 26th November when "Robin Gordon of Ballycuddy provoked much mirth by his humorous readings" for the Ballyhackamore Temperance Association. Early in the New Year, "Mr Robin Gordon, of Ballycuddy, was the lion of the entertainment" at the annual concert of the Drumbeg Flute Band on 9th January, 1879, according to the *Belfast Weekly News*. His relating of his adventures with *The Meer o' Belfast and his Proclamation*, and *The Twa Fechtin Dugs* "fairly brought down the house."

It would seem that "Robin" seldom varied his appearance. He did add the occasional flamboyant touch, though, as occasion demanded. This, from the *Newtownards Chronicle* after he had shared a platform in the Newtownards Assembly Rooms with the Rev Joseph Bradshaw, J. P. and other dignitaries:

> "Robin" appeared in what he was pleased to call "full dress," having donned white gloves and a white neck-tie, of somewhat large proportions.

I do get the impression that WG thoroughly enjoyed casting off his smart business suit and leaving behind the persona that necessarily went with it, to take to the stage once again as "Robin Gordon of Ballycuddy."

William Henry

After the publication of one of his stories in the *Newtownards Chronicle* back in October '78, WG was happy to accept an invitation from the newspaper's editor to come to Newtownards the following January to appear as "Robin" and help him raise money to aid the poor of the town. This occasion was to be the first time WG and William Henry met in person[87] and was the start of the two literary men's newfound friendship.[88] WG promptly wrote an amusing

---

[87] We know this from a comment Henry wrote in the *Chronicle* when reporting a subsequent appearance of "Robin" in Newtownards later in the year and comparing him to when he had "first seen him back in January."

[88] The friendship was not destined to endure; though, as we shall see, Henry would continue to dog WG's career for the rest of his life.

10 - ...AND ON STAGE...

account of that whole venture which became his second contribution to the columns of the *Chronicle*—"A Night in Newton." The piece appeared in the 18th January issue.[89]

Again, he included references to real people that many readers would have known. The Byers were a long-established family in North Down occupying "Grove Cottage" in Ballyboley since the 18th century.[90] The family became prominent members of the new Non-subscribing Presbyterian Church in Greyabbey. One of the current generation, Robert Stewart Byers, was known to one and all as Robin Byers and was renowned for the rickety state of his old cart. WG, as "Robin", pokes fun at him at the start of this latest story when he claimed to have accepted a lift into Newtownards from his Byers namesake:

> 'Wull ye hae a lift?' ses he, when he overtak me.
> 'I wull that, Rabin,' ses I, although it were a danger o' my life tae git my fit on the kar. He had the hinner en' o' it tied on wi' a lump o' a rape, an' whun I put my fit on the side, an' gied a spring, the wecht o' me very near coppit horse, kar, Rabin an' a'.'
> Ses I, 'Rabin, I hope it'll no gie wae wi' me.'
> 'No fear,' ses he. 'I hae carried wechtier men nor you on it.'
> 'Weel, it wasnae safe,' ses I.
> 'Deed it din my kar nae guid,' ses he. 'I used to hae Mister Elyit ridin' wi' me gie an' aften, an' I think the wecht o' him has knockit my kar a' tae pieces.'[91]

---

[89] "A Night in Newton" has now been published for the first time in a book, *Robin's Further Readings*, AG Lyttle, 2021

[90] Grove Cottage and the Byers family played an important role in the 1798 uprising. (Read more in chapter 20.)

[91] 'Will you have a lift?' says he, when he overtook me.
'I will that, Robin,' says I, although it were a danger of my life to get my foot on the car [cart]. He had the hind end of it tied on with a lump of a rope, and when I put my foot on the side, and gave a spring, the weight of me very near turned over horse, car, Robin and all.'
Says I, 'Robin, I hope it'll not give way with me.'
'No fear,' says he. 'I have carried weightier men than you on it.'

THE STORYTELLER

—thus taking a passing sideswipe at another, portly, local dignitary. These references, particularly when WG was reading them to live audiences already in jocular mood, always brought forth gales of laughter.

Apparently "Robin" survived the journey on his friend's horse and cart and was delighted to see posters all over the town announcing his imminent arrival and "the picture that Mister Massey tak o' me, in the shap wundaes."[92] (mirroring WG's own undoubted pleasure at being thus celebrated.) As mentioned in Chapter 2, "Robin" said here that he was pleased to be back "in his native town." But we have further evidence to WG having been born in Newtownards:

General Ulysees S. Grant had been touring Europe and interviews he had given were in the papers; he visited Belfast and Dublin on Wednesday 8th January, 1879. Always on the lookout for a topical slant for his stories, WG decided that "Robin" would wangle an interview with the American former president. He proceeded to write a new sketch in time for the February issue of the *Irish Templar*. An ad placed in the *Newtownards Chronicle* proclaimed that "General Grant Interviewed,"[93] a humorous reading by Robin, was in the current *Irish Templar*; copies could be obtained, it said, from Mr James M'Kee, 30, High Street, Newtownards. So the Lyttle's old family friend shared WG's enthusiasm for the Temperance movement and made copies of the journal available at his shoe shop.

In "Robin's" account of that night in January when WG performed to support William Henry's fund-raising event, he writes that, after the concert—

> *I stied a' nicht wae Mister M'Kee, an' him an' the mistress wuz terble kin' till me.*[94]

'Well, it wasn't safe,' says I.
'[In]deed it did my car no good,' says he. 'I used to have Mister Eliot riding with me very often, and I think the weight of him has knocked my car all to pieces.'

[92] the picture that Mister Massey took of me, in the shop windows.
[93] Alas, this is another of WG's stories whose text has not survived.
[94] I stayed all night with Mister M'Kee, and he and the mistress were terribly kind to me.

10 - ...AND ON STAGE...

It would seem that James M'Kee had offered to put up his friend for the night to save Wesley having to return very late to Belfast. This would, presumably, have been in the Ulster Hotel that Mrs M'kee ran. So Wesley got to stay once again in his old childhood home.

James M'Kee, unlike Wesley, was an Orangeman, the Worshipful Master (W.M.), in fact, of Newtownards No. 128 Lodge. The *Belfast Weekly News'* report of that lodge's meeting held the following month on Wednesday 5th February stated:

> *The members of this lodge held their usual monthly meeting in the Good Templar Hall... After the usual lodge business had been gone through the W.M. entertained the meeting to a reading by Mr Wesley G. Lyttle, better known as "Robin," entitled "General Grant Interviewed," which was highly appreciated, more especially as Mr Lyttle is a native of Newtownards.*

With Unionist opposition to the persistent talk of Home Rule for Ireland, the ranks of the Orange Order were increasing. Lodge members in the Newtownards area were bemoaning the fact that they had no Orange Hall in which to hold their meetings. Indeed, one Friday in February, according to the *Belfast Weekly News,* the No. 1055 Lodge had had to hold their soiree and ball in the premises of one of their members, Br. Alex. Doggart. "The room was decorated for the occasion with a number of flags and appropriate pictures. The attendance of members and their female friends was large," reported the *News.*

After tea had been enjoyed, and "under the chairmanship of Mr William Henry, editor of the *Newtownards Chronicle*", several speeches were made and a vote of condolence to Queen Victoria on the death, the previous December, of her daughter, Princess Alice, was passed unanimously. For entertainment a number of solos were rendered by various Orangemen and "a Worshipful Master from another lodge, Br James M'Kee, read two selections from 'Robin'."

THE STORYTELLER

Thus "buoyed and in jovial mood," the dancing was reported to have continued until five o'clock on Saturday morning.

Again we see WG's friend, Mr M'Kee, promoting his stories.

A new skill

Around this time WG was asked—probably by his friend, Alexander M'Murtry—if he would consider taking on the role of editor of the *Irish Templar*. The journal had survived a year under the joint guidance for four editors but it must have been felt that this was not ideal. WG's literary skills were well established; he had written many times *for* journals, why should he not be capable of editing one?

The *Newry Telegraph* reported upon the March 1879 issue of the *Irish Templar* thus:

> *Although much of the available space is occupied with the unhappy quarrel as to the exclusion of the Negro, the new editor, Mr. W. G. Lyttle has managed to turn out a number full of promise of even better things. The Editor's address "To our Readers" strikes a hopeful note, and is clearly and sensibly written... Our valued contributor, "Robin," contributes a sketch on "Speerits,"[95] which is amusing and pointed. The Irish Templar is now an acknowledged success, and with such a wary helmsman as Mr Lyttle, we expect to see it become one of the most popular Temperance periodicals of the day.*

As with most things that WG turned his hand to, his first foray into editorship seems to have been a success.

---

[95] Elsewhere, the *Newry Telegraph* reported that, at an IOGT Lodge meeting, "Br. Maleery favoured the meeting with one of "Robin's" humorous readings, "The Speerits," which appears in the current *Irish Templar,* and was received with enthusiastic applause. Sadly we have no extant copy of the text of "The Speerits."

10 - ...AND ON STAGE...

Theatre Critic

When not writing his stories, WG thoroughly enjoyed reading them on stage. But he also appreciated being entertained by others who also trod the boards. It seems he and Lizzie, no doubt employing her sister as baby-sitter, attended an English language performance of Victorien Sardou's French play, *Diplomacy*, which was presented at Belfast's Theatre Royal in February. Wesley had probably read a critique of it in the *Belfast News-Letter* or maybe the one in the *Belfast Morning News* and he subsequently had the idea of penning his own write-up, but in the narrative form of "Robin" describing his attendance at a performance of the play. He would derive much comedy from making it the first time the aging country farmer had ever stepped inside a "The-yater", since, along with many of his stauncher Presbyterian brethren, he had always considered such behaviour "a sin".

"Robin's" account includes this conversation with the friend who persuaded him to attend:

> *'There's fowk objecks till the theyater wi'out just raison. Accordin' till them,' sez he, 'it's wrang till change yer voice, till move yer face, till change yer claes, or dae a piece o' ressytashin.'*
>
> *'I knowed a man,' sez I, 'that wuz applyin' for a sityeashin, an' some o' the fowk objected till him because he went noo an' then till the theyater.'*[96]

Was WG that "man"? Was he talking, here, from bitter recent experience? Was this the reason his application for the post of Secretary to the Irish Temperance League was turned down?

But that was over and done with. WG's main strength, his writing, now had yet another outlet. The *Belfast Morning News* was happy to print his new story and "Dipplemassy—a Nicht at the Theyater Royal, Belfast" appeared in their 20th February, 1879 issue. A Belfast paper

---

[96] 'There are folk object to the theatre without just reason. According to them,' says he, 'it's wrong to change your voice, to move your face, to change your clothes, or do a piece of recitation.'

'I knew a man,' says I, 'that was applying for a situation, and some of the folk objected to him because he went now and then to the theatre.'

was more appropriate than the *Newry Telegraph* to review a Belfast show and WG was now appearing in one of the "dailies." He subsequently included "Dipplemassy" in *Robin's Readings, Vol II.*

A few weeks later the papers were full of ads for the annual Easter Pantomime at the Theatre Royal. The proprietor, Mr JF Warden had excelled himself for this year's production of The Sleeping Beauty, bringing in many professional burlesque and speciality artistes for the main roles—although Wesley noted that, as usual, the "principal boy", Prince Golden-Heart, would be played by the redoubtable Mrs JF Warden. He and Lizzie must have decided to take John and Agnes (now 12 and 10) to see the show. Perhaps little Eva, at four-and-a-half, persuaded her parents to let her come too, but the toddler and babe, Roland and Robina, would have had to remain behind in their Aunt Isabella's care.

They all enjoyed a great show with the traditional harlequinade at the end proving particularly splendid. Shortly afterwards, readers of the *Belfast Morning News* were learning all about "Robin Gordon's" experience of "The Pantrymine in the Theyater", WG's second article for the paper.[97]

Robin joins the North Down Rifles

WG also had an established outlet now for his writing in the *Newtownards Chronicle*. Earlier in the year he came up with the idea of a tale about "Robin" joining the "Newtownerds Mileeshy," an ideal story for the Newtownards newspaper.[98] Militias had been established throughout Ireland for the past hundred years, recruited on a county basis to augment the regular army during times of insurrection. The one "Robin" wished to join was the 24th Royal North Down Battalion,

---

[97] I have Philip Robinson to thank for first discovering WG's stories printed in the *Belfast Morning News,* three of which had never been published in any of WG's books. They can now be read for the first time in over 140 years in *Robin's Further Readings* by WG Lyttle, published by AG Lyttle, 2021.

[98] I am indebted to *Indexes to the Newtownards Chronicle, 1873-1900 and the Newtownards Independent, 1871-1873*, compiled by Kenneth Robinson for recording that "The Newtownerds Mileeshy" appeared in the *Chronicle* in three parts in April 1879 – a fact that I have since confirmed along with his other contributions to the *Chronicle.*

10 - ...AND ON STAGE...

known colloquially as the North Down Rifles. His story duly appeared over three weeks, starting on 12 April, 1879.

Of newspapers and editors

Easter Monday that year was the 14th of April and the Newtownards Orange Lodges arranged to hold a fund-raising meeting towards providing themselves with a much-needed building.

Many dignitaries shared the platform in the Good Templars Hall in North Street, which was hired for the occasion.[99] Every local lodge was represented and there were clergymen, a school principal, town commissioners and other men of prominence. Among them was one, "Robin Gordon, of Ballycuddy"—there not in any "Orange" capacity but, of course, as part of the entertainment. William Henry was among the platform party and was most likely the one who had again persuaded WG to come along as "Robin" to support a worthy cause.

WG's Good Templar involvement would have brought him into contact with members of the Orange Order, which also appealed for temperance among its members. However, he seems neither to have had the time nor the inclination to seek any involvement in that movement despite its growing popularity amongst the Protestant community. He tended to avoid sectarian confrontation or party politics. But he was happy to help promote their fund-raising event to oblige his friend and business colleague, and keen Orangeman, William Henry.

As WG headed down to Newtownards to attend the event his mind may still have been full of the wonders of his recent evening spent in the presence of *The Sleeping Beauty*. However, as Newtownards grew nearer he perhaps turned to pondering what he knew of the short history of his new friend's newspaper. The *Newtownards Chronicle* was first published only six years previously in 1873. It advertised itself as "the first Weekly Paper published in the County at One Penny" but WG was aware that, in fact, its predecessor, the *Newtownards Independent and County Down Advertiser* had sold for

---

[99] At that time in Victorian County Down, the Good Templars movement—in which WG was still prominent—was better supported than the Orange Order, although Orangism was on the rise.

THE STORYTELLER

a penny, although, had it survived, it had announced the price would increase to 2d in February, 1873. That had been a paper that had quickly, over its short life since July, 1871, come to be highly regarded throughout the county before the proprietors, as their readers were informed in its final issue on 18th January, 1873, "were compelled, through unforeseen circumstances, to suspend publication."

From what WG had heard, the new *Chronicle,* while popular enough, had not managed to capture the hearts of its readers to the same extent as had the *Independent*. Perhaps he alluded to these thoughts when conversing with William Henry when they met at the Orange Order fund-raising event and perhaps the editor took the opportunity of soliciting from WG the promise of more "local" adventures of "Robin" following on from the success of "The Newtownerds Mileeshy." For this was a proposition that WG was pleased to embrace and went on to fulfil, unaware at the time that his pleasant relationship with Henry would be short-lived and would eventually become decidedly acrimonious.

The programme that evening in the Good Templar hall, however, as the *Belfast Weekly News* subsequently reported on 26th April, "was fruitful in getting the proposal for a new Orange Hall for Newtownards agreed," with promises of help from some prominent individuals such as the Marquis of Londonderry, Viscount Castlereagh and, indeed, from William Henry, himself. The entertainment, which included a number of pieces from a choir in addition to several of "Robin's" humorous readings, "undoubtedly contributed to the success of the event," the *Weekly News* concluded.

For WG, the evening was a success on a number of levels. Although, as we shall see in the next chapter, he could ill-afford the time, he always enjoyed entertaining folk with his recitations and especially so when it was in support of a worthy cause. In addition to that, his conversation with the Newtownards editor would have helped to crystallise a number of thoughts that must have been running through his mind at the time. Firstly, his stories were appreciated not only by the readers of the *Irish Templar,* the *Newry Telegraph,* the *Belfast Morning News* and the *Newtownards Chronicle,* but by the newspapers' proprietors as well; they were helping sell papers. And secondly, that the folding of the *Newtownards Independent and*

10 - ...AND ON STAGE...

County Down Advertiser six years earlier had left a gap in the market that William Henry had somehow failed to fill. He had the impression that people still missed the style and charm of the *Independent* and that Henry's new approach to running a weekly journal was not as universally appreciated.

As he travelled home to Belfast late on that Easter Monday evening, he must have been wondering if there was an opportunity here. He had tried his hand at editing and was enjoying putting together the monthly Temperance journal. What about a weekly? Could he make a success of a second newspaper in Newtownards to replace the *Independent*? Tomorrow was his birthday; he would be 35, in his prime. Were he to embrace this venture, much time and effort in research and preparation would be required in the months ahead.

The possibility that such an undertaking might fail is unlikely to have crossed his mind.

Chapter 11 – ... AND IN A BOOK

1879

1879 saw a "Last" for Wesley Lyttle, the family man, and a "First" for W. G. Lyttle, the writer. It was the year Lizzie gave birth to what would prove to be the last of the couple's six children (five surviving.) No trace can be found of the birth certificate but the date of birth can be calculated from the 1901 census form completed on 31 March of that year. Then 22, the child must have been born between 1 April, 1878 and 31 March, 1879. Since Roland was born in mid-January, 1878, his younger sibling is unlikely to have arrived before the following January at the earliest, and quite possibly late February or March, '79. I can quite imagine Lizzie holding back the news of her happy condition until she was quite certain, particularly as Wesley was so preoccupied at the time with perfecting his look and delivery as "Robin." Perhaps she broke the news to him at the end of "Robin Gordon's" first triumphant stage appearance—a fitting and crowning culmination to all Wesley's hard work and achievement.

Whether or not that was the exact timing, it is clear that Wesley, straightaway, set his heart on a further son that he was determined to christen, Robin, in honour of his new alter-ego. In the fullness of time, however, the Lyttles were blessed with another daughter, not a son—and so *she* was blessed with the name, Robina.

It would seem that registering the new baby's birth slipped Wesley's mind, just as it had done nine years previously when her ill-fated brother, Robert, had been born. On that occasion it had been the child's own poor state of health that had put registering him clean out of his father's mind for just over a year. With little Robina it was outside circumstances that must have caused the lapse.

11 - ...AND IN A BOOK

WG's first book

And that was the other big event—the "First" of 1879. Ever since WG's stories started to appear in the *Irish Templar* and the *Newry Telegraph*—and, indeed, before that, even—people had been telling him that he ought to produce a book of them. Earlier in the year he had begun the process of doing just that. Much time was taken up in selecting which stories to include as he found he had many more tales than could reasonably be contained in one volume. He had to tighten up on their wording, make the odd adjustment to a local reference that might need a word of explanation, create minor changes to update the text where necessary—all time-consuming and exacting tasks.

At the same time, he was making enquiries as to how to get them printed up in book format and in the end chose a Belfast firm called Allen and Johnston with premises in Upper Arthur Street. All this work must have come to a head just at the time of Robina's birth. He would have received the galleys to proof-read, a painstaking task but an important one; he could not afford to have his book looking anything less than professional.

The volume was to be called, *Humorous Readings by "Robin"* and would contain twelve of his best stories[100] in a cloth-bound octavo book with a specially commissioned drawing of himself as "Robin" on the cover[101]. As was common in the period, WG arranged with the printers to offset the cost of producing the book by the sale of advertising space within its pages. On the inside front cover, for example, "Robin's" friendly Hatter, John S. Shaw, had a full-page ad. WG's friend, William Henry, took a full-page to advertise his newspaper, the *Newtownards Chronicle and County Down Observer* to give it it's full title.[102]

Humorous Readings by "Robin" is the only one of WG's books of which I have a first edition copy and, although the title page simply gives 1879 as the year it was printed, a few of the adverts are dated

---

[100] See Appendix C1 for the Contents List for Humorous Readings by "Robin."

[101] See Appendix E, Images of W. G. Lyttle, Figure 1

[102] No *Newtownards Chronicle* adverts appeared in WG's later publications as his brief friendship with Henry became distinctly cool soon after the launching of WG's own newspaper in 1880.

THE STORYTELLER

April, 1879. So its publication date could have been late April or, more probably, early May. With all the work involved and the excitement around the launch of his first book coinciding with Lizzie's confinement, we can, perhaps, forgive Wesley his oversight in failing to register their youngest child.

WG felt a great affinity with his public, so generous in their appreciation of his efforts to entertain them each time he stepped into the limelight. Some even wrote to "Robin" to express their enjoyment of his merry tales. So when it came to producing his first book of stories, he wanted to retain something of that intimacy. He thought hard about how best to do this; some form of preface? A letter of introduction? What he settled on was what he did best; what he had often amused his friends with since his youth. He wrote a poem to appear just after the title page. Or, rather, "Robin" wrote a poem—in his own quaint language—written directly to all his *friens* (This was how WG chose to spell the Ulster-Scot word *freens*—friends).

TO MY FRIENS

My friens, it was at your requist
I got this wee book prented
An' whun ye've read it till the en'
I hope you'll be contented
It tak me mony a day an' hoor
Tae pit it a' thegither
An yet I hae as muckle left
As ocht tae fill anither

So if ye'll jist dae what ye said—
Buy up them ivery yin—
I'll ken ye want tae see the nixt
An' very suin begin.
I'm shair there's fowk will lauch an' sneer
An' say my book's a' "stuff;"
That "Paddy" wuz a common boor,
That "Robin" is a "muff".

11 - ...AND IN A BOOK

My friens, I didnae write fur fowk
That think themsels sae nice;
Wha's hearts—if they hae got sich things—
Ir jist like lumps o' ice.
My stories ir but little worth,
I ken that's very true,
But tak them as they come, my friens,
I wrote them a' for you.

An' mony an hoor they've help't tae pass,
An' aft it din me guid
Tae hear hoo hearty ye cud lauch
Whun I got up tae read.
Jist for the sake o' these auld times
I've put my book in prent,
An' if it pleeses you, my friens,
Then "Robin" is content.[103]

---

[103] *TO MY FRIENDS*

My friends, it was at your request
I got this little book printed
An' when you've read it to the end
I hope you'll be contented
It took me many a day and hour
To put it all together
And yet I have as much left
As ought to fill another

My friends, I do not write for folk
That think themselves so nice;
Who's hearts—if they have got such things—
Are just like lumps of ice
My stories are but little worth,
I know that's very true,
But take them as they come, my friends,
I wrote them all for you.

So if you'll just do what you said—
Buy up them every one—
I'll know you want to see the next
And very soon begin.
I'm sure there's folk will laugh and sneer
And say my book's all "stuff;"
That "Paddy" was a common bore,
That "Robin" is a "muff".

And many an hour they've helped to pass,
And often it did me good
To hear how hearty you could laugh
When I got up to read.
Just for the sake of these old times
I've put my book in print,
And if it pleases you, my friends,
Then "Robin" is content.

THE STORYTELLER

The book was published with a cover price of one shilling, the equivalent of about £6 in 2021. The public loved it. Copies fairly flew off the shelves and the publishers were soon encouraging WG to finish editing more stories for Volume 2.

He promised himself he would do that, yet at the same time he was still full of ideas following his meeting with the editor of the *Newtownards Chronicle* at Easter, whose full page advert in "Humorous Readings" proclaimed that the *Chronicle* was the best newspaper and had the largest circulation in the County. In the following weeks he made it his business to find out all about the defunct *Newtownards Independent and County Down Advertiser* that it had replaced.

New ideas

He discovered that it had been run by a group of local businessmen including amongst them Mr James Caughey who ran a printing business on Francis Street in Newtownards, Mr Samuel Irvine, who looked after the paper's finances and his new colleague, William Henry, who had been appointed editor and business manager of the enterprise. WG learned of the bizarre "unforeseen circumstances" that caused the paper's closure: William Henry, it seemed, had injured himself by slipping on an orange peel.[104] Wesley never heard the whole story but only knew that after Henry was fully recovered, the old *Independent* was never resurrected. Instead, the *Newtownards Chronicle* was born, with William Henry as sole proprietor. Although the new paper proved popular enough, the vibes that WG picked up were that Henry's new editorial policies, no longer steered by a consortium of joint proprietors, meant his paper had not achieved quite the same appeal that its predecessor had enjoyed among its upper Ards readership.

---

[104] The strange circumstances of the demise of the *Independent* and establishment of the *Chronicle* are mentioned in Kenneth Robinson's *Indexes to the Newtownards Chronicle, 1873-1900 and Newtownards Independent, 1871-1873*.

11 - ...AND IN A BOOK

Wesley shared his thoughts with Lizzie and over the coming months their plans began to take shape. It would involve yet another move for the Lyttle family. A move, for Lizzie and the children, out of Belfast for the first time in their lives; it was going to be a big change. Lizzie had just got used to living back on the old streets where she grew up and close to her sister again. She wasn't sure how she would adjust to life in a sleepy little market town out in the country. But we can be confident Wesley would have assured her it was becoming a thriving community with plenty of good shops and churches.

'And forbye[105],' we can hear him say, 'They're tearing down our old city and forever making changes. It's not the same, living here anymore. Have you seen the state of Hercules Street? Demolishing the houses all down one side—to widen it and give it some hifalutin new name.'

'I heard it's to be called "Royal Avenue",' said Lizzie. 'I quite like the sound of that.'

'Ay, but it won't be like it was. Belfast's changing. It's time we changed, too. What we need is the good, fresh country air of Newton,' he told her, perhaps also recalling the distinctive odour of the weekly cattle market in West Street, just along from his school. 'An' Strangford Lough! Ye can tak a wee danner alang the shore and the weans can skite stanes on the watter and hoak fur crubbins. It's a gran' wee toon, so it is.'[106]

Lizzie smiled at her husband's lapsing into the vocabulary of his youth, when describing his old stomping ground.

---

[105] as well

[106] And Strangford Lough! You can take a stroll out to the shores and the children can skip stones on the water and dib for crabs. It's a grand little town, so it is.'

'An' A'll tell ye anither thing, Mrs Lyttle. The toon boasts its ain newspaper but rumour haes it that it'll soon hae twa.'[107]

'Will it, indeed?' said Lizzie, 'And I wonder if Mr Lyttle would have anything to do with spreading those rumours.'

Wesley chuckled.

In truth, he must have had mixed feelings about this new venture they were contemplating. It would be quite a wrench for him, too, to leave behind the hustle and fun of the city that he had known and loved for the past 15 years—all his married life. The city where he had carved out a career as an accountant and shorthand teacher; made a real difference in his community with his work for the Good Templars and provision of a circulating library; built up a substantial reputation as a popular entertainer right from his early days with Dr Corry's Diorama and on to presenting his own humorous stories and the creation of the hugely successful character of "Robin." And now he was a published author and the editor of a monthly journal, as well.

He would have to resign from editing the *Irish Templar* but, of course, he wouldn't be leaving "Robin" behind, or his writings. They would be an integral part of his new life as a newspaper proprietor. He had seen how the popularity of his stories had boosted the circulation of the *Newry Telegraph* and the *Newtownards Chronicle*. Why should he be promoting these other vehicles when his stories could be selling copies of his own newspaper? He had the ideal marketing aid; all he needed was something to market. He probably baulked at the idea of trying to compete with the Belfast papers, but a new provincial weekly? A revival of the sorely missed *Newtownards Independent* might be the perfect answer.

He discovered the *Independent* had serialised stories in its columns week by week and, judging from the correspondence, these had proved popular. There had been a tale of smugglers in the Ards peninsular set a hundred years ago called, "Merry Hearts of Down;"

---

[107] 'And I'll tell ye another thing, Mrs Lyttle. The town boasts its own newspaper but rumour has it that it'll soon have two.'

11 - ...AND IN A BOOK

this had been followed by "Clatterdom"—recollections of how the weavers fared during the Famine years in Newtownards; "Winds and Tide"—a story of Comber and Ballygowan and finally one called, "The Lost Ring." WG could see the attraction of running these longer stories that would keep his readers coming back each week for the next instalment.

He would make it clear in his first editorial that he intended to honour and continue these and other traditions of that short-lived but well-loved journal; he would promise independence of thought and clarity of vision, and a determination both to inform and to entertain. But he would change the name. It would continue the spirit of its predecessor but it wouldn't *be* its predecessor. It would be his newspaper; W. G. Lyttle's and his alone, proclaiming news and views to an ever growing readership. It would be a herald to the region.

A herald. Yes, but not just a Newtownards Herald. The new *Chronicle* had limited itself by its title. WG planned to cover the whole of the upper Ards. He would call his paper, *The North Down Herald*.

Preparations, performances and Presbyterians

The second half of 1879 was a hectic whirl of activity. Suitable accommodation had to be found in Newtownards—premises appropriate for the offices of a busy provincial newspaper business with living quarters for a family of seven—not an easy task. Talks with printers were needed. WG approached Allen and Johnson, who had produced his book and agreed, in principle, that they should print his broadsheet. Correspondents would be needed to supply interesting local news from each of the townships that the paper would serve. Links to national and international news agencies had to be established. WG didn't just have to arrange all this; he first had had to learn *what* was required and *how* to acquire it. His time at the helm of the *Irish Templar* must have helped but he must, surely, have sought advice from some friendly newspaper editor, too; probably someone, other than William Henry or the editor of the *Newry Telegraph,*. Those two would have been wary at divulging too many trade secrets to a writer who was currently a lucrative source of material to them both. Yet, learn the business he did and kept his accountancy firm running at the same time.

Nor did he neglect his reading public. He continued to supply the *Newry Telegraph* with new stories to appear each week while working away at odd minutes with editing and updating more of his earlier tales to be included in a second volume of *Humorous Readings*.

He wrote two more stories for the *Belfast Morning News* over the summer. the first was following another family trip to the theatre to see the amazing "Signor Boz", a magician of great skill and dexterity. Of course, it was "Robin's" visit that was written up in the paper and how he got called up on stage to assist with the tricks—to the accompaniment of hoots and cheers from people in the audience who knew him:

> *'Niver min' them, sur,' sez Mister Boz, takin' me by the han an' leadin me up till a nice cushioned cher. 'Jist sit doon there,' sez he.*
> *'Shair ye'll no play ony tricks on me, sur?' sez I.*
> *'Tricks, my dear sur!' sez he, 'that would be a poor return for your kindness.'*
> *Wi' that he touched my face as canny as ocht, an' it left sich a queer feelin' after it that I pit up my han an' rubbit it.*
> *'Is yer face sair!' sez he, 'hev ye teethache?'*
> *'Deed I dae feel a wee touch o' it,' sez I.*
> *'Let me see it,' sez he, an' afore I cud speak he whuppit apen my mooth an' keekit in. Then he lukit in my face an' lauched, an' sez he,*
> *'Dae ye live in the country, sur?'*
> *'Yes sur,' sez I, 'I dae.'*
> *'I thocht that,' sez he, an' wi' that he slippit his finger intill my mooth an' draws some big thing oot. My! If ye had heard the lauchs o' the fowk.*
> *'What wuz that?' sez I.*
> *'Luk fer yersel,' sez he, haudin' up a big hen egg.*
> *'Ye didnae get that oot o' my mooth,' sez I.*

11 - ...AND IN A BOOK

> *'Let us try agen,' sez he, an' afore ye cud hae said "Jack Robinson" he whuppit oot anither yin. I cudnae believe my een.*[108]

The big news throughout the British Empire that July was the defeat of the Zulus in Africa. There had been a brief boost to the British morale back in January over the heroic stand at Rorke's Drift but since then there had been tremendous fighting and terrible slaughter in Zululand. Finally, now, the tide had turned and King Cetshawayo's warriors had been routed at the Battle of Ulundi. Although many thousands more Zulus were killed than British soldiers, nevertheless they had taken a heavy toll, too. Back home, the Zulus were not seen in a good light.

Yet all the talk in Belfast was of this forthcoming appearance at the Victoria Hall. Wesley would have seen the advertisement in the *Belfast Telegraph*:

---

[108] 'Never mind them, sir,' says Mister Boz, taking me by the hand and leading me up to a nice cushioned chair. 'Just sit down there,' says he.

'Sure you'll not play any tricks on me, sir?' says I.

'Tricks, my dear sir!' says he, 'that would be a poor return for your kindness.'

With that he touched my face as ordinary as anything, and it left such a queer feeling after it that I put up my hand and rubbed it.

'Is your face sore!' says he, 'have you toothache?'

'[In]deed I do feel a slight touch of it,' says I.

'Let me see it,' says he, and before I could speak he whipped open my mouth and peeked in. Then he looked in my face and laughed, and says he,

'Do you live in the country, sir?'

'Yes sir,' says I, 'I do.'

'I thought that,' says he, and with that he slipped his finger into my mouth and draws some big thing out. My! If you had heard the laughs o' the folk.

'What was that?' says I.

'Look for yourself,' says he, holding up a big hen egg.

'You didn't get that out o' my mouth,' says I.

'Let us try again,' says he, and before you could have said "Jack Robinson" he whipped out another one. I couldn't believe my eyes.

THE STORYTELLER

> **VICTORIA HALL, BELFAST**
> **MONDAY, JULY 21ˢᵗ, AND FOLLOWING DAYS**
> **THE ZULUS**
> Six friendly Zulus, accompanied by
> Mr Redwood, Ex-Colonist
> **War Songs and Dances**
> **Fighting with Assegai and Shield**
> An Interesting Account will be given of the
> **Manners and Customs of the Zulus**

Wesley decided to go along and must have been impressed, not only by the skills demonstrated by the black warriors, but also by their demeanour and attitude when they spoke through an interpreter. He decided "Robin" should attend the show and express his thoughts to the readership of the *Morning News*. The article, "The Zoolyoos" appeared on the 1ˢᵗ August, 1879.[109] "Robin" got to talk back-stage with the six men and he concluded:

> *At last I bid them guid-bye, an' cum awa'. They invited me back, but I'm feared I'll no be able to gang. I cannae get yon men frae afore my een, an' I'm angery at mysel' noo fer the opeenyin I used tae hae o' the Zoolyoos. What a pity it is that sum ither way cudnae hae been ta'en wi' them nor tae shoot an' cut them doon in thousands, as if they wur brute beasts! Puir fellows! Their skin's dark, but they cannae help that, an'a black skin's no' as bad as a black heart.*[110]

---

[109] All three of these 'never before published' *Morning News* stories can now be read in *Robin's Further Readings* by WG Lyttle, published by AG Lyttle, 2021.

[110] At last I bid them goodbye, and came away. They invited me back, but I'm afraid I'll not be able to go. I can't get those men from before my eyes, and I'm angry at myself now for the opinion I used to have of the Zulus. What a pity it is that some other way couldn't have been taken with them other than to shoot and cut them down in thousands, as if they were brute beasts! Poor fellows! Their skin's dark, but they can't help that, and a black skin's not as bad as a black heart.

11 - ...AND IN A BOOK

Having now met some, WG apparently felt strongly that the natives of Zululand had been poorly represented to the British people.

Perhaps his Presbyterian sense of fair play caused him to take a small step to try to redress the balance. It is obvious from his writings that WG had developed an extensive knowledge of the inner workings of the Presbyterian Church. He used it to poke innocent fun at his fellow-churchgoers in many of his stories including "Kirk Music," "The Ballycuddy Precentor," "The Newtownbreda Harmoneyum," "The Ballycuddy Elders" and more. The General Assembly of the Presbyterian Church in Ireland held their annual conference each June to elect a new Moderator for the following twelve months and spend a week debating issues, both profound and minor, that affected the smooth running of their denomination throughout the land. Not only ministers but elders, as well, attended what was always a packed auditorium to listen to the sermons, speeches, wrangling and heckling that went on before a vote was taken upon each issue.

There had been quite an uproar this year, according to the lengthy accounts in the newspapers, over whether to allow the singing of paraphrases or even—dare it be mentioned—of hymns! The idea occurred to WG that "Robin Gordon" could report in his own inimitable style on the proceedings by the simple expedient of explaining he had been appointed an elder of the Ballycuddy Presbyterian Church and been asked to accompany the minister to the 1879 Assembly. "Robin's" ignorance of the ways and protocols of such meetings allowed WG to write amusing comments on the debates and the manner in which the delegates conducted themselves. "Robin" was quite upset by the amount of clapping and cheering and heckling that went on, which seemed to him like "a kin' o' desecrashin in a meeting-hoose."[111] He remarked upon it to his neighbour:

> *'Ye'll hear mair nor that afore ye gang hame,' sez the man aside me.*
> *'Wull A?' sez I.*

---

[111] A kind of desecration in a meeting-house [church]

THE STORYTELLER

> *'Ye wull that,' sez he, 'efter a while ye'll wonner if yer in yer ain cuntry, an' it'll tak Mr Watts [the newly-elected Moderator of the General Assembly] a' his time tae keep sum o' the fowk A see here in any kin' o' moderation.'*
> *'Dae ye tell me that?' sez I; 'A suppose that's what they ca' him the Moderator fur.'*[112]

A man standing with many others in the aisle next to where "Robin" was seated in the crowded hall, when any controversial point was mentioned, would shout, "Chair! Chair!" wishing to enter in the debate. "Robin" finally had had enough:

> *A grew that angry at the last that A spauk till him, an' sez I—*
> *'A dae wush ye wud houd yer tongue.'*
> *'What fur?' sez he.*
> *'Wha's gaun tae bring you a cher,' sez I, 'an'sae mony ither fowk stannin' roon ye? Sit doon on yer hunkers if yer tired, or else awa hame.'*[113]

The hottest topic of the week was reserved for Friday. It was on the introduction of a musical instrument to lead the worship and it caused a heated debate. "Robin" reported that most of the ministers

---

[112] 'You'll hear more than that before you go home,' says the man beside me.
'Will I?' says I.
'You will that,' says he, 'after a while you'll wonder if you're in your own country, and it'll take Mr Watts [the newly-elected Moderator of the General Assembly] all his time to keep some of the folk I see here in any kind of moderation.'
'Do you tell me that?' says I; 'I suppose that's what they call him the Moderator for.'

[113] I grew that angry in the end that I spoke to him, and says I—
'I do wish you would hold your tongue.'
'What for?' says he.
'Who's going to bring you a chair,' says I, 'and so many other folk standing round you? Sit down on your hunkers if you're tired, or else away home.'

were in favour of allowing instruments but was disappointed that the majority of the elders voted against it thus defeating the motion. But "Robin" declared, 'We haenae heerd the last o'it.'[114]

Although Presbyterian readers of the *Newry Telegraph* easily outnumbered all others, they proved more than happy to laugh along with WG at "Robin" and the antics of their governing body.

WG's personal appearances as "Robin" continued, although less frequently than he had been doing, judging by the reduced number of newspaper adverts for such occasions over this period. With so busy a schedule, WG decided to make fewer guest appearances and concentrate instead on occasional larger events such as one advertised in the *Belfast News-Letter* on the 11th November, 1879, under the heading "Robin" in Newry.

> *It is announced that "Robin," the popular contributor to the Newry Telegraph, has arranged to give a number of his amusing recitals in the Assembly Rooms, Newry, this evening. James Henderson, Esq, M.A., is to preside, and there is sure to be a crowded house.*

The same paper wrote on the following Monday that "Robin" would again appear in Newry the next evening "when there will be a large audience to greet the old man eloquent from Ballycuddy." For the occasion WG chose four of his sketches (according to an advert in the *Newry Telegraph*)—"Peggy, and Hoo I Coortid her," "Wee Wully," "Betty Megympsey" and an extract from "Paddy M'Quillan's Trip tae Glesco"—"Buying a Rid Hankerchy frae a Glesco Man."

However, if the people of Ulster saw a bit less of WG during this hectic time, they were not deprived of his stories altogether. Increasingly, since their publication in book form in *Humorous Readings*, others were delivering WG's words at entertainments around the province. According to the newspaper adverts for the events, those reciting his tales ranged from seasoned performers to

---

[114] We haven't heard the last of it.

enthusiastic amateurs, and from those of a mature age to young pupils at their annual school prize givings.

At a reunion of the Belfast Catholic Total Abstinence Association, noted the *Belfast Morning News*, a Mr R Burns contributed to the evening's entertainment with a reading of "The Tipperary Policeman" by "Robin," showing once again that such was "Robin's" fame among the people of Ulster it was no longer felt necessary to attribute the stories to W. G. Lyttle.

Some youngsters, bereft of the hefty sum of a shilling needed to purchase a copy of *Humorous Readings,* were known to write out the text in longhand in order to have their own copy of one of these sought-after stories. One such young girl was brought to my attention by retired Detective Constable, Ben Forde[115], sometimes referred to in Ulster as The Singing Policeman because of his love of performing Gospel songs in churches and concert venues throughout the province. Ben's cousin, Mildred Sergeant of Portadown, is still in possession of an old hardback notebook that belonged to her great aunt, Annie Margaret Sergeant. When Annie was thirteen she got hold of a copy of *Paddy M'Quillan's Trip tae Glesco* and copied the text into her notebook in a commendable hand for a young girl. I have seen her notebook, now well over a hundred years old, and have included this photograph of it and of the opening lines of the text Annie copied into

Annie's notebook and her signature which she wrote in 1899 and, below, the opening lines of WG's story in her own handwriting

---

[115] Ben Forde is the author, with Chris Spencer, of three challenging books about his experience as a Christian detective constable during The Troubles in Northern Ireland – *Hope in Bomb City, Love in Bomb City* and *Faith in Bomb City,* published by Marshalls Paperbacks, 1979, 1982 and 1984 respectively. An updated and extended edition of *Hope in Bomb City* was published by Drumcree House in 2012 and is also available on Kindle.

11 - ...AND IN A BOOK

> *One morning when I was at my brakfast, siz I, Ma, I'm thinkin about goin from home for a bit. It's not very far a hope, siz she, for there's a good tack if the pritties to be dug out yit, & ye can't be spared, whar ar ye goin. Am goin over the shough ta Glasgow, siz I. Yer goin ta the mischef, siz she, Whar's that, siz I, if its in any part if Glasgow all be there, for a mane tee see all thats worth lukin at, yil not go one fut, siz she, not the linth if yer toe, if ye do all lock up yer clothes, Well if ye do, siz I all go & list, a will as sure as deth. A hedint another word ta say. Whinever ma ma refused me anything, a jist thratened ta list an then a got what a wanted.*

it. It stands as a further memorial to the fondness WG's contemporaries had for his writings, not least young Annie Sergeant, pictured here as an adult with her own little son.[116] I am grateful to Ben Ford and Mildred Sergeant for allowing me to include these photographs.

Praise for "Humorous Readings"

Life for the Lyttles, and Wesley in particular, grew increasingly frenzied. He realised he had neglected to provide William Henry with any further copy for the *Chronicle*. But he and Lizzie had had a rare day out to visit the Newtownards Flower Show and he had promised Henry that "Robin" would provide an account of it for his paper. He added, jokingly, "Particularly, as Peggy took 1st Prize for her butter!" (Peggy was "Robin's" fictitious wife.) However, the weeks passed and WG had not found the time to write up the story.

---

[116] As an adult, Annie married and moved to Manchester in England, before emigrating to Denver, Colorado where this photograph was taken with her little son, Earl. He would grow up in America to become a multi-millionaire—a far cry from his mother's childhood when she couldn't afford her own copy of *Humorous Readings by "Robin."*

THE STORYTELLER

On 20 September, an item appeared in the *Newtownards Chronicle* which caught his attention. It related to his book and how well it was being received in Scotland, too. The report opened with a verbatim quote lifted from the Glasgow edition of the *Daily Mail*:

> *"Robin," A COUNTY DOWN HUMORIST.*
> "Mr William Perrett, of 625, Duke Street, sends us a quaint sample of North of Ireland wit in the shape of "Humorous Readings by Robin," a production of the Belfast Press. The writer of the volume would seem to be popular in Ulster as a public reader; he is described as appearing on the platform in the attire of a well-to-do County Down farmer, and carrying everything before him. We do not wonder at this if his power as an orator approaches the force and vigour he displays as a writer. His home-spun is mirth-provoking in a high degree. It is impossible to follow Paddy M'Quillan in his trip to Glasgow, and through the adventures which he had in our city, without enjoying many a hearty laugh. This is especially true of the scene in the police court, which is described with genuine dramatic power. "Robin" is an earnest teetotaller, and loses no opportunity of denouncing strong drink. The dialect in which he writes bears the strongest possible resemblance to that of the West of Scotland; yet we are assured it is a pure reproduction of the speech of the common people in County Down, where the author was brought up and still resides. Except that he is a little more free in the use of tender and endearing terms, especially to the members of his own family circle, he might be an Ayrshire man."— North British Daily Mail.

This was followed by the *Chronicle's* own comments:

> *Our friend "Robin" is very well known in Newtownards and district, and it is not the first time his productions have appeared in our journal, to the*

11 - ...AND IN A BOOK

intellectual amusement of "all concerned." We have personally said so much in his favour on former occasions, as to preclude us from doing so just now, especially as we have been informed that "Peggy," his excellent and well-known sober spouse, not only visited the recent County Down Show, but actually carried off a prize in the exhibition of her butter. Where was "Robin" then? Our suspicion is he has had enough of the Good Templars, has kicked them aside and that when in "Newton" kept too close company with "Old Cummer,"[117] otherwise we would have had one of his inimitable sketches of "Peggy's" victory and the proceedings of the various shows generally. "Robin" was formerly attached to our literary staff but since he joined the Royal North Down Rifles we have had no good of him. "Oh, "Robin," "Robin," as ye wud sae, "what's cum o'er ye?"

This is of interest on three counts: firstly, it further evidences the widespread appeal of WG's writing. Secondly, and significantly, it identifies, perhaps, the start of a schism in relations between WG and William Henry, the proprietor of Newtownards' only newspaper. That odd phrase, "We have personally said so much in his favour on former occasions, as to preclude us from doing so just now..." has a slightly bitter ring to it. The editor was still waiting for "Robin's" promised account of the Flower Show. He goes on to have a dig at WG's well-known teetotalism and suggests he has fallen off the wagon to account for the absence of a story about how Peggy had won a prize for her butter.

It seemed to rankle that he had had no further contributions from WG after the final instalment of his *Newtownerds Mileeshy* (the North Down Rifles) series; "Robin was *formerly* on our literary staff..." Had

---

[117] "Old Cummer" was a locally distilled whiskey made in Comber, County Down.

THE STORYTELLER

he already heard rumours that WG was considering starting up his own newspaper?

Before we leave this article in the *Chronicle* it is also of interest to note how it came to my attention. It was actually quoted in an item that appeared some seven years later in the letters column of WG's own *North Down Herald*. This read:

> *Dear sir,—Looking over a heap of newspaper cuttings the other night, I came upon one from the Newtownards Chronicle, of 20th September, 1879, regarding your good self. I enclose you the cutting and would be glad to see it in your next issue. Truly yours, A Constant Reader. Newtownards, 30th October, 1886.*

It duly appeared in a November issue of the *Herald*.

As a trivial footnote to all this, on discovering the clipping from the *Herald* (in the North Down Museum in Bangor) I sent a copy of it to the, then, editor of the *Newtownards Chronicle,* Ismay Woods, who printed it in a subsequent edition. So the 10th August, 2017 issue of the *Newtownards Chronicle* carried the November 1886 item from WG's *North Down Herald*, which, in turn, had reproduced the article from an 1879 issue of the *Chronicle* that had quoted an earlier report from the *Daily Mail* which itself was all about *Humorous Readings by "Robin"*!

Charity event has "Robin" recounting his visit to the Newton Flower Show

WG took no outward offence at the flippant remarks published by William Henry, whatever he may have thought privately. He took it as a timely reminder, in fact, that he had committed to sending another article to the *Chronicle*. As it happened, a big fund-raising evening in Newtownards was to be held a few weeks later to help reduce an outstanding debt on a local charitable building, according to the *Newtownards Chronicle* of October 17th, 1879. The paper unfortunately chose not to name the premises in its columns. The building's trustees had sent WG an invitation urging "Robin" to

11 - ...AND IN A BOOK

please attend as a sure crowd-puller for their event. He decided to accept and agreed to donate his time for this worthy cause. He even promised to come with new material. Since it was for a Newtownards audience he determined to write the long-awaited account of "Robin's" visit to the Flower Show.

It was a prestigious event and the Newtownards Assembly Rooms overlooking Conway Square were packed to the doors. Many dignitaries were present and presiding in the chair was the Rev Joseph Bradshaw J.P. (none other than the official VIP who had judged some of the entries at the Flower Show a few months earlier.) In his introductory comments the Rev Bradshaw said how much he had been looking forward to meeting his old friend, "Robin," again but remonstrated with him that he had not yet received an invitation to visit him in Ballycuddy, nor been introduced to his good wife, Peggy. This went down well with the audience so WG, dressed up in "Robin's" country finery, added an impromptu response to his Reverence in his own opening remarks. In a strong voice, according to the report in the *Chronicle*, he spoke "in a broad, homely dialect that could be distinctly heard in every part of the building."

> *Mr Chairman an' dear friens I'm reel glad tae see ye here agen in this nice place, for mony a time I hae thocht aboot the gran' nicht we spent here afore, an' I hope it was usefu' and did guid, and I hope this meetin' will dae guid, tae.*[118]

WG paused, as this drew some applause from the audience, and then continued:

> *It dis me guid tae see sae mony nice, weel-dressed fowk comin' oot fur an nicht's divershun, an' I hope*

---

[118] Mr Chairman and dear friends I'm real glad to see you here again in this nice place, for many a time I have thought about the grand night we spent here before, and I hope it was useful and did good, and I hope this meeting will do good, too.

THE STORYTELLER

> *we'll hae twa plaisint hoors, an' that ye'll a' gang hame sayin' that ye wudna a missed it fur anything.*[119]

This had the audience laughing out loud before WG turned to the chairman and said:

> *An' it's a gran thing, sur, till see a nice, weel-respected gentilman, like your honor pursiding at this meetin'. I neednae tell the Newtownards fowk hoo muckle yer thocht of in the Coonty Doon, but I wud like fer tae tell ye, sur, that iver since that day o' the Flower Show, that ye ordered the rid ticket fer till be pit on Peggy's butter fer furst prize, she thinks there's no sich anither gentilman in Coonty Doon.*[120]

The audience roared at this and the Rev Bradshaw smiled in acknowledgement as "Robin" started in on a recital of "Peggy, and Hoo I Courted Her" drawing forth frequent applause and hearty laughter from the appreciative audience. This was followed by a selection played by the band of the North Down Rifles, readily volunteered by Captain George R. Hamilton who played along with the joke and said how much he had been looking forward to meeting again with his old friend "Robin Gordon" who, of course, had recently joined the Militia. The band was followed by Mr R. D Agnew, a well-known elocutionist from Belfast, who read "The Execution of Montrose," before it was "Robin's" turn again. This time WG took out the manuscript of his account of the Newton Flower Show and had his audience in stitches with copious amusing references to locals whom

---

[119] It does me good to see so many nice, well-dressed folk coming out for a night's diversion, and I hope we'll have two pleasant hours, and that you'll all go home saying that you wouldn't have missed it for anything.

[120] And it's a grand thing, sir, to see a nice, well-respected gentleman, like your honour presiding at this meeting. I needn't tell the Newtownards folk how much you're thought of in the County Down, but I would like to tell you, sir, that ever since that day of the Flower Show, that you ordered the red ticket to be put on Peggy's butter for first prize, she thinks there's no such another gentleman in County Down.

11 - ...AND IN A BOOK

"Robin" had met either on his way to the show on in the grounds—and, of course, including Peggy's triumph with her homemade butter.

Altogether, the evening was declared to be a great success and WG, as he had arranged, handed a copy of his latest manuscript to William Henry, who was there reporting the proceedings for the *Newtownards Chronicle*. The whole account appeared in the paper over the next three weeks. So WG's efforts not only raised money for the charitable event but also boosted Henry's sales: an announcement in Henry's own columns heralded the forthcoming series of articles by "Robin" and added, "Agents requiring extra copies of the *Chronicle* containing the above will please forward their orders at once."

The third piece, which he entitled, "The Newtownerds Dug Show an' Horse Jumpin'"—events that were run alongside the Flower Show—appeared on the 8th November, 1879. This was the last time WG would write an article for the *Chronicle*. However, the following month, perhaps looking forward to Christmas and in a benign frame of mind, he sat down one evening and penned one final letter to 'the Editor.' He wrote as "Robin".

Ballycuddy,
Desaymber the foart, 18 & 79

Deer Mister Henerey,—I wuz quer and glad fur till heer that yer bizzy getting' reddy yer new Aulmanak fur echteen hunner an' echty, an I want ye, if ye please sur, fur till pit doon my name fur a cappy, bekaus I very neer missed it last yeer, an' I sen' ye rowled up in a wee peece o' paper, fower penny stamps, which I hope ye'll get safe. If it coasts any mair nor it did afore I can settle wi' ye the nixt time I'm in Newton. I hope it'll soon be reddy, fur Peggy and me ir thinkin' quer lang till see it, an' wee Paddy wunners what the picters wull be aboot this time...

I'm shair it gie's ye dredfu' bother gettin' up the Aulmanak, an' I dae not ken hoo ye can sell it sae chape. It keeps the fowk aboot heer reedin' fur weeks, an' there's no a hoose ye gang intil but ye see it either lyin' in the bauk o' the chimley, or the wunday, or a

THE STORYTELLER

bit o' string put throo it an' it hung up in the corner. Ye hae nay noshin hoo usefu' it is, an' it's nae wunner Peggy says that ye hae the gran' heed on ye, an' that she's shair yer mistress is gie an' prood o' ye. Hoo in the wurl yer heed contains sae muckle I dae not ken...[121]

WG went on to have "Robin" praise all the diverse content of the Almanac in what amounted to a hearty endorsement for the publication and then, aware that he would soon be setting up in opposition to the *Chronicle,* and hoping to remain on good terms, finished by saying,

I beg yer pardin, sur, fur takin' up yer time, but I hope ye'll excuse yer auld frien an' wull wusher,
Rabin Gordon

---

[121] Ballycuddy,
December the fourth, 1879
Dear Mister Henry—I was very glad to hear that you're busy getting ready your new Almanac for eighteen hundred and eighty, and I want you, if you please sir, to put down my name for a copy, because I very nearly missed it last year, and I send you rolled up in a little piece of paper, four penny stamps, which I hope you'll get safe. If it costs any more than it did before I can settle with you the next time I'm in Newtownards. I hope it'll soon be ready, for Peggy and me are longing to see it, and little Paddy wonders what the pictures will be about this time...
I'm sure it gives you dreadful bother getting up the Almanac, and I do not know how you can sell it so cheap. It keeps the folk about here reading for weeks, and there's not a house you go into but you see it either lying in the back of the chimney, or the window, or a bit o' string put through it and it hung up in the corner. You have no notion how useful it is, and it's no wonder Peggy says that you have the grand head on you, and that she's sure your mistress [wife] is very proud of you. How in the world your head contains so much I do not know...

11 - ...AND IN A BOOK

> *P.S.–I hope yer mistress an' family's in guid health. Peggy sens her kin' regards an' hopes yer wee son's better.   R.G.*[122]

In January, the *Chronicle's, Newtownards and County Down Almanac* appeared, heralding in the new decade when, in a few short months WG would be returning with his family to live again in his native town and to establish his very own weekly newspaper. From now on, any further utterances of "Robin" in Newtownards would be gracing the columns—and boosting the sales—of the *North Down Herald*.

---

[122] I beg your pardon, sir, for taking up your time, but I hope you'll excuse your old friend and well-wisher,
Robin Gordon
P.S.–I hope your mistress [wife] and family's in good health. Peggy sends her kind regards and hopes your little son's better.
R.G.

THE STORYTELLER

Chapter 12 – LIVE AND LET LIVE

1880 – January to July

The family would have been preparing to move out of the city to take up residence in their new home early in the spring of 1880 in order for all the preparations to be completed in time for the planned summer launch of the new newspaper.

Inevitably, much of the burden of packing up must have fallen upon Lizzie. Wesley would have helped, of course, where he could, but he still had his accountancy business to run. He planned to keep this on after the move, employing a manager to look after the firm's business and keep it going when WG eventually withdrew to become a fulltime editor and newspaper proprietor. During this period, too, he was busy with the proofs of fifteen more of his stories for the second volume of *Humorous Readings by "Robin"*[123] which was duly published in March, 1880, probably just as the move to Newtownards was taking place. To coincide with this, the publishers, Allen and Johnson, produced a second edition of Volume I, the first having sold out during the previous year. While the first volume had the drawing of "Robin" on its cover, Volume II was adorned with a similar portrait of "Robin's" wife, Peggy.[124]

"Robin" writes to the *Newry Telegraph*

WG had been so busy that winter that he realised he had been neglecting his readers amongst those who took the *Newry Telegraph*. Back at the end of January he decided to pen a note to the editor from "Robin".

---

[123] See Appendix C2 for a list of the stories contained in Humorous Readings by "Robin" Vol 2

[124] For an image of "Peggy" on the cover of Vol 2 see Appendix E, Fig.2.

12 - LIVE AND LET LIVE

LETTER FROM "Robin".
Ballycuddy, Coonty Doon,
Janyeary the Thirty-One
18 & 80

Deer Mister Editur,
A wud like fur till tak my excuse till ye fur my lang spell o' quiteness, but I harly ken hoo fur till set aboot it. Railly an' truly, sur, efter a' yer grate kindness till me a feel ashamed fur till think that a didnae as muckle as drap ye a line fur till wush ye a Happy New Year. But, sur dear, this is a wurl o' trubble, an' we hae oor share o' it in Ballycuddy as weel as ither places. We had a spell o' terble frostay wather, an' Peggy was neer wrang in her min' wi' the roomytics, an', the crater, a did a' that a cud fur till gie her releef, fur she's the kin' wuman till me when there's ocht wrang wi' me, an' it wud be il becommon no till be attentif till her when she's poorly.
Well, sur, yin trubble niver cums on its lane; like the craws, they aye cum in flocks.[125]

"Robin" went on to recount an accident in which his daughter, Susannah's husband fell and broke his shoulder after firing "Robin's"

---

[125] LETTER FROM "Robin", Ballycuddy, County Down, January the Thirtyfirst, 1880

Dear Mister Editor, I would like to make my excuse to you for my long spell of quietness, but I hardly know how to set about it. Really and truly, sir, after all your great kindness to me I feel ashamed to think that I didn't as much as drop you a line to wish you a Happy New Year. But, sir dear, this is a world of trouble, and we have our share of it in Ballycuddy as well as other places. We had a spell of terribly frosty weather, and Peggy was nearly wrong in her mind with rheumatics, and, the creature, I did all that I could to give her relief, for she's the kind woman to me when there's anything wrong with me, and it would be ill becoming not to be attentive to her when she's poorly.

Well, sir, one trouble never comes on its own; like the crows, they always come in flocks.

old Queen Anne gun with too much powder in it. "Robin" had to cart him off to the General Hospital (now the Royal Victoria Hospital.) And then, apparently, "Robin's" "granwean" [grandchild], Paddy had a bad fall, too, that needed four stitches in his forehead. He explained that it was partly all these troubles that had kept him from writing.

The letter continued, touching upon some issues of the day: The Land Question; whether the Newtownards Town Commissioners should buy the Gas Works; the new "Eleck Trick Licht;" the merits of Champion "prittaes" [potatoes]. He even tells the editor, if he has a garden, he'll send him some of the "darlin' seed potatoes" so he can grow his own. He suggests the editor sends one of his "importers" to take notes in shorthand and report on a particular meeting that's due to take place. He then pokes fun at himself regarding shorthand:

> My! It's quer writin'. Ye showed it till me whun a was in Newry, an' it's fur a' the wurl like a hen scrapin' amang sand.[126]

He signed off with:

> Hopin' till hae the pleeshir o' sendin' ye a story afore long, a remain, sur, yer humble servint,
> Robin Gordon.
> P.S.—Ye'll be glad till hear that a' my books ir sell't, an' the printers ir busy at a second yin.[127]

Rev Isaac Nelson

"Robin's" letter appeared in the *Newry Telegraph* on Thursday 5th February, 1880 and, indeed, it wasn't long before WG, in spite of all the busyness in his life at the time, couldn't resist taking time out to

---

[126] My! It queer writing. You showed it to me when I was in Newry, and it's for all the world like a hen scraping amongst sand.

[127] Hoping to have the pleasure of sending you a story before long, I remain, sir, your humble servant, Robin Gordon. P.S.—You'll be glad to hear that all my books are sold, and the printers are busy at a second one.

12 - LIVE AND LET LIVE

put pen to paper once more when an idea for another story of a particularly topical nature presented itself.

Just across and up the road a little from St Anne's Church (now the Church of Ireland Cathedral) where Wesley and Lizzie were married, stood Donegall Street Presbyterian Church. It was only a fifteen minute walk from where the Lyttles used to live before they crossed the Lagan to leave behind the ever-present threat of sectarian strife and to be nearer Lizzie's sister. With Wesley probably coming from a Presbyterian background, I should imagine he and his family might well have visited the church from time to time. Although their closest Presbyterian church was the Rev Hugh Hanna's St Enoch's at Carlisle Circus, which had a very large congregation of seven or eight hundred affiliated families, Wesley may not have been much attracted by the rabble-rousing anti-Catholic, anti-Home Rule rhetoric from "Roaring Hanna," as the clergyman was irreverently known.

Donegall Street, on the other hand, had the attraction of being led by a calmer cleric, although equally notorious and controversial. So the minister, the Rev Isaac Nelson, was a gentleman who would have been well-known to Wesley, at least by reputation and quite possibly from his having, at times, gone along to hear him preach. Ordained in 1837 at First Comber Presbyterian, the Rev Nelson moved in 1842, two years before Wesley was born, to Donegall Street where he had remained ever since. An ardent abolitionist in his younger days, speaking out against the evils of slavery, he later gained notoriety following the 1859 Ulster Revival, which put much emphasis (some claimed over-emphasis) on assurance of salvation received through an outpouring of the Holy Spirit. Nelson supported the Rev W Dobbin in refuting this "theology" and hence the whole revival movement and became rather *persona non grata* amongst the Presbyterian hierarchy.

Unusually, too, for a Protestant, the Rev Nelson was a strong advocate of Home Rule for Ireland—an issue which united many an Irishman and divided as many others. WG, from the very little we have preserved of his writing on the topic, seems to have kept an open mind. The subject was frequently in the news at this time and particularly so in the run up to the General Election due to take place that spring. Nelson was quite forthright about it. Indeed, WG could have been forgiven for believing that the reverent gentleman was, by then, more of a politician than a theologian. It wouldn't have come as much of a surprise to him when he heard rumours that the cleric was going to stand for Westminster when Disraeli went to the country during March and April, 1880.

Nelson decided to fight the election in County Mayo, knowing he would stand little chance of winning in a Belfast constituency. The big majority of his fellow Presbyterians in Ulster were staunchly Unionist. They had backed the outspoken Presbyterian minister, Dr Henry Cooke in 1841 when he had strongly refuted Daniel O'Connell's arguments to repeal the Act of Union and establish a Catholic, independent Ireland. Now, four decades on, there was a distinct possibility that the Whigs—probably with the help of the Irish Parliamentary Party—might defeat Disraeli's Tories, who were strongly Unionist in their Conservative politics. The chance that Gladstone, if he came to power, could be persuaded to introduce legislation to bring about Home Rule for Ireland was very real.

"Robin" Meets Rev Nelson

WG had largely steered clear of political themes in his stories, although he saw in the Rev Nelson's standing for parliament an opportunity too good to miss. Such a forthright orator was much in demand in other pulpits. It occurred to WG, when he learned that Nelson was about to become even more newsworthy, that "Elder Robin" should invite him to preach one Sunday at Ballycuddy. And so the story, "A Crack Wi' Izek Neelson"[128] was written over a few dark evenings early in February. We know this because it is one of the few stories where WG has provided the date after the title: "Written in February 1880." Perhaps this was the moment that Nelson announced

---

[128] A Conversation with Isaak Nelson. This is the title of the story as it was first written for the *Newry Telegraph*. When it subsequently appeared in an anthology of WG's stories, *Humorous Readings by Robin—Vol II* and later in another, *Robin's Readings—Vol III* it had been re-named, "Izek Neelson at Ballycuddy." WG wrote a second Nelson story that appeared in the *Telegraph* a week later, which was then called "Another Crack wi' the Rev. Izek Neelson." When that one subsequently appeared in *Readings by Robin—Vol III,* its title was simply, "A Crack wi' the Rev. Izek Neelson." It is included in the newly published, *Robin's Further Readings,* published by AG Lyttle, 2021.

12 - LIVE AND LET LIVE

his intention to stand as an Irish Parliamentary Party candidate and WG wanted to emphasise the contemporaneity of his tale.

In preparation for his writing, WG headed back to his old haunts and walked up the Shankill Road past a row of houses in a poor state of repair that were referred to, irreverently, as *Home Rule Terrace*—though not by the indignant Protestant residents. For the Rev Nelson, himself, had had these homes built next to his own rather grander dwelling with big bow windows and steps leading up to the front door. As WG looked upon the home of the object of his research, he found himself thinking that even it had a neglected air about it.

We know all this from what WG subsequently wrote. From the material he gathered about Isaac Nelson he ended up with enough to fill at least two stories,[129] which he accommodated by the simple device of having the minister take a shine to "Robin Gordon" when he came to preach at Ballycuddy. So much so that he invited "Robin" to drop in to see him the next time he was in Belfast. This, "Robin" duly did and we have "Another Crack Wi' Izek Neelson"[130] as a result.

Three consecutive adverts in the *Belfast News-Letter* on Monday to Wednesday, the 23rd to 25th February, 1880 heralded the forthcoming publication in that Saturday's *Newry Telegraph* of this second story about the Rev Nelson. The first one had been printed the previous week on Saturday the 21st and had to be reprinted in the Tuesday 24th edition, so vast was the demand for copies. Over 1000 were sold in Belfast alone. The popularity of "Robin's" stories prompted the *Newry Telegraph* to reprint the second story the following Saturday, running a series of ads in the *Belfast News-Letter* on Tuesday 2nd March ("...will appear in the *Newry Telegraph* on Saturday"), Friday 5th March ("...will appear in the *Newry Telegraph* tomorrow"), Saturday 6th March ("...appears in the *Newry Telegraph* today"), and three further ads the following week saying that the story

---

[129] "at least two"—We have two stories preserved that both appeared in February editions of the *Newry Telegraph*. In April, 1880 the *Newry Telegraph* ran an advert headed "CRACKS WI' THE REVEREND IZEK NEELSON (No. 3) BY 'ROBIN'," which would appear the following Saturday. It is unclear whether the "No. 3" implies this is a third Nelson story, or more probably, that the "Cracks" in the title means that both the original stories, "A Crack..." and "Another Crack..." were being reprinted in April in (at least) three instalments.

[130] See previous Note on the titles of WG's two Isaac Nelson stories.

had appeared in last Saturday's *Newry Telegraph*. "Robin's" fond blethers[131] were undoubtedly still selling newspapers and, yet again, one of WG's ventures—this time into political satire, had paid off handsomely.

Anything written about Home Rule at the time would have been read with much interest. However, it was WG's bouncing Nelson's Nationalist sympathies off "Robin's" naïve thinking that they both shared traditional Presbyterian and Unionist principles—done with such humour—that made his stories so popular. When the notorious Belfast cleric came to the Ballycuddy pulpit WG drew excruciating humour from the innocent naivety of "Robin" and the solidly Unionist, Presbyterian congregation who assumed that the visiting clergyman must hold views similar to their own. The Rev Nelson's erudite, but impenetrable, two-hour sermon left them impressed but quite oblivious to his strong views on Irish Nationalism. The result was some highly amusing talking at cross purposes. This, for example, when the Ballycuddy elders and their visiting preacher had enjoyed lunch back at "Robin's":

> *Sez Neevin Erthurs, "Ah wuz wonderin, sur, if ye wud give us a lekter in the skulehoose sum nicht. "We hae an Orange Ludge that meets here, and we were thinking of biggin a Hall, an A'm shair we cud sell a queer wheen tickets if your reverence wud gie us a lekter on the Battle o the Boyne."*
> *Mister Neelson begood a crackin' his heels on the hearth-stane. A declare A heerd his teeth skringin'. He spauk at last an' sez he—*
> *"Orangeism is the bane o' the country, sur!"*
> *"It is that sur," sez Jamey Menyarry, "baith bane an' muscle; An A'm glad till heer that yer yin o' the richt soart."*[132]

---

[131] blethers - chatter

[132] Nevin Arthurs says, "I was wondering, sir, if you would give us a lecture in the schoolhouse some night. "We have an Orange Lodge that meets here, and

12 - LIVE AND LET LIVE

It is clear from the second Nelson tale that WG was familiar with the location and appearance of the minister's house. Indeed, he describes the interior as well. While this could be purely from his imagination, it is quite likely that WG arranged an interview with the cleric and sat in the same "darlin' big erm cher" where "Robin" would subsequently be entertained.

He could also, of course, have gained knowledge of the Rev Nelson's thinking from the gentleman's book, *Year of Delusion*. He describes this publication as a green-backed book about the size of a *Confession of Faith*, so he was obviously acquainted with it. Upon "Robin" being shown a copy in the Rev Nelson's parlour, WG has him say:

> *'It's bigger nor a thocht it wud be,' sez I.*
> *'Yis, it contains a vast amount o' matter,' sez he.*
> *'It wud tak ye a quar while tae write that book, sur,' sez I.*
> *'No as long as ye wud think,' sez he; 'the pen o' a reddy writer can akomplish wunners.'*
> *'A wush a had yin,' sez I; 'for a hae a dale o' writin' till dae, an' a fin' it tiresome wark.'*
> *'Ye wush ye had yin what?' sez he.*
> *'Yin o' them reddy writin' pens ye spauk aboot,' sez I; 'a hae heard o' "Reddy Rekiners," but a never heered tell o' the tither.'*
> *He just lauched. Then he got a pen an' ink an' wrote inside the book cover:-*[133]

---

we were thinking of building a Hall, and I'm sure we could sell quite a number of tickets if Your Reverence would give us a lecture on the Battle of the Boyne."

Mister Nelson began cracking his heels on the hearth-stone. I declare I heard his teeth grinding. He spoke at last and said—

"Orangeism is the bane of the country, sir!"

"It is that sir, says Jamey Menary, both bone and muscle; And I'm glad to hear that you're one of the right sort."

[133] 'It's bigger than I thought it would be,' says I.
'Yes, it contains a vast amount of matter,' says he.

THE STORYTELLER

"Presented to
Mr Robert Gordon, of Ballycuddy
Accompanied by the best wishes of his friend,
Isaac Nelson.
Honi soit qui mal y pence."

A hae copied it letter fur letter oot o' the book, fur it's as plain as prent. A suppoas the last words will be Latin or Haybroo. A didnae like till shew my ignerance or A wud a axed him, so whun onybuddy axes me what it means A tell them that it's a compliment till Peggy, fur that it means—
"Honey's sweet, an' so is Peggy!" A'm shair that's jist what it is.[134]

To Newton

"A Crack Wi' Izek Neelson" was one of the last, maybe *the* last story WG wrote in Belfast before the move. For around about the time of little Robina's first birthday Lizzie was bundling up all the belongings they had accumulated over the years and getting her children ready for this major upheaval. Neither Robina, nor two-year-old Roland will

---

'It would take you a considerable while to write that book, sir,' says I.

'Not as long as you would think,' says he; 'the pen of a ready writer can accomplish wonders.'

'I wish I had one,' says I; 'for I have a deal of writing to do, and I find it tiresome work.'

'You wish you had one what?' says he.

'One of them ready writing pens ye spoke about,' says I; 'I have heard of "Ready Reckoners," but I never heard tell of the other.'

He just laughed. Then he got a pen and ink and wrote inside the book cover:...

[134] I have copied it letter for letter out of the book, for it's as plain as print. I suppose the last words will be Latin or Hebrew. I didn't like to show my ignorance or I would have asked him, so when anybody asks me what it means I tell them that it's a compliment to Peggy, for it means—

"Honey's sweet, and so is Peggy!" I'm sure that's just what it is.

12 - LIVE AND LET LIVE

have been much bothered by all the goings-on, but Eva at five-and-a-half must have revelled in the excitement of it all. Her big sister, Agnes, now nearly 12, and brother, John, going on 14, would have been roped in to help with all the packing and in making decisions about what could be thrown out or given away.

Eventually, however, the whole family was ready and fond farewells to Aunt Isabella and to neighbours were made. The removal people had loaded up all their furniture and packing cases. I wonder if WG used the services of W. W. Kennedy & Co., a removal firm who subsequently took out advertising in one of his publications.[135] He may well have done, as their premises were located on Academy Street where he used to teach shorthand when he first moved to Belfast, so he would have known of them and may even have used them for previous moves.

The seven Lyttles were finally leaving behind the cries of the costermongers and the rattle of cart wheels on Belfast's cobbled streets—sounds and sights the children had known all their lives. With their entire worldly goods already *en route* by road, they would have boarded the Belfast and County Down Railway train that was to take them out of the smoke and grime of the city. That would transport them to their new, rural life in Newtownards where they would be surrounded by fresh air and open countryside, with Scrabo Tower on its hill overlooking the sparkling waters lapping on the shores of Strangford Lough.

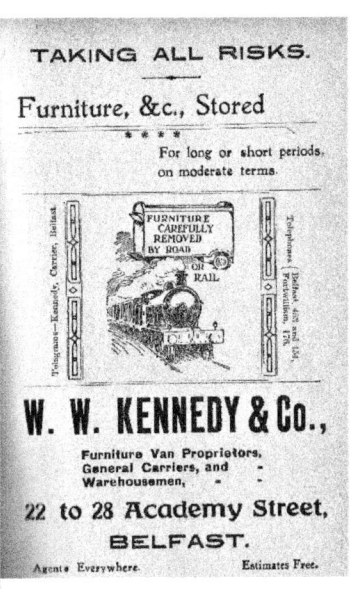

Advertisement from ***Robin's Readings*** for W. W. Kennedy & Co., Removals

---

[135] An omnibus edition of Robin's Readings, Volumes 1, 2 and 3, First edition.

THE STORYTELLER

As the train chuffed out of the station, we can just imagine Lizzie's thoughts of all they were leaving behind. Probably apprehensive, aware that this would be the farthest move she and Wesley had ever made, fully ten miles to the east of the city. Wondering about how the family would adapt to the premises Wesley had been able to rent on the High Street right at the heart of the little market town's busy centre. Did she glance at her husband sitting back, perhaps with his eyes closed, the repetitive clickety-clack of the wheels crossing each joint in the track an urgent lullaby to her contemplations? Was she wondering if Wesley, too, was picturing their new residence that was just a stone's throw from the ancient Market Cross, so familiar to him in his youth?

Until recently, No 32 had been home to Samuel M'Cutcheon, General Agricultural Equipment and Machine Warehouse,[136] so it was to see quite a change when the Lyttles moved in and converted it to a newspaper office. It was right next door to Hugh Donnan's fine showrooms for glass, china and fancy goods that also sold general hardware, house furnishings, seeds and farm implements. Mr Donnan took out advertisements in WG's publications and as a result we have this photograph of his shop frontage. On the other side, No. 30 High Street, was the Ards Boot and Shoe Warehouse, the premises of WG's old friend, James M'Kee who had quite likely first made him aware that No. 32 was becoming available. A nice serendipity that, on his return to Newtownards, WG should move in next door to the premises of the man who took over

The premises next door to **the Herald** office.

---

[136] We know the previous occupier of 32 High Street from an advert in the *Newtownards Independent*.

12 - LIVE AND LET LIVE

his old childhood home on Regent Street and perpetuated the family business.

To see today where the new newspaper offices stood we must bear in mind that since that time the numbering of High Street premises has been altered twice. The location of the original newspaper office is where No. 38 now stands[137] (occupied in 2021 by Berlin Clothing.)[138]

We know from further adverts that other nearby businesses included John Simmons' General Drapery Warehouse across the road at Nos. 49/51, and the Ards Flour and Bread Company, Limited. WG's new enterprise would sit comfortably amongst these stalwart traders and soon become what he was determined would be not only the country's newest, but its finest weekly journal.

Encouraging support

Once established in his new premises, WG set about putting in place all that was necessary to produce the sort of newspaper that would capture the hearts of its readership and leave them wanting more. There were ads to be placed in the Belfast newspapers for Correspondents in Bangor, Donaghadee and Downpatrick and other centres of population to provide him with local news and gossip and, in due course, interviews to make suitable appointments. He planned to publish the first issue in July and as the summer approached, amongst all the business correspondence that arrived on his desk at No. 32, letters of support started to appear. One, from Bangor, read:

> *I have just heard a rumour that you are going to revive the Newtownards Independent. Please say if this is so. It was, indeed, a popular paper and we have seen nothing like it since. When I hear from you in confirmation of this report, I shall do what I can in the way of circulating it for old times' sake.*

---

[137] I am grateful to Terence Bowman for his detective work in establishing the location of the original *Herald* office.

[138] Appendix F—Fig 5 shows the site of the *Herald's* original office in Newtownards.

THE STORYTELLER

Another ran:

> *I was told today that the Independent, under some other name, is about to be started again. We were very fond of that paper in our district, and looked for it eagerly every Saturday. I hope the Old Man that lived on Scrabo will drop us a line now and then... I wish you every success.*

A writer from Donaghadee said:

> *If you make your paper anything like what it was in the hands of the former proprietors, the people in this district will subscribe largely. Don't forget to give us a local story.*

WG received a score of letters of encouragement from folk living in and around Newtownards. One wrote:

> *Kindly put down my name as a yearly subscriber. I have no fear of your success. In fact, if your paper is conducted with any kind of moderation and judgement at all, it must succeed. From what I have heard, I have no doubt your paper will confer a great benefit upon our town and be advantageous to yourself.*

A letter, which particularly touched WG when he read it, included the following:

> *J--- C--- wants to join me in getting your new paper. Please send it to me, as I am to get the first reading, and then I'll hand it to him. I send you the 6½d, the half a quarter's subscription, and J---C--- will send you the other half. If he don't, then please send me the half of the paper that contains "Robin's" letter.*

12 - LIVE AND LET LIVE

WG was so encouraged by all the messages wishing him well in his new venture that he decided to print these few examples in the first issue of the *Herald*. He couldn't resist including, also, the following, written jocularly, he presumed, in a dialect for which, he said, "we own a fondness":

> *Dear sur—so yer gaun tae prent a paper on yer ain acoont. The Fowk that I hae been talkin' till ir rael glad till hear it. Oor Tammy says he'll carry papers for ye. Heth I hope he'll no get hurt wae the fowk pu'in them frae him. I suppose ye'll gie us sumthin' gran' ivery week.*[139]

To conclude his column of correspondence, the new editor wrote: "With many thanks to all those who have thus cheered us as we enter upon our labours, we ask their kind indulgence, and we promise to do our best to gratify their wishes, and to realise their anticipations."

Printing the paper

Contrary to what has been written over the years about the start-up of WG's newspaper, he did not own a printing press at that stage. The copy was all sent up to Allen and Johnson's in Belfast where the paper was produced each week. As evidence of this we have the, admittedly ambiguous, statement in the first edition that the newspaper was "Printed and Published Weekly *for* (my emphasis) the Proprietor, W. G. Lyttle at the Office, 32 High Street, Newtownards, to whom papers

---

[139] *Dear sir – so you're going to print a paper on your own account. The Folk that I have been talking to are real glad to hear it. Our Tommy says he'll carry papers for you. Faith, I hope he'll not get hurt with the folk pulling them from him. I suppose you'll give us something grand every week.*

and business communications… are to be addressed."[140] The use of the word *for* rather than *by* suggests the newspaper was not printed at No. 32 High Street. Allen and Johnson were making good money from "Robin's" books, so should have been happy to extend WG credit to produce the first copies of his newspaper before the revenue from their sales and advertising came in.

But further, definitive evidence comes to light some time later in an account of a libel action brought against the newspaper and its publisher, which refers to "the defendants, Mr. Robert S. Allen, and Mr Wesley G. Lyttle, publisher and proprietor, respectively, of the *North Down Herald…*" It wouldn't, in fact, be until some years after he moved the paper to new premises that WG was able to install a printing press of his own. But we are getting ahead of the story.

Saturday, 17th July was set as the date for the first edition. WG had handbills printed announcing the launch of the newspaper. These were distributed to all and sundry at the Newton fair held earlier in the month. I imagine he roped in his children to compete with each other for who could hand out the most flyers.[141] On Wednesday, 14th July, he placed an advert for the new journal in the *Belfast Telegraph*. The same advert appeared on the Thursday and Friday and on Saturday the 17th, as well. The ad led with: " 'ROBIN'S' NEW READING—The General Assembly o' Echteen Hunner and Echty".[142] This was the eye-catcher—everyone knew "Robin." Reading on, they would see

---

[140] This is the notice that appeared in the first edition of the *North Down Herald*:

> Printed and Published Weekly for the Proprietor, W. G. LYTTLE, at the Office 32 High Street, Newtownards, to whom papers and business communications—in every case free of expense—are to be addressed
> SATURDAY, 17th JULY, 1880.

[By kind permission of the British Library: Microfilm – shelfmark MFM M14050 (1880)]

[141] We know this from a letter that appeared in the second issue of the *North Down Herald* that started: "Sir, When I got one of your proposals, or playbills or whatever you call it, on the fair day in Newton…"

[142] The General Assembly of Eighteen Hundred and Eighty

12 - LIVE AND LET LIVE

that the story would appear in the *North Down Herald*. The advert looked like this:

> **"ROBIN'S NEW READING,**
> THE GENERAL ASSEMBLY O'
> ECHTEEN HUNNER AN' ECHTY
> See
> **NORTH DOWN HERALD**
> **Of Saturday, 17th July.**
> PRICE ONE PENNY
> Belfast Agents—Henderson, Castle Place;
> Mayne's Donegall Square East.

By September, WG's adverts would be leading with the name of the newspaper, by then established in the public's mind, and continuing with information about the "Robin" story it contained. Another advert in the *Belfast Telegraph* ran:

> **THE**
> **NORTH DOWN HERALD**
> **Of Saturday, 4th Sept.,**
> Will contain a humorous sketch entitled "THE FAUGH A BALLAGH PLEECEMAN AND HIS BATON" (an episode of the recent riots), by "Robin," author of the "Tipperary Policeman," the "Meer's Proclamation," the "Fechtin' Dugs," &c, &c, as published in *Newry Telegraph*.
> On sale from Friday evening at Henderson's and Robb's, Castle Place; Edward Johnston's, High Street; Reid's, Victoria Street; Mayne's Donegall Square East; and other Newsagents.
> PRICE ONE PENNY

The first issue

The office in Newtownards will have seen increasingly feverish activity as Publication Day approached. Reporters being lined up to attend the Newtownards and Bangor Petty Sessions, meetings of the Board of Guardians, and local events; national and international news sources scanned for items to reproduce in the *Herald*; advertisements placed in the Belfast papers promoting the new journal and seeking personal ads for publication; advertising contracts agreed with numerous companies who took out space—many for the front page, which, traditionally, consisted entirely of advertisements at that time.

This meant the front page could be set up in advance. It contained adverts for Bangor Steamers that brought day-trippers from Belfast; American Line, carrying passengers from Liverpool to Philadelphia; Anchor Line—Glasgow and Londonderry to New York; Cunard Line (Royal Mail Steamers)—Liverpool to New York and Boston, Wednesdays and Saturdays.

Other ads were of more local interest—Geo. A Kennedy, Builder, South Street, Newtownards; James A. Brown, Drapers, High Street, Newtownards who announced their Summer Sale, while Kurlew & Co. of Ann Street in Belfast advertised their "India-rubber Garments." There were adds from Photographers, Watch and Clock Makers, Hotels and Restaurants ("with private room for Ladies")—and one from Francis Ritchie & Sons, "Manure and Felt Manufacturers".

Inside, on page 2, was a full column ad:

Cloth limp, 1/- By Post, 1/2
Boards, 1/6 By Post 1/8.
HUMOROUS READINGS by "Robin" Vol I,
with portrait of "Robin".

Beneath the heading was listed each chapter with a brief synopsis of its contents. Under this was:

Now Ready—Second Volume—
Price 1s By Post, 1s 2d
With Handsome Portrait of "Peggy".

This was followed by a complete contents list of Vol II.

The advert for his two books took the whole of the first column of the seven-column broadsheet. Next was a column of more assorted adverts and then—what was to set the tone for the future life of the *North Down Herald*—WG's first editorial. He must have spent

12 - LIVE AND LET LIVE

considerable time mulling over what he should write and gone through a number of drafts. He had noted how his predecessor in the *Independent* had always headed his editorials with the phrase, "Be just and fear not" and perhaps it was that that it inspired him to come up with his own editorial strapline. So, from the very first issue, his editorials always commenced with a slogan he felt portrayed the attitude he proposed to adopt in his reporting—"LIVE AND LET LIVE." A fine aspiration but, although he always retained the slogan week after week, there would be times—particularly when he reported on what he saw as the shortcomings of the Town Commissioners, for example—when readers might have questioned his commitment to *laissez faire,* certainly when it came to hints of inefficiency, skulduggery or oppression of the downtrodden. Indeed, his outspokenness against such things was what would make his journal so popular.

Editor Lyttle's first editorial

Eventually the great day dawned and the *North Down Herald*, hot off the presses, hit the streets of Belfast, Newtownards and surrounding towns. Eager hands throughout the whole of North Down turned the pages; eyes in every townland scanned the columns. Soon hundreds were reading WG's editorial that he had taken such pains to get just right.

The North Down Herald
"LIVE AND LET LIVE"
NEWTOWNARDS: Saturday, July 17, 1880
To all our readers,
In the last issue of the Newtownards Independent *its readers were informed that its proprietors were compelled, through unforeseen circumstances, to suspend, for a time, the publication of that journal. The* Newtownards Independent, *during the entire period of its existence, was held in high esteem by all classes of readers in this broad county. It seemed as though an old friend had gone from our midst, when that popular newspaper was discontinued. There was*

a blank which up till the present had not been filled to the satisfaction of the reading and thinking people of our town and neighbourhood. They miss the tone of the old favourite and have been calling loudly for its revival. We rejoice to have the privilege of responding to that call, and the letters of congratulation which have poured in upon us during the past fortnight have been most encouraging. We shall do our utmost to merit the confidence and approbation expressed on all sides and to secure and retain the support of the people of County Down. We adopt a new name, but in other respects the North Down Herald *will be identical with the* Newtownards Independent. *We resume the pen as our predecessor in the editorial chair put it down. The old lines shall be followed strictly. Devoid of party politics of an aggressive nature, we shall know no man. Our former principles are our principles of today, and in keeping with our motto of "Live and let live," we shall, as has been hitherto done in the columns of the* Newtownards Independent *earnestly support what we believe to be right, and strenuously oppose what we may consider to be wrong in all questions affecting our neighbours or ourselves. We shall subscribe to no set policy, pander to no clique, be led by no party. To follow with blind complacency the mandates of a master-mind, whether it be a Beaconsfield or a Gladstone, is not our idea of independence. To be proud to follow any man, however exalted, will not form any portion of the principles of this journal. Sir Joseph Porter, of H.M.S. "Pinafore," has boasted of how he attained his eminence. He always*

"*Voted at his party's call,
And never thought of thinking for himself at all*"

There are no Sir Joseph Porters on the staff of the North Down Herald.

12 - LIVE AND LET LIVE

WG had cleverly garnered all the good will and affection attained by his paper's predecessor that had not, it seemed, been picked up to a significant extent by his rival publication, the *Newtownards Chronicle*. He appropriated it for the *Herald* instead. In doing so, though, he had included an implied sideswipe at the *Chronicle*. Amidst all the approbation the *Herald* was receiving, there was at least one Newtownards citizen less than adoring—the editor of the town's other newspaper.

William Henry sent his reporter and leader writer, a Mr Magee, to the *Herald* office to procure copies of the first issue and subsequently pronounced that the *Herald's* claim to be a reissue of the *Newtownards Independent,* which he had formerly edited, was libellous and threatened to bring an action against the paper. But it was all bluster; he never did.

Be that as it may, WG's first editorial continued by saying that each subject would be considered on its merits and how it could best be "for the advantage and welfare of our town and district." It raised the Land Question as an example (an issue that had remained in WG's mind ever since his childhood when he watched Scrabo Tower being constructed as a memorial to Lord Londonderry, one of North Down's biggest land owners.) It said the paper would "contend until a healthy measure of Tenant Right has become law," but recognised the fine balance between the rights of tenants and the just requirements of landlords. And, far from leaning towards one political party or another (commentators down the years have asserted the *Herald* to have been "a strong Liberal paper and Home Rule supporter") the fact of the matter is that it advocated an occasional change of government between Liberals and Conservatives as "likely to be of greatest advantage to the people" as each party granted concessions, eager for the popular vote.

Hitherto, WG was known throughout North Down, Antrim and beyond as "Robin", the inoffensive and amusing stage performer, and as the emollient occasional chairman at Belfast public events. Overnight, as it would have seemed, he had metamorphosed into an assertive opinion former, in command of Westminster politics, yet independent of them, and an authoritative purveyor of news—local, national and international. Many must have found the transformation remarkable. But with it, he never lost his sense of humour. His wit would frequently encroach upon his journalism. It was probably that, more than anything, that would always endear him to the vast majority of his readership.

Other content

Readers found a good write-up of the annual celebrations held on the 12th July by the Orange Order, with a stirring account of the marches and speeches. There was plenty of other local news: an account of the previous Friday evening's meeting of the Comber Total Abstinence Society sat, uncomfortably, adjacent to an item headed, "Fatal Accident at Comber" about a man who had been killed by falling from one of the chimneys of the Comber Distilleries.

Further afield, there was a report from the House of Commons, and international items were as diverse as to include an account of an earthquake in Switzerland, a paragraph about an exhibition in Cincinnati showing all the processes undergone in the making of bread and an update on the Russo-Chinese war.

Then, of course, there was what a large number of the purchasers of the paper were looking for, a brand new story by "Robin." His piece about the General Assembly had been well received last year and WG had been right in predicting that the introduction of musical instruments was an issue that would be on the agenda again in 1880. He decided that "Robin," who, the previous year, had "niver sat as long in a meetin'-hoose at yin time afore, an it's no likely that iver A wull agen,"[143] would, nevertheless, turn up at this year's assembly and provide WG with a tried and tested format for his first "Robin" story to appear in the *North Down Herald.*

---

[143] "never sat as long in a meeting-house [church] at one time before, and it's not likely that I will ever again"

12 - LIVE AND LET LIVE

The front page of the very **first edition of the *North Down Herald*** published on Saturday 17 July, 1880 [by kind permission of the British Library – sheffmark MFM M14050 (1880)]

THE STORYTELLER

"Robin", himself was prevailed upon to address the Assembly on the matter of instrumental music and his argument was that, perhaps, they should not seek to legislate against the use of instruments; that only made congregations rebellious. If they left the decision to individual churches, many may decide against it, themselves. By way of illustration he told the gathered church dignitaries all about his cow:

> *There's that moily coo o' mine that A had tae keep lamgled an' tethered fur mony a year fur brekin' intil the squire's clover. The sorra a tether or langle cud A get in Newton, but what she cud brek, an' she wuz neer brekin' my heart intil the bargain, so yin day A loused her an' tuk her intil the clover fiel', an' sez I till her, 'there, noo, Spotty, eat till ye burst yersel'.' A declare she jist turned roon an' followed me oot o' the fiel' wi' her heid hingin' doon, an' frae that day till this she never needed langel nor tether.*[144]

A vote was called for on whether a ban should be introduced and it was only by the narrowest of margins that it was agreed to hold the matter over for another year. In WG's account the matter was decided by a single vote—"Robin's".

The story appeared as planned in the first issue, with the sub-title, "A Reading by 'Robin' author of 'Cracks wi' the Reverend Izek Neelson,' 'The Newtonbreda Harmonium,' 'The Londonderry Banquet,' &c. &c. (Written for the *North Down Herald*.)"

---

[144] There's that hornless cow of mine that I had to keep fettered and tethered for many a year for breaking into the squire's clover. Not a tether or fetter could I get in Newtownards, but what she could break, and she was near breaking my heart into the bargain, so one day I loosed her and took her into the clover field, and says I to her, 'There, now, Spotty, eat till you burst yourself.' I declare she just turned round and followed me out of the field with her head hanging down, and from that day to this she never needed fetter nor tether.

12 - LIVE AND LET LIVE

No longer "written for the *Newry Telegraph*" or "written for the *Newtownards Chronicle*," WG's stories were now promoting the sales of his own newspaper.

And, whether due to "Robin's" input or not, the number of sales of the first issue far exceeded even WG's optimistic expectations. Anticipating a big take-up, he arranged for an enormous print run. In spite of this, as a reward for all the months of hard work and his faith in himself and the good people of Down, the printers had to go to press again for a second run, such was the overwhelming demand for the first issue of WG Lyttle's, and Ulster's newest weekly.

Chapter 13 – UNIVERSAL ACCLAIM —ALMOST

1880 – August to December

Wesley must have been delighted with the enthusiastic reception given to his new enterprise and all the more so because it had brought him back to his roots, the town where he had spent his formative years. There would have been tinges of sadness as sights and sounds recalled incidents from his childhood with his parents who were no longer with him. But to counter those, Wesley must have enjoyed exciting opportunities to show Lizzie, and particularly his children, all the places that he fondly recalled from when he was their age—starting, no doubt, with the premises in Regent Street where their grandfather had been a cobbler, now the Ulster Hotel.

Seeing the sights

John, with his technical mind, would have been intrigued by the unique, octagonal-shaped Market Cross just down the street from his new home; it may even have inspired him to immortalise it on canvas, using his other developing skill as an artist. Roland and Eva would have thrilled to hear about the rumoured secret passage beneath the inner chamber that I'm sure Wesley could not have resisted passing on to his youngsters. A passage, if it ever existed, which may or may not have emerged somewhere amongst the ruins of the nearby Old Priory.

Agnes, would surely have enjoyed looking around the Priory's ancient site with its ivy-covered tower still standing, to the memory of its founding Dominican Order. If she did, Wesley may well have taken her further out of town to visit the remains of Movilla Abbey, too. We can imagine her running her hands over the rough old stonework of the two remaining gable ends of a later, 15th century

13 - UNIVERSAL ACCLAIM—ALMOST

Augustinian church built on the site, listening to her father telling her about the Abbey:

> 'Chap by the name of St Finnian founded the place in 540 AD,' she would have heard him say. 'Continued as a place of worship for over a thousand years! Right up until the Dissolution of the Monasteries in 1542, as I recollect.'

Agnes traced a worn etching with her finger that had been carved on the surface of a stone hundreds of years before, as her father continued.

'But way back in the 7th century Movilla Abbey was one of the greatest monasteries in the whole of Ireland. Think of that; right where you're standing. Yon St Finnian fellow had the right idea. Got it off to a fine start by bringing a copy of the Latin Vulgate version of the Bible back from Rome.'

'The vulgar version?' said Agnes.

'Vulgate. Same Latin root. The Versio Vulgata—the version commonly used. At that time, it was the only complete copy of the Bible in the whole of Ireland.'

Wesley went on to tell his daughter about St Colmcille and his monks who wanted to make a copy of the text but St Finnian wouldn't lend it to him; he would only let them read it at the abbey. However, the monks managed surreptitiously to copy it while they were studying it and when St Finnian found out he took St Colmcille to the high court of the land—before King Diarrmaid—demanding that they hand over the copy. The king found in St Finnian's favour with the famous ruling: "To every cow, its calf; to every book, its copy."

Agnes said, 'I think I'll go and look at the tombstones,' and wandered into the adjacent cemetery

THE STORYTELLER

before her father started in on any more ancient history lessons.[145]

Reporting the events

Apart from revisiting the haunts of his youth and trying to enthuse his children with what used to excite him as a boy, WG set about becoming part of the scene in modern Newtownards. His job as a journalist brought him entry to all sorts of happenings around the town. Although some of the work was delegated to his reporters, WG attended as many events as he could manage, to get to know the local dignitaries and to become better known, himself, outside of his other persona of "Robin" whose fame, of course, preceded him.

A note on the Newtownards Dog Show Society graced the pages of the *Herald's* first edition. In just under two years' time, as recorded in the Belfast News-Letter on the 11th May, 1882, WG would be chairing the Dog Show committee. Also in that first edition was a full account of the doings of the Newtownards Board of Guardians and, of course, of the cases occupying the minds of the magistrates at the Petty Sessions. The Belfast courts were covered, too, and one interesting item involved Mr Thomas Gallagher, the tobacco manufacturer, who successfully sued the Great Northern Railway for negligence when a case of tobacco they were transporting for him lost part of its contents *en route*. (Tom Gallagher would go on in, 1896, to open the largest tobacco factory in the world on Belfast's York Street.)

News items reported ranged from the discovery of stone circles in the Pyrenees to the dates of next week's Fairs that would take place around the Ards. There was an article about the Harem of the Turkish Viceroy in Egypt and a short obituary for Tom Taylor, "the genial editor of *Punch*." I wonder if that item caused WG to make any conscious decision to emulate something of Mr Taylor's style in his own journalism. WG's impish sense of fun and love of telling a good

---

[145] Incidentally, the ground where Agnes may well have walked in that ancient graveyard was destined, some 75 years later to become the last resting place of, arguably, Newtownards' most famous son, the decorated war hero and co-founder of the SAS, Lt-Col Blair Mayne.

13 - UNIVERSAL ACCLAIM—ALMOST

story was frequently to creep into his articles and, on more than one occasion, land him in hot water.

All at the newspaper office at 32 High Street settled into their new routine of garnering the news and writing it up for inclusion in the next week's paper. For his second editorial, WG opened by quoting Lord Justice Fitzgibbon's remarks to the Grand Jury at the Downpatrick Assizes the previous week where he noted the significant drop in crime levels in County Down. WG went on to contrast this with other counties in Ireland, mentioning some in the South and West where the courts were often overstretched trying to process all the misdemeanours. He said the people should be proud of their homeland.

> *"Let strangers say what they will, County Down occupies a high and distinguished position in our country, not alone for its broad acres of rich and well-tilled soil, and its varied and charming scenery, which have won for it the title of the Yorkshire of Ireland, but also for the high moral character of its thrifty, contented and prosperous people."*[146]

Over the following few weeks the *Herald* covered such diverse items as The Afghan Massacre—attributed to the Russians; a Report from the India Viceroy; the Recall of Sir Bartle Frere from South Africa; and, reprinted from the *American Review*, an article on the Prussian Prince Bismarck and his friendly relationship with America.

Closer to home, the Flying Scotsman was reported to have had a bad accident, with the engine, tender and several carriages derailed, killing the driver, fireman and two guards but, mercifully, no passengers. A "Serious Illness of Mr Gladstone" was noted—he took ill the previous Friday, suffering from a fever and congestion at the base of his left lung. A day by day account of his progress and those asking after his health was printed; the Queen and the Prince of Wales were kept informed; by Wednesday, it seems, he was over the worst of it.

---

[146] *North Down Herald* editorial, 24th July, 1880

THE STORYTELLER

Local items included a "Hints for Farmers" column, taken from the *Farmers' Gazette*; prices at the Newtownards and Belfast markets; the doings of the Newtownards Town Commissioners; reports on various churches, and this year's Flower Show complete with Dog Show and Horse Jumping Fete. There was a poem in each issue by a local poet and, of course, a story by "Robin".

In his Live and Let Live editorial on 7 August WG spoke out against the recent blanket distribution of an Income Tax Demand warning of the dire consequence of not paying what was owed. This was causing much anxiety amongst ordinary people who had never had to pay income tax due to the low level of their earnings. WG assured his readers that all with an income below £500 a year could safely ignore the "Demand." It should only ever have been received by those on a higher level of income, he said, and he decried the fact that the letter had lazily been sent to all and sundry.

Preserving copies of the *North Down Herald*

In the week following the publication of the fifth edition WG was reminded that, for the past eleven years, since 1869 in fact, it had become a legal requirement for newspaper publishers to send one copy of each issue to the British Museum in London. Accordingly, he bundled up copies of all five editions and sent them off, no doubt intending to supply that central depository of all printed material with further editions month by month.

We do not know if WG continued, dutifully, to dispatch copies throughout his lifetime and these copies were eventually transferred, in 1903, to the British Museum's new facilities in North London (the forerunner to today's British Newspaper Library) only to be numbered amongst the estimated 6000 volumes lost on the night of October 20th, 1940 to a Luftwaffe bomb. But however it came about, sad to relate, the only known surviving complete copies of the *North Down Herald* are those first five editions from the 17th July to the 14th August, 1880.

These copies have all been microfilmed and their contents can be viewed at the British Newspaper Archive in the British Library at St Pancras, London. However, it is not possible to see the original newspapers. They are now stored at the purpose-built facility in Boston Spa, West Yorkshire, to preserve the old and delicate paper copies. WG's five editions have been shrink-wrapped to protect them from the atmosphere and are kept in an environmentally controlled warehouse that is hermetically sealed with no direct access by humans. A robotic selection and delivery system brings required items to an air locked access hatch designed to prevent any contamination entering the storage area.

That such should be their fate, or that they would even still exist over 140 years on, could hardly have entered WG's head. His mind was much too occupied with the day-to-day business of running Newtownards' latest newspaper.

WG pokes fun at a "fictitious" newspaper editor

Another sketch by "Robin" appeared early on in the life of the *Herald*—one, unfortunately, that did not make it into any of WG's books where it would have been preserved through the years. It was called *At Hame in Ballycuddy* and, writing about it subsequently, WG explained it "introduced, as one of the persons attending the 'At Hame,' a certain Abner Byng, a newspaper proprietor whose abilities as a liar, boaster and blusterer had never been excelled." As a clever publicity stunt for the *Herald*, WG had posters pasted up on derelict walls around the town which read as follows:

> *CAUTION*
>
> *WHEREAS, I attended an "AT HOME" recently, given in connection with the BALLYCUDDY FARMERS ASSOCIATION;*
> *AND WHEREAS in response to the toast to THE PRESS I delivered a speech, being at the time considerably under the influence of PALE SHERRY, and labouring under strong mental excitement;*
> *AND WHEREAS my reporting and editorial staff decided upon the suppression of my said speech inasmuch as it contained a number of very extraordinary statements, the truth of which it would be difficult to establish, and my chief editor inserted in*

THE STORYTELLER

the columns of my journal a speech such as I had intended to deliver;

AND WHEREAS a certain MUSHROOM GROWTH called the NORTH DOWN HERALD has recently made its appearance in the world of press literature, and is with dangerous and alarming rapidity spreading over the whole of North of Ireland;

AND WHEREAS I have reason to believe that the said MUSHROOM GROWTH will, on SATURDAY NEXT, the 2nd April publish what purports to be a verbatim report of the speech delivered by me as aforesaid, but in a vulgar dialect spoken only by showmen, clowns, the lower orders, and ignorant farmers, but utterly unknown to literary gentlemen of standing and experience:

BE IT THEREFORE KNOWN UNTO ALL MEN that I,

ABNER BYNG

of Ballycuddy in the County of Down, Gentlemen, I hereby COMMAND all intelligent inhabitants of County Down to abstain from purchasing said NORTH DOWN HERALD of next Saturday, and I hereby offer

ONE POUND REWARD

for every copy of said paper brought to my office, accompanied by a written Declaration, duly perfected and sworn before a Justice of the Peace, to the effect that my speech, if reported in said paper, has not been read by any person whatsoever.

Signed,
ABNER BYNG,
Sole Proprietor of the Ballycuddy Observer, the first penny paper published in Ireland, and the most influential journal in the world.

13 - UNIVERSAL ACCLAIM—ALMOST

The next Friday, an indignant William Henry turned up at WG's printers with a copy of the poster, claiming that it was supposed to be about him. He said, "If you publish that I'll bring an action against you for £5,000 damages." The irate editor was laughed at; the skit appeared in the *Herald*. Once again, no lawsuit followed but ther was, doubtless, an extra-large uptake of WG's newspaper.

Land League

News coverage wasn't only local. WG would have kept his readers up to date, for example, on the progress of the Land League who were active in Ireland in recent times seeking to banish landlordism and give the land back to the tenant farmers. As that summer was drawing to a close, he may well have reported how one Land Agent in Mayo, a Captain Boycott, had been particularly harsh on the tenants, denying them a rent reduction following a poor harvest. The whole community, therefore, refused to have anything to do with him, including refusing help to bring in his own harvest. He had to pay Orangemen from Ulster (the Orange Order was opposed to the Land League) to come and do the work. WG's article would not, however, have included what was perhaps the most interesting outcome of this story because, at the time, it had not yet become established. The hapless Land Agent has the peculiar honour of giving his name, throughout the English-speaking world, to the practice of ostracising something or someone—of boycotting them.

Lyttle's Almanac

By the autumn of that year, 1880, WG had received "assurances from all over North Down that a good, reliable and useful almanac was much needed." [147] If he could fill that gap a large circulation was predicted. So on top of everything else, WG set about producing *Lyttle's North Down Directory and Almanac*, an octavo-sized booklet of over 100 pages containing often fascinating anecdotes, articles and information, many illustrated with wood engraving pictures of famous locations, or scenes from the stories. Included, too, were some of his

---

[147] Quoted from WG's introduction to the 1888 edition of his almanac.

own tales by "Robin." He even had "Robin" attempt to describe just where Ballycuddy was located in the Ards Peninsular but in such a vague manner as to leave his readers none the wiser.

The directory covered the main centres of population in North Down—Bangor, Newtownards and Holywood, with an alphabetical listing of the names and addresses of persons entitled to vote at the Election of Commissioners in each town. Later editions added Downpatrick and, eventually, short sections on Conlig, Donaghadee, Greyabbey, Groomsport, Kirkcubbin and Portaferry were all included as well. For the main centres it named the town commissioners and noted when each was due to retire or stand for re-election; it gave the salaries of various public officials; it listed places of worship and their incumbents, schools and their head teachers and various other prominent organisations, clubs and societies at each location. For Newtownards, it provided the names and addresses of all the elected and ex-officio members of the Newtownards Board of Guardians; the ex-officio members were all Justices of the Peace.

The calendar section devoted two pages to each month with the dates on the left hand page along with the rising and setting times for the sun and moon each day. It was a mine of information on famous events that had taken place on the various days of each month throughout history, with the facing page containing fuller accounts of some of the most interesting items relating to the month in question.

The new Almanac was, indeed, well received. The *Belfast Telegraph* had this to say in its 31st December, 1880 edition: "The North Down Almanac. We have received a copy of this publication, and it reflects great credit upon the compiler and publisher. It contains a vast amount of information relative to the Ards, and the description of the various towns are well written and exceedingly interesting. The location of 'Ballycuddy,' regarding which speculation has been so rife, is dealt with by old 'Robin,' himself, but we, like the editor of the almanac, would, we fear, have some difficulty in finding out the place. The almanac is sure to be popular, and it is a marvel of cheapness."

And so it proved. Its circulation was to grow from year to year as, encouraged by its success, WG continued to publish it annually.

It is strange that in all of the references to WG's works down the years *Lyttle's North Down Directory and Almanac* is seldom, if ever, mentioned, even though these annual publications represented a

13 - UNIVERSAL ACCLAIM—ALMOST

considerable effort on his part and contain some fascinating articles, poems and other contributions, including those from "Robin." Copies of only two editions have survived in the family—1888 and 1894, plus one other, published after WG's death, as the *"Herald" Almanac and County Down Directory* in 1913, still being produced by the newspaper staff.

Given their wide circulation to "virtually every household in North Down" and given that they were produced annually from 1881 to at least 1913, of the thousands of copies that must have been printed, it is hard to believe that the three in my possession are all that remain of these Almanacs.[148] If anyone reading this biography knows of the existence of any other editions I should be delighted to hear from them.

In competition

In the Foreword to the 1888 edition WG wrote:

> *In presenting to the Public this Eighth Yearly issue of the "North Down Almanac," the Proprietor of the "North Down Herald" respectfully tenders his warmest thanks for the large measure of encouraging support which has, from year to year, been so ungrudgingly bestowed upon his Newspaper and Almanac.*
>
> *Towards the close of the year 1880 he received, from many parts of North Down, assurances that a good, reliable, and useful Almanac was much needed. He was told that nothing worthy of the name, or in any way suited to the tastes of the people, had ever been published locally; and liberal support was predicted for a suitable North Down Annual.*

---

[148] Guy Beiner in his book, *Forgetful Remembrance* (Oxford University Press, Oxford) mentions an article on "The Execution of Rev. James Porter, of Greyabbey, Co. Down: An Incident of the Irish Rebellion of 1798", which appeared in "Lyttle's North Down Almanac and Directory (Bangor, Co. Down: North Down Herald, 1892)." So a copy of that edition must also have survived.

THE STORYTELLER

> *The attempt was made; the public were satisfied, and the publisher was rewarded. Year by year the demand for the North Down Almanac increased, and it quickly attained a circulation and popularity which even Belfast publishers envied. Since then numerous imitators have sprung up, but the "North Down" holds the premier position, and will continue to maintain it.*

The second paragraph of this 1888 foreword reads as though it is being quoted from a foreword to the first issue in 1881. As such, it disparagingly dismisses the efforts of William Henry, proprietor of the *Newtownards Chronicle* who had been producing the *Newtownards and County Down Illustrated Almanac and Directory* since 1875. That was a publication which had, as a matter of fact, received some favourable reviews from other sectors of the press and, indeed, from WG himself, writing as "Robin" only the previous year.

However that friendly gesture was spurned, it would seem. It is interesting to note that I failed to find any reference in the columns of the *Chronicle* to the launch of its rival newspaper in Newtownards in July, 1880. On the contrary, as we have seen, Henry took every opportunity to seek legal redress against the impish pen of WG Lyttle. His feelings towards an erstwhile contributor to his own journal, who had unexpectedly emerged as a competent rival editor, were no longer benign. These feelings could hardly have been softened by reading WG's comments in his new Almanac, published, again, in direct competition to Henry's own. Whatever cordiality may once have existed between the two newspaper men was now dead and buried.

The far-reaching consequences of this was destined to change the future for Wesley and his family, and for the *North Down Herald*, itself.

Chapter 14 – ADVERSARIES

1881

With all the activity involved in setting up and running a provincial newspaper it's hard to imagine how WG found time to give attention to his accountancy business but *Slater's Royal National Commercial Directory of Ireland (1881)* lists Lyttle W. G. & Co. accountants as still at 27 Victoria Street in Belfast. What is more, there is a subsidiary entry: Lyttle Wesley G. accountant (W. G. Lyttle & Co.) Downpatrick. So, with the help of his Belfast manager, he had opened up a second branch in the town where he first started his working career.

Speaking engagements continued to occupy many an evening for Wesley either as "Robin" or in his own right. Early in the New Year of 1881 WG was a guest speaker at an annual soiree held by the Presbyterian church in Carrowdore near where, as a youth, he is believed to have attended a Punch Ball. The following month, according to the *Belfast Telegraph,* the patrons of St Malachy's Total Abstinence Association greeted the "now famous 'Robin' with a most enthusiastic reception… and during the delivery he kept the audience in a continual roar of laughter." WG remained as Grand Worthy Secretary of the Good Templars. The "Good Samaritan" lodge he started was, no doubt, still in the safe hands of his fellow Worthy Chief Templar, Dr M'Murtry, but since leaving Belfast, WG, himself, seems to have withdrawn from active lodge membership. This, in spite of Newtownards having a Good Templars Hall on North Street that was used by a number of lodges. Some of these remained affiliated to the original Right Worthy Grand Lodge in America, but some were now part of the Right Worthy Grand Lodge of the World.

WG still continued, as we see, to support various groups advocating abstinence.

Newtownards now had, too, an Orange Hall in Mary Street which served over a dozen different lodges but failed to attract much interest from WG. There was also a Masonic Hall, on Regent Street not far from where Wesley had been brought up and it was sometime during this period that he started sending out feelers about the possibility of joining the Freemasons.

Limelight show for the workhouse

Soon after returning to Newtownards, Wesley thought he would like to do something for the residents of the town's Workhouse. Although he had been too young at the time to remember, he would have learnt in later years what splendid work had been done there, during the terrible famine years, in helping to alleviate the suffering of the poor and invalided. (He may also have been acting in the grateful knowledge of the care his father, and possibly his mother, too, had received there during their last days.)

He had in mind a presentation of the diorama that he used to lecture with for Dr Corry but that proved to be too problematical and, besides, a new and much more portable method of displaying Ireland's beautiful scenery was now available. He contacted Mr William Erskine Mayne, the publisher of the Irish Templar and son of the founder of the chain of bookshops that now bore his name. Erskine Mayne's was also a city agent for the *North Down Herald*. Mr Mayne agreed to provide his services along with his amazing new lantern and slides.

WG roped in other new friends from around the Newtownards area to help. Captain George Hamilton was happy to lend the services of the splendid band of the Royal North Down Rifles which made the event go with a swing. According to the *Belfast News-Letter*, a Miss Waters presided at the harmonium and songs from Miss Jones and Messrs Sailes, Waters and Doggart were heartily applauded.

Illuminated by limelight, Erskine Mayne's lantern was able to project images onto a large screen. Successive spectacular views were presented, accompanied by descriptive readings from Captain Hamilton and WG. And not to forget the younger members of his audience, WG had arranged "a supply of oranges, presented by a lady friend, [which] added much to the comfort of the little ones." The *News-Letter* does not reveal the identity of the "lady friend" but I do wonder if this was Lizzie's touch. WG could well have been too preoccupied with all the other arrangements to have thought of such a gesture towards the children.

The show, presented on 9th February, 1881, was a resounding success, thoroughly enjoyed by all, and WG and his friends received an enthusiastic vote of thanks.

Five days after that, and it was off to Banbridge where "Robin" was due to entertain a gathering at the Seapatrick Church Temperance Union. There, he received another hearty vote of thanks, according to the press report, this time from the Venerable, the Archdeacon of Dromore, who presided during the evening.

"Robin", the Bangor Town Commissioners and some big fish

Meanwhile, the day job went on. Regular ads for the *Herald* had to be placed in the Belfast papers, which always included reference to the next story by "Robin" that was due to appear. These tales, that had done so well for the *Newry Telegraph* and the *Newtownards Chronicle* were still working their magic but now boosting the circulation of the *North Down Herald*.

WG had reporters covering the Bangor Town Commissioners as well as those serving the Newtownards community. In May the *Herald* informed its readers about an ambitious project being undertaken in Bangor—in fact three simultaneous projects: a new reservoir to supply clean water for all the inhabitants, a proper sewerage system and an extension of the gas distribution and street lighting. For this the commissioners had to negotiate a loan of £17,000 (over £2,000,000 in 2021). It was an enormous undertaking fraught with difficulties and not without opposition. WG, however, said that this did not deter the rulers from the discharge of their duty.[149]

---

[149] This quote from the *North Down Herald* was copied in the resignation letter of a Bangor Town Commissioner, which was reported in the *Belfast News-Letter* in November, 1885.

THE STORYTELLER

The paper caused a minor sensation in June of '81 when a news item it ran was picked up by the dailies. The *Belfast Telegraph* reported:

> NEW FISHING GROUNDS
> *Considerable excitement (says the North Down Herald) has, during the past week, existed around the neighbourhood of Ballywalter, Millisle, and Donaghadee, in consequence of a rumour freely circulated that a fish of remarkable size and value has visited our northern waters. Small fishing boats were out in great numbers, and numerous "takes" were reported. The fish are said to measure several feet in length and some three feet in diameter. Their flavour is delicious, and they bring prices varying from four shillings to twenty shillings each. A correspondent informs us that one of these "big white fish," as they are called, which he had an opportunity of inspecting shortly after its capture, turned out to be a bag of flour washed from the wreck of the Macedonia on the Scotch coast.*

This was just the sort of hoax story with which WG delighted to amuse his readers.

Coffeehouse gossip

When he had first returned to his native town, Wesley had been pleased to find that one of the new coffeehouses had been opened on Regent Street.[150] These were providing practical alternatives to the numerous public houses and he and many others thought them to be a welcome improvement to merely *talking* about the advantages of abstinence. Frequenting the one in Newtownards, WG would

---

[150] The *Newtownards Chronicle* reported that the business had secured "a commodius house and yard in Regent Street opposite the old brewery" They provided "broth, coffee and lemonade... newspapers and magazines and a bagatelle table. In the rere [sic] there is a large yard opening out to Mill Street, and there is excellent stabling accommodation for a large number of horses."

doubtless pick up the latest gossip, which would then find its way into the columns of the *Herald.*

One such paragraph to appear gave some particulars about an otherwise anonymous, gluttonous fellow who was represented to have "so gorged himself with liquor at a free banquet on board a pleasure steamer that after driving from Bangor to Newtownards he fell from a car[151] and got taken in charge by the police. A summons was afterwards issued and the case was dealt with by two local magistrates who connived to having it hushed up." When William Henry saw the paragraph, true to form and ever eager to find an excuse to sue his rival, he lost no time in accusing WG of libelling him. I must say the expression, "If the cap fits…" comes to mind. However, yet again, nothing came of his blustering protestations.

It may well have been in the coffeehouse one afternoon when the leaves on the trees were on the turn that WG found himself chatting over a cup of the aromatic brew with one of the town's most prominent citizens, the mill owner, George Walker. In the course of their conversation Mr Walker must have mentioned that he was about to retire from the Board of the Town Commissioners and casually threw out the question as to whether WG had thought of standing. Three more commissioners were at the end of their three year tenure and another, Edward M'Call, had been disqualified some months ago for non-attendance at meetings, so there would be five vacancies to fill in the October election. Mr Walker, it seems, said he'd be happy to nominate WG should he care to have his name put forward.

Whether or not WG had previously considered standing for a seat on the Board, we do not know, but when it emerged that William Henry of the *Chronicle,* who had tried and failed to gain a seat at the previous election, was rumoured to be standing once again, Wesley's interest was aroused. It seemed the other three retirees, James Clarke, James Finlay and John Ramsay, would all be seeking re-election, but with five vacant seats, George Walker encouraged WG to consider seriously going for one of them. As they rose to leave the coffeehouse, George likely reminded his friend that nominations had to be in by Thursday 6th October, which wasn't far off.

---

[151] horse carriage

THE STORYTELLER

A Town Commissionership may well have already crossed WG's mind. What better way to associate himself with the essence of Newtownards life than to serve on its governing body?
The previous October he hadn't been living in Newtownards nearly long enough to be eligible to stand—but now, another twelve months on...

He must have thought hard about the news that his arch-rival, Henry, planned to try again for a seat. The *Chronicle* editor probably stood a better chance of being elected this time as his popularity in the community was growing. WG had recently heard he was now on the organising committee of the new "Ards Rifle Association" that had just been established. Where would all this leave the editor of the town's other newspaper? He would have wondered if a relative newcomer like himself could realistically hope to become a Town Commissioner. Wesley had much to discuss with Lizzie over tea that evening.

Guns

Round about the same time, the latest news in the coffeehouse was that some residents in nearby Comber were hoping to open a similar establishment and would be holding a Sale of Work Bazaar over two days to raise funds towards the venture. Thoroughly supportive of these new venues, Wesley contacted them and volunteered to help in any way he could. Guns for a shooting gallery at the event were being supplied by a local gunsmith who couldn't man the stall himself.

As it happened, Wesley had been talking to the gunsmith about the possibility of purchasing a firearm for personal protection during his many journeyings, often alone in a pony and trap. It would usually be very late when he was returning from one of his performances. In spite of the comparatively low crime rate in the county it was common practice for citizens travelling alone to arm themselves.

Perhaps thinking of the latest string to William Henry's bow, and maybe even because of it, Wesley now suggested he could run the stall if he was given a quick lesson in loading and firing small-bore, single-action Gallery Guns. He then thoroughly enjoyed a couple of days off from working in the *Herald* office while he manned the stall at the Bazaar. He relished encouraging the Comber locals, and the many visitors who arrived by train from Belfast and Newtownards, to part with their coppers and test their shooting skills. Indeed, according to the *Belfast Telegraph* he spent time teaching youngsters how to aim and fire the guns—no doubt recalling crack shot, Johnnie M'Closkey who had taught him when he was their age.

The occasion served to remind Wesley that he had not yet followed the advice of his friends to arm himself when he ventured abroad. He returned to the gunsmiths and purchased one of the modern guns known as revolvers—possibly a little Remington, for it fitted easily into an overcoat pocket.

Nomination papers

With all this going on, the deadline for submitting nomination forms to the Town Commissioners was almost upon him. WG had decided he would stand against William Henry and the other candidates. He hastily completed his application papers. Against his name, under 'Description' he proudly wrote "Newspaper Proprietor." George Walker duly signed the papers as Nominator, along with another sitting Town Commissioner, William Reid. WG hand-delivered his nomination by the Thursday deadline. The die was cast. He sat back to await developments.

They were not long in coming.

WG was informed that William Henry had lodged an objection to his nomination form, which would be ruled upon by the chairman of the Town Commissioners, Mr R Caughey, acting as Returning Officer, the following day, Friday 7th October. If the objection was upheld WG would be disqualified from standing for election; there could be no appeal.

In his last minute haste, had WG made some vital error in his application? Had George Walker or William Reid not signed properly? He could do nothing but await the adjudication. He duly turned up at the appointed hour of two o'clock in the Regent Street boardroom of the Town Commissioners. Two other nominated candidates, James Finlay TC and David Stormont were present along with Mr Andrew Menown TC, who was to assist the chairman in reaching a decision, and William M'Gowan, the Town Clerk. The final person in the boardroom that ominous Friday afternoon was the objector, Mr William Henry.

The editor of the *Chronicle* read from his copy of his points of objection: WG's name appeared on the list of voters as "Little" but on his nomination form as "Lyttle;" the wording of the nomination paper used was not in conformity with that prescribed by the Ballot Act; in particular a column that should have been labelled, "rank, profession, or occupation", had been labelled with the vague heading, "description." On the strength of these irregularities he demanded that the application be rejected.

William M'Gowan said that he had supplied the nomination papers; they were all the same and correctly drawn up. He also accepted responsibility for the discrepancy in the spelling of WG's surname on the voting list.[152] Mr Henry requested the Town Clerk not to interfere and proceeded to make a lengthy statement in support of his objections. Finally he stopped speaking.

WG must have realised there was little substance in his adversary's objections; that they appeared to be purely mischievous. Yet they were put so forcibly that he had to accept that they might be taken seriously and his aspirations of becoming a commissioner could end in the next few moments.

The brief period of silence after Henry's tirade was becoming unbearable.

Mr Caughey cleared his throat and made his ruling. He said that the spelling of the name could not be held to affect the nomination. As to the papers and their wording, he declared them to comply accurately with the recent Municipal Elections Act of 1879.

But Henry, who had used the wording prescribed by the earlier act of 1872 (presumably the same as he had used for his previous application when he had been an unsuccessful candidate) said he would appeal the chairman's decision. David Stormont entered the debate with the sweet voice of reason, suggesting that, in the light of

---

[152] It seems quite probable that the clerk, Mr M'Gowan, would have known Wesley as a child and as a member of the Little family. Hence his inadvertent use of the old spelling of his name, and further evidence that Wesley was, indeed, born a 'Little.'

14 - ADVERSARIES

Mr Caughey's statement, if asked, might Mr Henry consider withdrawing his objections to allow the election to proceed.

WG glanced up at this.

It looked as though Henry wouldn't budge but after further persuasion from Mr Stormont he relented and said he would.

Only then did WG speak up. The *Chronicle* editor's objections had been overruled and now it was being suggested that they be brushed under the carpet, as it were, as though they had never been made.

'I strongly oppose such a withdrawal,' he said. The tense anxiety he'd been put through was giving way now to indignation. Henry had been overruled. He should not simply be allowed to pull back as though he had attempted nothing untoward. 'If the objections had been sustainable,' said WG, 'they would have been proposed and ruled upon. I want to have the Chairman's ruling in writing to Mr Henry's objections.'

Mr Menown, Mr Stormont and Mr Caughey urged that the matter should be allowed to drop, which Mr Henry must have been relieved to go along with, but WG, the injured party, was proving harder to persuade. The attack on his good name could not just be brushed aside and ignored. He refused to drop his demand for a written ruling. Eventually, however, he agreed to a compromise. He said he would be satisfied with a verbal statement from the chairman that the objections were withdrawn because they could not be sustained. This, Mr Caughey readily did and the meeting finally concluded.

Belfast paper reports on Henry's action

We know the details of what occurred in the boardroom of the Town Commissioners on that Friday afternoon thanks to an account that appeared in the *Belfast News-Letter* the following Monday, 10th October—an account that William Henry suspected (probably quite correctly) had been submitted by WG, himself, although Henry merely suggested, "by one of the candidates." It seems, however, that Henry's own recollection of events differed from the *News-Letter's* version and he wrote a long letter, dated 11th October, attempting to justify himself. This was printed in Thursday's issue of the paper.

THE STORYTELLER

He denied objecting to the wrong spelling of the name, saying, "on the contrary, I distinctly said that I passed it over." Regarding the form of nomination papers he spelled out in some detail how they were required to adhere as closely as possible to what was laid down in the Ballot Act, though he made no mention of the subsequent Act to which Mr Caughey had referred.

Mr Henry then told how Mr Stormont, "in a most kindly and gentlemanly manner" had asked him to withdraw his objections to allow the election to proceed in harmony. He replied that he would "have no objection to do so, as he was not personally afraid of the result." He stated that all the objections were read, however, and on being asked a second time by Mr Stormont, he withdrew them. His written statement had been handed back to him by the chairman, who, Henry claimed, had made no ruling on the matter at all. "How could he, when the objections had been withdrawn?" This was contrary, Henry concluded, to what the account in Monday's issue had stated.

And there, with the poll only two days away, the matter might have rested. Except—on the day of the election, Saturday 15th October, the *News-Letter* carried a further letter dated 13th October:

> *NEWTOWNARDS TOWN COMMISSIONERS*
> *Sir,– Referring to a letter under the above heading, which appeared in your issue of today, we beg to state that we were present in the boardroom on Friday last during the sitting of the returning officer, and we say that the paragraph concerning same which appeared in the News-Letter of the 10th inst. is true in every particular. The verbal statement made by the chairman was: "The objections are withdrawn because they cannot be sustained," and with this Mr Lyttle was satisfied.—Yours, &c,*
>   *James Finlay, T.C., P.L.G.*
>   *David Stormont,*
>   *W. G. Lyttle*
>   *Newtownards, 13 Oct, 1881*

So thanks to William Henry's attempt to justify himself, WG was able, after all, to have the ruling and his exoneration put in writing for all to see. Whether the whole sorry episode cost William Henry any votes or gained any for WG we have no way of telling. Even before these events were reported, the Belfast papers were announcing the forthcoming municipal elections in Newtownards with reports that a vigorous canvass was going on. They were anticipating a keen contest. Certainly, it seems that the Newtownards voters had caught the excitement of the occasion, no doubt spurred on by conflicting editorials in the town's two newspapers. But WG would have realised that his rival newspaper man's popularity was growing daily. Although his friends assured him that he stood a good chance of being elected, privately he must have been wondering if he had over-reached himself.

The election

Like every Saturday, 15th October was market day in Newtownards. The day broke fair, which was good; inclement weather could keep the polls low. Two polling booths were set up in the Commissioners' office on Regent Street and throughout the day people were abandoning their places of business or other commitments on a busy market day and coming to exercise their voting rights in support of their chosen candidates. There were seven, in all, competing for the five vacant seats: Messrs Clarke, Finlay and Ramsay, all seeking re-election, and Messrs William Henry, W. G. Lyttle, William Dobbin and David Stormont.

It was, of course, WG's first experience of such proceedings but at the close of the poll he was assured by the others that there had been an excellent number of voters attending throughout the day, the highest they had ever seen in Newtownards. Then came the agony of awaiting the result of the count. Townsfolk had begun to gather on the street outside the office, anxious to be among the first to hear the outcome. We can be sure Lizzie and the children would have been there in that jostling crowd as the hour of 7 o'clock approached when the Returning Officer would make his announcement.

583 names appeared on the list of eligible voters in Newtownards at that time. Of those, it was estimated that there would be about 500 who could actually vote, the others being either dead, out of the country or unable to attend for other reasons. In the event, 460 voters

THE STORYTELLER

posted ballot slips—an unprecedented turnout, indeed.[153] Finally they were all counted.

A sudden hush descended upon the awaiting throng on the street outside as the sash of the central window of the first-floor boardroom was dropped and the Returning Officer appeared to address the people. After a few introductory comments, Mr Caughey got to the part they had all been waiting for.

'The results of the voting, in alphabetical order, are as follows:
    Mr James Clarke   249
    Mr William Dobbin   132
    Mr James Finlay   222
    Mr William Henry   303—'

At this, there was loud cheering from parts of the crowd, but Mr Caughey was continuing:
    'Mr Wesley G Lyttle   169
    Mr John Ramsey   146
    Mr David Stormont   243

'And I therefore declare that Messrs Henry, Clarke, Stormont, Finlay and Lyttle are duly elected to serve as Town Commissioners for the next three years.'

The crowd erupted once more into wild cheering, each for their own man and I have no doubt that little Roland, now nearly four, and Robina, two-and-a-half, cheered just as much as their older sisters, Eve and Agnes and their big brother, John, along with their mother. According to the report in the following Monday's *Northern Whig* the crowd then "were addressed by several candidates." This would have undoubtedly included the victorious William Henry and I'm sure that WG would not have missed the opportunity to speak out and thank his supporters.

On the evidence of the voting, however, the night deservedly belonged to William Henry. Upon his emerging from the Commissioners' office he was hoisted upon the shoulders of his jubilant fans and carried all the way up to his home in Great Frances Street. After entering his house he reappeared, briefly, at one of his

---

[153] It will be noticed that the total votes allocated to candidates comes to 1464, so obviously each voter was allowed to vote for more than one candidate, since there were five vacancies.

14 - ADVERSARIES

windows and thanked the people again for contributing to his success. He asked them all to disperse quietly, which they did in fine good humour.

At various points around the town tar barrels were lit and fireworks set off to release the tensions of the last few days' run-up to the election. The victorious candidates could finally relax in the knowledge that their hard efforts had not been in vain. As for the two gentlemen who came bottom of the poll, well, like William Henry last time, they would no doubt live to fight another day.

Although WG only came fifth, he had nevertheless been elected to the Town Commission and, as a newcomer in town, could feel justifiably proud of his achievement. Let us walk with him a while and share in his triumph:

> As Wesley headed home along Regent Street that Saturday night in October, 1881, with his excited family around him, they all stopped and watched a sky rocket soar above the rooftop of the Ulster Hotel—the building that had once accommodated the humble shoemaker's shop his father had run and where he had lived during his formative years. He squeezed Lizzie's arm, which was linked through his own and she looked up at him.
>
> 'You may have only moved to the other side of Conway Square, Wesley,' she said, 'but you've come a long way since doing the messages for your Da in his wee shop.'
>
> Newtownards' newest Town Commissioner regarded his five children and his fair wife for a moment before starting off, once more, in the direction of the office of the *North Down Herald* and home. He replied in "Robin's" broad Ulster-Scot vernacular, which always delighted his youngsters:
>
> 'Ay, wife, deed A hae—a gye lang wye. An' ye micht see me gang a brave bit yit.'[154]

---

[154] 'Yes, wife, [in]deed I have—a very long way. And you might see me going a good bit yet.'

THE STORYTELLER

Chapter 15 – MOVING ON

1881–1882

A churchman, a commissioner and a freemason

The smell of spent gunpowder still lingered over Newtownards on Sunday morning as the town's good citizens were strolling along to their respective places of worship. The Lyttle family could have been seen heading down past the Old Cross towards the Presbyterian Church in Greenwell Street to give thanks to the Almighty for the previous days' success and, it is to be hoped, to pray for each of the town's commissioners, new and old, that they may all be enabled to fulfil their municipal duties with integrity.

That the Lyttles attended Greenwell Street Presbyterian, we can surmise from the fact that the following evening, Monday 17th October, 1881 saw Wesley there again helping with the annual treat for the children attending the Church's Sabbath and Day schools. Over 300, including, no doubt, at least three of his own, were served with tea, sandwiches and cakes and, during the evening, Wesley and two of the other helpers delivered 'instructive and entertaining addresses' according to the write-up in the *Belfast News-Letter*.

There were now, of course, Town Commissioners' meetings to attend regularly, as well. At his first one, WG took the oath, 'I Wesley Greenhill Lyttle, do solemnly declare that I will faithfully and impartially, according to the best of my skill and judgement, execute all the powers and authorities reposed in me as a Commissioner, by virtue of the Towns' Improvement (Ireland) Act, 1854, and in accordance with the Local Boards Act, 1880, and that I am not an ecclesiastic of any religious denomination.' As a new boy, he would have read up on just what those "powers and authorities" were and quite probably took the others to task from time to time if he felt they were in danger of exceeding their powers or neglecting their responsibilities.

A week after the Sunday school treat, on Monday 24th October, WG was giving his services again, this time at a masonic meeting in Bangor. Rather than join either of the Newtownards lodges, WG had become a member of the Bangor Freemasons, perhaps at the invitation of his old school pal, George Dickson (see chapter 3), who was also a brother with the 746 Bangor Union Masonic Lodge. Always ready to use new experiences as a source for his light-hearted stories, we find that on this occasion "Br. W. G. Lyttle" was asked to read his tale about an "aspirant to Masonry," which the *News-Letter* reported as causing much laughter.

WG later adapted the account to be told by "Robin" and entitled it, *How I became a Mason*. He recited it on other masonic occasions (including at a concert on 1st September, a couple of years later in 1883) but as far as I have been able to ascertain it has never appeared in print—perhaps it would have revealed some "masonic secrets." He does seem to have been well established as a Brother at 746 Lodge. His name appears on the guest list of a Masonic Installation Supper that was held in the Royal Hotel in Bangor on the 28th December, '81.

WG writes an address for the Lord Lieutenant of Ireland

Prior to that, at the annual meeting of the Newtownards Town Commissioners on 14th November, Robert Caughey, presiding, stated that his term of office as chairman had expired and asked the Board to appoint a successor. It was proposed and seconded that he should be re-appointed for a further year but an amendment was moved and seconded that William Henry should be elected chairman. I should imagine WG particularly enjoyed being part of the "large majority" that defeated the amendment and Mr Caughey was duly re-elected.

The meeting continued and, amongst other matters, selected a sub-committee to prepare an address to his Excellency Earl Cowper, the Lord Lieutenant of Ireland, on his visit to Ulster the following week. The six-man committee included both Henry and WG, so that must have made for a fun week for its members.

The address they agreed upon was subsequently read by the Town Clerk, William M'Gowan, to Earl Cowper when he attended

Clandeboye House, Lord Dufferin's mansion near Bangor. It referred to the town's long-standing loyalty to their sovereign and went on to praise new legislation going through parliament to improve Tenant's Rights and looked forward to better relationships between the owners and occupiers of the land throughout the country. It mentioned that in Newtownards, "They have the happiness to reside on an estate where the principle of 'live and let live' [surely WG's phrase, quoting his editorial strapline] has ever been observed, and where the rights and interests of the cultivators of the soil have ever received kindly recognition from the members of the Londonderry family."

The full address was quoted in the *Northern Whig* on 23rd November. The Commissioners also took the opportunity to mention the amount of "home industry" going on in the town and the extent of the work of its flax, cotton and wool manufacturers. "In no part of the United Kingdom is capital more secure, labour more abundant, or is there a better field presented for manufacturing enterprise," it claimed.

Another matter raised was about Newtownards' prestigious rifle range, "one of the best in Ireland, and Newtownards would be in all respects an admirable place for the formation of a musketry instruction ground for the military forces stationed in the North of Ireland."

Hopefully, the Lord Lieutenant was, in the fullness of time, able to act upon some of this, for in his reply he included the remark that he had received several such addresses on his visit, "but none of them have I received with greater pleasure than that which you have just read from Newtownards." WG, along with his fellow committee members who had penned the address, must have been duly gratified.

Commissioners' validity questioned

The work on publishing the *Herald* each week continued and WG would have been extremely busy, too, in updating and finalising his second annual almanac. The *Belfast Telegraph,* who received an advance copy, spoke of it in glowing terms—"exceptional merits…cannot fail to obtain the appreciation of the public…seldom seen such a complete and valuable work." It contained, again, several contributions by "Robin" and built upon the success of the first issue, ensuring its place as an ongoing annual publication.

15 - MOVING ON

The new year saw WG back at the seaside resort on 26th January, where "Robin's" humorous readings brought a contrast to vary the entertainment provided by the Bangor Musical Society at their first concert of the year.

This made for a pleasant start to the New Year, but 1882 was not to continue in such a vein. There are few details to go upon but it would seem that in his zeal to ensure the Town Commissioners were acting in full propriety, WG questioned whether one board member, Mr SC Kelly was, in fact qualified to sit on the Board. The *Belfast Morning News* reported:

> *"At the monthly meeting of [the Newtownards Town Commissioners] on Monday [6th March] Mr. R. H. Caughey presided. Mr. S. C. Kelly, having called attention to the fact that it had recently been asserted that he was disqualified to sit at the board, the chairman said he had not the slightest hesitation in stating that Mr. Kelly was a duly and properly qualified member of the Board."*

There is nothing here to say that it was WG who made the assertions (apparently erroneously). The paragraph was published, however, just after an earlier letter had appeared in the *Newtownards Chronicle* on 1st March which was to have grave repercussions for that paper's rival editor. It strongly implied that the one laying the assertions about Mr Kelly was WG.

The writer used a nom-de-plume but William Henry was happy to print it anyway.

> *THE QUALIFICATION OF TOWN COMMISSIONERS.*
> *To the Editor of the "Newtownards Chronicle".*
> *Sir,–The editor of a local publication has lately been parading his legal lore in connection with the above question. It would be a poor compliment to pay you to assume that you are at least as well qualified as the individual in question to give an opinion on the*

THE STORYTELLER

following matters, but I will thank you to do so for the edification of the electors:–

By the 25th section of the Towns' Improvement Act, 1854, which deals with the qualification in question, it is set out as follows:– "Every person who shall have been, for twelve months preceding the 1st day of January in the year in which such election is held, the immediate lessor of lands, tenements, and hereditaments within such town ... of the value of £50 or upwards, according to the last Poor Law valuation ... not being an ecclesiastic of any religious denomination, shall be eligible to be elected a Commissioner for the purposes of this Act, &c."

It strikes me, therefore, that a person elected in October, 1881, to act as a Commissioner is not entitled to do so unless he had ... resided within the boundary ... for twelve months prior to January, 1881—that is, in January, 1880. One of our Commissioners is thus disqualified, as he did not come to reside in Newtownards until several months after January, 1880, and by the Commissioners' Clauses Act, 1847, is liable to a penalty of £50 for every time he acts. Both his nomination and return was a mistake. However, as I have intimated, I submit the question to your superior knowledge, and commend it also to the personal consideration of the individual referred to.–Yours, &c., RIP VAN WINKLE

Newtownards, 1st March, 1882.

[Without in any degree pretending to be gifted with the "legal lore" assumed by the individual to whom reference is made, we have no hesitation in stating that the Commissioner in question is disqualified and liable to the penalties he has incurred since he made his declaration—Ed. N.C.]

"The individual referred to," clearly identified in the opening sentence as the editor of the [only other] local publication was left to

15 - MOVING ON

"personally consider" his position. It must have come as a severe blow to WG who was just beginning to find his feet as an active contributor to the work of the Board. That the twelve months' residency requirement had to be counted back from the January of the year of election had been completely overlooked by George Walker and, indeed, by everyone else involved until now. I have found no further references in the press to the situation. It was an embarrassment to all the Town Commissioners, none of whom had noticed the discrepancy in WG's qualification to stand. There was clearly no fraudulent intent and possibly no fines were imposed. But from subsequent events, as we shall see, we can infer how upset WG must have been that the *Chronicle's* revelation resulted in his having to vacate his hard-won seat on the Board.

Another blow

Two weeks later, Editor Lyttle received another body blow. Whether influenced by his disqualification from the Board we cannot say, but the tender of the *North Down Herald* to publish county advertising was not accepted. The report of the Sheet committee showed that the *Belfast News-Letter, Newtownards Chronicle, Downpatrick Recorder, Banbridge Chronicle,* and *Newry Telegraph* were selected to carry the county advertising. This represented a major loss of potential income for the *Herald.*

Two massive setbacks within two weeks, one personal and the other to his business, must have set WG thinking hard about the future.

He carried on: running his newspaper, fulfilling his commitments, living his life. He was coming to realise that perhaps it had been a mistake to start up a new weekly in the same town as the *Chronicle*, particularly as that newspaper's editor had taken such a dislike to him. It would have been affecting his family, too. Maybe not so much the younger ones but John and Agnes must have known about their father's troubles and Lizzie's health was suffering.

Assassination attempt

WG would have realised that in the grand scheme of things there were others who had to contend with greater difficulties than his. At least no one had tried to shoot him. In the midst of his own troubles he would have been preparing a news item for the next issue of the *Herald* with the headline:

"EIGHTH ASSASSINATION ATTEMPT ON THE QUEEN"

Perhaps he paused for a moment to count his blessings before continuing to write, reminding his readers that throughout her long reign their dear sovereign had already survived no less than seven attempts upon her life at the hands of deranged gunmen. Now, he recounted, as recently as Thursday 2nd March 1882, another such attack has been carried out whilst Queen Victoria and Prince Albert were being driven from the station at Windsor up to the castle. The route, according to WG's source, had been lined with cheering boys from Eton College. From their midst emerged a man, later identified as Roderick Maclean and mentally disturbed, aiming a revolver at the carriage. Mercifully, his shot missed and the man was overpowered by the schoolboys who pummelled him with their umbrellas before he was arrested and taken away. WG probably bore a wry smile as he pictured that last scene he had just described.

At the next meeting of the Town Commissioners, on a motion of William Henry seconded by Mr Menown, a resolution was unanimously adopted to send a telegram to "her Most Gracious Majesty the Queen expressive of the great indignation felt by the commissioners and the people of the town generally for the dastardly and traitorous attack made upon her life Thursday last by a would-be assassin, and our gratitude to God that her Majesty has been again providentially preserved to her loyal and loving subjects."

When the *Herald* came out, perhaps WG read his own headline and reflected further upon his situation. No, no one has tried to shoot him. Nevertheless, he likely made a mental note not to forget to carry his own revolver when he was out and about. But besides all that, he can no longer have been finding much enjoyment living back in his home town.

15 - MOVING ON

Bangor beckons

At the same time, circumstances in recent months had taken him frequently to the little watering place known as Bangor. It was a small town but one that was growing and would be becoming ever more popular now that its smelly old sewers were being replaced. WG had just written in the *Herald*, again, about their construction projects, comparing the speed at which the Bangor Board appeared to be achieving their goals with the cumbersome progress made in Newtownards on the erection of a single pump.[155]

WG could only see Bangor continuing to grow, particularly in the summer months when its population swelled enormously due to vacationers and day-trippers. WG was of the opinion that it would not be long before Bangor became a sizable town.

And it did not have a newspaper.

Throughout their married life, on average, Wesley and Lizzie had lived in each of their homes for just over two years. It was coming up to two years since they moved to Newtownards. Was it time for another change of address? It wasn't just the family, now, though. Upping sticks and moving the seven of them presented problems enough, but he would be moving the whole newspaper enterprise, too. Could he do that? Find new accommodation, set up a new business address, new letterheads—maybe new staff, if his existing employees didn't want to work in Bangor. But these were all logistical problems that he was confident he could handle. The more subjective troubles surrounding him in Newtownards, if he stayed, he was less sure about.

He would have talked it all through with Lizzie, of course. She may have been happy to support whatever decision he made, but possibly agreed that the sea air might be good for her. She hadn't been feeling on top form for some time.

The main hurdle would be suitable premises—big enough to accommodate his family and his newspaper. By excellent good fortune an ideal property, owned by a Mr James Skillen, of Belfast, had just become available. It was a three-story house at the top of

---

[155] This account from the *North Down Herald* was also copied in the resignation letter of the previously mentioned Bangor Town Commissioner, which was reported in the *Belfast News-Letter* in November, 1885 (see Chapter 14).

THE STORYTELLER

Ballymagee Street [now High Street] on the corner of a little lane that would eventually be widened to become Clifton Road. It even had a small garden for the children and a number of garages and workshops at the rear, which WG immediately thought of as accommodating his own printing press at some future time. But could they afford the rent on such a place?

WG did his sums and determined that, provided the *Herald* continued to prosper and grow, and he could keep selling plenty of copies of "Robin's" tales, they could meet the higher overheads, including, he had decided, retaining an office in Newtownards.

On Wednesday 11th May, according to the *Belfast News-Letter*, WG chaired a meeting of the Newtownards Dog Show Society; he had become quite a dog-lover during his association with the club. It would be his final reported function as a citizen of Newtownards, and it was, no doubt, a pleasant last duty for him to perform before moving on.

A month later, in June, 1882, the Lyttles and the newspaper had taken up residence at 110 Ballymagee Street in Bangor. WG renamed his newspaper, the *North Down Herald, Newtownards Argos and Bangor Gazette* and the tall white building where it was produced, sitting at the top of the hill above Bangor Bay, his new home, he renamed, "Mount Herald."

WG was destined to remain there for the next twelve years—the longest time he ever lived at one address since leaving his parental home. Indeed, he would remain in Bangor for the rest of his life and it is as a Bangorian that he is still largely remembered today.

Chapter 16 – TOASTED

1882 – June to August

Previous mini-biographies of WG have always said that he moved the newspaper to Bangor in 1883 but, as we have seen, this was not the case. An article about the Bangor Town Commissioners in *Lyttle's North Down Directory and Almanac, 1888* starts thus:

> *The municipal history of Bangor is possibly without parallel. From the formation of the first Board of Town Commissioners—upwards of twenty years ago—until the month of June 1882, the existence of such a body was scarcely known. At the period named (June, 1882) the proprietor of the North Down Herald changed his headquarters from Newtownards to Bangor and added Bangor Gazette to the name of his paper. He immediately turned his attention to the affairs of the town and devoted much time to the Town Commissioners.*[156]

There is, moreover, in the Monday 7th August, 1882 edition of the *Belfast News-Letter* a report on a Grand Masonic Ceremony, held in Bangor the previous Saturday, at the conclusion of which Lord Clanmorris proposed a toast to "The Press, coupled with the names of Br. Jas. Alex. Henderson, proprietor of the *Belfast News-Letter* and Br. Lyttle, proprietor of the *Bangor Gazette*."

---

[156] No mention is made in the article of the third name he also added to his newspaper at that time, the *Newtownards Argos*, as that part of the name seems to have been used only in the Newtownards edition.

THE STORYTELLER

We can also see from the passage in Lyttle's Almanac, quoted above, that it confirms his decision to maintain an office in Newtownards when it uses the phrase that he "changed his *headquarters* from Newtownards to Bangor" [my emphasis].

Settling in

"Mount Herald" occupied a delightful position at the top of Ballymagee Street with a view down to Bangor Bay in one direction and out to the open fields of Ballymagee townland in the other. The street linked seaside with countryside and "Mount Herald" sat on the cusp between the two. Lizzie must have felt that at last they had arrived, as she set about turning their new house into a home for the family. Its spacious accommodation provided enough bedrooms for the children and she and Wesley enjoyed a fine bay window in theirs, overlooking the small front garden.[157] Wesley had his newspaper office on the second floor with sloping ceilings and dormer windows. He would take his time sorting out and deciding upon the use of the workshops behind the house, though one of the lock-up garages would make good stabling for his pony with another for the trap.

We are fortunate that my grandfather, Roland, often recalled details of his childhood at "Mount Herald" to my father, who passed them on. Our knowledge of the house, itself, is further augmented by an article written by Robin Page for the *Ulster Tatler*[158] at the time of "Mount Herald's" eventual demolition.

The family had a sunny front room with a big bay window under the main bedroom, but Lizzie loved best her fine dining room at the back with its polished wood flooring. It held a large table at which she looked forward to entertaining friends when her health improved. Indeed, with all the excitement of the move and setting up home and, she imagined, the change of air, too, she was already feeling stronger.

The children liked the dining room best, too—because of its secret trapdoor. Concealed beneath a rug that could be folded back, the trap covered the top of their own private well. Just below floor level was a hand pump that brought up crystal-clear spring water to a faucet from which vessels could be filled. It was so much easier than in

---

[157] See Appendix F for photos of "Mount Herald" (Figs 6 and 7)
[158] *County Down Portrait 1988-1989* – an Ulster Tatler Publication

16 - TOASTED

Newtownards where they'd had to go out in all weathers to fetch in water from a pump in the street. Throughout their time at "Mount Herald," even after the longest periods of drought, there is no record of the spring ever running dry.

Pets

As the weeks became months and, eventually years, the family knew they had found their home. They grew to love Bangor and living in a seaside town. Wesley couldn't have been more pleased for Lizzie and the children. At some point they had acquired two family pets. The first was a parrot called Captain Sharrat that Wesley might have picked up from an old sea dog he may have met when they were living near the River Lagan in East Belfast.

The other was a lively cocker spaniel. We know that Wesley was a dog-lover from an editorial he wrote for the third edition of the *Herald* on 31st July, 1880. It was mainly about the risks of contracting hydrophobia from dogs allowed to run free and un-muzzled and the "sinfulness" of owners who do not look after their pets properly. He included this advice:

> *"The dog master should consider his dog as his friend, and should see that he receives the amount of attention to which he is entitled, and of which he stands in need. Let the dog be well fed, have plenty of pure water, a good bed, with sufficient exercise, and he will hardly ever be ill."*

It is possible that Wesley got his dog as a puppy from someone in the Newtownards Dog Show Society, either while they still lived in that town or, perhaps around the time of their move to Bangor where, for the first time, they would have a home with a garden. Wesley trained the dog well and it would always obediently come to his side when he whistled.

THE STORYTELLER

Here I must confess that I have had to make an educated guess as to the breed of the Lyttles' pet. Our family lore only recalls that they had a dog; a dog that young Roland grew up with and would have loved. So in later years, when he had children of his own, might he not have bought them the same breed of dog he played with as a child? And we do have a photograph of Roland's cocker spaniel which was reproduced as the frontispiece of the *"Herald" Almanac and County Down Directory, 1913*.

Roland Lyttle's cocker spaniel

From around 1909, HMV Records, or His Master's Voice, started to use what became their widely-known logo, a picture of a black and white terrier sitting listening to his master's voice reproduced through the horn of a gramophone. By 1913, the logo had become world-famous. Roland's picture is of his dog sitting with a rolled up copy of the *North Down Herald* in his mouth with the caption, "His Master's News".

Spaniel or not, Wesley's dog hated the parrot. For a start, unlike the dog, the exotic bird was allowed to eat its meals with the family. It had a thick perch on a stand which was brought up to the table at dinner time and its food dish was placed on the table just like the plates in front of each of the family members. It would eat the same food as the others, the vegetables at any rate. Stepping onto the table top, the parrot would tilt his head to one side to inspect his dish before walking around the table, eyeing each of the other plates. If he saw something on another plate that was not on his, he would steal some of it and carry it back to his own dish.

The spaniel could probably have lived with this, preferring his own meaty food in a bowl on the floor by his basket, anyway. But what really brought out his loathing was the bird's ability to mimic. It had WG's whistle off to perfection. At random moments during the day, wherever its perch might be placed, it would recreate his master's distinctive call. The dog would prick up his ears, jump up at once and come running, tail wagging vigorously—only to find no one there but the parrot, which would burst into cackles of human-sounding laughter, copied from the children. The dog would slink away with its tail between its legs.

But the early years at "Mount Herald", what with taking the dog for walks, trips to the beach, entering into the social life of the developing little resort of Bangor, together with living in a new big house with a garden, were perhaps the happiest time of their lives for the Lyttle family.

Meeting the Bangor Town Commissioners

As he had done two years earlier in Newtownards, WG made himself known to the town's organisations and societies whose activities he reported on in the columns of his newspaper. He started to attend meetings of the Bangor Town Commissioners who were, perhaps, a little taken aback when he showed up to their hitherto private meetings. They couldn't forbid him entry in his capacity as reporter without appearing to have something to hide, so instead they cut their losses and extended to him a public and cordial welcome to their boardroom. Such friendly relations, however, were destined to cool when they read some of WG's subsequent editorials, sparked by what he saw as their inefficiency and ineptitude.

The 746 Masonic Lodge

A few weeks after they had moved into their new home—Saturday 5th August—Bangor hosted a most prestigious event. The *Belfast News-Letter* described it as, "the grandest and most imposing demonstration ever witnessed in this ancient seaside town." The occasion was the laying of the foundation stone for a masonic hall to accommodate the brethren of Lodge 746, under their Worshipful Master, Captain Samuel K Cowan. About a thousand Masons from all over the North were to be present. The fine weather on the day encouraged the arrival of huge numbers of visitors in horse-drawn cars, on boats and by trains that had cheap, excursion-rate tickets available. It was estimated that the ceremony was witnessed by fully six thousand people.

On the Saturday morning, WG awoke to a clear blue sky with bright sunshine slanting in through the east-facing pane of their bay window. It was going to be a big day and the weather looked perfect. He arose promptly and breakfasted; a normal day's work for a

THE STORYTELLER

Saturday had to be compacted into just a morning. Throughout the hours until dinnertime he found it hard to concentrate, his thoughts returning repeatedly to the grand occasion that would take place in the afternoon and all that had led up to it.

The 746 had been formed comparatively recently as a small and insignificant Masonic Lodge. Then, in 1878, a prominent freemason and member of the nobility, the 5th Baron, Lord Clanmorris from Galway, married Matilda, the daughter of Edward Ward of Bangor Castle.[159] He joined the 746 in addition to his Galway lodge and it was largely through his efforts that the membership and prosperity of the Bangor lodge grew rapidly over the next few years. To such an extent that, with membership now around a hundred, a dedicated meeting place was much needed,

It was Lord Clanmorris's initiative that was bringing that about, too. The site for the new hall had been generously donated by Mr Ward, his father-in-law. It was located behind St Comgall's Church on Hamilton Road[160] and would be separated from the church by a new road (Ruby Street) about to be constructed. Clanmorris, himself had already raised half the required £1,200 building costs. As WG tried to fix his mind back on the work he was supposed to be doing, he had a passing thought that he ought to be able to help raise some more funds towards the outstanding amount; he had helped plenty of other fundraisers over the years.

---

[159] The marriage conveniently united his title with her wealth. Their third son, Edward Barry Bingham became a Naval Commander and was awarded the Victoria Cross in 1916 after the Battle of Jutland. His decoration is on display in Bangor Castle, his childhood home. The Clanmorris finances became increasingly straitened, however, and when the widowed Matilda died in 1941 her son, the 6th Baron sold the Castle to the town of Bangor to be used as municipal offices. Interestingly, her grandson John, 7th Baron Clanmorris, had a career as a spy with MI5, where, in odd free moments he wrote thrillers and was inspirational in setting his colleague, David Cornwall, on the road to writing. Cornwall used the pen name, John Le Carré and even based his most famous fictional character, George Smiley, partly upon John Bingham.

[160] Then called Hamilton Street but by 1894 it had been changed to its present name, Hamilton Road. For clarity the name, Hamilton Road, has been used through the rest of the book.

Procession

At last the time came for Wesley to head off to Bangor Castle—the marshalling grounds for the enormous number of people who would be taking part in the procession through the town. Lizzie and the children would set out a little later to find a vantage point near the building site to watch the ceremony.

Wesley made his way through the town, probably finding himself among a horde of people coming up from the pier where a Belfast steamer had recently docked. Then, on Main Street he likely met crowds more coming in the opposite direction, from the station, where a train had just pulled in. He had never seen the town so full, but he struggled through the throng, carrying what he needed for the procession, until he reached the Castle grounds. He met up with all the other brothers and joined them in donning his masonic regalia.

It wasn't long before he heard the Abbey clock chime the hour of four and he watched as a brother mason, wielding a drawn sword, headed the procession that moved off exactly on schedule. He still had quite a few minutes to stand before he too would commence the march through the town to the site of the new masonic hall.

In the vanguard of the parade were representatives of 67 other lodges from Belfast, Antrim and Down, who lined up as they were ranked on the registry, in order of importance. WG would have recognised quite a few familiar faces in the melee: friends from Belfast and Newtownards—he noticed William Henry from the *Newtownards Chronicle*, amongst others—and a number of Good Templar acquaintances, too, from Belfast and further afield.

Then came the standard-bearer for 746 accompanied by two stewards with white wands. WG may have given his own wand a quick polish to enhance its pristine look as he observed brothers from various lodges, including 746 marching off carrying assorted paraphernalia—two with globes, three with silver candlesticks, and a setsquare, level and plumb rule. Each of the brothers was escorted by two others with white wands. Then came two carrying a velvet cushion between them. WG knew that on it rested a Holy Bible, square and compasses. He stretched his muscles after standing waiting for so long and prepared to take his place. The Secretary and Treasurer of 746 joined the procession escorted by two more brothers

THE STORYTELLER

with wands, one of whom was WG's friend, George Dickson from the Newtownards rose gardens. He grinned at Wesley as he moved off. Then came the Junior and Senior Wardens preceding the Worshipful Master of 746, Brother Captain Samuel Cowen. WG and another brother stepped into place behind him with their wands, as his escorting deacons.

Of the hundred or so members of Lodge 746 just 20 were chosen to play particular roles in the parade and WG felt honoured to be among them.

Behind him, he knew, were marching the officers of 746 followed by Lord Clanmorris and dignitaries from other lodges with another Standard-bearer and Sword-bearer. The rest of the brethren of Lodge 746 brought up the rear of what was, undeniably, a grand and imposing demonstration, the like of which Bangor had never seen before.

When they reached the site, the massed brethren formed a hollow square around the foundation stone, which was currently suspended on a tripod ready for laying. Already waiting, on a raised platform was an immense crowd of onlookers. As WG arrived and took his place he must have searched amongst them to try to spot Lizzie and the children, but he didn't have long as the ceremony was about to commence.

Laying the foundation stone

It opened with a masonic ode that the Worshipful Master had composed for the occasion. The rector of Bangor, the Rev E Morrow, then offered a prayer that concluded by asking the Lord to grant "that the sublime principles of Freemasonry may so subdue every discordant passion within us, and so harmonise and enrich our hearts, that the entire Craft throughout the world may ever humbly reflect that order, wisdom, strength and beauty, which reign forever before thy throne."

The foundation stone was then lowered into position. Within a cavity in the stone was placed a hermetically-sealed casket containing, as the Provincial Deputy Grand Master announced, examples of the current coinage, a parchment on which was inscribed the names of all the brethren of Lodge 746 and the roles played by individuals in

16 - TOASTED

today's ceremony, and copies of newspapers and other matters of current historical interest.

Was WG remembering a similar ceremony that had taken place on the summit of Scrabo Hill a quarter of a century earlier?[161] He must have felt immense pride as the present casket was fixed into place, knowing that this time it contained a copy of his own newspaper—the *North Down Herald and Bangor Gazette,* preserved for posterity.

The ceremony was proceeding, involving the three Masonic symbols—the square, "To square our actions by the square of virtue and prove our work;" the level, "Morally, it reminds us of equality and its use is to lay horizontals;" and the plumb line, "Morally, it teaches rectitude of conduct and we use it to try perpendiculars." These answers were given by the Worshipful Master, the Senior Warden and the Junior Warden, respectively, to questions put by the Provincial Deputy Grand Master about each symbol in turn. Each was applied to the foundation stone and it was found to be correct in every aspect.

Let us, for a moment, join Lizzie as, in the company of hundreds of other onlookers, she observes the ceremony.

> During this lengthy procedure the younger Lyttles became weary of the seemingly endless prayers, ritual responses and speeches. They had soon lost interest in trying to wave to their father seated down among the Masonic Brethren.
>
> Growing restless, they asked their mother if they could go off to the seashore to look for crabs in the seaweed and clamber over the rocks at the Big Hole;[162] maybe see one of Moore's paddle steamers docking at the pier and watch all the daytrippers disembarking who had responded to the Brothers Moore's slogan of "Bangor and back for a bob"[163]. Lizzie allowed them to

---

[161] See Chapter 3, Scrabo Tower

[162] Normally called the "Long Hole" today and situated at the start of Seacliff Road.

[163] A bob was slang for a shilling, or 12 old pennies (five new pence). It would be worth just under £6 in 2021.

THE STORYTELLER

go but made Roland and Eve promise to stay close to their big brother and sister.

"And everyone, including you, Agnes, must do what John says. Now, off with you," she said. Little Robina, much to her disgust, had to stay with her mother.

As the older children left, the National Anthem, in its Masonic setting, was announced. Lizzie was intrigued by the unfamiliar second and third verses, which ran as follows:

> Hail! Mystic light divine,
> May'st thou ne're cease to shine
> > Over this land;
> Wisdom in thee we find,
> Beauty and strength combined,
> Masons are ever joined
> > In heart and hand.
>
> Come then, ye sons of light,
> In joyous strains unite,
> > God save the Queen;
> Long may Victoria reign
> Queen of the azure main,
> Masons resound the strain,
> > God save the Queen.

Before Lizzie could ponder too long about what, exactly, her husband had become involved with, her attention was taken by a short address from the Provincial Deputy Grand Master of Antrim. He was emphasising Masons' faithfulness to the laws of the country, their obligation to erect magnificent buildings and to fear God, the great Architect of the Universe. This all sounded more reassuring to Lizzie until her ears caught the word "secrets"...

"... which cannot be divulged," the speaker said, but he assured his listeners that they were "lawful and honourable and not in any way repugnant to the laws of God or man." They had been entrusted to Masons from ancient times and would be passed from generation to generation in perpetuity. Lizzie again felt a slight unease which wasn't helped by listening to the final verse of the Masonic anthem, which followed the closing of the address:

> Hail! Masonry divine,
> Glory of ages, shine,
> > Long may'st thou reign!
> Where e're thy lodges stand
> May they have great command,
> And always grace the land,
> > Thou art divine.

The ceremony complete, the crowds prepared to depart, Lizzie among them. As she and Robina made their way home she was trying to recall the words of the First Commandment from her Sunday School days. It was something about having no other gods before Me, she thought. She pondered upon this and wondered if, perhaps, she had misunderstood the implications of that last verse.

Ceremonial dinner

Any such implications did not seem to be of concern to WG nor, indeed, to many of his brother Masons, who accepted the ritualistic language and statements of their fraternity without delving too deeply into their intent. They all began to disperse. WG accompanied around half of the brethren who were returning to the Castle grounds. There a huge marquee had been erected for the members of Lodge 746 to entertain about 400 guests to dinner. It was a splendid occasion and WG was able to catch up with many old friends. After the meal there was the inevitable proposing of numerous toasts, each with their attendant acceptance speeches. These often provoked further speeches of thanks for the gracious manner in which the toast had been received but eventually the evening was drawing to a close. Brother Lord Clanmorris offered the final toast, "The press," naming the editors of the *Belfast News-Letter* and the *Bangor Gazette*. The Belfast man had had to leave before the end so it was Brother Lyttle who responded on behalf of the press.

As he resumed his seat he was amused to see Brother William Henry of the *Newtownards Chronicle* rise to reply, too. Although not mentioned in the toast, the Chiel[164] wasn't going to be upstaged by WG.

Wesley had had to look up the word "chiel" and found that it meant "good fellow, one of the lads;" but it could also mean "child," which he considered rather more fitting. He had taken habitually to referring to his rival as the Chiel, because when he used the word it was always with its juvenile connotations in mind.

---

[164] Chiel—a soubriquet Mr Henry used for himself for one of his regular newspaper columns

Chapter 17 – THE DUEL

1882 – 1883

Scurrilous claims

The *Newtownards Chronicle* was to keep cropping up in WG's story. Later in the year, it seems they printed some allegations made by a lady called Rachel Baxter. It's hard to be certain of the exact nature of these from the little surviving evidence we have but what is clear is that they involved WG Lyttle.

Mrs Baxter claimed to have read certain letters and documents addressed to WG and then voiced her accusations to "numerous persons in Bangor and Newtownards" including William Henry of the *Chronicle* but we do not know what the allegations were—only that Henry referred to them as her "woeful tale." They must, however, have been damaging in nature, and quite false, for WG felt constrained to take action to remedy the situation.

With a witness, he visited Rachel Baxter to discover why she had been speaking out against him. Much to WG's relief, the result of his visit was that the woman retracted all that she had been saying. She had been under severe strain and now upon calmer reflection couldn't account for her actions. She agreed that WG could print a public statement from her to that effect. It seems this is what he did and sent a copy of the circular, under registered post, to the *Chronicle.*

We have only this public statement remaining from which to deduce the whole story. This is how it appeared in the Newtownards newspaper:

THE BANGOR SCANDAL
The following unique production in the form of a printed circular reached us, by registered letter,

THE STORYTELLER

addressed to our public office, in the handwriting of W.G. Lyttle, on Tuesday morning last:–

"Bangor, 11th November, 1882

"I hereby declare that the statements made by me to numerous persons in Bangor and Newtownards, and amongst others to Mr William Henry, of the Newtownards Chronicle, regarding Mr W. G. Lyttle, to the effect that I had read certain letters and documents addressed to him, are entirely untrue; that the letters were not addressed to him, nor were they written by the person whose name I used. I say that I made such statements while labouring under strong mental excitement brought on by family troubles and other causes with which Mr Lyttle had no connection whatsoever, and I hereby express my deep sorrow for my conduct, which was unjustifiable, and which now in my calmer moments appears to me utterly unaccountable.
"Signed,
   "Rachel Baxter.
"Witness present,
   "J. Gaw."

We do not understand why our name should have been dragged into this matter at all. We never sent for the woman, and never asked for her confidence. All we can say is, if she was labouring under mental excitement at the time she told her "woeful tale," she seemed to us, and to others to whom she related the same story, perfectly calm and collected. Comment on the document, which, though signed by Mrs Baxter, is probably not her own composition, is needless. "Qui s'excuse, s'accuse."—Ed. N.C.

It is amusing to see how Henry managed to include two scathing comments in his closing remarks about how "comment on the document is needless."

17 - THE DUEL

So the whole episode is still something of a mystery but, patently, WG survived to continue his illustrious career with his reputation untarnished, for he was invited the following month to contribute to the entertainment at a Christmas fund-raising event organised by the principal teachers of the Bangor Parochial (National) Day Schools.

Researching a heroine

As I have mentioned, WG had long been fascinated with the movement of the last century known as the United Irishmen. Their tenet of embracing both Protestants and Catholics within their ranks would have appealed to his "Live and let live" approach to life without his necessarily subscribing to their goal of driving the English out of Ireland. Although he never showed any interest in joining the Orange Order with their staunchly Loyalist credo, neither did he show much enthusiasm for favouring Home Rule. At the same time, his son, Roland, who would follow him into the newspaper business and must have learned much from him as he was growing up, would eventually marry a Roman Catholic girl. This would suggest that WG may have been as equally open-minded in religion as in politics.

Looking into the tales of the United Irishmen he was intrigued by stories of some of the participants in the uprising who came from nearby parts of County Down and Antrim. One, in particular, captured his imagination for sheer determination and bravery—and, not least, because this one was a woman renowned for her beauty. In researching the subject WG built on all the local oral tradition he had picked up over the years by visiting the places with historic links to the rebellion and speaking with many relatives of those involved in the uprising. He listened to all their stories and in so doing he discovered that the brave and beautiful woman—Miss Elizabeth Gray—was born and raised not far from Bangor in a cottage at Gransha near Six-Road-Ends. This was contrary to folklore perpetuated in William McComb's popular poem[165] that she had been a Killinchy lass known as "Bessie Grey" [*sic*]

---

[165] The poem was included in a section all about the Battle of Ballynahinch in McComb's *Guide to Belfast* that was published in 1861. It repeated Mary Ann McCracken's original assertion that "Elizabeth Grey" [*sic*] came from Killinchy.

THE STORYTELLER

For some time, he had been playing with the idea that he would write a book about what led up to the rebellion of 1798. He would incorporate the stories he had picked up over the years since his youth, that lived on in the memories of families whose forebears had been participants in the insurrection. From the shorthand notes he undoubtedly kept, he had already tried writing a few scenes that might one day find their way into the finished novel. For it would be a novel, he decided, not a history book. He had a ready-made heroine—his love interest—the beautiful young girl from Gransha who had been a camp follower at the crucial Battle of Ballynahinch. But more than just a camp follower. From what he could ascertain from contemporary and later written accounts, young Betsy Gray—as she had been known around Gransha—was in the thick of the fighting at the end. Maybe he'd use her name for the title of the book—he'd have to think about that.[166]

Although his would be a fictionalised account of those terrible times, he wanted to make it as authentic as he could—hence his interviews with so many people and his visits to the historical locations, to ensure the accuracy of what he wrote. He was already familiar with the Belfast public house in Sugar-house Entry, not far from where his Accountancy firm's office was. That had been the venue for a clandestine meeting of concerned individuals in 1791 that resulted in the formation of the United Irishmen. He met up with the postmaster at Ballygrainey, George Moore, who took him to the smiddy where Mat M'Clenaghan had fashioned pike heads for the rebels (Matt would become a significant character in the book). The two stood by the old forge as George related all he could remember of what his father had told him of those stirring times.[167] He visited, too, Hans Gray's nearby cottage at Gransha where Betsy had lived.[168]

---

[166] The book, when published, was called Betsy Gray, or Hearts of Down – a Tale of Ninety-Eight.

[167] The elderly George Moore, himself, recalled the details of this meeting in a letter to the *Newtownards Chronicle* that Kenneth Robinson mentions in his article, "Betsy Gray Revisited," published in the 2000 issue of the Journal of the Upper Ards Historical Society.

[168] See photos in Appendix F, Figs 10 and 11 when I, too, visited Betsy Gray's cottage.

17 - THE DUEL

Not everyone, of course, was happy to talk about having rebel ancestors. North Down, staunchly protestant, staunchly loyalist and staunchly unionist was no longer—eighty years on—a hotbed of insurrection. The talk of Gladstone introducing a Home Rule Bill had antagonised the current brave "Hearts of Down" who feared it could lead to only one thing—a break from the British Crown to form a republic. However, fortunately for WG's research, in the minds of most people the long passage of time since the United Irishmen had fought the British had lent enchantment. While they wouldn't have embraced their forebears' political aspirations, they looked upon their bravery and their exploits with a degree of familial pride. That wouldn't have been the case had the rebellion been a more recent event.

WG decided—audaciously, some might say—that enough time had passed, even with strong feelings generated by the Home Rule debate, for him to be able to make his readers warm to a romanticised re-telling of the struggle for Irish rights, in spite of his protagonists fighting for freedom from British rule and his local villain—an informer—being a steadfast loyalist. Would determining to write such a novel at such a time prove to be a rash decision?

A site visit

One fine day in the spring of 1883, in pursuit of his research, WG decided to try to find a certain spot that he had heard about and set off in his pony and trap in the direction of Ballynahinch. When he finally reached the little town he turned right along the Lisburn Road towards Ballykine.

As he drove along the narrow road he kept a sharp lookout for his goal and it wasn't long before he spotted it—a willow tree in a field, set back about ten yards from the road. He could see that it was growing on a raised area with the remains of a stone retaining wall, about three feet in height, surrounding it. He knew he had found the last resting place of a wealthy farmer from Greyabbey, a Mr Adair, who had fought bravely alongside the rebels only to be cut down and hewn to pieces by the Hillsborough Yeomanry. It had happened at this very spot, as Adair tried to escape after the United Irishmen lost their last battle at Ballynahinch. The field, where some friendly hands had buried him, belonged then to Alexander Douglas who, himself, built the wall and planted a willow sapling to mark the spot.

WG got down from his gig and approached the sally.[169] He estimated it now to be a good fourteen feet in height. He gazed at the turfed mound and the little wall and paused for a moment to reflect on Adair and the others who lost their lives all those decades ago. On a whim he took out his penknife and cut a short, firm twig from a branch before returning to where his patient little horse was chomping some long grass by the verge.

Back at his office in "Mount Herald" that evening he sat and examined the twig he had taken as a souvenir. With his penknife again, he started to whittle at it until he had fashioned for himself a sturdy pen-holder. Taking a fresh piece of paper, he dipped the nib of his new pen in the inkwell and began to write:

> *Some twenty-five years ago [Adair's] grave was opened—with what object cannot be said. It was found to contain the skeleton of the unfortunate man. Hat, boots and clothing were in a perfect state of preservation. The coat, which was of a superfine green broadcloth, and long skirted, the waistcoat, knee-breeches, and green silk kerchief had suffered but little by their sixty years subjection to the soil under which they and their wearer had been laid.*[170]

In this short passage WG has told us that he was already starting to draft at least this section of his famous novel in 1883.[171] In a footnote to the above passage WG added,

---

[169] Sally: the Ulster-Scots term for a willow tree and still commonly used in Ulster.

[170] Quoted from Betsy Gray or Hearts of Down, by WG Lyttle (chapter XXXVI)

[171] Adair's grave was opened 60 years after his burial in 1798. That would have been in 1858—which, WG tells us was 'some 25 ago'. So he must have been writing this in 1883.

17 - THE DUEL

The author of this story has visited the grave of Adair. While there, he cut a twig from the sally, and from it manufactured the pen-holder which he used in the writing of this tale.

WG knew he had many more incidents and locations to investigate and people to interview before he could hope to complete his novel and he was prepared to take as long as it took. In the meantime he had an idea for another story which he thought about from time to time, piecing it together in his mind before he would start to pen that tale, also. Like many a first-time novelist, he would set this one at the time of his own youth and in locations he had been familiar with as a child. It would be set amongst the tenant farmers of County Down, many struggling to make a living from the soil. They were entirely dependent on the land and the seasons, these "sons of the sod." In his mind, he had that as its working title.[172]

Archibald Thompson

Reporting the meetings of the Bangor Town Commissioners for his newspaper often provided WG with some diversion. Their offices and boardroom were on Ballymagee Street, only just down the road from "Mount Herald".

A newly elected commissioner was causing ructions at the Board meetings. Archibald Thompson was actually an acquaintance of WG, as he was Congregational Secretary at First Bangor Presbyterian Church, where the Lyttles had started worshipping upon moving to the resort. Wesley had been intrigued when Archibald told him that the big weeping ash tree in front of the church building had been planted in 1844, the year of Wesley's own birth.[173] He soon discovered that Thompson was a man disinclined to keep his opinions to himself. He had stirred up something of a hornets' nest when he was elected as a commissioner the previous November.

---

[172] This book would eventually be published first, before "Betsy Gray," under the title, "Sons of the Sod, a Tale of County Down."

[173] See photo of First Bangor Presbyterian Church with the weeping ash tree, in Appendix F, Figure 23.

THE STORYTELLER

At their monthly meeting held that May, Mr Thompson demanded to see correspondence between the board and their solicitor. This was because of previous questions he had raised about the legitimacy of the purposes to which the ratepayers' money was being devoted. Most of the board felt that his statements on that occasion (which must have been put in writing) amounted to libel against them and they had consulted the board's solicitor. That worthy had written to Mr Archibald Thompson requesting that he retract his insinuations, but Thompson had merely put the matter in the hands of his own solicitor with instructions to await the action of his fellow commissioners and then take whatever steps were necessary to justify the position he had taken.

The *North Down Herald and Bangor Gazette* now recorded that Archibald Thompson, rather than showing any signs of wishing to placate the other commissioners, wanted to debate the matter again, When this was refused, he objected to every item brought forward. He even objected to the "garbled reports" of their meetings in the newspapers. WG was, in fact, careful to insist his reporter always jotted down Thompson's exact words. Archibald's request to view the letters was pointedly ignored, as was his subsequent attempt to make a speech. The chairman, John M'Meekan declared that he would manage the affairs of the board as he pleased. There was some further attempt to carry out the business of the day but eventually two of the commissioners had had enough and left the room.

This rendered the meeting inquorate and it had to conclude.

In his editorial WG would surely have made it clear just what he thought of the town's Commissioners.[174]

---

[174] As mentioned before, we do not have any copies of the *Herald* over this period. The details in the foregoing account are taken from the *Northern Whig*. WG would, undoubtedly, have covered the story, too, and his attitude to these events, which I have attempted to convey, are based upon his actual accounts of later similar occurrences that have been preserved for us in the scrapbooks of newspaper cuttings held at the North Down Museum in Bangor, and upon the nature of the skit that he subsequently wrote about the "Doings of the Bangor Town Commissioners."

17 - THE DUEL

The Parable of the Rulers

Indeed, such was the bizarre conduct of the members of the Board that WG decided to write a skit on their proceedings, chapters of which he published from time to time in the columns of the *Herald*. It was later reproduced as *The Parable of the Rulers* in a travellers' guide he wrote called *The Bangor Season*. It was amusingly written, mostly in the style of the King James version of Old Testament with some of the language of the New Testament added for good measure. WG must have been familiar with his Bible to be able to mimic its language so well and so humorously

In the opening skit he spoke briefly of Bangor's growth from a little fishing village until latterly:

> *...Then did the people multiply and their habitations did greatly increase in number.*
>
> *And the Commissioners, or Rulers, beholding these things did rejoice with exceeding great joy. And they took council [sic] one with another and did borrow moneys, yea, exceeding great sums, and did expend them in the gathering of streams of water for the town, and in the digging of drains for discharging the common offal into the sea* [referring to the construction of a reservoir and sewer.] *Then did the people look on in wonder, saying in their hearts— 'Who shall pay for these things?' And the place prospered; the steam horse did bring people to visit it; and a mighty merchant, whose name was Moore, did sail his great steam ships thither, carrying large multitudes whose number was even as the sands of the sea.*
>
> *And it came to pass in those days that Archibald, whose surname was Thompson, came down from the Mount of Oriel [Thompson's Bangor abode was called "Oriel House"] and stood amongst the people. And when he had come down he opened his mouth and spake with a loud voice unto the citizens in this wise: 'Men and brethren, ye are befooled by our*

> *Rulers. Their breath is in their nostrils; they are even as smoke; they are fools, being ignorant and blind. For lo! they have borrowed moneys having nothing wherewithal to pay the same. And, moreover, I say unto you, that they cannot count, nay, not even upon their fingers, and they have plotted against you to lay upon your shoulders grievous taxation, which cannot be borne. And they will not so much as touch your burdens with their little finger; and ye shall be called upon to pay their debts, yea, twice told.'*
>
> *And the people held up their hands in astonishment, and cried with a loud voice saying—'What shall we do to escape this great evil?'*
>
> *And the Prophet of Mount Oriel said unto them—'Here am I; put me among your Rulers, making me the chief thereof, and I shall set all these wrong doings aright.'*
>
> *And the people answered saying—'We will do even as thou sayest, and may it be well with thee and thine after thee for ever.'*
>
> *And Archibald returned to the Mount; and the people did gird up their loins for work. And in due season they demanded a poll, and it was given them. And they did vote; and did select Archibald as the first in order.*

Archibald Thompson, came top of the poll that November but, as reported above his attempts at righting the perceived wrongs were not received well by his fellow Commissioners. His self-imposed task of cleaning up the work of the Board was proving rather more difficult than he had, perhaps, imagined. Still, from WG's point of view, the accounts of his efforts sold newspapers.

The new Masonic Hall

A few months later, in August, exactly a year since the magnificent procession through the town for the laying of the foundation stone of the new Masonic Hall, there was another, equally splendid turnout for

17 - THE DUEL

its grand opening. The occasion served to remind WG about his idea that he could help in some way with the building fund, which was still not cleared. It had rather slipped his mind in the intervening months, but he now set about enlisting the services of friends from near and far, who could help to provide a splendid evening of entertainment. As to a venue, well, of course, it could now be held in the brand new Masonic Hall on Hamilton Road. He knew that the reading and billiards rooms could be combined to use as a concert hall. WG's entertainment, held on Wednesday 29 August, was one of the first events to be hosted in the new premises.

Bangor **Masonic Hall**, Hamilton Road
(Photo courtesy of Trevor Low, Bangor]

The evening included a mix of fifteen musical items, solos, recitations and readings. Numbered amongst the ten artists who took part were last year's Worshipful Master, Captain Samuel Cowan, well-known as a poet and elocutionist, who read a selection of his own verse, and Mr JG Swanston, an actor who used to tread the boards of Belfast's Theatre Royal, who gave a moving recitation in character.

WG was well received when reciting one of his poems entitled, *"What the People Say in Bangor."* He later returned to the stage dressed as "Robin" to read, *"How I became a Mason."* A couple more songs brought the successful evening to a close.

Lord Clanmorris, Worshipful Master, Lodge 746 presided over the evening and he said how gratified he was at this unsolicited assistance to him in the efforts he was making to provide suitable accommodation for the Masons of Bangor and its vicinity. The venue was packed to capacity, so WG must have raised a goodly sum in support of those efforts.

THE STORYTELLER

A strange occurrence at the North Down Rifles Encampment

On a Sunday afternoon around this time, Wesley took his family back to Newtownards to visit the Encampment of the North Down Rifles—a pastime enjoyed by many, especially on Sundays, to see friends in the corps, or just out of interest, and in the hopes of enjoying a free drink of porter in the canteen or, for the gentry, something stronger in the officers' mess.

The gossip around the field was all about an ignorant fellow of the American cowboy ilk. He wore his hat at the table, ate with his knife and was seen to put the ice intended for his champagne into his curry. Apparently he had been abusing the hospitality of the good officers of the North Down Rifles and more than once had had to be carried from the field after consuming too much liquor. Wesley was told that just recently he had been refused an audience with Lord Clandeboye and had lost his temper. He challenged any and all to a duel, the outcome of which convinced Wesley, the storyteller, that here was a skit for the *Herald* that would practically write itself.

At that moment, I wonder if he spotted the editor of the *Newtownards Chronicle* who happened to have chosen the same Sunday afternoon to visit the militia. And as he watched him swagger through the crowds looking rather pompous and ridiculous, did a mischievous thought begin to take shape in his mind?

Five years later, in 1889, WG would write an article in his newspaper[175] claiming that the skit he wrote in the summer of '83 was based entirely upon the gossip he had heard about the uncivilized "cowboy." While it is clearly true that it was based upon what he had heard, did he slant it a little so that readers could, if they so wished, see a different character as the centre of ridicule? Of course William Henry wasn't named. WG wrote a complete fable about a foreign count visiting the Encampment but why, I wonder, did he choose, not once but twice, to mention that he wished to *chronicle* the events that took place?

The article appeared in the *Herald* the following Saturday under the heading:

---

[175] The article appeared in three parts in three consecutive issues of the *Herald* from 22nd February to the 8th March, 1889.

17 - THE DUEL

> *Exciting Duel with Swords Between a Member of the Downs and a Foreign Count. (By our special wire.)*
>
> *Downs Encampment, Sunday—a remarkable duel occurred here today. By the merest chance I happened to be on the grounds at the same time and am therefore in a position to supply full and accurate details.*

After some introductory remarks about the Encampment being open to visitors WG then referred to,

> *... a distinguished foreigner whose doings I am about to chronicle ... His approach was heralded by a slim youth whose slender limbs seemed absolutely to fly over the ground.* [A metaphor, perhaps, for his own young newspaper whose circulation was growing rapidly as the copies flew off the press and was always ready to "herald" any misdeeds of his rival editor?]
> *'The Count!' he gasped, 'the Count!' and sank, breathless into the arms of a bystander.*

The Count

WG continued with a wild description of this 'Count' whose

> *large unwieldy trunk stood upon massive legs and ponderous feet, spread well apart, and supported a head, whose phrenological developments a somewhat shabby hat concealed to the eye of the physiognomist. ... The small eyes were full of cunning cruelty and meanness...*

This uncouth caricature of a man demanded of a passing soldier that his card be taken to "my noble friend, Clandeyman" [Lord

THE STORYTELLER

Clandeboye.] While awaiting a response, he accepted a drink from a three quart can of porter proffered by "a dirty looking half-drunken fellow." He assured nearby doubters:

> *'Yes, I am a Count, the Count Rhinosera.* [Did Henry, perhaps, have a prominent nose?] *I am no interloper here, and as has been very justly remarked, I do dress well. In fact the Prince of Wales employs my tailor, and I lead the fashions for him.*

Snubbed

He then continued with a story about how he often dropped in to visit Wales, which, in WG's account, was interrupted by the first soldier coming back.

> *What was to follow I am unable to chronicle, for at that moment the messenger returned, saying that the noble Clandeyman was nowhere to be found.*
> *'Go, then, to the next in command,' said the Count, 'and say that the Count Rhinosera, bearing letters of introduction from Victoria, Wales, Lorne, and all the crowned heads of Europe, from Gladstone, Bright, and other members of the House of Lords and Commons, from the Lords Hollow and Castlerain* [Lords Hill and Castlereagh], *the Marquis of Dondonderry* [Londonderry], *and a host of others too numerous to mention. Say that I have come to dine here today, and to display some of my mighty feats at arms.'*

Forced to wait once more, the Count addressed "the gaping, wondering crowd." He was a self-made man, he told them, his father being a humble cobbler who died in a workhouse. [Had William Henry, perhaps, once cast aspersions at WG's own humble beginnings as a shoemaker's son? And might Wesley Little Snr, actually have been confined to the Newtownards Workhouse infirmary during a terminal illness?] The Count continued to address his admirers:

17 - THE DUEL

> *'Yes, that's how it goes, mine is the tongue of a Demosthenes; women hear me and melt into tears; men listen to me and catching me up bear me upon their shoulders in a frenzied excitement.'* [A mocking reference to the Election Night of two years ago?]
> *'Give us a speech,'* cried the crowd.
> *'After dinner,'* said the Count.

Just then the messenger returned with news that the officer declined to receive the Count on the grounds that "you take tea with your curry, wear your hat in company and otherwise conduct yourself in an unseemly fashion." This drove him into a rage and he demanded satisfaction:

> *'They lie,'* roared the Count. *'Go back and tell the fellows I challenge them each and all to mortal combat.'* The man did not move. *'I must have blood,'* screamed the Count. I have been insulted, and blood alone can wipe out the disgrace.'

The duel

A private stepped forward and offered to fight the Count, who scoffed, "I'll split you in a jiffy. Bring swords."

Within a ring of spectators the two combatants commenced their duel. It was soon obvious that Count Rhinocera was not much of a swordsman and the private was playing with him. After a while the soldier pulled back and then made a rapid forward sweep at his opponent's head. The Count's hat fell off, cut clean in two and the Count, with a shriek, staggered and collapsed.

The crowd held its breath as the apparently lifeless body of the Count was examined:

> *It was found that the skull was cracked in several places, as the result, probably, of previous encounters, but in the present instance he had not been wounded. He had simply fainted. Restoratives of a spiritual*

THE STORYTELLER

character were applied, and at a late hour, supported by a number of the sturdy Downs, the Count was able to reach his hotel.

Thus ended the story as it appeared in the next Saturday's *Herald*. How much WG had William Henry in mind as he wrote the sketch we do not know, nor indeed, how many readers inferred from his writing that he was poking fun at the Newtownards editor—if, indeed, he was. But William Henry, when he read it, was in no doubt that he was the butt of WG's satire. From the subsequent article in the *Herald*, written some years later, we do know that it was generally well received, causing "the most unbounded merriment in civil and military circles" with Lord Clandeboye, himself, personally complimenting WG on the skit.

I am quite sure he thoroughly enjoyed writing the piece and, no doubt, hundreds of his readers would have loved it. Just not all of them.

WG would later come to regret having a laugh at his rival editor's expense. But for now he was happy to receive the plaudits from his friends and all those who appreciated the jape. For the time being, he forgot all about it in the excitement of what he was planning. The Lyttles were about to go on holiday.

Chapter 18 – THE BLACK GHOST OF BALLYGARVAN

1883 – September

Wesley was a down-to-earth man, not subject to superstitions or susceptible to tales of the paranormal. So when his children swore to him that they had seen a ghost he pooh-poohed the idea and attributed it straightway to childish imaginations. Their mother wasn't quite so dismissive but Wesley was pleased that she, nevertheless, supported him when he made light of the youngsters' claims and told them just to enjoy their holiday. He would have done better to be guided by Lizzie's natural instinct for caution.

The following account is a dramatic reconstruction of real events. All the salient details about the aparition are as passed down through my father from my grandfather, who, as a young boy with his siblings, personally experienced what I am about to relate. It occurred while eldest son, John, was still living at home, probably about 1883 and likely in late summer. The children would have enjoyed sunny days on Ballyholme beach in July and August and rides on the carousel and swing boats when the big funfair arrived, as it did each year to a field on the edge of the town off Clifton Lane. The distinctive music from its steam organ wafted across the width of Bangor Bay when the wind was in the right direction, delighting children and adults, alike, throughout the resort with its promise of gaiety and laughter.

However, the summer attractions of Bangor also brought a threefold increase in its population from around its usual 3,000 to over 9,000, so spending some time in the peacefulness of the countryside was not without its attractions. Wesley decided to take a house "somewhere down the Ards Peninsula" for a couple of weeks to give

THE STORYTELLER

Lizzie and the children a bit of a change. Exactly where this was, I cannot say. I shamelessly chose Ballygarvan for the alliterative nature of its name in providing my chapter title. But it would have been to somewhere in that vicinity that, with their bags packed and loaded onto a barouche hired to take them, the Lyttle family set off, quite unsuspecting of the ominous events that awaited their arrival.

Five-year-old Roland felt squashed sitting between his father and big brother. He had been waiting by the gate and was first to see the barouche pull up outside "Mount Herald", having just been driven up the hill from James Fletcher's, Undertaker and Coachbuilder, who also hired out vehicles from his premises lower down Ballymagee Street.

The well-sprung carriage was pulled by two hefty horses and was meant to carry four adults—two pairs facing each other, but the leather seats were generously proportioned and the family soon had themselves sorted out. Wesley and his 17-year-old son, John, took up most of one seat but there was still room for little Roland between them. The child strained his neck to look past his mother opposite, and under the high seat of the coachman, at the big rear ends of the horses that would take them off on their adventure. He grinned at his little sister, Robina, on their mother's lap, as fifteen-year-old Agnes on her right and Eva, now nearly nine, on her left wriggled about trying to get comfortable.

Their driver took the road to Donaghadee and, from there, headed south along the coastal route towards Millisle. The sun shone on the open barouche, as he pointed out an immaculate garden along the way that he told the Lyttles were open to the public and worthy of a visit. Roland wondered if "the public" would come to visit their garden at "Mount Herald".

18 - THE BLACK GHOST OF BALLYGARVAN

St Patrick's Well

A little later, approaching a small cemetery between the road and the sea, the driver called out to his passengers,

'Thon's Templepatrick graveyard. Yis can see the footprint of St Patrick, himself, and his horse in the rocks down by the shore.'

'Really? Can we stop and see them?' asked Eva. 'Please; can we?'

'Well...' her mother hesitated.

'There's St Patrick's well, too, if any of yis are thirsty,' the driver added and, anticipating the response, pulled back on the reins. 'Whoa! there.'

Roland saw his parents nodding at each other in agreement. It wasn't until much later that he learned that his father had planned on breaking their journey here all along; Wesley had had a quiet word with their driver before they set off. It was why they had chosen this route. He wanted to see the famous well for himself, for he was gathering information that he planned to include in his travellers' guide. As a result of this family visit to the ancient site he later told all about it in the booklet he called, *The Bangor Season*.[176]

---

[176] This is what he wrote (extract from *The Bangor Season* by W. G. Lyttle, 1885):

"Leaving Donaghadee and emerging on the Millisle road, the fine public gardens of Mr Connolly are certain to be admired. After passing a mile of charming ocean scenery we come upon Templepatrick graveyard, thickly studded with gravestones, and on and among the adjacent rocks can be pointed out the prints of St Patrick's foot and his horse's hoof; but better—a thousand times better is St Patrick's well—pure, sparkling, overflowing, flowing and running over for hundreds of years, yet as full as ever. We don't ask strangers to believe that either St Patrick or his horse were so heavy footed, as that they left the prints of their feet in the rock; but we do ask them to believe that this well, no matter who built it, is limpid, sparkling, pure and better for quenching thirst than all the intoxicating liquors ever distilled or brewed.

"Stranger! If you are thirsty drink, and if you are not thirsty, we would, nevertheless, respectfully ask you to drink, that you may be able to say in all

THE STORYTELLER

Everyone sampled the water from St Patrick's well and agreed that it was wonderfully refreshing on a warm sunny day, but Roland thought the water from their own well at "Mount Herald" was every bit as good.[177]

The house at Ballygarvan

Leaving the bubbling waters behind them, they continued their long journey across the Ards Peninsula and were eventually rewarded with a first glimpse of the house they were to occupy for the next fortnight. It lay just outside the village of Ballygarvan, set back from the road and remote from other habitations. Roland tried to peer through the tall trees and caught a glimpse of a forbidding house that loomed out of the shadows. The surrounding grounds were unkempt and overgrown with patches of brambles and nettles and long grass. Wild thorn bushes in a neglected shrubbery clawed and scraped against the ground floor windows near where their barouche now came to a standstill. The horses whinnied and stamped their hooves as though anxious to be gone from the place.

'This is spooky,' said Eva, struggling with her valise up the steps to the large front door.

'It gives me the shivers,' Agnes agreed.

Roland stayed close to John who ruffled his hair and said, 'Don't listen to them, they're only girls. There's nothing to be scared of. It's just a house.'

---

future time, 'the purest water ever I drank was out of St Patrick's well, near Donaghadee.'"

[177] The pure water from St Patrick's well continued to flow uninterrupted for another century, during which time some private dwellings were built on adjacent land. More recently, with changes in ownership, the well became "an inconvenience." Sadly, it has now been filled in and never again can a weary traveller quench his thirst from St Patrick's spring.

18 - THE BLACK GHOST OF BALLYGARVAN

'Here's the key, right where the agent said it would be.'

Roland watched with some apprehension as his mother retrieved it from behind an urn which contained a dried-up climbing plant that had long since perished from lack of care and attention.

Once inside, however, his curiosity got the better of him and he raced ahead of the others. He passed a big grandfather clock that stood sentinel in the hall and had a solemn and sonorous tick. As he ran on, he heard his mother commenting that she found the house a little dark but was pleased to see that the accommodation appeared to be spotless. Each room they entered she proclaimed to be spacious and comfortably furnished, and the kitchen quarters equipped with all they were likely to need. When they went upstairs she said that the large bedrooms were just as described to them and would suit the family perfectly.

Roland watched as Agnes and Eva, who seemed to have forgotten about the "spookiness" of the outside of the house, rushed over to an enormous four-poster bed that they were to share in what their mother was referring to as "The Girls' Room." They jumped onto the counterpane and sank into the depths of the wel-stuffed mattress as everyone surveyed the rest of the chamber. Continuing the oversized nature of the solid mahogany furniture, there was an impressive tallboy in the window recess and a massive wardrobe against the wall in the corner. Two big leather armchairs and a bedside table completed the room, apart from a modern crib that looked rather out of place but would be just right for little Robina. In later years, it would be the big wardrobe and the four-poster that endured most strongly in Roland's memory.

"The Boys' Room" was similarly furnished but with two single beds. Roland jumped onto his and was disappointed not to find the mattress as bouncy as the girls'. There was another big double room for Lizzie and Wesley.

'I'm just sorry, ' Lizzie said, 'that I will be sleeping alone in this big bed tonight.'

They all knew that Wesley had important business to attend to at "Mount Herald" the next day and was returning to Bangor in the barouche. He would drive back down late tomorrow in his gig.

The ghost

The following evening, dusk was already settling when Wesley pulled back on the reins to bring his horse to a standstill by the steps of the house in Ballygarvan. He removed the travelling rug from across his knees and leaned forward in his seat to look around the edge of the gig's leather canopy. The shadowy old house, silhouetted now against a darkening sky, held little in the nature of a welcome. He wondered about the wisdom of agreeing to take it, unseen, just because the rental was such good value.

But his misgivings were short-lived, as the front door swung open and four of his children raced down the steps to greet him. Everyone seemed to talk at once.

'Father! You're back.'
'You'll never guess.'
'Guess what?'
'The house is haunted!'
'What? Poppycock!'
'It is! There's a ghost, honestly.'
'We've all seen it; it was really scary.'
'I saw it first.'

18 - THE BLACK GHOST OF BALLYGARVAN

'Did you, young Roland? I expect that explains a lot—you and your imaginings.'

'I didn't 'magin' it,' said Roland with as much dignity as he could muster, surrounded by his older siblings.

Lizzie appeared in the doorway holding Robina's hand. The child was already in her nightgown. Lizzie said, 'They do seem to have seen something; it quite upset them.'

They all went inside and sat in the big drawing room, variously occupying two sofas, a leather armchair, a hassock and a thick-piled rug on the floor.

'Now, then. What's all this nonsense? What did you see, or think you saw?' said Wesley.

Roland opened his mouth to answer but John beat him to it:

'We don't think; we definitely saw it.'

'Him,' said Eva.

'You saw a man? Where? It was probably the gardener. The place certainly could do with one.'

'He was in our bedroom. A black man,' said Agnes.

'Your bedroom!'

'Half a black man,' said Roland.

'What, he was half black and half white? This is preposterous. You're all making it up. I'll not have it.' Wesley gave his children a stern look.

'Roland's right,' said Eva. 'We only saw half of him.'

Agnes explained, 'It was this afternoon. We were all sitting on our huge bed—'

'Well, four of us; Robina was with Mother,' said John.

'We were playing Five Stones[178],' Agnes continued, ignoring her brother. 'Eva and John and me were still in. Roland was out; he always drops the ball.'

---

[178] A game, played one-handed, usually called Jacks nowadays, involving throwing up a ball and picking up the jacks, or stones, before catching the ball again in the same hand.

'I don't always!'

'Well, maybe not *always*.'

'It's a boring game, anyway,' said Roland. 'I stopped watching the others and was looking round the room and that's when I saw him. He was behind the wardrobe, watching us on the bed!'

'We all heard Roland shout out, "Who's that man?" and we turned to look,' said John.

'But, as soon as we did, he disappeared,' said Eva.

'We all saw him, but. Didn't we?' said Agnes.

They were each adamant that they had seen the man before he disappeared. Their description was of a huge and well-muscled black African, bare-chested and peering out at them from behind the big wardrobe—the wardrobe that sat in the corner of the room leaving a gap of no more than two inches between itself and the wall.

'Wait a moment. Behind the wardrobe? No one could hide behind that massive piece of furniture.'

Roland felt that his Father didn't believe them. 'He did, I tell you; I saw him—well, his top half. It was his legs that were hidden behind the wardrobe. But when he saw that we'd seen him he went away.'

'What, through the door onto the landing?'

'No. Just went. Agnes screamed and he disappeared.'

'I didn't *scream*.'

'Yes you did!' the others chorused, bringing the colour to Agnes's cheeks.

Their father said, 'That room is dark even in mid-afternoon, and full of shadows. It was most probably a trick of the light.'

'It was a big black man,' Roland insisted.

His father looked unconvinced.

18 - THE BLACK GHOST OF BALLYGARVAN

Icy grip

That night it took the children a long time to fall asleep. Their mother had gone along with Wesley's scepticism and tried to put thoughts of hauntings out of their minds, but for Roland, at least, the fearsome image of the huge ebony head and torso, apparently leaning out from behind the wardrobe, remained etched in his memory.

After a long time all was quiet in the house except for the rhythmic ticking of the grandfather clock in the hall and the occasional creak common to all old buildings. There was, too, the intermittent scraping of thorns against a downstairs windowpane.

Everyone slept.

Then Roland's eyes snapped open. Something terrible. He was instantly wide awake. In the darkness it came again. A scream. Tears seeped, unbidden, from his eyes. He heard John jump out of bed. Together, the brothers stood in their room, some faint moonlight throwing up weird shapes and shadows in the near blackness surrounding them.

Roland could hear footsteps hurrying across the landing. John opened their door and, gripping his hand, Roland followed him into the pool of flickering light cast by their father's candle where he stood in the girls' open doorway. From behind his parents, Roland could see Agnes sitting up in bed, her arms holding Eva close. The younger girl was sobbing against her sister's chest. Her mother rushed over and Eva turned from Agnes and flung her arms round Lizzie's neck.

It was some time before she calmed down enough to explain why she had screamed and all the while the menfolk could only stand and watch from the landing. But Roland would always remember his sister's frightful words.

'I woke up feeling his grip tight around my ankle. It was like an icicle had formed around my leg; an icicle with fingers that wouldn't let go.' Eva started to cry again.

'It's alright, darling; it's alright. There's no one here.' Roland saw his mother hug Eva again.

'He's not here now,' sobbed Eva. 'As soon as I screamed he let go and vanished.'

'Vanished? So you saw him, then. Gripping your ankle?'

'Well, I could only see a vague shape in the dark, Father, but I knew he was there and then, when I screamed, he wasn't.'

Roland watched as his father held the candle aloft and said, 'Well, you can see there is no one else here, now. I'm afraid all that silly talk of ghosts last night has been giving you nightmares. Back to sleep, now, all of you. You boys get back to your own room.

But Eva and Agnes insisted they could never get back to sleep until, finally, Lizzie agreed to share their big bed, too. Roland would have liked to have his father share the boy's room but said nothing as he pulled the blankets up over his head and squeezed his eyes tight shut. It was a long time before the ponderous tick-tock, tick-tock in the hall faded and he drifted into unconsciousness.

The final encounter

Some of the shocking events that occurred the following day, Roland only heard about after it was all over as he listened to his parents converse in low tones, but he remembered them all his life.

The family awoke tired after the alarms of the night but it was a fine bright morning and things always seem better in the sunshine. There were some people Wesley had to see further down the peninsula so he would be gone until mid-afternoon. The children played in the garden but never strayed far from where they could see their mother through the kitchen window preparing dinner.

By the time the meal was finished the sky had grown dark and all the leaves were showing their backs as a strong breeze whipped though the branches. The thorn bushes were scraping against the drawing room windows and the wind was whistling in the chimney.

'It's scary in here,' said Eva, 'let's play upstairs.'

The others were quick to agree and they all trouped up to the Girls' Room.

It was about an hour later that Wesley tugged on the horse's rein and turned his gig into the driveway. It had been threatening rain all afternoon and the first drops were just beginning to fall. The overcast sky left the house shrouded in an unnatural gloom for the time of day. Wesley hurried up the steps and opened the big front door.

The stairs were immediately opposite and something drew his glance up to the shadowy landing above. He couldn't be certain... but... was there someone standing up there? Just outside the Girls' Room? He advanced to the foot of the stairs and started to climb. His head cleared the landing. There—unmistakeable, even in the poor light—he saw it. Or him. Undeniably. A powerful bare-backed man, the muscles of his black torso tense as he leaned towards the door in a listening stance.

Wesley shouted and reached into his travelling cape. His hand emerged gripping the revolver he always carried when journeying alone. The figure turned towards him bearing a frightful expression. Fear? No,

THE STORYTELLER

malice! The intruder took a step towards him. Without hesitation Wesley raised his weapon and pulled the trigger. The report was deafening and the flash momentarily lit up the empty landing.

A landing devoid of a body; devoid of blood spatters. A landing with nothing but splinters in the doorframe where the bullet had embedded itself.

But Wesley knew what he had seen. Clearly, with his own eyes. Not his children's wild imaginings or frightened nightmares. The apparition had faced him not six feet away and with clearly malevolent intent.

He determined the family would not spend another night within that house. Arrangements were made, belongings packed up and the Lyttles were soon in another barouche, with Wesley following in his gig, heading back through a steady drizzle towards Bangor. No one spoke as they drove. Everyone felt the relief of listening to the reassuring clip-clop of the horses' hooves on the damp road surface, taking them ever further from the Black Ghost of Ballygarvan.

The details of the three encounters with the ghost are exactly as my grandfather, Roland, related them to my father, and he to me. The experience was obviously deeply embedded in Roland's childhood memory with the facts no doubt re-enforced by the recollections of his older siblings as he grew up. As to the origins of the haunting? It is true that a few rich families in the Ards were slave-owners in the 18th century. Could some tragic death have occurred in the house? There is no record that WG ever tried to find out. Indeed, in all his writings, I have not found a single reference to his experience of the supernatural. It was an episode which, unable to explain, he chose not to re-visit. It was probably also the only time he ever discharged a firearm in self-defence. He never wrote of that either.

Chapter 19 – THE LITIGANT

1883 – 1884

Summonsed

Wesley got back from the family's brush with the supernatural, only to be faced with more unwelcome news. It came in the form of a writ from the High Court. This time, he actually *was* being sued for damages by William Henry.

I imagine his first reaction on reading the summons was to laugh out loud. He'd have known immediately that it was over his "Count Rhinocera" fable. Can't the man take a joke? he would have thought. Apparently not. We know from the article WG subsequently wrote in 1889 (mentioned in chapter 17—"A strange occurrence at the North Down Rifles Encampment") that the writ didn't bother him. He merely "tightened his belt and prepared for battle." And in the event the writ was withdrawn, with Henry's solicitor, Kelly, a notorious Newtownards lawyer, bearing the costs.

Was that to be the end of the matter? WG hoped not. He was fed up with Henry's constant searching for an excuse to bring an action and wanted the opportunity of roundly defeating him in court. Any time he bumped into one of the *Chronicle* editor's acquaintances he would urge them to encourage Henry to press his case. Henry, in the meantime, was taking merciless chaffing for having identified himself, in his own eyes, as the Count Rhinocera. But how had that become public knowledge? Well, WG printing Henry's writ of summons and statement of claim in the *Herald* might have had something to do with it. In the end, whether by now reluctantly or not, William Henry felt obliged to take the matter further.

A new summons was issued, this time jointly suing both WG and his printer, Robert S Allen—a cunning piece of legal skulduggery, advised by Kelly, to help his client win his case; if WG refused to crack, his printer might. The sum sued for was £1,000—the equivalent of about £118,000 in 2021. WG was now forced to take the matter seriously and secure the services of a solicitor, himself. Time had passed and the preliminary hearing was to take place in the High Court in Dublin on Thursday 22 November, 1883.

WG talked it over with his lawyer and devised their defence—they would simply deny libel; the story complained of was a fairytale, the Count was clearly identified as foreign. How could this be libellous to an Irish newspaper editor? And the amount of damages sought was ludicrous; surely no court would grant such a sum. The advice was to sit back and wait for the hearing and leave it to the barristers.

WG felt much better. So much so that he couldn't resist referring to the pending case in the *Herald*. He even, rashly, printed a pretend interview with the notorious 'Count Rhinosera' in which the count admitted to having once put ice on his curry as it was so hot. His *faux pas* was the subject of much mirth among his companions but the Count explained that the people amongst whom he had been brought up knew but little of the modern ways of civilisation. He had not seen much of the world at the time the incident occurred. WG's loyal readers enjoyed the joke.

In Dublin Court

It was Henry who had demanded the hearing be in Dublin, perhaps fearing a local jury might side with the defendant, a celebrated and popular humourist. Or he may just have been reluctant to have any more publicity given to the lampooning article in his own locality. In that, he would have been disappointed, however. We have the *Belfast News-Letter* of the 23rd November, 1883 to thank for its detailed coverage of the hearing which reproduced, in its entirety, the alleged libellous article that appeared in the *Herald,* from which I have quoted extensively in Chapter 17, above. The Ulster newspaper industry was taking a keen interest, much, I'm sure, to Henry's annoyance, and the *News-Letter* report provides us with a clear account of the court proceedings.

19 - THE LITIGANT

These opened by first establishing that the plaintiff, William Henry, was the proprietor of the *Newtownards Chronicle* and the defendant, WG Lyttle was the proprietor of the *North Down Herald, Newtownards Argos and Bangor Gazette*.[179]

At this point the judge intervened to ask, with a measure of incredulity, 'Do you mean to say there are *two* newspapers in Newtownards?' The barrister replied, 'There are indeed, my Lord.'

After the preliminaries, the QC acting for the defendants stated that the libel was denied and immediately asked for the case to be tried in Belfast which would be a much more convenient venue and less costly, too. The defendants would be calling upon ten witnesses including magistrates, sub-inspectors and others—all from Belfast and Newtownards. The plaintiff's legal representatives objected to any change that would delay the trial.

Further debate took place about the nature of the libel, the question being, said the judge, whether or not the statements made in the newspaper article referred to the plaintiff. They plainly do, answered Henry's barrister, drawing, I should imagine, a look of highly mixed feelings from his client. The legal man continued by drawing attention to the spurious interview with the Count that had been published since the writ was issued. This was manifestly written, the barrister claimed, to hold the plaintiff up to ridicule and show he was a vulgar fellow.

'The question will be,' said the judge, 'whether it points to the plaintiff? Is he to step into the witness-box and say, "Is this a picture of me"?'

I can imagine William Henry cringing in his seat. He was in the original "Catch 22" situation, a century before Joseph Heller came up with the notion. To prove WG's fantasy story was really about him and have it declared libellous and untrue, he would have to show how the wicked descriptions actually *could be* a depiction of himself, and true.

The judge was of the opinion that the publication of the writ of summons and statement of claim in the *Herald* might amount to a contempt of court. If an application were made for an attachment,

---

[179] This is the only reference I have come across to the 'Argos' title in WG's newspaper. It seems to have been dropped fairly soon after this time.

strong reasons would have to be shown why it should not be granted. Further discussion ensued but in the end, the judge agreed that the case should be tried in Belfast. A date was set for the end of March, 1884.

Lizzie

Following his newspaper's philosophy of 'Live and let live,' WG put all this aside for the next few months and got on with his life. He was more concerned about Lizzie. Her perking up on their move to Bangor proved only temporary and she just didn't seem to be herself in the months since. The disastrous holiday, far from helping, had probably made her feel worse since returning, and worrying about the court case can't have things any easier for her. Wesley tried to reassure her on the latter but he was worried about her. Her sister, Isabella, claimed she had never been the same since leaving Belfast.

During the long winter evenings Wesley was loath to leave her for long with all the children to look after. There was one event, however, that had been arranged for some time on Saturday evening the 16th February that he would have been reluctant to miss. Lizzie assured him she could manage fine. We have the details from the *Belfast News-Letter's* write-up the following Tuesday. Wesley and two friends had promised to provide entertainment for the invalids at the Throne Hospital in Belfast. The three showed a series of limelight pictures of beautiful Irish scenery with a collection of comic images, too, to amuse the younger patients. They were all accompanied by suitable songs, readings and recitations. It was similar to the event Wesley had organised for the Newtownards Workhouse and was equally well received. The Matron, in thanking them, said how she hoped "others might imitate their very successful efforts to relieve the dreary monotony of the sick bed." WG was only too pleased to have been able to help. (He had no notion then, that one day his great-granddaughter, my sister, Lorna, would start her pre-training as a nursing cadet in that same hospital.)

In Belfast Court

Before long it was March. WG was relishing having his day in court. Denying the libel in the Dublin court had put the onus on Henry to

19 - THE LITIGANT

prove his case and WG imagined this would be causing him to think long and hard about his position. He would have to stand in the witness box, or have others do so on his behalf, and swear how like William Henry the fabled "Count Rhinocera" actually was. He would be a laughing stock.

But Kelly's ruse was to avoid all that. On the morning of the trial, four of Henry's friends buttonholed Robert Allen, WG's printer, as he arrived at court. Whatever they said to him, offered him or cajoled him with, he was persuaded that his best path was to settle out of court. Henry would withdraw his action and the defendants would withdraw the imputations complained of by the plaintiff.

When WG heard this, he refused point-blank to have any part of such a deal; he was confident of winning in court and called for the case to be tried. Allen, however, was adamant. 'If you don't settle,' he said, 'I won't print your paper on Friday.'[180]

What could WG do? To his utter disgust, he was forced to relent and spare Henry his undoubted blushes. He drew up the statement himself which was accepted "with a few minor amendments"—this according to WG's own account. It was handed to Kelly to have typed up for all parties to sign and present to the court, which was duly done.

The *Ballymena Observer,* on Saturday, March 29, 1884 reported on the outcome:

> *The case which was an action brought at the instance of Mr. William Henry, proprietor of the* Newtownards Chronicle, *against the publisher and editor of the* North Down Herald, *was settled out of court today on the following terms:—*
>
> *In the High Court of Justice in Ireland, Exchequer Division—William Henry, plaintiff; Robert S Allen and Wesley G Lyttle, defendants:— It is hereby consented and agreed by and between the plaintiff and defendants, testified by the signature of themselves and their respective solicitors hereto annexed—that*

---

[180] WG quoted his ultimatum, verbatim, in the article already mentioned that appeared in the *Herald* in 1889.

the record in this action be withdrawn; and the defendants withdraw all the imputations complained of by the plaintiff, and regret the publication of the same; and the defendants undertake to pay the plaintiff's costs.

Swindled

There followed the names of the plaintiff and his solicitor, and those of the defendants and theirs. WG explained in his 1889 article that he and Allen had simply signed the typed version that Kelly returned to them, without reading it. The duplicitous solicitor had changed the wording "party and party costs"—a legal term implying that certain cost would be borne by the plaintiff—to read "solicitor and client costs," thereby putting the whole of the costs on the defendants. Sharp practice to say the least, but as WG put it, "forgetful of the person with whom we were dealing," they had signed it without reading it through. It was not until a fortnight later when the bill of costs came through that WG realised the swindle. And what a bill! It was for nearly £200 (about £24,000, today.)

WG determined to attend the Dublin Court when the bill came before the Taxing Master. Kelly's agent in Dublin was most surprised to see the defendant in the case present in court, especially when he proceeded to denounce the whole fraud that had been practiced upon him. However, the court decreed, whatever the circumstances, the document was legally signed and witnessed; the bill must be paid.

As to the amount of the bill WG had more to say. He challenged various items amounting in total, he claimed, to "about £200" (although the actual total must have been rather less than that otherwise there would have been nothing left to pay at all) and demanded that Kelly should be brought to court to swear that such expenses had been incurred. The case was adjourned pending an affidavit from Kelly. Kelly, was apparently unable to affirm that these particular expenses had been incurred and the items were struck off the bill.

We don't know the final costs that WG and his printer had to pay between them. It must have been only a fraction of the original demand but it would still have been a blow to the Lyttle coffers.

19 - THE LITIGANT

William Henry's triumph

It was enough, however, for William Henry to claim a magnificent victory and hype it up in his paper for all to see. Describing the scene after the out-of-court settlement had been rendered legally binding, the *Newtownards Chronicle* reported:

> *When the plaintiff in the action came from the Record Court with his solicitor and counsel into the hall he was warmly congratulated by his numerous friends at the satisfactory termination of what would otherwise, no doubt, have been a prolonged trial. It may be mentioned that Viscount Clandeboye came at considerable inconvenience from London to give evidence on behalf of the plaintiff, and that his respectable uncle, Captain and Adjutant George Rowan Hamilton, JP, were present...*
>
> *To his lordship and the other witnesses subpoenaed on behalf of the plaintiff, Mr Henry begs to tender his warmest acknowledgements for their faithful attendance at Court, and the interest they took in the case, which has terminated to the plaintiff's entire satisfaction...*

This was followed by a glowing account of his reception by the townsfolk upon returning home. It was headed REJOICINGS IN NEWTOWNARDS:

> *When the result of the action became known in Newtownards a large number of the respectable inhabitants made arrangements to give the plaintiff a fitting reception on his arrival from Belfast. About eight o'clock the Castlereagh True Blue Flute Band, accompanied by a large crowd, proceeded to the railway station, and, on the arrival of the train at 8.20 p.m., Mr Henry was greeted with loud cheering. On reaching the head of North Street he was met by a*

> *large concourse of people carrying an immense tar-barrel on a portable platform, and, having been surrounded by a number of his sympathisers, he was carried to his residence in Frances Street, followed by the band playing a selection of lively airs, including "See, the Conquering Hero Comes."*
>
> *The scene presented a most picturesque appearance from the glare of the several tar-barrels which had been lighted opposite the Chronicle Office, where upwards of 2,000 people had assembled to give him a hearty reception...*
>
> *Mr Henry appeared at one of [his] drawing room windows, and when the cheering had subsided said— It affords me very great pleasure indeed to find that I have such a large number of friends and supporters in Newtownards, a very strong contingent of whom are present tonight to congratulate me on my great victory today. (Cheers.) I have had a victory of a most agreeable character because of the fact that I was in the right and the libellers in the wrong... In my action against the defendants I have undoubtedly been successful, and I do not therefore want to crow over it. (Cheers.)*

He went on to mention his "great friends" Lord Clandeboye and Lord Dufferin, thanking them, along with all his legal team and everyone present, for their support.

> *I beg to thank you very much for your kindness which show me that the* Newtownards Chronicle *is still the local paper for the district, and in nowise have I, throughout this litigation, shown a vindictive feeling against any individual, no matter how little he may be. (Loud and continued cheering.) Cheers were then, at the request of Mr Henry, given for the Queen, and the vast assemblage separated, after the band had played the National Anthem.*

19 - THE LITIGANT

Two sides to every story

Henry obviously felt he had had his day in court—despite the fact that the action was never heard, as he had withdrawn his allegations of libel. He played it for all it was worth. How much exaggeration there was in his account of the reception given him we can't be sure; perhaps it was completely factual. It certainly rankled with WG who had been denied *his* day in court which, if granted, he was certain would have resulted in an altogether different outcome. That it so rankled, we can tell from the fact that five years later, when he came to write the 1889 article previously mentioned, he could still put his hand on his copy of the *Chronicle* account upon which to comment.

WG's version of the events of Tuesday 25th March, 1884 was rather different. Regarding the presence of distinguished witnesses, he wrote:

> *The Chiel had boasted in his article that "Viscount Clandeboye came at considerable inconvenience from London to give evidence on behalf of the plaintiff," and "that he and his respected uncle, Captain and Adjutant George Rowan Hamilton, JP, were present..."*
>
> *We can tell the Chiel and his friends what he and they possibly know, that the witnesses he names and many other respectable witnesses he does not name, while complying with the law, considered it gross impertinence on his part to have them served with subpoenas commanding them to attend in court. But the Chiel... is not the one to hesitate at serving a subpoena upon a youthful Viscount or upon a good natured Captain and Adjutant. He served subpoenas right and left, his object being to keep out of the witness box himself, and to seek to prove through the respectable and reliable witnesses that he was the blustering, lying, swaggering, vulgar and drunken fellow described as the Count Rhinocera! ...*
>
> *All the witnesses were promised golden rewards from five guineas per day down, but he never paid one*

of them. Had Allen remained firm, the Chiel would either have bolted from the courthouse, or else he would have made such an exhibition of himself as would have caused any jury to scoot his ridiculousness and impertinence out of court. No Ulster jury would have given him a verdict.

A passing word must be said regarding the "rejoicings in Newtownards," about which the Chiel prates. He made his arrangements in advance. The corner boy brigade, which is ever ready for a few glasses of whiskey, to do duty for him, either as the interrupters of public entertainment, or in carrying him at great personal risk upon their shoulders, was in full force when the Chiel reached Newtownards. He, himself, ordered the few tar barrels and had them lit outside his office, and when a crowd of the unwashed had gathered to hold their sides at the mouthing of a mountebank, he, from the "drawing room" window, bellowed his bad grammar and unsavoury billingsgate.

Archibald Thompson again

It must have been a relief for WG, a fortnight after his court attendance, to be reporting in the *North Down Herald and Bangor Gazette* upon someone else's legal problems rather than his own. It was Archibald Thompson once more.

On this occasion Thompson had accused a member of the Kirk Session of First Bangor Presbyterian Church, Mr M'Meekan, of misappropriation of funds whilst carrying out his duties as Town Clerk and Rate Collector. The Kirk Session had ruled that it could not judge the matter as it did not have access to the Town Commission's books. Thompson appealed their decision to the Ards Presbytery who upheld the session's view, so he appealed to the General Synod. They heard evidence that a Local Government Board auditor had found nothing irregular in Bangor Town Commissioners' books. Nevertheless after a long debate the outcome of Thompson's appeal was that the Synod agreed to set up a committee to look further into his accusations.

As he filed his report, WG was probably thinking about writing another chapter of his skit about Archibald and the Rulers—and future copies of the *Herald* flying off the newsstands.

Plans for the paper, for Lizzie and a new anthology

In the aftermath of his litigious battle with William Henry, and his being so let down—not to say held to ransom—by his printer, Robert Allen, WG resolved to take steps never to be in such a position again. He had been considering for some time the possibility of setting up his own printing press; he had the premises, all he needed was the machinery and the skilled operators to run it. He determined to formulate a definite plan to take matters forward. In the meantime he parted company with Robert S Allen and Son, having arranged for the printing of the *North Down Herald and Bangor Gazette* to be undertaken by W. & G. Baird, Telegraph Printing Works, 10 & 12 Arthur Street. W. & G. Baird were the printers and publishers of the *Belfast Evening Telegraph*.

Working upon his plans for the paper and the daily grind of producing a new edition each week helped to take Wesley's mind off Lizzie but he was still worried about her. She seemed to have little energy and tired easily. He had had a word with the children and asked them to assist as much as they could and not leave everything to their Mother. John helped when he was there, but now 18, he had started going up to Belfast each day where he was attending lectures on Steam, Machine Construction and Drawing, and Applied Mechanics at Engineers' Hall in College Street. John was beginning to lead his own life, preparing to enter the professional class, thus continuing the social advancement achieved by his father in his generation.

So it was rather left to his sixteen-year-old sister, Agnes, to be the main help for her mother. She sang as she went about her chores. "She does me a power of good, that girl, just listening to her," Lizzie would say. Wesley thought she looked brighter, too, when Agnes was around.

THE STORYTELLER

But as the summer wore on the Doctor came to the conclusion that what she needed was complete rest in order to let her recover. Her heart wasn't strong and that was causing shortness of breath and constant tiredness. She needed bed rest. Her sister, Isabella, who had remained a spinster and was still living in their old Madrid Street family home, straight away offered to have Lizzie for a few weeks. She could have complete rest, free from all the concerns of motherhood, running the household—and being a wife to the ever busy Wesley.

And so it was arranged. About a year after the infamous holiday at Ballygarvan, Lizzie would have another holiday—a proper one this time—with Isabella waiting on her hand and foot. Wesley assured his wife that the children would be safe in his care. She should just concentrate on getting well and didn't he have Agnes to help with running the home and looking after the younger children. They'd be fine.

He was much relieved by this plan, convinced it was just what Lizzie needed and, perhaps, even the return to Belfast and her old home, would prove a tonic in itself. WG was able to carry on with the work of producing the paper and even make some appearances at events, whether as himself or "Robin", to entertain his ever-adoring public. He was still with the Good Templars, too. An account in the *Belfast News-Letter* described him as Brother Lyttle when reporting on his giving one of his readings at a meeting of the Ballywalter Temperance Association. Apparently it "greatly contributed to the evening's enjoyment."

He heard from Isabella who said that she thought she saw a slight improvement in Lizzie but for her to get any real benefit from the rest she really should stay longer. Wesley went up to town to visit them. We can imagine how the conversation would have gone. 'I don't want to impose upon your good nature,' and his sister-in-law reassuring him, 'Och, she's hardly any bother at all and it's lovely to have her to talk to. Having her here is doing *me* good, so it is. Let her bide a wee[181] and we'll see how it goes.'

So Lizzie remained with her sister and WG managed to finish off a project he had been working on. He was bringing together all his

---

[181] Stay a while

19 - THE LITIGANT

stories about Paddy M'Quillan, most of which, along with a miscellany of other stories, had been included in the first volume of *Humorous Readings*. He intended to publish them in one volume that he would call *Robin's Readings Vol 1, The Adventures of Paddy M'Quillan*. He planned to have further volumes of *Robin's Readings*; and aimed to bring out the second one next year. That one would contain only stories about "Robin Gordon." He allowed himself a year as it wasn't just a case of lifting the stories from the various volumes of the *Humorous Readings* series. He carefully edited and, where necessary, updated or amended each one before it was ready to include in the new anthology. He must have been thrilled when the proof copy of *Robin's Readings* arrived from R. Carswell & Son in that autumn of 1884.

He was still researching, too, when he could get the time, for the two novels he was writing. He wanted to have a long yarn with a Ballyboley man about his boyhood recollections, to help him with the background for *Sons of the Sod*. He would also enquire about the gentleman's father and uncle who, he was told, had been United Irishmen. WG wanted to know all he could tell him about their involvement in the 1798 Rebellion. He wrote to his acquaintance and arranged to drive over the following week.

Agnes was doing a good job in her new role as homemaker and seemed to enjoy being "in charge", but her father was aware that the family could not go on like this indefinitely. The news from Isabella was not encouraging. All she could say was that Lizzie had not grown any worse since starting her rest cure. While she remained away Wesley was trying not to leave the children for long periods too often, but on the day of his planned visit he would have bade them farewell with strict instructions to the younger ones that they were to behave and do what Agnes told them.

We can imagine the horse in harness as he took his seat in the gig and flicked the animal's flank with the driving whip, waving good bye to the children all crowded in the bay window, waving back.

Moving off at a sedate pace, he little realised what life-changing consequences would result from an afternoon's crack over a cup of tea with William Byers of Ballyboley.

THE STORYTELLER

Chapter 20 – DEMOTED

1884 – September

Just for a moment we need to leave Wesley to enjoy in peace his leisurely trot along the narrow lanes of North Down, as he takes the Greyabbey Road, heading for Ballyboley. We have other matters to consider before he reaches his destination.

The Bankheads

WG's future granddaughter, my father's sister, was named Anne Bankhead Eveline, although she was always known in the family as Eveline. "How I was disgusted with that 'Bankhead' bit when I was young," she once wrote to my sister. "I was told it came from an illustrious ancestor who was physician to Queen ?? [sic] ages ago. Fancy even female descendants having to be thus burdened in order to perpetuate the distinction!"

How she actually came to be landed with such a name is an intriguing part of WG's story, worthy of record.

Charles Bankhead MD, born circa 1767, was the third son of the Rev John Bankhead, long-serving minister of the Non-Subscribing Presbyterian (NSP) Church in Ballycarry, County Antrim. In his capacity as a doctor, Charles became personal physician to the Prince Regent who later, as George IV, continued to engage him as *physician extraordinaire*. He was also believed to be the personal physician of Lord Castlereagh, the Foreign Secretary, who committed suicide in 1822. It is said that Dr Bankhead was hastily summoned on that occasion but arrived too late to save him. So this was the so-called "illustrious ancestor" of whom my Aunt Eveline wrote, although, in fact, it was not he, but one of his sisters, Anne Campbell Bankhead

20 - DEMOTED

who is linked into the Lyttle family tree due to her marriage to a farmer called William Byers Snr.

In the late 1700s, when he was still single, William Byers, a Ballyboley man, lived with his mother and brother, Alexander, in the historic "Grove Cottage." We do not know how he came to meet Dr Bankhead's sister, Anne—perhaps her father came as a visiting preacher to Greyabbey—but, however it happened, the two did meet, fell in love and were married towards the end of 1798. This was a momentous year in the Byers family as, indeed it was in the whole of Ireland.

"Grove Cottage"[182] was being used as a clandestine meeting place for the United Irishmen, who were determined to overthrow their despised English overlords by a nation-wide uprising. As WG would later record in his book about the rebellion, *Betsy Gray*, rather than risk losing both of her sons to the cause, old Mrs Byers persuaded her boys to draw lots to determine which would go off to lead the Ballyboley contingent into battle. The lot fell to younger brother Alexander, who sadly became one of the casualties of the ill-fated rebellion.

Thus it was that William survived the uprising of '98 to take Anne as his bride some six months later and, over the years, she bore him six children. It was his fourth child, Robert who would grow up to father no less than nine children of his own. His youngest daughter, Anne Bankhead Byers, was born in the December of 1846.

At that time, a few miles to the north-west, in Newtownards, a youngster named Wesley Little would soon be approaching his third birthday.

Interview with the Byers

Now, some 38 years later in 1884, that same Wesley, having completed his journey from Bangor, found himself sitting in "Grove Cottage" in Ballyboley. Since Robert's passing a few years ago this was now the home of his younger brother, William, the last surviving offspring of William Byers Snr, who had plotted with the United Irishmen in the very room in which they now sat.

---

[182] Photos of the much modernised "Grove Cottage" can be seen in Appendix F, Figs 12 – 14.

THE STORYTELLER

During the course of a long chat William was able to supply Wesley with all sorts of interesting information and anecdotes to help him with his novels and, on hearing that William and Robert used to attend Punch Balls, Wesley promised to include such an event in *Sons of the Sod* and give them both a mention. And, of course, when he was told how the house and its former occupants were involved in the lead up to the 1798 rebellion he assured William that both his father and his Uncle Alexander would feature in his Tale of '98.

As Wesley's formal research questioning was drawing to a close, we can imagine the scene, with William's wife joining them with tea and cake, served on fine bone china. Let us eavesdrop for a moment on the conversation, as subsequent events suggest it may well have developed:

'Very kind of you, Mrs Byers, very kind.' Wesley said, as he accepted the proffered cup.

'Jane. Do call me Jane. And some cake?' Mrs Byers handed him a plate.

'Thank you... Jane. I'm not used to such finery; most obliged.'

'Och, nonsense. I'm quite sure Mrs Lyttle's tea service is every bit as fancy as these.'

'I'm afraid Mrs Lyttle hasn't been at all well of late; it's a long time since we've had out the best china.'

'Oh, I'm sorry to hear that. I hope she recovers soon.'

'Nothing serious, I trust,' said William.

Wesley had not intended mentioning Lizzie, it had just slipped out. Now he found himself sharing his worries about his wife's poor health and his 16-year-old daughter's enforced labours looking after the family.

'You need to get yourself a housekeeper,' said William.

'Housekeeper. Yes, I suppose I do.' He had been so busy, he hadn't really thought about that as a solution. 'How d'you go about getting one of those?' he asked.

20 - DEMOTED

'Problem would be finding one I could trust with my younger children.'

He saw Jane glance at her husband as she inquired, 'How many children do you have, Mr Lyttle?' She picked up the teapot and offered him a refill.

'Thank you. Just a top-up. And it's Wesley, Mrs... er, Jane; Wesley. Four—five, including John, but he spends a lot of his time up in town, now. Studying engineering. The others are Agnes, Eva, who's 10, Roland, six and that just leaves little Robina, who is four.'

William Byers cleared his throat. 'We don't know each other well, Wesley; not personally, I mean but, of course I know a lot about you by reputation and from your writings. Very witty. And you're going to give us a mention in your book, now. Perhaps we can do you a favour in return.'

Wesley gave a slight bow of acknowledgement, wondering where this was leading.

The elderly gentleman's teacup rattled in its saucer as he put it down and continued, 'We might just be in a position to help you. One of Robert's girls, our youngest niece, Anne—I mean, she's a mature woman, forty... one –'

'Two, dear. Anne's 42; 43, come December.'

'Is she, really? We have so many children and nieces and nephews, I find it impossible to keep track. Well, like I said, a mature and capable woman. Lots of experience with small children. She's housekeeper to a family up in town at the moment, but she was saying only the other day, that that position will be ending shortly. I'm sure she'd be happy to help you out—until your wife is recovered.'

Four weeks later Anne Bankhead Byers proudly took up temporary residence at "Mount Herald" in her new position as housekeeper to the proprietor of the *North Down Herald and Bangor Gazette* and carer to his offspring.

And Agnes found herself demoted to being a child again.

Chapter 21 – ARCHIBALD THOMPSON

1884 – 1885

All Wesley's children must have been missing their mother terribly; the visits to see her in Belfast would have seemed to them to be too few and too far between. In one way, though, for the three youngest, it was probably an exciting change having Agnes in charge. She would have been more fun than their mother and let them get away with things when their father wasn't around. But there'd be other times when Agnes would have insisted that chores had to be done; they wouldn't have enjoyed that so much. We can imagine her asserting, 'Everyone must help. You heard what Father said,' and sounding, probably, just like her mother.

But by and large they would all have become used to the new family routine. And, Father would keep reassuring them that it was only for a little while longer until Mother was quite well again.

Then Miss Byers arrived.

Imagine their reaction. Miss Byers was old. While parents' ages don't particularly signify with children, anyone else of similar years is definitely old. At 42, Anne Byers was four years older than their mother, so must have seemed positively ancient to Robina and Roland. However, as Wesley introduced her to the children she would have greeted each of them with a big smile and a friendly hug and said how much fun they were going to have together. The two youngsters would have been prepared to take this at face value and grin back at her; Eva probably smiled politely and wondered what Miss Byer's idea of fun would turn out to be. If Agnes held her body stiff and unyielding to the new housekeeper's embrace, it was probably a momentary incident soon forgotten.

THE STORYTELLER

A new routine

Wesley must have felt the relief of having another adult in the household to look after his domestic affairs. He had been reassured by Miss Byer's obvious competence, confirming what her aunt and uncle had told him of her abilities. Now that she was settling in, he was finding her easy to talk to and work with. I'm sure he thanked Agnes for all her help before the new housekeeper arrived but he may well have been unaware of her resentment at having her position suddenly usurped by a stranger. All credit to Anne Byers, though—the household was managed well and the family were soon all getting along fine, at least on the surface.

It would have been a relief, too, for Lizzie knowing that her children had a responsible woman to look after them in her absence, particularly since she still felt she really couldn't face taking up her old routine again back at "Mount Herald", not yet; she just couldn't do it. She must have been so grateful to Isabella for allowing her to stay as long as she needed to. She and Wesley would have discussed the situation and Wesley would have talked with his housekeeper about the 'temporary' nature of her employment. Was she able to continue for the foreseeable future until Lizzie's health improved? It seems Anne Byers was glad to stay as long as she was needed.

Wesley's dog would have been happy to treat the newcomer as a friend as soon as she first put down a dish of food for him. Captain Sharrat, I believe, was more wary. At the first family meal that the new housekeeper had prepared she was surely horrified when Agnes brought the parrot's perch up to the table, hygiene being one of the many duties her role embraced. I can hear the chorus of protests from all the children—not to mention the squawk of indignation from the bird—when Miss Byers attempted to remove him. However, the children, with their father's support, must have won the day and Captain Sharrat continued to enjoy his meals with the family. But according to Roland, thereafter, the parrot always kept one beady eye on the housekeeper whenever she was around.

21 - ARCHIBALD THOMPSON

An upset at the polls

There was some excitement just down the road from "Mount Herald" on Monday, 20th October, 1884. It was Polling Day and a small crowd had gathered outside the office of the Town Commissioners about a quarter to five in the afternoon. From the subsequent reports in the papers we are able to join WG as the results are about to be announced.

He would have donned his top hat, and with a call to Miss Byers that he may be late for tea, stepped out from "Mount Herald" and hurried down Ballymagee Street. He would have had little time to admire the view of the bandstand across Bridge Street at the bottom of the hill, and on over Bangor Bay to Pickie Terrace, before joining the large knot of people milling around the office where polling had been taking place all day until four o'clock. The Presiding Officer, Mr M'Meekan, was just starting to address the people as WG arrived, full of interest to hear how the voting had gone.

Three sitting members, James Bowman[183], David Harvey and Hugh Furey had put themselves up for re-election but three other candidates were standing against them. One of these was Archibald Thompson, who had resigned his seat the previous year but had been persuaded to stand again. He had been vociferous during this election campaign, in accusations of misconduct by the Board. WG was intrigued to see if he had managed to oust one of the 'Clique' as he tended to think of the town's core rulers, who kept getting re-elected and seemed to be a law unto themselves.

'And the results are as follows.' Mr M'Meekan's words drew WG's attention back to the proceedings. 'Mr James Bowman—151 votes; Mr John Boyd—101 votes; Mr David Harvey—155 votes; Mr Hugh Furey—155 votes; Mr Charles Neill—66 votes; Mr Archibald Thompson—134 votes. Messrs Furey, Harvey and Bowman are therefore all duly re-elected.'

There were loud cheers from sections of the crowd and Mr Furey proposed a vote of thanks to the Presiding Officer and the agents who had conducted the poll in a business-like and non-partisan manner. Mr Harvey seconded the motion and thanked the voters for electing him

---

[183] James Bowman is not thought to be related to the retired editor of the Mourne Observer, Terence Bowman who helped me with my early research.

once more, for the ninth year in succession. One of the disappointed candidates, Mr Thompson, then spoke up, also in support of the motion:

'I am not sorry on my own account about this result but I am disappointed on behalf of the town that they should have supported the men who have been returned before they have cleared themselves of the charges which I have brought against them. As for me, both personal and church interests have been brought into the electioneering field to influence electors. I heard one individual ask another, "Would you vote for Thompson?" "Why, he would sink an Orangeman in a spoonful of water!" ' This produced cheers and laughter from the crowd.

Next, James Bowman, in support of the motion, thanked the electorate for returning him and said, 'While I remain at the Board I will most anxiously endeavour to retain your confidence. I will spare neither time, trouble, nor thought in order to keep the rates as low as possible and to improve the town. I had not meant to refer at all to Mr Thompson, but inasmuch as that gentleman has thought it proper to refer to certain charges circulated in a pamphlet, I feel it my duty, on behalf of myself and my brother Commissioners, to repudiate the statements contained in it. I don't need to tell you that the pamphlet is a reiteration of misrepresentation and falsehood which Mr Thompson has been repeatedly asked to prove, which he cannot do.'

'Name the falsehoods,' cried out Thompson. 'What about your unpaid rates?' This brought cheers from some and groans from others in the crowd.

'It is an infamous lie.' Mr Bowman declared.

'I call upon the Clerk to produce the books.' Archibald Thompson raised his fist and drew more cheers from his supporters.

James Bowman shouted over the noise from the crowd, 'Mr Thompson has thought it proper to use my name in reference to the rates being unpaid–'

'Rates against your property.'

'I have nothing whatsoever to do with the payment of rates upon my property. The tenant pays the rates.' The cheers now were coming from Bowman's supporters. He continued, 'In order to misrepresent the matter to the ratepayers he has put down my name in his pamphlet as not having paid the rates.'

21 - ARCHIBALD THOMPSON

'The rates are against your Kinnegar property.'

'I repeat, the payment of those rates is not my responsibility. Over and over, as I have been canvassing, I have been told that I owe rates and each time I have been obliged to explain the true state of affairs. As to the other charges brought by Mr Thompson, they are, in my opinion, calculated to injure the town. But the ratepayers have pronounced their verdict and placed Mr Thompson in a position as dishonourable as he deserves.'

WG would have smiled at this and wondered, I'm sure, if coming a fairly close runner-up to the strong, ruling clique, was quite as dishonourable as James Bowman was making out. He probably didn't think much of Thompson's accusation about the rates, but as he walked back up the hill to where he hoped his tea would be waiting, he must have shared Archibald's disappointment that the town, like sheep, had settled once more for the status quo.

As he turned in at the gate of "Mount Herald" and took out his keys, his mind would already have been formulating next Friday's editorial. We can imagine the front door opening to sounds of childish chatter around the tea table, drowned out by Captain Sharrat's raucous and most human-like laugh, with Anne Byer's calming voice maintaining a degree of order. Removing his top hat as he entered, Wesley would be met by the spaniel rushing to greet him in the hall, ears flopping and tail wagging, banishing all further journalistic thoughts from his mind. Wesley went in to join his family.

The *North Down Herald and Bangor Gazette* was reporting on the antics of Archibald Thompson again the following month. The gentleman was challenging the recent election of Messrs Furey, Harvey and Bowman on the grounds that the maintenance of the voters list had been highly irregular. The newspaper quoted Thompson's claims that ratepayers previously entitled to vote had been struck off the list without informing them and that when some turned up to vote they were not allowed to do so. Others, who should not have been entitled to vote because their rates had not been paid by the due date, were allowed. One person, Thompson claimed, was even allowed to vote for his sister who wasn't able to attend the polling station. For these and other similar reasons Archibald Thompson asked that a proper scrutiny be carried out and only legitimate votes be counted and that if he should then be found to have a majority he should be duly elected. Alternatively, the election should be declared illegal and, once the voting list had been prepared properly a further poll should be held.

Thompson was petitioning in court for a ruling upon the matter.

More books in preparation

Letters to the Editor on this controversy no doubt kept up the sales of the newspaper over the winter months and kept WG and his staff busy. In addition, though, to compiling or editing reports for his paper, WG was hard at work on no less than three different books as the church bells around the countryside rang in the New Year. 1885 would see the publication of his guide to Bangor for the summer visitors, around May time, and by the end of the year the serialisation of *Betsy Gray* would have commenced in his newspaper. This was destined to bring him even more lasting fame than his renowned *Robin's Readings*.

The third book was *Sons of the Sod* which is generally thought to have been serialised in the *Herald*, too. However, there are no extant copies of the *North Down Herald and Bangor Gazette* available over that period and I have been unable to discover any other evidence to confirm that it was serialised. Whilst it is not impossible that it could have been, I believe this to be unlikely because of the timing of its publication.[184]

Just as WG wrote about many real individuals in *Betsy Gray* who played a role in the '98 rebellion, even though his was a fictionalised account, when writing *Sons of the Sod*, he introduced many characters as "extras" in his tale who really did live in the area at the time of the events he relates. This must have helped enormously to popularise the

---

[184] *Sons of the Sod* was published as a book in November, 1886. *Betsy Gray* had been serialised in the *Herald* from 7th November, 1885 to the following September. So if *Sons of the Sod* were to have been serialised, too, it would have had to run from no later than June, 1885 in order to finish by October before *Betsy Gray* started in November. The problem with this is in explaining why WG waited over a year after serialisation before publishing *Sons of the Sod* in book form. It seems more likely that the text was not ready until the autumn of '86 just prior to publication. In that case it could not have been serialised first in the newspaper.

21 - ARCHIBALD THOMPSON

book as readers spotted themselves or people they knew among the pages.

One such character who WG mentioned on a number of occasions was Wully Yeaman. Gaynor Kane, the Belfast poet,[185] recalls that her great grandfather, William James Yeaman of Carrowdore was Wully Yeaman's grandson. And William Edgar, now living in Newtownards, who was born in Greyabbey, is proud to be the great-great-grandson of Eliza Askin of Ballyboley. She was one of a crowd of lasses that WG names as attending the big party given for his two heroes and their new brides towards the end of the book. The late Robert Byers and Robert's brother William also both get a mention for attending the dance, just as WG had promised William they would.

William James Yeaman of Carrowdore. (1882–1954), grandson of Wully Yeaman who features in *Sons of the Sod.* (Photo courtecy of Gaynor Kane, Belfast)

Much as he undoubtedly enjoyed writing his novel, WG still had a weekly newspaper to produce. He had run an interesting paragraph in his paper towards the end of '84 on behalf of a correspondent who was anxious to obtain a copy of an out-of-print book entitled "Killinchy." In January '85 the seeker was duly rewarded from a most unlikely source. A letter addressed to "the Editor of the *Bangor Gazette*" was received all the way from Pittsburgh, Pennsylvania. John Thompson, the writer, explained that a friend often sent him copies of the *Gazette* which he always read with interest, having been born on Ballymagee Street in 1806 and lived there until he emigrated in 1838. The reason for his letter was that the Board of Publication of the United Presbyterian Church of Pittsburgh had recently reprinted "Killinchy" which, he wrote, "is read with interest by many of the

---

[185] Gaynor Kane's full works "Venus in Pink Marble" 2020, is published by Hedgehog Poetry Press.

North of Ireland people in this country, particularly by those raised in the Ards."[186]

Mr Thompson said he had sent the editor a copy of the book through the Post Office and if, in return, he could be sent a copy of "Humorous Readings by Robin" he would be very pleased. He also asked to be informed of how much a subscription to the newspaper would be, with postage and promised to send a Postal Order for that amount in order to ensure he continued to receive his copy.[187]

Archibald Thompson's petition

Soon WG's attention was turned from Mr Thompson of Pittsburgh to a Thompson much nearer home. The following month, on Friday 13th February the Dublin courts were due to hear Archibald Thompson's petition. We can be sure that the *North Down Herald and Bangor Gazette* covered the story fully, but not having any copies from that period, I am indebted to the reporters of the *Belfast Weekly News* and the *Northern Whig* for the account of what took place. It seems the judge was convinced early on of the irregularity of the voters list. Proof of whether those struck off should not have been was not required. The judge was more concerned about Thompson's claim that a man had voted for his sister. Lengthy arguments were made by counsel and evidence given:

- three men were named who had voted for their wives who were the ratepayers;
- four named women voted for their husbands;
- a named woman voted for her mother (deceased);
- thirteen men and women were named who were on the voters list but did not have the statutory period of occupancy;

---

[186] Quoted from a clipping from the *Gazette* of John Thompson's letter contained in the scrapbooks held by the North Down Museum, Bangor.

[187] Mr Thompson was just one amongst a host of Americans who regularly read the *North Down Herald and Bangor Gazette*. In his story "My Brither Wully," *Robin's Readings Vol III,* WG has the returning emigrant, Wully, say, "A wush ye seen hoo mony *Bangor Gazettes* ir sent till Ameriky noo." ["I wish you saw how many *Bangor Gazettes* are sent to America now."]

21 - ARCHIBALD THOMPSON

- others were on the list whose premises were under £4 valuation;
- men were named who should have been on the voters list but weren't;
- further allegations were made that a number of people on the list were not entitled to vote as their rates had not been paid by the due date (but these could not be substantiated as the petitioner had been denied access to the books.)

In delivering judgement the Chief-Justice said that, at an early stage of the proceedings, the respondents had abandoned the right to uphold the election, inasmuch as more than a third of those who voted were females. According to the decision in the Queen v. Crosthwaite, women could not vote, so under these circumstances it would be impossible to sustain the election.[188]

Thompson, however, was not satisfied with this judgement, based solely on women voting. He wanted the judge to rule on the actions of the Town Clerk and Returning Officer in mishandling the maintenance of the all-important voters list, so that he could claim costs against them. The Judge, though, still majored on the fact that "It appeared, however, to be a common impression in Bangor that all females had a right to vote." The respondents clearly were under that impression, as too, the Judge suspected, was the petitioner. He declared the election void; that a new poll was to be held; that the Town Clerk was to prepare a new and proper list of voters and that all parties should bare their own costs.

As a result, a new election took place in March when Messrs Furey and Bowman were again re-elected but Mr Harvey lost his seat to a triumphant Archibald Thompson.

The Bangor Season, May 1885—the first production on WG's own printing press

Whilst reporting on the doings of the Town Commissioners and other choice titbits that had his readers queuing to buy each latest edition of

---

[188] This was several decades before the Representation of the People Act of 1918 was passed, giving women over the age of 30 the right to vote.

THE STORYTELLER

the *North Down Herald and Bangor Gazette* WG was making plans to transfer the printing of the newspaper once again. There were always hassles with printers, and W. & G. Baird were no better or worse than the others, but the only way to be hassle-free would be to print the paper himself. He finally had his own printing press installed, hired from a firm in Great Britain. The machine took up residence in the big shed to the rear of "Mount Herald," while the typesetting was all prepared up in the second floor offices of the tall house. The newspaper's reporting staff was now supplemented by typesetters and a printer along with some new apprentices.

The first production of the newly established "North Down Print Works" was probably WG's travellers' guide which he called, *The Bangor Season—What's to be seen and How to see it,* and whose cover stated it was "Compiled and published by W. G. Lyttle, Bangor, Co. Down."[189] It was most likely published in May to be in time for the bulk of the summer visitors.[190] It includes a plethora of interesting information not only about Bangor itself but of many nearby destinations that can be reached during a short tour from the resort by those spending a season in the town:– Ballywalter, Conlig, Crawfordsburn, Clandeboye, Donaghadee, Groomsport, Greyabbey, Helen's Tower, Millisle and Newtownards are all covered.

The little booklet, measuring about seven inches by four-and-a-half, ran to over a hundred pages, including many adverts to offset the production costs. *The Bangor Season* contained such delights as WG's account of St Patrick's Well at Templepatrick (see chapter 18, above) and a description of Helen's Tower. WG drew upon his literary knowledge and included two poems that Alfred Lord Tennyson and Robert Browning had written in the tower's honour. The guide also proffered suggestions such as one advising lady readers that they would be "well repaid by a visit to M'Kenzie's Irish Embroidery on Ballymagee Street whose exquisite needlework was famed throughout the world and had won the patronage of her Majesty the Queen." This contrasted with fascinating facts such as the "Bangor Castle"—one of

---

[189] I have found no copies of the original publication, only an abridged facsimile copy published by Appletree Press in 1977.

[190] The book contains reference to the death of a prominent Bangorian in April, 1885 so it must have been published later than that.

21 - ARCHIBALD THOMPSON

the two paddle steamers that daily brought Belfast's summer visitors to Bangor—being originally commissioned from its Clydebank shipbuilders to run the blockades of New Orleans and other southern ports during the disruptions of the late Civil War in America, and, just for good measure, that the crews of the two steamboats were all tee-total.

WG was normally a stickler for detail and accuracy (unless writing some satirical piece, of course, when all such conventions were derisively cast aside.) Unaccountably, however, *The Bangor Season* does contain a couple of factual errors in the section dealing with Newtownards. He describes the town as standing "at the southern end of Strangford Lough," when, in fact, it is situated at the northern end of that vast inlet from the Irish Sea. The second is similar in nature. He writes, "At the southern extremity of the square [Conway Square] stands the parallelogram-shaped building called the Assembly Rooms, or, more commonly, the Market House." This building actually forms the northern edge of the square. I can only surmise that the typesetter misread WG's handwriting of the word "northern" and the two instances escaped the proof-reading stage.

There is another typo in a footnote about M'Kee's famous "Scrabo Shoes." WG gives the address of the Ards Boot and Shoe Warehouse as 80, High Street, when it should have been 30, as evidenced by a full page advert for the shoe shop in the same publication. As it was right next door to the original office of the *North Down Herald* he should have got that right, but, again, it was probably a transcribing error—a poorly written 3 could look like an 8.

But, in spite of a few errors, his travel directory proved popular. To give it added appeal, WG opened the book with what he called, "The Parables of the Rulers," a reprint of all his skits upon "the doings of the Bangor Town Commissioners." He hoped visitors would appreciate the humour as much as the townsfolk had when the sketches appeared in the *Gazette*—which abbreviated name for the newspaper now tended to be used, rather than the *Herald*, when it was referred to colloquially. There is even an advertisement in the travel guide, not for the *North Down Herald and Bangor Gazette,* but simply for "the *Bangor Gazette."*

THE STORYTELLER

More self-publishing

Having successfully produced the *Bangor Season* on his own press and now also printing his weekly newspaper, WG decided to self-publish a second edition of the first volume of *Robin's Readings—The Adventures of Paddy M'Quillan* to coincide with R. Carswell and Son bringing out *Robin's Readings Volume 2—the Adventures of Robin Gordon*. They were most likely produced in the latter half of 1885.[191]

During this hectic year WG was also trying to get his third volume of *Readings by Robin*[192] ready before Christmas, though it was looking as though that deadline may to have to slip by a month or two.

A news item that would undoubtedly have appeared in the columns of the Gazette in 1885 concerned some ground-breaking work in the study of diseases and their prevention. WG would have made reference to his editorial on the subject of hydrophobia, or rabies, as it is more commonly called, that appeared in the third edition of the *North Down Herald* on the 31st July, 1880. He would have been pleased to announce to his readers that now, just five years later, a French scientist by the name of Louis Pasteur had developed a vaccine that had saved a little boy's life when he had been badly bitten by a rabid hound.

Commissioner Thompson upsets the Board

Apart from international news, there was, of course, always plenty happening on the home front, not least of which was covering the on-going saga of the doings of Archibald Thompson.

Perhaps not surprisingly, his presence back on the Board was not universally welcomed by the other eight Town Commissioners. A report of their monthly meeting in May in the *Belfast Weekly News*

---

[191] We know both these books appeared prior to the publication of the third volume of *Readings by "Robin"* in May, 1886 because that book contains footnotes which read, "See Robin's Readings Vol 1, 2nd Edition" and "See Robin's Readings Vol 2."

[192] The 1st and 2nd editions of Vol I were entitled *Humorous Readings by Robin*, as was the 1st edition of Volume II. By the 2nd edition of Volume II, however, WG changed the title to just *Readings by Robin*, which he used for the 1st and subsequent editions of Volume III, as well.

21 - ARCHIBALD THOMPSON

tells us that "owing to a series of unpleasant passages between Mr Thompson and several members of the Board, the chairman vacated the chair, and the meeting broke up in confusion."

Throughout June and July there was plenty for WG's reporters to submit for publication following each Board meeting. There was Thompson's investigation into the payment of a cheque for £5 19s to a labourer, one R Legg, to cover his invoice for £1 15s. Mr Legg paid the difference in cash to the Town Clerk. On another occasion Mr Thompson strongly opposed an application for a loan to cover various unpaid invoices.

He called a public meeting in Bangor Courthouse on Wednesday 15th July, which all the Town Commissioners were requested to attend and accused them of misappropriating a loan that had been procured to re-lay the gas main through the town. No new pipes had been laid. In relation to the loan he had, in common with all the other ratepayers, been led to believe that the capital and interest would be paid off at the rate, and over the period, that had been quoted. However, on taking up office as a commissioner he had discovered that the reported payments only covered the interest and no facility was in place to repay the capital.

Another speaker at this public meeting said of the commissioners that, while "in their individual capacity as men he respected them very highly, as a Board, he had no confidence in them." He commented on the fact that their meetings were often adjourned with business uncompleted and alleged that sometimes it had even been arranged that there would not be a quorum present so no business could be transacted. He moved the following resolution: "As it appears evident to the ratepayers who have recently attended the meetings of the Town Commissioners that the affairs of the township are not being conducted satisfactorily, we hereby call upon the Chairman and other Commissioners who are acting in concert with him to resign their seats unless they can show that they are not responsible for the present state of affairs owing to the baneful influence exerted by their colleagues and officers."

From the report in the *Northern Whig* it would seem that no other commissioners attended the public meeting although a Mr Brown, the Clerk of Works for the sewage scheme was a vociferous presence. Brown was eventually ejected from the meeting for his continuous interruptions. But the Bangor Town Commissioners' days were numbered. As we shall see in the next chapter, they would not long survive these public expressions of no confidence.

Sued for libel

WG reported the woes of the Town Commissioners week by week as factually as he could. While not being overtly anti-commissioners—or, more specifically, the Clique amongst the commissioners—he was most certainly pro-ratepayers. His paper's reputation amongst the general readership was thus high but held in a degree of contempt by certain of the Town Commissioners.

He found himself reporting again upon Archibald Thompson a fortnight after the infamous public meeting. Commissioner M'Meekan had taken out a libel action against Thompson the previous year following the accusation of embezzlement he had made against him. The case finally came to court in the summer of 1885. M'Meekan, who had been training for the ministry but dropped out after a year, was claiming £1,000 in damages.

His barrister presented all the evidence to the court on Monday 27th July and the next day Archibald Thompson mounted his defence. Unlike WG who, albeit reluctantly, had agreed to apologise for his alleged imputations against William Henry, Thompson strongly defended his position, attempting to prove to the court that his allegations were true and, therefore, not libellous.

The judge, however, was not convinced and said, that by his submissions to the court Thompson had perpetuated the libel. Judgement was given against him with damages set at £75. This was nothing like the £1,000 claimed, but was still a hefty sum for Thompson to find, being equivalent to around £9,000 in 2021. Indeed, it was to prove a crushing burden upon his finances, as we shall see. It must have helped boost the circulation of the *Gazette*, though.

The launching of *Betsy Gray*

WG had been writing *Betsy Gray*, on and off, since 1883 and researching for it well before that. His hard work was nearing completion. *Betsy Gray or Hearts of Down, a Tale of Ninety-Eight,* as he had decided to call his novel, was an historical documentary

21 - ARCHIBALD THOMPSON

thriller/romance about the 1798 rebellion in Ireland. WG needed a framework of factual accuracy upon which to hang his fanciful tale of the beautiful heroine who fought alongside her brother and her sweetheart, and spurred on the rebels at the fateful Battle of Ballynahinch. Whereas *Sons of the Sod* had a background set in a period that he knew well from growing up in the Ards in the '50s, WG did not have that advantage with *Betsy Gray*. To provide the authentic details of everything that led up to that terrible battle and its horrific aftermath he turned, initially, to a number of written sources.

CH Teeling's *Personal Narrative of the Irish Rebellion of 1798*, published in 1828, and the Rev William Steele Dickson's *Narrative of his Confinement and Exile*, published in 1812, were two such books which could have first come to WG's attention gracing the shelves of his circulating library in Belfast. The influence of the poets, Shelly and Byron, who portrayed Lord Castlereagh as a cold and heartless tyrant, could account for WG's own references to the cruelty of the Londonderry family at the time.[193]

WG's account of the martyrdom of William Orr was informed by a history written by the Young Irelander, Thomas MacNevin.[194]

So, as the autumn nights were drawing in, WG was putting the finishing touches to his novel. Having already borrowed successfully from Charles Dickens' example of reading his own stories on stage, he had decided also to follow the late English writer's practice of serialising his work in a weekly journal prior to publishing it in book form. As I have mentioned, there is no evidence that *Sons of the Sod* was serialised first before being published. So, when the first chapter of *Betsy Gray* appeared in the *North Down Herald and Bangor Gazette* on 7th November, 1885, WG would have waited with some trepidation for the public's reaction.

---

[193] I am indebted to historian, Kenneth Robinson, whose research has established the above-mentioned books and poets as being WG's sources. Robinson mentions, for example, that WG repeats Teeling's error of calling Archibald Warwick "William Warwick".

[194] This comes from the research of Guy Beiner in his book, *Forgetful Remembrance* (Oxford University Press, Oxford) He also quotes bibliographer and librarian, Stephen Brown, of Holywood, County Down, who noted that Lyttle "has gone over every inch of the ground, and has hunted up old documents and old traditions indefatigably."

THE STORYTELLER

He needn't have worried. From the start it was well received, with readers writing in with their own families' recollections of the period. The unfolding tale helped to boost sales of his newspaper and, no doubt, its advertising revenue, right through to the completion of the story the following September.

While all was going well with his newspaper and his writing, a matter of continuing concern to Wesley was the health of poor Lizzie. She just didn't seem to be able to start picking up again from her illness and, while some days were better than others, Wesley thought he saw, if anything, a gradual decline in his wife's condition. Lizzie and he were so grateful to her sister, Isabella, who continued to look after her.

Back at "Mount Herald," Anne Byers ran Wesley's household with consummate efficiency. While the two older children's attitude to her never seemed to progress beyond restrained politeness, and this at Wesley's insistence, Anne got on well with the three younger siblings who must have appreciated her presence and ministrations while their mother's health continued to prevent her return.

So Wesley's home life, whilst as good as could be expected under the worrying circumstances, nevertheless must have put something of a damper on his business successes.

Bankrupt

On the Monday of the week that the first chapter of *Betsy Gray* appeared in Saturday's *Gazette* the Bangor Town Commissioners met following the previous month's elections. Archibald Thompson had been re-elected and at the meeting on Monday 2nd November, 1885 he was appointed chairman of the Board.

In his business life, however, eight months after his punitive fine by the courts, Thompson was not faring so well. By March, 1886, WG was reporting in the *Gazette* that, under the provision brought in by the Bankruptcy (Ireland) Amendment Act of 1872, Thompson had applied to the courts to have himself declared bankrupt. He had sold all his furniture to his brother, James, for £130 and assigned him his six-bedroomed home, Oriel House, for £50. The bulk of this money went to pay off a bank overdraft of just over £118. He was, he told the court, possessed of very little property. His creditors claimed the

21 - ARCHIBALD THOMPSON

house was worth £300 and this was just a ploy to avoid meeting his debts.

As WG wrote up this latest account of one of Bangor's most notorious citizens, did he feel a touch of sympathy at all for the outspoken commissioner? He would probably have found it hard to empathise with him, or imagine how Archibald Thompson must have been feeling as he walked out of Belfast's Bankruptcy Court on a cold day in March, wondering how he was going to rebuild his life.

There would come a time, however, when WG would know exactly how he felt.

THE STORYTELLER

Chapter 22 – HOT OFF THE PRESS

1886

WG was editing the stories that would form the contents of the third volume of *Readings by Robin*. What with all the work involved in preparing *Betsy Gray* for serialisation, his original, self-imposed Christmas deadline had come and gone, as he had feared it would; in the New Year of '86 he was still putting together the anthology. Church music remained a contentious issue with some strongly held views from both the traditionalists and modernists among the local Presbyterian congregations. The controversy had provided WG with plenty of scope for satire and three of the first four stories of the new volume had it as their theme. "The Newtownbreda Harmonium" was about the introduction of this keboard instrument to play the tunes for the Newtownbreda congregation. "Robin" writes:

> *Ye ken A'm terble fond o' music, an' a guid wheen fowk in Ballycuddy thinks me waur than an infidel acause A want them till get a harmoneyum fur oor meetin'-hoose. Mebbe it's acause it's a sin that sae mony fowk ir taen on wi' it. Sum grate man yince said in a book, "music haes charms till smoothe the savage breest," an' that's rael true. Mebbe A'm a bit o' a savage whun A'm sae fand o' it. A ken this, that whun A get oot o' sorts at ony time a birl o' the fiddle jist pits me richt.*[195]

---

[195] You know I'm terribly fond of music, and a good number of folk in Ballycuddy think me worse than an infidel because I want them to get a harmonium for our meeting-house. Maybe it's because it's a sin that so many folk are taken on with it. Some great man once said in a book, "music has

22 - HOT OFF THE PRESS

Then there was the story of how the matter was addressed at the General Assembly that we looked at in Chapter 12, "Other content." The third tale was about the Ballycuddy Precentor, who took the huff and resigned from his job of starting off the singing—raising the tunes—of the Psalms at the Sunday services. WG's account of that was amusing and light-hearted, as always, but even he would never have written in his fictional tales what he found himself reporting in the *Gazette* that February while he was still polishing up his fantasy about the Ballycuddy Precentor.

Prayer meeting disrupted

The congregation of First Bangor Presbyterian Church had recently appointed one of their members to be their precentor and raise the tunes at their meetings, the Church not yet having embraced the modern notion of using an organ. Now this was a task that Archibald Thompson had been used to carrying out on a voluntary basis. What with one thing and another, not least the bankruptcy case looming over him, he had not been attending his church so regularly and was unaware of the new appointment.

He turned up to a mid-week prayer meeting in early February and when the first Psalm was announced he started it up. This happened again with a second Psalm. When it was time for a third Psalm, the new Precentor stood up and said he would start this one, which he proceeded to do. Incensed, Archibald Thompson promptly started a different tune and half the worshipers tried to sing along with him while the other half gamely continued to follow the Precentor's tune. The resultant musical disharmony developed into physical discord, too, and Thompson had to be ejected from the meeting by two of the congregation, whom he subsequently sued for assault. They countersued and the whole story was revealed in court and reported by the local press and as far afield as the Dundee Advertiser. The magistrate ruled against Thompson, fining him 10s and bound him over to keep the peace.

---

charms to sooth the savage breast," and that's real true. Maybe I'm a bit of a savage when I'm so fond of it. I know this, that when I get a bit out of sorts at any time a twirl of the fiddle [tune on the violin] just puts me right.

THE STORYTELLER

As that particular item went to press, WG must have been thinking his fans would never have believed him if he had made up such a story about the good Presbyterians of Ballycuddy.

Thompson's unguarded tongue

It was only a month later that the other Town Commissioners were to read in the *Bangor Gazette*, with concerned interest, the news that their chairman was now a bankrupt. They called a special meeting in April to consider their position.

On the 9th of the month the commissioners duly turned up at their meeting room on Ballymagee Street and, along with other members of the press, the *Gazette* had a man there to record the events. Archibald Thompson took the chair, as was his custom, but another commissioner, Samuel M'Cormick objected to this, as the purpose of the meeting was to discuss Thompson's position. It was agreed the clerk should act as chairman *pro tem*. Commissioner Morrow then proposed that Samuel M'Cormick be elected chairman. Commissioner Robinson seconded this and the motion was passed.

The *Gazette* reported Thompson as saying that Robinson was an old humbug who would be guided by anything Morrow suggested. Thompson stated that he was surprised that Morrow had proposed a branded thief as their chair, to which Robinson responded by calling Thompson a liar. 'Of course,' Thompson added, 'I understand why one brother [freemason] would nominate another.'

The exchange continued and became heated. Thompson's words were such that, when quoted verbatim in the *Gazette* the next day, Mr M'Cormick felt obliged to issue a summons against Thompson for using insulting language towards him.[196] In court Thompson conducted his own defence, as usual, but reason prevailed and he agreed to apologise to Mr M'Cormick and that his apology should appear in the *Gazette*.

WG printed Thompson's statement in the next issue, without a hint of embarrassment at having, perhaps, been partly responsible for

---

[196] Whilst, unfortunately, we do not have a copy of that issue of the *North Down Herald and Bangor Gazette*, all of the foregoing was reported in the *Belfast News-Letter's* account of the ensuing court case, including the fact that Thompson's outbursts were recorded in the *Gazette*.

M'Cormick suing Thompson in the first place (would he have done so if Thompson's insults had not been made public in the Gazette?) It ran: "I apologise to Mr Samuel M'Cormick, of Bangor, for the language used to him at the meeting of the Bangor Town Commissioners of the 9th April, and published in the *Bangor Gazette* of the 10th April, 1886, and regret having used it." The whole debacle—the court case and the apology and how it all reflected on the Bangor Town Commissioners, would, I feel sure, not only have been reported as a news item but would have featured in WG's editorial that week, as well.

It is interesting to note that about this time the *North Down Herald and Bangor Gazette's* rival newspaper, the *Newtownards Chronicle* carried in its April 3rd edition a new column headed 'Bangor Notes and News.' It was preceded by this statement:

> *We beg to inform our readers that we have made special arrangements for the publication of NOTES AND NEWS FROM BANGOR and its neighbourhood in the CHRONICLE. We have taken this step at the request of many respectable inhabitants of Bangor, who are anxious that their local news should be published in a paper of established reputation and extensive circulation.*

—an obvious sideswipe at the *Gazette*. The news items covered appear to be accurately reported but lacking in spice or individuality. I doubt if WG lost any sleep over this new departure—nor his newspaper many sales.

A third volume of humour

The next month, May 1886, finally saw the publication of *Readings by Robin—Volume 3* by University House, Allen, Son and Allen (formerly, Allen and Johnston, who had published the first two volumes of *Humorous Readings*.) So WG must have forgiven Robert Allen for letting him down in the libel case, or at least let business interests prevail.

THE STORYTELLER

In the preface to the book, writing as "Robin," he said:

> *My dear Friens,*
> *Whun A tell't ye a wud hae the Third Volyum reddy aboot Krismas, a no had ony idea that it wud be langir; but my! hoo the wurld diz flee, an' time rins wae it. A wunner whaur they hae gaun tae? A ken mony o' ye hae been axin' ivery whaur fur this volyum; but noo ye can tak yer fill o' the "Oyster Supper" an' the "Hither Dew"[two of the stories in the book.]...*[197]

Following a few more comments about the contents, he finished by touching on politics and the first Home Rule Bill, saying that the General Assembly would be discussing the "Instraymental" question (church music) this year for the last time,

> *afore the Hame Rool Bill diz cum intil pooer; fur Peggy sez—'Weemun wull hae their Richts.'*
> *Your auld Weelwisher,*
> *Rabin Gordon*
>
> *Ballycuddy, County Down,*
> *May the saxteen, 188sax.*[198]

This latest batch of stories was received with much enthusiasm. Its popularity rekindled public demand for WG's tales and, in July, the publishers brought out a large second edition of Volume 2; they must still have had stock of the second edition of Volume 1, published in '83. In a short preface to this second edition of Vol 2 WG wrote (as

---

[197] My dear Friends, When I told you I would have the Third Volume ready about Christmas, I had no idea that it would be longer; but my! how the world does fly, and time runs with it. I wonder where they have gone to? I know many of you have been asking everywhere for this volume; but now you can take your fill of the "Oyster Supper" and the "Heather Dew".

[198] ...before the Home Rule Bill does come into power; for Peggy says– 'Women will have their Rights.' Your old Well-wisher, Robin Gordon Ballycuddy, County Down, May the sixteenth, 188six.

"Robin") that "A hae no' been weel fur sum time," presumably reflecting WG's own state of health. It would be another reason why he failed to keep his promise of the previous Christmas deadline for his third volume.

In the same year R Carswell & Son Ltd published a third volume of WG's stories in the "Robin's Readings" series.[199]

Riots

"Robin's" reference to Home Rule was, of course, topical. Ulster was experiencing a period of considerable political unrest. In February, the Conservative MP Randolph Churchill delivered a rousing speech to a packed Ulster hall about the need to stand against any attempt to introduce Home Rule in Ireland. An autonomous Irish parliament in Dublin, he claimed, would favour the agricultural South over the industrialised North, promote the majority Catholic religion in the South over Protestantism in the North and lead to the eventual breakup of the Union. His speech appealed not only to Orangemen but to prominent protestant churchmen, many Tory MPs and solid middleclass citizens and farmers, too. In an open letter to a Glasgow Liberal unionist in May, Churchill coined the phrase, "Ulster will fight and Ulster will be right!" and this became the rallying cry amongst Ulster's protestant unionists for nigh on the next hundred years.

Gladstone, re-elected as Prime Minister, introduced what became known as the First Home Rule for Ireland Bill in April, 1886. As it turned out, the Bill was voted down on its second reading in the Commons on the 8th June and the Liberal Party was soon relegated to the opposition benches once more. Protestant shipyard workers celebrated the Bill's defeat by taunting Roman Catholic co-workers and fighting broke out that escalated into full-scale rioting over the next few days—the worst that the streets of Belfast had ever known. Catholic homes and businesses in the city were attacked. Largescale police and army reinforcements had to be brought in to re-establish the peace. Further rioting erupted a few weeks later during the 12th July marches. Feelings in the city continued to run high on the

---

[199] See Appendix B for a complete list of WG's works

question of Home Rule, loyalty to the Crown and Protestant versus Catholic dominance. Sporadic skirmishes went on until September. Right or not, Ulster *will* fight.

There had been earlier skirmishes that had also resulted in the police breaking up the crowds—with varying degrees of force. They had prompted WG to write a story in which "Robin" witnessed an incident of police brutality. He described some officers as "doon-richt savages." "Robin" wrote:

> ...amang ither things a seen a man frae Glesgo gettin' his heid brauk, an' if it hadnae been that my son-in-law an' anither man hel' me, A wud a tuk the peeler's stick frae him an' gien him a thoro' guid threshin'.[200]

WG's feelings were running high. "Robin" gives evidence in court against the offending policeman, who, he says, yelled out an Anglicisation of an old Irish battle cry as he laid into the Scotsman—Faugh-a-ballagh![201] However, in spite of "Robin's" eyewitness testimony, the case was dismissed and WG ends his story on a satirical note of sarcasm:

> It bates ocht, this law! It luks tae me sumtimes as if it wuznae jistis; but a suppoas that maun be my ain ignerance.[202]

And that story, "The Faugh-a-ballagh Pleeceman and his Baton" appearing in WG's third volume of *Readings by Robin* in May 1886 was being read around the Province over the next few months while Belfast police were trying to control the city's worst ever rioting.

---

[200] ...among other things I saw a man from Glasgow getting his head broken, and if it hadn't been that my son-in-law an' another man held me, I would have taken the policeman's stick from him and given him a thoroughly good thrashing.

[201] Pronounced Faugh (to rhyme with lough) – ay – bal-aa (emphasis on the last syllable) and meaning, Clear the way!

[202] It beats anything, this law! It looks to me sometimes as if it wasn't justice; but a suppose that must be my own ignorance.

Once again, the timing of one of WG's publications couldn't have been more fortuitous.

The rioting and the whole Home Rule controversy also occurred during the serialisation of WG's *Tale of '98,* the story of the rebellion of the United Irishmen almost 90 years earlier, where Protestants and Catholics fought side by side against the British. But he had been right. The passage of decades had separated the historical tale from current events in his readers' minds and, against all the odds it would seem, in spite of the current political state of the country, *Betsy Gray* remained a favourite read in the columns of the *Gazette* every week.

Engineering success—and failure

While Wesley's books were hitting the newsstands, his eldest son, John, was busy studying for his exams. Later in the summer, the *Belfast News-Letter* of Thursday, August 19, 1886 reported on the 'Successes Gained by the Students' attending Science and Technical Classes, Engineers' Hall, Belfast under the tuition of WJ Fforde. I am quite sure, although no copy survives, the *North Down Herald and Bangor Gazette* of Saturday, August 21st, 1886 carried the same report.

Amongst the names of successful scholars was that of John Wesley Lyttle. He is listed four times; first, under Machine Construction and Drawing, Elementary stage—First Class; next, Steam, Elementary stage—First Class; then, Applied Mechanics, Elementary stage—First Class; and finally, City and Guilds of London Institute of Mechanical Engineering, Ordinary grade—Second Class. All in all, a worthy achievement and a fine way to celebrate his 20th birthday a few days later on the 24th. His academic prowess must have made his mother and father very proud of him and Lizzie would have brightened up in spite of her poor health when she heard how well he had done. On the strength of his results John was soon able to secure a good job for himself with the railways.

Just three weeks later the news from Belfast was of a much more sombre nature. As WG was growing up he had learned that the 'new' Queen's Bridge was opened the year he was born, but the Albert Bridge, he knew, was some ten years older, having been opened in

THE STORYTELLER

1834. The 18th September edition of the *Gazette* carried the appalling news that two spans of the multi-arched Albert Bridge had collapsed into the River Lagan at around a quarter to eight the previous Wednesday evening with the loss of at least two lives and others injured. The reporter had discovered that the bridge had recently shown signs that parts of it were slowly sinking and work had already been started to remedy this, alas, too late for Wednesday's victims.

Just rewards?

The collapse of the Bangor Town Commissioners followed barely a month later. Since the ratepayers' declaration of no confidence in them, the Board had finally been forced to resign and Bangor's affairs were now temporarily in the hands of the Newtownards Board of Guardians. The *North Down Herald and Bangor Gazette* recorded the event at the time in WG's usual satirical style. He drew a picture of a graveyard monument and under it inscribed:

IN MEMORIAM
Bangor Town Commissioners
WHOSE BRIEF CAREER
TERMINATED ON
FRIDAY 15TH OCTOBER, 1886

Clipping from the *North Down Herald and Bangor Gazette* held in the "North Down Huseum"

There followed these two verses:

Kind reader pause and drop a tear
The Board is dead, alas, alas!
How true the words you oft-times hear–
"Our life is short, all flesh is grass."

Some day the Board may rise again,
If so, kind reader, ask this boon–
That they reduce the rates–and then
They cannot leave their graves too soon.

SALUS POPULI SUPREMA EST LEX

His Latin proclamation that the safety of the people is the highest law confirms his newspaper's stand for the best interests of the ratepayers.

WG prints his first novel

While *Betsy Gray* continued to be received with enthusiasm each week by the readers of the *Gazette,* WG was working hard on his other novel. Not just the final editing and proof-reading but starting to get the typesetting done for each of the 150 or so pages. For *Sons of the Sod, a Tale of County Down* was to be printed and published by the North Down Printing Press in WG's own workshops behind "Mount Herald".

After the final episode of *Betsy Gray* had appeared in the 4th September, edition of the *Gazette,* people were soon asking when *it* would be available as a book. And so, eager to please his public, WG started to work, too, on editing his serialised tale of the '98 into book format. As the nights began to draw in once more during the autumn of 1886, WG's time was split between reading the galley proofs for *Sons of the Sod* and overseeing the typesetting for *Betsy Gray.* Then, of course, there was the day job of running and producing the newspaper each week and, amidst all of this, catching the train to Belfast as often as he could to visit Lizzie.

She would have been so pleased at the early success of *Betsy Gray* in the paper, but Wesley would have particularly wanted her to see his

THE STORYTELLER

first published novel.[203] When he called with her in November he would have told her all about it and promised to have a copy to show her when he next visited. As he was leaving, Isabella probably whispered that he should not delay too long.

WG and all his staff worked hard and finally *Sons of the Sod,* his debut novel, started coming off the press. The books were carefully bound and stitched with a hardback cover and looked every bit as "professional" as the volumes of his "Readings" produced by the big Belfast publishers. But this wasn't just another collection of inconsequential short stories, popular as they were. This was a proper, 60,000 word novel of which he could be justifiably proud. He sat re-reading it in the train as it chuffed and puffed through Holywood on its way to the city. He couldn't wait to show it to Lizzie.

* * *

27th November, 1886, Elizabeth Evelyne Lyttle, peacefully in her home at 80, Madrid Street, Belfast, after a long illness. Sorely missed by her loving husband and family.

---

[203] Although *Betsy Gray* had been finished earlier, WG's first published novel would be *Sons of the Sod.*

Chapter 23 – FIRST EDITIONS
Sons of the Sod and *Betsy Gray*

1886 – 1887

Lizzie's death certificate gives the cause of death as heart disease over a two year period and shows that Isabella was present when she died. It confirms her age as 41, making 1845 her year of birth and putting her a year younger than Wesley.[204]

The *Northern Whig* carried an advert for "*Sons of the Sod,* by Robin.[205] Price 1s. at all Booksellers" on Friday 26th November. So Wesley did have the book ready to take up to show Lizzie before she passed away on the Saturday. Indeed, that occasion may have been the last time they were together. Lizzie would have been so happy for him.

Sadly, Wesley was not able to share any of the subsequent reviews with her. The *Whig* wrote on the following Saturday:

> *The reputation which the author of this story gained by his "Humorous Readings" will be sufficient to ensure for his new book a wide circle of readers. The author is quite at home in the County Down vernacular, faithfully describes many local scenes, and gives interesting glimpses of the manners and customs of the neighbourhood with which he deals.*

---

[204] This, as mentioned earlier, is contrary to what they declared on their marriage certificate, where they both claimed to be 21 when Wesley was, in fact, only 20 and Lizzie, it seems, just 19.

[205] On the front cover, the book's author is shown as W. G. Lyttle (Robin). WG must have believed his alter-ego could sell as many copies of his novel as could his own name.

THE STORYTELLER

There is a good sprinkling of that characteristic humour which has popularised the "Readings," but the general reader will be inclined to say that the extensive use of trade advertisements introduced into the story—a system inaugurated in recent times in Colonel Burnaby's "Ride to Kiva"—might with advantage have been dispensed with.[206]

Yours truly, holding a **first edition copy of Sons of the Sod,** courtesy of the British Library, shelfmark YA.2000.a.43197

WG knew all about product placement a century or so before the movie industry would start to practice it in earnest. That it didn't appeal to the *Whig* reviewer, though, was probably of little matter to Wesley reading it while still grieving over the loss of his dear wife.

Her death, although long expected, would have come as a sad blow to the Lyttle family. Wesley's work would distract him, though it must have been difficult carrying on with his daily routine knowing that never again would he hear the sound of Lizzie's soothing lilt. The joke "Memorial" to the Town Commission he published a few weeks earlier must have rung hollow now.

The children would have adapted as only children can. Devastated at first, they would have gradually come to terms with their loss, the younger ones, at least, finding solace from the care and attention given them by the housekeeper.

Anne—or Annie, as her employer had taken to calling her, perhaps after one of his own heroines, Squire Brown's daughter, Annie, in *Sons of the Sod*—would have accepted that her services to the family were needed now more than ever. The manner in which she fulfilled her role seems to have been much appreciated, certainly by Wesley and the younger children. John and Agnes probably found

---

[206] *Northern Whig,* Saturday 04 December, 1886

comfort in each other's company, never having managed to bond with Miss Byers the way their younger brother and sisters had.

Sometime soon after the funeral Wesley must have had a conversation with her on her future:

> 'Annie, you've been a real godsend to the family over these past months,' Wesley said to her over tea one evening. 'I hope you will be able to continue with us.'
>
> 'I should very much like to. I enjoy working here and of course I'll stay, if you still want me.'
>
> 'I do—we do. You're like part of the family. We'd be lost without you.'

So Miss Byers—Annie—stayed, and life at "Mount Herald" gradually returned to normal.

The end of The Clique?

On Thursday, 9th December WG was reporting on another meeting of Bangor's thoroughly dissatisfied ratepayers. He chose it as the topic for that weekend's editorial. Under the paper's motto of 'Live and Let Live' it appeared with the heading, 'BANGOR AFFAIRS:

> *The people have spoken. They will no longer be dormant, but will have a voice in the affairs of their town. The meeting on Thursday night was large, enthusiastic, and unanimous. There will either be a new Board of men prepared to work energetically and openly, or the town will remain as it is, under the government of the Newtownards Poor-Law Guardians. The Clique are not in it. They have defeated themselves. Working men of Bangor are the men who are most interested in this question, and we are much mistaken if they are not now about to make their power and influence felt. The large property holders did not put in an appearance at the meeting, but they had representatives there, and today they are sneering at the puny power of the humble Ratepayers.*

Beyond his demanding role as a newspaper proprietor, along with all the other irons in the fire of his busy life, we see just after Christmas that year a reminder that WG had kept up his secretaryship of the Independent Order of Good Templars. The *Belfast News-Letter* of Wednesday 29th December reported on the meeting of IOGT Sunbeam Lodge held on Monday 27th where, it informs us, 'Br. W. G. Lyttle, G.S. [Grand Secretary] gave the address.'

Assault

1887 got off to a rousing start. In January, in his official capacity as journalist, WG attended a function at the Courthouse. As he was arriving, Archibald Thompson turned up but was refused admission by the attendants at the door; he apparently didn't have a ticket.

As WG watched, Thompson tried to force his way in but was stopped. He then placed himself in the doorway, saying he would prevent entry to anyone else until he was allowed in. At this juncture, much to WG's private amusement, the leader of the displaced Clique, James Bowman, arrived and tried to go in but couldn't because of Thompson's presence. WG didn't hear him ask Thompson to move aside, as Bowman later claimed to have done; he simply saw the ex-Town Commissioner grab Archibald by the throat, drawing some blood by his fingernails, and throw him down the steps where he fell against another man, knocking him over.

It all made for an interesting diversion from what could otherwise have proved a lacklustre event. But it did result in WG being called as a witness for the prosecution the next month, when Thompson sued Bowman for assault. Bowman's defence was his claim to have asked Thompson to step aside to allow him entry to the Courthouse. When Thompson refused to budge, Bowman said he gripped him by his coat collar to make him move out of the doorway. WG lost no love on Archibald Thompson (other than for the sensational copy he always provided), but, along with some other witnesses, he described in court what he had seen, which did not show Bowman in the best light. The magistrates, however, decided to dismiss the case.

23 - FIRST EDITIONS

Bangor Rule

Also in January, the townsfolk decided they had had enough of being governed by the Poor Law Guardians in Newtownards and voted at a meeting to have their own Town Commissioners again. In due course elections were held and many of the old regime regained their seats—no doubt, much to WG's disgust. In the run-up to the elections WG's editorial commented, in a sideswipe at Ireland's Nationalists, that calls from Bangorians for a return of the town commission was an obvious instance of a desire for "Home Rule," while "Union" with Newtownards was not to be tolerated!

Automation

When workmen came, later in the spring of 1887, to install a gas engine to replace the manual power that turned the big flywheel on the printing press at "Mount Herald", Roland had just turned nine. He would almost certainly have been accustomed to having a go, from time to time, helping the operator whose job it was to keep the heavy flywheel turning so the printer could operate the press. So he would have been keen to see how the new engine could do the same job much more easily. His father told him that the gas to supply the engine would cost 1s 2d a week compared to the 15s a week he had been paying the manual operator and the press would work at twice the speed it had before.[207] Even as a nine-year-old, Roland would have been impressed by the figures and the fact that his father said they would have the finest home-printing press in the land. The following advert appeared in the *North Down Herald and Bangor Gazette* on 4th April –

> *TO PRINTERS: WANTED A MACHINE MAN who understands working gas engine; also two smart Turnover Apprentices. Apply immediately to W. G. Lyttle, Bangor Gazette, Bangor.*

---

[207] The comparative figures that WG mentioned were quoted in a newspaper report later in the year.

THE STORYTELLER

With the installation of his new gas engine WG was anticipating an increasing workload, hence two more apprentices. And he didn't want novices either. A turnover apprentice was one who was part-way through his apprenticeship and was "turned over" to a new employer to broaden his experience.

First edition

Betsy Gray was one of the first works to be printed using the new engine, which, as anticipated, did indeed speed up the process considerably. WG already had much of the typesetting for *Betsy Gray* done when *Sons of the Sod* was published. He included in that book an advertisement for *Betsy Gray*. It was, it said, "In the press and would shortly be issued," quoting the price at 1s, or by post 1s 2d and adding that it "may be ordered from the Publisher, W. G. LYTTLE, Bangor, County Down." Now this advert appeared in November 1886, so if *Betsy Gray* was already "in the press," its first edition must have been published in 1887.

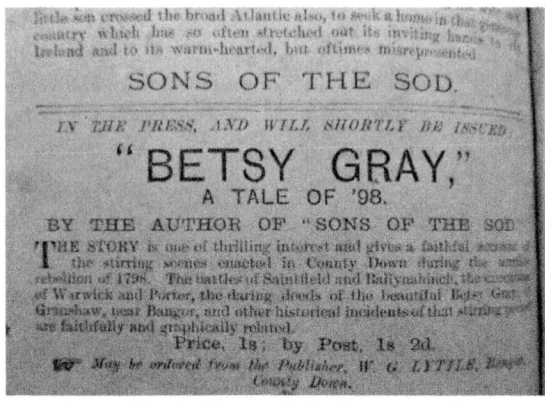

The November 1886 advert that appeared in the first edition of *Sons of the Sod* immediately following the end of the story (reproduced, with permission, from a copy held at the British Library, shelfmark YA.2000.a.43197)

This is contrary to all previous accounts, which claim that it was first published in 1888. A copy of the 1888 edition used to be on display at Library Headquarters in Ballynahinch labelled as a "First edition" but, sadly, that has since been lost. Mark Thompson of Portavogie, however, still has an 1888 copy, actually the second edition, showing it was "printed by the author at his North Down Printing Works and priced at sixpence."[208]

---

[208] See Appendix C8 for a photo of the front cover of the 1888 edition of *Betsy Gray,* along with other editions.

23 - FIRST EDITIONS

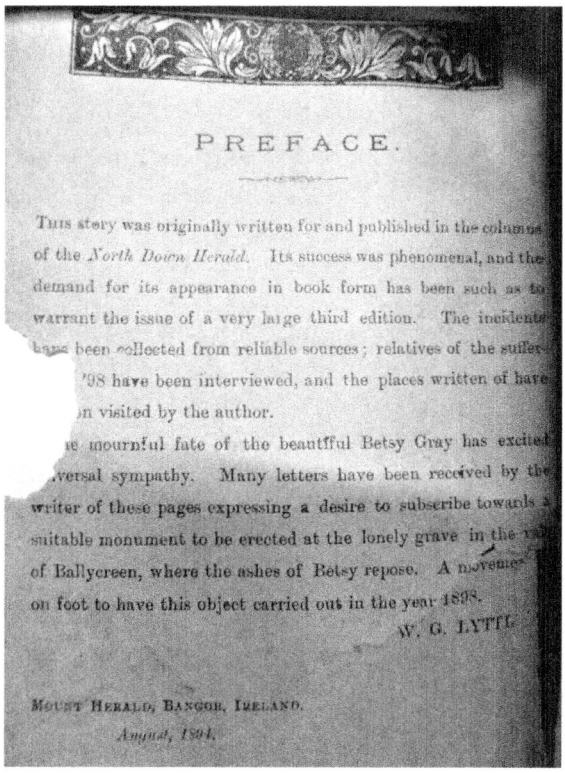

Preface to the **3rd edition of *Betsy Gray*,** from a copy held at the Linen Hall Library, Belfast, reproduced with permission.

There are still copies in existence of the third edition printed by WG in 1894. In the Preface to that edition he wrote that the success of *Betsy Gray* "had been phenomenal and the demand for its appearance in book form such as to warrant a very large third edition."

So we jump from an alleged first edition, dated 1888, to a third edition published in 1894; plenty of time, it might be argued, for a "second edition" to have been produced in the interim. But I have been unable to find any trace or mention of an edition dated between '88 and '94. The explanation is simple. The '88 version *was* the second edition. *Betsy Gray* was first published in 1887, as advertised in the November '86 first edition of *Sons of the Sod*.

As further evidence of this we have the *Sons of the Sod* advert quoting the price as one shilling. The 1888 edition was marked at sixpence; clearly not the same edition. With the story's serialisation in the *Gazette* only recently finished WG would have been cautious in his estimate of the number of copies of the tale he might sell in book form. With a small print run he must have felt he needed to charge a shilling a copy to cover his set-up costs. However, such was its immense popularity that the first print run must have quickly sold out.

THE STORYTELLER

As soon as he could, he produced a second, larger run—the 1888 edition, which he was thus able to sell at just 6d a copy. This lasted a few years but still sold out with demand continuing; hence the 1894 edition.

Demand for this, the most enduring for WG's books, was destined to continue over the decades to the present day with the latest, 14th edition still available as print-on-demand. A list of all the editions of *Betsy Gray,* along with WG's other works, is included in Appendix B.

In May of the year he published *Betsy Gray*, WG attended a retirement celebration for a long-standing teacher from Helen's Bay where the chair for the evening was occupied by the Rev. John Quartz—none other than the minister of Ballygilbert Presbyterian Church, who WG had written into *Sons of the Sod* as the officiating clergyman at a wedding in his story. The report of the occasion lists, among the toasts, one to "The Press, coupled with the name of Mr. W. G. Lyttle," who would, certainly, in his reply, have mentioned their literary connection.

Sparring match

Back in the early part of 1887 WG had no idea of the success that lay ahead of him through his second novel and how it would be received by the public—a success that would outlive him by over a hundred years. Once copies started to sell he turned his attention to the next job, which was to produce a second edition of his tourist booklet, *The Bangor Season*. That had also proved popular and was now out of print, so he had his team in the print shop run off more copies ready for the summer.

These hit the newsstands just as the first of the season's visitors started to arrive in the seaside resort. Later on it received just a cursory mention in an early July issue of the *Belfast News-Letter*. But WG was not one to let that affect his mood. Let us, therefore, watch him in a lighter moment in an episode that always remained in my grandfather's memory:

> 'Well, they could have given *The Bangor Season* a bit more of a write-up than that,' Wesley remarked to his

23 - FIRST EDITIONS

housekeeper, putting his copy of the *News-Letter* aside. 'Never mind. I must go and have a word with the new printer chap.'

Anne stepped ahead to the front door and opened it for him.

'Oh, listen. Do you hear it?' She cocked an ear and caught Wesley's arm just as he was leaving to go round to the print shop. 'The music; can you hear?'

As the door had opened, the unmistakable hurdy-gurdy sound of a distant steam organ had drifted by on the summer breeze. 'Aye, indeed,' said Wesley, 'the funfair's back in town. Perhaps you and I could take the youngsters along on Saturday afternoon.'

'Oh, they would love that, Mr Lyttle, I know they would.'

'And you, Annie?'

'Oh—Why, yes... of course. I should be happy to accompany you.'

Wesley was amused to see the colour rising in her cheeks.

As he walked round to have a chat with his printer he felt the warmth of the sun on his back. He had a jauntiness in his step, perhaps for the first time since the dark days of winter following the death of poor Lizzie.

He could hear laughter and, as he rounded the corner, he saw some of the apprentice boys larking about. They hadn't noticed his approach so he stood and watched. Two of the lads were indulging in a sparring match, a favourite pastime in their lunchbreak. They would prance around the yard outside the print shed seeking to score points by landing a light slap on their opponent's cheek whilst trying to protect their own.

As he watched, the bout came to an end and the others suddenly noticed they were being observed. The apprentice boys quickly moderated their behaviour as befits being in the presence of their employer. But WG, far from telling them off, laughed and challenged the winner.

The sparring started off with the younger lad seeming to have the upper hand as WG retreated gradually between the big doors of the print shed. At one point his opponent had him backed up against the table with the ink rollers and the trays of type ready for printing. WG put a hand behind him to steady himself and then seemed to rally. He was scoring points now with his fingers breaking through the apprentice's guard to land strokes on his cheek.

The young lad couldn't understand why his pals were sniggering. He felt he was giving as good as he got, but each time WG landed a slap there would be more laughter. Eventually, they called it a draw and the mystified apprentice was led to a mirror hanging inside the print shed. His face was covered in streaks of black ink that WG had secretly dipped his fingers in when he allowed himself to be backed up to the table.

Young Roland was there, laughing along with the other apprentices at Wesley's antics. He always remembered the occasion, maybe because he was happy to see his father in a light-hearted mood once more, or maybe just because it was a sunny day and he could hear the magical sound of the funfair beckoning from farther afield. Years later he would tell the story of the sparring match to his own son, Gerald, my father, who, in the fullness of time, told me, just as I have related it here.

Laughter

In the summer months the children would often bring Captain Sharrat outside, tethered to his perch. The apprentices enjoyed his company as they worked in the open shed or sat out in the sun eating their piece,[209] spread with jam, for their lunch. The parrot would whistle and the cocker spaniel would come running only to be greeted by a raucous laugh from the pitiless bird. This brought roars of laughter from the lads which, in turn, caused the parrot to mimic them and laugh even louder.

No one knew how old Captain Sharrat was, but he could have been well over 50 by now and Wesley would have warned the children that the parrot wouldn't be with them forever. On one of these laughter-filled occasions the bird was thoroughly enjoying himself—laughing at the lads, who would laugh back at him. He would laugh louder; they would laugh back even louder. So Captain Sharrat laughed louder still. This went on until, suddenly, the bird stopped in mid-cackle. He keeled over and fell from his perch. The poor thing had burst his aging heart with laughter.

Maybe not a bad way to go.

---

[209] Slice of bread

THE STORYTELLER

Chapter 24 – THE BATTLE OF THE EDITORS

1887 – June

WG's relationship with his old adversary, William Henry, the editor of the *Newtownards Chronicle*—the Chiel, had not improved. The *Bangor Gazette* editor, as we know, often liked to speak his mind through the voice of "Robin" and perhaps got away with casting more aspersions on the establishment in that manner than he might have done through his "Live and Let Live" editorials. Perhaps prompted by the *Chronicle's* BANGOR NOTES AND NEWS that had commenced the previous year, the *North Down Herald and Bangor Gazette* had recently started a new regular column headed THE OLD TOWN CLOCK in which WG gave a voice to the clock above the Market House that looked down upon Conway Square in Newtownards.

> *For a hundred years I've been looking down*
> *By day and by night on the dear old town;*
> *Speaking to men of the flight of time*
> *As I ring out the hours with silvery chime;*
> *And the Square, like a huge stage, stands in sight,*
> *Where no curtain falls save the curtain of night!*

The clock, it seemed, was privy to all that passed beneath his lofty gaze. From his high vantage point, he claimed to see all that went on in the town and he "wrote" to the *Gazette* offering to pass on his observations, weekly. WG thus had another third-party voice through which, in all innocence, he could share delightful snippets of gossip with his eager readers as well as interesting news items. It was often written in WG's whimsical style, so it was much more appealing to his readership than the *Chronicle's* dry reporting of Bangor events.

In the latter half of June, 1887 The Old Town Clock reported the cutting of the first sod for the building of a new road to run from East Street to the Newtownards railway station. On the same day he also mentioned seeing Major Hamilton [of the North Down Rifles] preparing the Square for a muster of the troops on the 27th. He wondered, "Will old Robin go in for training this year?" There then followed an account that reflected badly on the *Chronicle's* editor:

In the aftermath of a tragic and fatal accident, the previous year on the 12th July when a workman named John M'Nabb was killed, the public donated generously to a subscription in support of his widow.

'I'm told,' the Clock reported, 'that though nearly a year has elapsed, the poor widow has never yet received the money which was subscribed. It is said "The Chiel" holds it, and that Mrs M'Nabb, who lives in Belfast, comes down frequently and asks for the cash. Her expenses amount to about two shillings every journey, and she is sent away with a paltry instalment of five shillings or so! Is not this monstrous! Has the widow no friend to step forward and procure her that which the public gave, and which she should have received in the month of August last year?'

The final item of that week's column read, somewhat cryptically, 'The Chiel is trying to kick up a fuss about some bill of sale but I'm not very clear whose it is.'

Relations between the two local newspapers were at a low ebb and over the following weeks, stemming from this bill of sale which involved WG, accusations and counter-accusations would appear in their respective columns.

Objective reporting in question

WG had submitted a bill for printing and advertising carried out for Bangor's previous Town Commissioners before the affairs of the town had been placed in the hands of the Newtownards Guardians. The Town Clerk had passed the bill on to the Guardians to pay. There was now a new board of Commissioners in Bangor and the chairman, Mr Bowman, lost no time in writing to the Guardians to say they had no authority to pay Lyttle's bill; nor did he see any obligation for the new

THE STORYTELLER

Board to do so. However the Guardian's cheque had already been cashed so the debate was rather academic. How this was all reported in the *Gazette* in May prompted a scathing attack in the columns of the next edition of the *Chronicle*:

> FALSE AND MALICIOUS REPORTING
> To the editor of the "Newtownards Chronicle".
> Sir,– The mode of reporting pursued by the Bangor Gazette is unique in my experience of journalism... ... One might search in vain for its compeer for scurrility. If not engaged in defaming the characters of some of the best men in the community, its brazen puffing of "publicans and sinners" of all descriptions out-herods anything I have ever known. No person of honourable reputation appears to be safe from its attacks. No one is too vile for its praise...
> ...
> What I wish to draw attention to is its infamous system of reporting for a purpose. In last Saturday's Gazette a discussion at the Board of Guardians on the mysterious Lyttle's cheque business is apparently reported. Every line almost is made to bear a meaning the very reverse of what was intended by the speakers, and speeches which were never uttered are manufactured for gentlemen, as I said, to serve a purpose.

The letter claimed the *Gazette* reported that Mr James Pollock, of the Newtownards Board of Guardians, complained of how he was reported in the *Chronicle,* when, according to the letter-writer, Pollock's complaint was about how *others* had been reported in the *Gazette*—"two very different things"—in the mind of the correspondent. The writer also claimed that the *Gazette* quoted the chairman of the Board of Guardians as wishing, "that the *Chronicle* would report the proceedings correctly, and he hoped that a report like that of which he now complained would never appear again." But the correspondent claimed that the chairman was not even present at that

24 - THE BATTLE OF THE EDITORS

meeting and that he later stigmatised the words as a "pure concoction".

Moreover, the writer said that the *Gazette* twisted people's remarks to appear, "as if they had actually bolstered up and defended the manner in which Mr Lyttle's cheque was obtained." The letter concluded,

> *I think I have proved my case, that the report in question [in the Gazette] was false and malicious, and in justice to myself I request you, sir, to publish this letter. Your Reporter. May 12, 1887.*[210]

The above was, apparently, not the only defamatory letter from the Bangor "reporter" to be published in the *Chronicle*. Faithful followers of the *Gazette* were, no doubt, early to their newsagents on Saturday next to see what WG's response would be. They would not have been disappointed as they turned over the front page of advertisements to find this column inside:

> *THE LYING SCRIBE*
> *There were Scribes and Pharisees in olden times. They exist still, and, though their calling and nationality may be different, they enjoy the same unenviable notoriety. The Chiel and his Bangor scribe are types of these classes and are admirably suited to run in double harness. The latest issues of the* Newtownards Chronicle *fairly bristle with lies, deliberately concocted to injure the reputation of the proprietor of the* Bangor Gazette. *The scribe is an ink-slinger of the lowest species; the Chiel can't write at all so he kicks up mud. They may both amuse themselves to their hearts' content. The object of their malice can afford to treat them with supreme contempt, and brands them as a brace if impudent, ignorant liars.*

---

[210] From a scrapbook clipping held in the North Down Museum.

THE STORYTELLER

> *Their cause must be weak indeed when they write reports of meetings never held, quote correspondence never read, and utter statements that have no foundation. The Chiel might, with advantage, look after his business, and the scribe may be assured that the American ham trade or the cleansing of Bangor streets and sewers will suit him better than literature, even of the* Chronicle *type. Why doesn't he start a newspaper and get the Ratepayers to work it as they do the gas? Such reports as he has been supplying to his Newtownards friend should get a much wider circulation as specimens of barefaced, malicious falsehood.*[211]

It would seem the *Chronicle's* article about WG, whether false or perhaps containing half-truths and exaggerations, had hit a nerve to prompt such a venomous reply.

WG's rates unpaid?

The *Newtownards Chronicle* must have been delighted to have further occasion to report on the affairs of their rival editor not long afterwards. In early June, '87 they ran their story under the headline:

THE "LITTLE" NEWSPAPER MAN'S ARREARS OF RATES

It used a soubriquet that William Henry liked to employ when referring in his columns to WG—just as WG used "The Chiel" rather than print Henry's actual name. The report was about a meeting of the Bangor Town Commissioners at which WG was present to address some allegations made at previous meetings, including that his rates bill for an earlier year remained unpaid.

When the *Gazette* reporter had returned from covering the previous Board meeting it was the first WG became aware that they were claiming he still owed rates—from 1884, it seemed. He had never received an overdue demand from the Board and as far as he

---

[211] From a scrapbook clipping held in the North Down Museum of the *Bangor Gazette*, 21st May, 1887.

24 - THE BATTLE OF THE EDITORS

knew the original bill had been paid by his solicitor. Other allegations were made, too. There were six in all:

1. That his rates for the year 1884 were still unpaid
2. That a letter he wrote to the Clerk was an insult to the entire Board
3. That he stated to Mr Brice that he would not pay anything so long as the town of Bangor was not under a Board of Commissioners
4. That he had erected a gas engine which entailed a serious consumption of gas
5. That he gave no security for the gas thus being consumed
6. That his gas account was in arrears.

WG felt obliged to defend himself against these charges and decided to attend the next meeting of the Board.

In the following account all the words attributed to each speaker are as reported, verbatim, in the columns of the *Bangor Gazette* and preserved for us in a scrapbook clipping held in the North Down Museum.

WG must have marched down Ballymagee Street to the Commissioners' Office at the allotted time and sat through all the tedious business of the day, noticing, as time went on, that the chairman, Mr Bowman, glanced frequently at his pocket watch. Eventually, the chairman rose and said he must retire. He asked Mr M'Cormick to take the chair.

WG jumped to his feet and addressed the Board, 'Gentlemen, before your chairman leaves, you will, perhaps, allow me to be heard for a few minutes. I have come here tonight to refer to certain statements that, in my absence, were made against me. You all know to what I refer. I presume, if any ratepayer is mentioned at a public meeting of your Board and statements made against him, you have sufficient sense of justice and fair play to allow him an opportunity of defending himself. Gentlemen, I await your permission.'

Most of the Board members nodded their approval and the Chairman stated, 'It is out of the usual course, but I, personally, have no objection to Mr Lyttle making an explanation—'

'Then it ought to be the usual course,' WG interrupted, claiming that if the Board made allegations they had an obligation to allow a defence to be heard.

WG went on to list the six charges that had been made against him and said that he deemed it his duty to offer explanation.

'First, then, as regard my rates of 1884, for reasons which I need not now explain, I postponed their payment. I frankly admit that the collector frequently asked for the amount and that Mr Dinnen [the Town Commissioners' solicitor], who was then my own solicitor, processed me, and here I wish to ask your Clerk a few questions.'

Addressing the Clerk, Mr Francis Pollock, WG asked, 'Do you keep a cash book, Mr Pollock?'

'I do,' came the reply.

'Do you keep a ledger?'

'I do.'

'Have you an account with Mr Dinnen, solicitor?'

'I have not.'

WG surveyed the Board and then turned back to Mr Pollock to ask, 'If any commissioner asked you how much you have paid Mr Dinnen for law costs during the last five years, could you tell him?'

The Clerk looked a little uncomfortable. 'I could not,' he said.

WG continued, 'Did Mr Dinnen pay you my rates?'

'He did not.'

'Have you entered all monies paid by Mr Dinnen?'

'I have not.'

Turning to the Board, WG said, 'Gentlemen, you possess sufficient business qualities to understand that your accounts cannot be properly kept in that way.'

Ignoring this, the Chairman protested, "It is not fair that Mr Lyttle should cross-examine Mr Pollock in this way.'

WG said he was merely establishing the facts and that as far as he was aware his solicitor, Mr Dinnen had paid his rates bill. If the Board's book-keeping was so poor as not to show it as paid, that was not his responsibility. If he *was* in arrears why had he not been asked for the amount alleged to be owing along with his 1885 and '86 rates demand?

After further heated exchanges WG moved on to the next accusation and said, 'It was stated at your last meeting that my letter

24 - THE BATTLE OF THE EDITORS

of the 7th inst. was an insult to the whole Board. Gentlemen, it was not so intended. It referred to the Chairman alone. It was also stated that Mr Brice said I refused to pay. Mr Brice, did I ever refuse to pay?'

Mr Brice responded readily enough, 'No, you did not.'

At this the Chairman insisted, 'Mr Brice said that you refused to pay your gas account.'

'Mr Brice, is that true,' asked WG, raising an eyebrow in mild astonishment.

'No, it is not.'

WG moved on again. 'Now gentlemen, I come to the gas engine. It was stated by your Chairman that I had erected a gas engine, which meant a large consumption of gas. I requested the Clerk to have the gas meter in my printing house examined. He did so, and I find the consumption amounts to the very large sum of one shilling and tuppence per week.'

WG paused, as this raised a ripple of laughter.

He then continued, 'I had formerly been paying a man fifteen shilling per week to drive my printing machine by a flywheel. The gas engine enables me to turn out double the quantity of work, so I shall probably be able to pay the one shilling and tuppence per week.

'Your Chairman also stated that I had not given any security for my gas. May I enquire of the Clerk if it is the custom of the Board to ask security?'

'It is not,' replied the Clerk.

'Was I asked for security?'

'No.'

'Then, gentlemen, the statement of your Chairman was most uncalled for, to say the least,' adding that, in fact, the Board currently owed *him* the sum of £22 for twelve months of printing and advertising.

The Chairman said that he was not aware of that.

'You should have been aware of it,' WG shot back. 'It's too bad to make such unfounded statements.'

Ignoring this, the Chairman went back to the question of outstanding rates and further argument ensued with the Board asking WG to produce proof that he'd paid and WG stating that it was not his place to have to do so; the state of their books was such that they were unable to prove that he had not paid. He acknowledged that the current, recently elected Commissioners were not personally responsible but they nevertheless represented the Town Board.

Mr M'Cormick said that since they now had quite a new Board they would prefer to be friendly with Mr Lyttle, if he would allow it, but WG had had enough of what he saw as their inefficiency and baseless accusations.

He responded, perhaps injudiciously, 'I care not a fig for your friendship or your enmity. I am neither to be bribed nor intimidated.'

The account in the *Gazette* concluded, "The chairman then entered upon a rambling, incoherent statement, evidently meant as a defence of the ridiculous position in which he found himself, but which was simply a vituperative and prevaricating tirade interrupted by Mr Lyttle who pointed out that he was flatly contradicting his previous utterances." There, apart from some further arguing over whether or not the Newtownards Board of Guardians should have been authorised to pay the *Gazette's* bill that WG had alluded to, the matter rested.

The Chronicle's account

The *Newtownards Chronicle's* reporter chose to relate the events of that same meeting from a markedly different stance. Under its aforementioned heading about "The 'Little' Newspaper Man", it read as follows:

> *After the special meeting an adjourned meeting was held at which Mr W G Lyttle of the Bangor Gazette was present and asked to be allowed to make an explanation to the Commissioners with reference to his arrears of rates.*
>
> *Mr Lyttle then entered into an explanation and after a patient hearing the Chairman requested Mr Lyttle to produce his receipt for the arrears of 1884, which he alleged he had paid to Mr John Dinnen, solicitor. Mr Lyttle refused to do so, and stated that he would produce it at the proper time.*
>
> *After some further remarks, Mr Lyttle inquired of the Clerk if he had a cash book and a ledger, to which Mr Pollock replied in the affirmative.*

24 - THE BATTLE OF THE EDITORS

> *Mr Lyttle—Have you a ledger account with Mr Dinnen?*
> *The Clerk—We have.*
> *The Chairman—This is really going too far, Mr Lyttle, to cross-examine the Clerk in this fashion.*

Another Commissioner suggested WG should simply produce proof of payment

> *but Mr Lyttle refused to do so.*
> *The Chairman—I am confidant you have no such proof, as I hold a letter from Mr Dinnen which states that Mr Lyttle had not paid any rates, and I now read it to the Board.*
> *At this Mr Lyttle waxed indignant, and was beginning to be obstreperous, when he was politely informed by the Chairman that if he did not conduct himself properly he would ask him to retire.*
> *Mr M'Cormick—We are all friends of Mr Lyttle, and would like to continue so, and I would be very sorry if anything should happen at the Board that would cause any other feeling than that of friendship to exist.*
> *Mr Lyttle (interrupting and snapping his fingers)—I don't care that for your friendship or enmity.*
> *Mr Lyttle then made some sneering remarks with regard to the manner in which the books were kept.*
> *In regard to the gas-engine which Mr Lyttle had erected, he stated that it only took 14d per week to work it, to which Mr M'Cormick replied that he would keep a strict watch on it in future.*
> *After some further discussion, the matter dropped, Mr Lyttle having failed to prove to the Board that he had paid his arrears.*

In another article the *Chronicle* ran with THE "LITTLE" NEWSPAPER MAN ONCE MORE, and quoted the letter of James

THE STORYTELLER

Bowman, Chairman of the Bangor Town Commissioners, to the Newtownards Board of Guardians in which he wrote: "I am surprised to find this day that an account was passed by your Board on Saturday last in favour of Mr. W. G. Lyttle, *Bangor Gazette*, for advertising local notices &c, in connection with having the town placed under the provisions of the Town Improvements (Ireland) Act, 1854. This account should not have been furnished to you, and passed by you, as it was contracted under the Town Improvements (Ireland) Act, and besides, the Commissioners are alone acquainted with the items, and have the authority, under the Act of Parliament, to pay these and similar accounts. I consider it to be my duty to give you this information to prevent the amount being surcharged upon the Board of Guardians, or signatories of the cheque—I remain, yours faithfully…'

Bowman also, it seems, considered it his duty to send a copy of his letter to the *Chronicle* who continued the story at length about how WG's bill had apparently been paid by the wrong official body.

And all the time the Old Town Clock above the Market House in Conway Square kept an eye on the blustering in the office of the town's weekly newspaper and simply remarked in his next column in the *Bangor Gazette*, "The Chiel is trying to kick up a fuss about some bill of sale but I'm not very clear whose it is."

Chapter 25
RELATIONSHIPS—BROKEN AND FORGED

1887 – July to October

All the blustering and journalistic jousting were not doing William Henry's health any good. He may or may not have come near to "apoplectic fits" on occasions, as WG sometimes suggested in his columns, but his doctor was recommending that he take a sabbatical period away from the daily cut and thrust. He prescribed a leisurely sail across the Atlantic Ocean.

On the 16th July the *Chronicle* editor congratulated his readers "on commencing, with the present publication, the fifteenth year of [the newspaper's] publication." At the close of a short article on the paper's history, Henry wrote:

> *I have decided upon taking a short tour through the United States and Canada; and will leave Ireland on Friday next on the magnificent steamer Furnessia, of the Anchor Line. I expect to return in about two months in invigorated health and with additional newspaper experience.*[212]

The same edition contained an account of a "Complimentary Supper to Mr William Henry T.C." held in the Ulster Hotel the previous

---

[212] The *Furnessia* sailed from Glasgow but also picked up passengers at Moville, County Antrim, on the northwest shores of Lough Foyle, which seems to be where William Henry joined the ship. It was a fairly small steamer with just one funnel and fitted with sails as subsidiary power.

THE STORYTELLER

Thursday. A large gathering of his friends met to wish him *bon voyage* on his proposed trip. They were well catered for by the proprietress, Miss M'Kee, the daughter of Mrs M'Kee who had run the enterprise when it was first converted to a hotel. Not listed among the guests was the man who had been born in the very place where friends were now raising their glasses to the town's only surviving newspaper editor. WG, it appears, was not invited.

Satirical poem

Freed for a season from the constant sniping from Newtownards, WG sat down and wrote some humorous verse. An advert that appeared in a Belfast newspaper on Friday, 26 August, 1887 asked,

> *Where will Archibald Thompson, the Editor of the Bangor Gazette, and other local celebrities be in 1907?*

The advert promised that readers would hear the answer if they attended the entertainment to be held that evening in the Good Templar Hall, Bangor. Those who did were treated to a witty and entertaining poem of some 43 verses written and recited by WG. It started by explaining that, like Rip Van Winkle, the writer had been asleep for twenty years and awoke to find the Bangor he knew changed in many ways. Amusing references to how current situations turned out and to the fates of many named individuals kept his audience in roars of laughter.

He included himself in the jests:

> *"You had a paper here, 'twas called Gazette,*
> *Have you it still? Is Lyttle living yet?"*
> *"We have the paper still amongst us here,*
> *I'm told it's worth five thousand pounds a year.*
>
> *By Lyttle, some ten years ago, 'twas sold,*
> *He went abroad, is living yet, I'm told;*
> *Some say he's dead and gone where such men go,*
> *All editors, I'm told, are sent below.*

25 - RELATIONSHIPS—BROKEN AND FORGED

WG published his poem in the *Gazette,* and also included it in his next (1888) *North Down Directory and Almanec* so we have the text preserved.[213]

Banned

Now that James Bowman had re-established himself as chairman of Bangor Town Commissioners and the old Clique was back in power, it seems he had had enough of the *Gazette's* style of reporting and WG's critical editorials. After the usual business had been transacted at their meeting on the 19th August he announced the closure of the session. The reporters left, including the man from the *Gazette* and at least three commissioners. But Bowman had one more item on his private agenda which he introduced behind closed doors. It resulted a few days later in the following letter arriving at "Mount Herald" (reproduced here exactly as subsequently quoted in the columns of WG's newspaper:

> Bangor Commissioners Office
> Bangor 24th August, 1887
> Dear sir,—I am directed by the Town Commissioners to forward to you the following copy of a Resolution which was passed at their meeting of the 19th inst.—Yours truly,
> Francis Pollock,
> Town Clerk
> W. G. Lyttle, Esq.
>
> ———
> *(Copy)*
> "Resolved unanimously
> "That whereas the Notices of the Proceedings "at the meeting of this Board, appearing in the "Banger Gazette," have been uniformally [sic] misleading and untrue. [sic] and as such are calculated to disturb the public spirit of the Town, and to bring this Board into

---
[213] The full poem can be read in *Robin's Rhymes*, AG Lyttle, 2021

THE STORYTELLER

contempt and ridicule, and that although cautioned, such misrepresentations and misstatements have not only been continued with increased pertinacity and virulence, but have been enlarged upon in leading articles accompanied with direct personal attacks upon members of the Board.

It is hereby resolved, that in order to protect the interests of the Ratepayers and to defend this Board from being thus falsely reported and maligned, that the representatives of the above-named Journal shall not hereafter be permitted to be present at any of the meetings of the Board, or have any access to any Books, Documents or Accounts belonging thereto, and that the Chairman be and is hereby authorised and required to carry this resolution into effect."

The following Saturday's *Gazette* reproduced this, and I quote, "*verbatim et literatim*" going on to ask "the intelligent, educated section of our readers whether a resolution so grossly illiterate, ignorant and ungrammatical ever before emanated from any public board." The paper pointed out that no mention was made of who proposed or seconded this resolution of "an unprincipled clique" but had no doubt it was "framed by the butcher's son" [Bowman]. The secrecy under which the resolution was passed was fully revealed, finishing by stating that "it had been carried, through the same underhand, sneaking dodgery by which the Chairman regained the position from which he and his clique were, not long ago, ignominiously swept by public opinion."

WG defended his paper's reporting as always being fair and "as full as was necessary… If all the twaddle talked at the board meetings were published it would, sometimes, fill all the pages of the *Gazette*. Our reporter is a trained shorthand writer, and we have always instructed him to report impartially." Indeed, any tampering with the reporting was by the Board, itself, which, on more than one occasion, told the paper's representative that such and such should not be reported.

By way of explanation to his readers, WG stated:

25 - RELATIONSHIPS—BROKEN AND FORGED

> *We first incurred the displeasure of Bowman and his party at the time of Mr Archibald Thompson's election to office, and when, as in duty bound, we reported and published the astounding disclosures which the new member made. From that day to this day Bowman and his clique have been our inveterate enemies, and now, having by trickery, secret plotting, and barefaced impudence regained their position, they resort to the expedient of excluding the local organ from their deliberations. We don't blame them. They are, doubtless, ashamed of themselves. Let a veil be drawn over them for the brief space during which they shall hold office. We leave the Ratepayers to draw their own inferences…*

The usual column header appeared in the next week's paper:

BANGOR TOWN COMMISSIONERS

the column itself, however, was blank. The blank column continued to appear over the next weeks, emphasising the absurdity, not to say duplicity, of the Board's position.

Early in September an official announcement appeared in the *Newtownards Chronicle* informing Bangor's ratepayers that their Board had drawn up and passed new byelaws and applied to the Newtownards Board of Guardians to have them approved; they were available to be viewed by the public at the Boards premises. That this notice did not appear in the town's own newspaper, as would normally have been the case, was due to the *Chronicle's* editor, returned from his American jaunt, approaching the Bangor Town Commissioners and offering to carry their notices for free. The chairman, James Bowman, jumped at the opportunity to do WG out of the business but was shrewd enough to get a written confirmation from William Henry that he would publish the notice free of charge.

As soon as WG saw it, he wrote in his editorial about how the Clique were acting covertly to keep Bangor citizens in the dark. He at once drew the matter to the attention of the Local Government Board, stating that such a notice *must* appear in Bangor's own newspaper.

THE STORYTELLER

The circulation of the *Chronicle* generally, and in Bangor, in particular, did not come close to that of the *Gazette*. The Board agreed with him and, armed with their ruling WG marched down the road and bearded the Clique in their den.

How he got an audience under his existing ban, we do not know, but he did manage to get in and reluctantly the commissioners agreed to post the notice in the *Gazette* the following Saturday. Back home, WG took a fresh sheet of paper and began to draw on it. Although not an artist like his son, John, he was a dab hand at quick pen and ink sketches with which he occasionally illustrated an article in the paper.[214] The cartoon he drew appeared alongside the Board's notice in the next issue of the *Gazette*. It portrayed them as braying donkeys and himself—"the Editor victorious"—as a strutting cockerel. The captions read (top left to bottom right):

At the Boardroom, "May I come in?"

*

Certainly not, we can't admit him!

*

Now that he's in let them have it out. Ten to one on the little fellow.

*

The Boss Donkey Ruminates.

*

The Editor Victorious.

From a clipping of the *North Down Herald and Bangor Gazette* held in the "North Down Museum."

---

[214] That WG was the artist of such sketches is lent credence by this quote from his story, "A Crack Wi' the Prince of Wales." Robin Gordon has written an Address to be presented to his Royal Highness and says, 'Weel, we got the *Bangor Gazette* man tae illumerate [illuminate] the address. It lukit darlin'.'

304

25 - RELATIONSHIPS—BROKEN AND FORGED

Annie

Over those weeks, while WG was enjoying poking fun at the Town Commissioners, he was feeling particularly beneficent. Could his housekeeper have had a hand in that? Let us imagine ourselves, for a while, in her presence and eavesdrop upon a conversation which must, undoubtedly, have taken place around this time.

> Annie was having an afternoon off. She quite liked how Wesley had taken to addressing her as Annie. She thought about her employer's name, Wesley. It suited him: efficient and business-like but with a hint of kindness and humour about it, too. She had asked for the time off and Mr Lyttle—Wesley, she smiled to herself—had agreed as he had a lot of writing to do and would be in the house all day to keep an eye on the children.
>
> It was a dull August day in Bangor and the pavement was damp underfoot from earlier rain. In spite of this, Annie was wearing her best bonnet as she walked with a jaunty step along Hamilton Road, heading for No. 7 where her sister, Jane, had lodgings. It was only a few minutes away from "Mount Herald" and Annie had insisted she didn't need an escort just to walk around the corner. Whether the brief presence of a lady alone on the streets of Bangor outraged any prying Victorian eyes, she cared not.
>
> Annie came from a large family of nine siblings. Sadly five were already deceased and Jane, a few years older, was now her only sister. She was ready when Annie knocked, dressed equally resplendently, and together the ladies strolled on down Hamilton Road.
>
> Two females walking together, etiquette was now restored. Annie glanced across the road at the hedgerow and green fields beyond and thought they

were looking a little brighter. 'I do believe the sun's trying to come out,' she observed.

Jane glanced skyward. 'It might be trying but I doubt very much that it will succeed,' she said. 'I'm glad we shall be indoors again quite soon.'

'Well, I think it's a lovely day.'

'A lovely day to be sitting in the Ava Hotel enjoying afternoon tea,' laughed Jane, as they left the fields and a copse of trees behind and strolled on past the brickworks.[215]

'Oh, yes! How decadent. Imagine us—taking Afternoon Tea. It is most enterprising of Charles to introduce the custom at the Ava.'

'Just like some of the big London hotels, he told me.'

'And so kind of him to invite us.'

Charles, one of the sisters' two younger brothers, had married Sarah Carroll, the daughter of John and Jane Carroll, who owned the Ava Hotel at the top of Main Street in Bangor. He was now the hotel's manager.

When the ladies arrived they were ushered through to a lounge area where they were told Mr Byers would join them shortly. They were barely seated when a waitress in a long black dress and white pinafore brought in selections of finger sandwiches, petit fours, and gateaux which she placed in front of them on a low, carved ebony table. The waitress was followed by an elderly waiter in tails, carrying an ornate tray that held an elegant silver teapot together with a silver milk jug, sugar bowl and tongs, and silver tea strainer. The waitress returned with cups, saucers and plates of fine bone china and little pastry forks.

---

[215] Bryce's brickworks would close within a decade and the Ward family, who owned the land, would grant it to the people of the town. It would become the recreational green area known to this day as Ward Park.

25 - RELATIONSHIPS—BROKEN AND FORGED

'This is all quite excellent. Thank you,' Jane said, as the waiter poured their tea. Once he had departed she turned to her sister and said, 'Now, Anne, you said you had something to tell me.'

'Oh, we must wait for Charles.'

She had no sooner said it than their brother hurried in.

'I do apologise for not having been here to greet you.' He took the proffered hands of each of his sisters in turn, both clad in long satin gloves, and touched his lips to their fingertips. 'I hope I haven't kept you overlong. But I see you have been well taken care of.'

Charles lifted one of the plates and offered Annie and Jane a sandwich before sitting down and stirring two lumps of sugar into his tea with a delicately etched, silver teaspoon.

'Anne has some news she wants to tell us,' Jane prompted, looking hard at her sister.

'Have I? Oh, yes. Well...'

'You're blushing, Anne,' Charles broke off a piece of cucumber sandwich and popped it in his mouth. He continued, with rather less clarity, 'Mm, do tell us what you have been doing?'

'It's not so much what *I've* been doing.'

'Well who then, or what?'

'I'm trying to tell you, Jane.' Annie hesitated before blurting out, 'I... I'm to be married.'

'You are? Why, that's wonderful!' Charles clapped his hands in delight.

Jane was somewhat more restrained in her enthusiasm. 'What do you mean, married? At your age?'

Annie knew that Jane expected to remain a spinster for the rest of her days. To have her younger sister propose changing her single status must come as an unwelcome shock to her.

Annie said, quietly, 'I'm only 46,' then added, 'and Wesley's just 43.'

'Wesley!' Charles' teacup remained, hovering next to his lips. 'Wesley Lyttle, the editor of the *Gazette*?

'Your employer!' Now Jane *was* shocked.

Annie's eyes remained demurely downcast as she answered, 'Yes. Wesley and I are to be wed in October.'

It must have seemed expedient to Wesley to marry the woman who had essentially been mother to his children for most of the last two years. She had stepped into the role soon after Lizzie had gone to be looked after by Isabella. His appreciation of all Miss Byers had brought to the family during that time had surely engendered a growing fondness for her. He knew there would be those who would say it was too soon after Lizzie's death to be taking a new wife but he was never one to dwell overlong on other people's opinions. He must have been delighted at Annie's ready acceptance of his proposal.

Following some discussion, they agreed upon an October wedding, regardless of what the town's busybodies may think. Annie, with her feminine insight, may have feared the source of any opposition might be closer to home.

Family heirloom

Somewhere around this period WG acquired this most impressive silver-plated pen and ink stand decorated with a splendid silvered stag

25 - RELATIONSHIPS—BROKEN AND FORGED

and complete with a crystal inkwell. It is one of only two artefacts of his, apart from some early copies of his books, that has survived. This reminder of my great-grandfather sits in pride of place on my desk as I key these words. Stamped in the base is the name of the manufacturer, James Deakin & Sons, Sheffield, dating it to within an eleven year period from 1886 to 1897.[216]

Could it have been bought earlier as a gift from his first wife, Lizzie? Such a fine piece of silverware would certainly have been purchased in the city. She could have asked her sister to buy it for her in time to present it as a special commemorative item to mark the forthcoming publication of her husband's first novel.

Perhaps Wesley selected the item himself, as he was writing the final chapters of *Betsy Gray* It would have made a perfect holder for the pen he fashioned from a twig cut from the willow tree that grew by Adair's grave in Ballykine.

Or might it not have been a loving wedding gift from Annie? The other surviving memento we have is a few serving spoons, monographed with the initials WGL, from a canteen of silver cutlery that seems subsequently to have been divided up between WG's various children and grandchildren. But could the cutlery have been Wesley's wedding present to Annie in return for the beautiful stag pen and ink stand? We can only speculate, but it is good to have both the stag and the spoons and to know they were once used by WG, himself, over a hundred and twentyfive years ago.

Of interest here is that, although commercial typewriters were by now just beginning to become more common in Britain's offices, I have found no evidence that WG ever advanced beyond using the trusty pen and ink. Indeed, in Chapter 33 we refer to the existence of some typos in an edition of *The Bangor Season* as late as 1895, the explanation for which seems to be the typesetter misreading WG's handwriting. It is odd that the man who embraced innovation in other ways did not appear to do so in this instance.

---

[216] James Deakin's company was founded in 1866 but it wasn't until 1886 that the company's name changed to include his sons. Then in 1897 they became a limited company and the name changed again to James Deakin & Sons Ltd. So the inkstand must have been manufactured between '86 and '97.

THE STORYTELLER

The wedding

There was much more to arrange for the forthcoming marriage than just the matter of presents for each other. Perhaps because First Bangor Presbyterian Church held too many memories of Lizzie, Wesley came up with what he must have considered the ideal solution for where they should be married. His Annie, just like her namesake in *Sons of the Sod*, would be married in the popular country church at Ballygilbert.[217] (Incidentally, this is the church where in 1960, or thereabouts, WG's own grandson, my father, would be invited to preach as a guest speaker, and where I sat as a young lad listening to his sermon on a balmy, late summer Sunday evening where a setting sun cast ruddy shadows across the aisle in the darkening sanctuary; the very aisle, though neither of us knew it at the time, that our illustrious ancestor had walked down with his new bride some seven decades before.)

WG had researched the church for his *Sons of the Sod* and this is what he wrote about it:

> *Ballygilbert Presbyterian Church has always been a favourite place for the celebration of marriages. It occupies a retired and pleasant site upon the country road leading from Belfast to Bangor, about a couple of miles distant from the latter town.*
>
> *At the period of which I write, The Rev. John Quartz, a native of County Down, had just been ordained to the ministry and installed at Ballygilbert. Never did pastor and people become more rapidly knit together in the bonds of Christian affection and love. Gifted with a richly cultured mind, an eloquent delivery, a pleasing and prepossessing presence, the young minister rapidly acquired immense popularity. Wherever he preached crowded congregations listened with breathless attention to the chaste language, the glowing poetic imagery, and the burning eloquence which distinguished him as a*

---

[217] For photographs of Ballygilbert church see Appendix F, Figs 15, 16.

25 - RELATIONSHIPS—BROKEN AND FORGED

preacher; wherever he visited, old and young received him with every manifestation of pleasure, regarding him not only as their affectionate spiritual teacher but also as their true earthly friend and advisor.[218]

The Rev Quartz was still the minister at Ballygilbert Presbyterian over 30 years later and WG had met him from time to time at various functions. It was to this gentleman, therefore, that WG turned to seek to make arrangements for his planned nuptials.

Having just been given such a splendid write-up in the recently published *Sons of the Sod*, the Rev Quartz, perhaps not surprisingly, was happy to unite the two in the bonds of holy matrimony. And united they were, on Thursday, 20th October, 1887, as evidenced by their marriage certificate. It also shows that Annie's sister, Jane Carson Byers was one of the witnesses, presumably acting as her bridesmaid. The other was a friend of Wesley's, James Rippard; his Best Man, probably.[219]

We have no further details of the happy occasion. We don't know what was sung during the service but we do know, from the church records, that Ballygilbert had not yet embraced the use of musical instruments at that time. The tunes at the wedding were raised by a precentor.[220] But the singing would have been lusty, I am sure, as there would probably have been quite a large turnout for the wedding of such a prominent Bangor citizen. Many friends and business acquaintances and even readers of the *Bangor Gazette* with time on their hands, would have been happy to go to see the town's newspaper editor tie the knot.

Did these good folk, perhaps—as WG described the occasion of the wedding in *Sons of the Sod*—see the bridal party arrive in "several handsome carriages, each drawn by a couple of magnificent white horses, dashing along at a rattling pace"? And after the ceremony,

---

[218] From *Sons of the Sod—a Tale of County Down*, WG Lyttle, 1886

[219] On WG's second Marriage Certificate, unlike on his first, his father's surname is spelt with a "y." This is, no doubt, due to the Rev Quartz assuming that WG's father would have had the same surname as his son.

[220] I am grateful to Molly McConaghy of Ballygilbert Presbyterian Church for researching this information for me.

when the pair had struggled through the crowd of well-wishers and finally reached their carriage, were they "followed by showers of rice, old shoes and slippers and a cheer such as has rarely been heard so near the sacred precincts of a church" as they were whisked away for the wedding breakfast?

Wesley's children would, doubtless, have been among the cheering crowd, although whether 21-year-old John and his 19-year-old sister, Agnes were there under protest—perhaps just to look after their younger siblings—or whether they boycotted the event altogether, we do not know. But the marriage did not meet with their approval and what semblance of a relationship there had been between Wesley's two elder children and their erstwhile housekeeper was now broken completely.

Young Eva, Roland and Robina were happy to embrace their father's new wife as a mother figure and, in time, came to love her as they had Lizzie. But Agnes and John could not empathise with their father's own needs and feelings. To them, his remarrying just eleven months after burying Lizzie seemed callous. Identifying with their mother, they must have felt, somehow, abandoned. And, of course, it was all Miss Byer's fault; she had bewitched their father; stolen him from them.

We can imagine Annie's attempts to make friends with Wesley's two older children on her return from their honeymoon, and we can, perhaps as easily, hear the rejection from John and Agnes: 'You are *not* our mother; you never will be.'

Chapter 26 – A SETBACK

1887 – 1888

The strained relationship between his new bride and his elder children must have pained Wesley but he probably realised there was now little he could do about it—having made the decision and married Annie. John had recently become of age; his 21st birthday was in August. He would soon be leaving home permanently as he was being transferred to Larne with his engineering design job with Great Northern Railways.

On his departure from Bangor he would have taken his fond farewells from his siblings. The exchange with his father may have been cooler and with Annie, non-existent.

Two Hours with "Robin"

Nevertheless, a few months later, in early December, 1887, John most probably managed to get a seat in Larne's M'Garel Town Hall when it was packed to capacity for an entertainment entitled, "Two Hours with Robin." This was a new venture for Wesley where, instead of merely providing a reading or two as part of a variety concert, he—or rather "Robin"—was the star of the evening with just one other performer to give "Robin", and the audience, a brief break.

According to the newspaper report, amongst the pieces he read, was a comical poem WG had written "especially for the occasion all about Larne in 20 years" time, entitled, *Larne in 1907*. Well, some of the verses would certainly have been penned specifically for Larne, but this was clearly WG's poem, *Bangor in 1907* with the local references changed to reflect life in the Antrim town, instead. From his travels around the Province he must have become familiar with a number of its more prominent citizens. The poem's gently humorous style still delighted his audience who received it with as much enthusiasm as had the Bangor folk back in the summer.

As he took his final bow to the cheering applause of the crowded auditorium, was he remembering a time when he was part of an Ulster Hall audience showing similar appreciation to the celebrated Charles Dickens? An occasion that maybe played a part in propelling him along the theatrical path he had chosen. He had first seen Dickens perform exactly twenty years ago, in 1867. His son, little John Wesley was just beginning to toddle then, and now, as a Larne resident, John was out there in the audience, a full-grown man, clapping his father's achievement. As Wesley left the stage with the applause ringing in his ears, he could be forgiven for thinking that, whatever the next twenty years might hold, he had come a long way in the last two decades.

Such was his growing prestige that he had been invited over to Glasgow a week later to take part in the annual Ulster Reunion, just before Christmas. WG chose to read two poems by other Irish writers, *God bless the hills, the Irish hills,* and *Gi' me your han' we're bruthers a'.* Why did he not appear as his arguably more famous alterego, "Robin" and read some of his own poems? The main speaker was Sir James Haslett, the prominent Ulster businessman, Conservative MP and current Mayor of Belfast, who had a robust figure and full beard, and bore a remarkable resemblance to a slightly posher version of "Robin," himself. Perhaps caution, for once, constrained WG's exuberance.

Right to vote

In the following February WG received a letter complaining about the inaccuracy of the Bangor voting list contained in his newly-published 1888 Directory and Almanac. This gave him the opportunity to reassure readers that his list was "almost" an exact copy of the Town Clerk's official sheets; "almost," because he had actually made a few corrections to the official list to include *all* those entitled to vote, regardless of whether they had previously exercised their right. Although the October elections were still some way off, he encouraged everyone with the right to vote to confirm that their names

26 - A SETBACK

were listed in order to ensure that the three commissioners who would be standing for re-election could be "crushingly defeated".

Writing the paragraph for the *Gazette* set WG to thinking. If Bowman and his cronies in the Clique were to be ousted there would need to be others to stand against them. His thoughts turned back to his brief time on the Newtownards Board of Commissioners.

An ungrateful Chiel

But other matters were soon occupying his mind. An intriguing editorial appeared in the *Gazette* in March under the heading, "The Chiel is ungrateful." It seems that the editor of the *Newtownards Chronicle* had come under some criticism of late. Henry was charged, according to WG's report, "of violating a written promise, betraying bosom friends, attempting to extort money from an over-taxed body of ratepayers." In the previous issue of the *Gazette* WG had, he claimed, "defended him to the best of our humble ability... We declared him to be, in our opinion, utterly incapable of such dishonourable behaviour, and declared our conviction that when the matter should be brought under his notice he would crush his would-be calumniators under his iron heel."[221]

WG's support of Henry would seem laudable, until we realise that in "defending" the Chiel against these charges the *Gazette* was in fact giving wide publicity to them and to this Henry apparently took great exception. His "ungrateful" response cannot better be described than in WG's own fair rhetoric:

> *In return for all this we have been most shamefully treated. When our newspapers were being bought up with lightning rapidity in Newtownards, he dashed through the streets like one demented, throttled the*

---

[221] What had brought about these accusations was Henry's furnishing his "bosom friends"—the Bangor Town Commissioners and hence, indirectly, the "over-taxed ratepayers"—with a bill for publishing the notice in the *Chronicle* that he had offered to carry free of charge some months back. When his offer had failed to deprive the *Gazette* of the revenue after all—as the notice appeared subsequently in the Bangor paper, too—Henry, apparently, didn't see why he should be left out of pocket.

newsboys, tore the papers from their hands, stormed at and shelled them until the frightened and overawed urchins ran for their lives. He threatened our agents with all the pains and penalties of the law if they did not instantly suspend the sale of the North Down Herald, Newtownards Argos, *and* Bangor Gazette, *while all the time people clamoured for copies* [note WG's use of the full title of the Newtownards edition of the paper.]

But that was not all. On Saturday he went to Belfast, and, calling upon a solicitor who has inaugurated for him countless abortive lawsuits, had a voluminous summons drafted, calling upon us to appear at the Bangor Petty Sessions on Wednesday, the 21st day of March, in the year of our Lord one thousand eight hundred and eighty eight, to shew cause why we should not for the next twelve months enjoy the retirement of a prison cell, the luxury of water, gruel and dry bread, the exhilarating exercise of picking oakum, and the delightfully refreshing slumbers of a plank bed.

Armed with this formidable document, and nursing his wrath to keep it warm, the Chiel was, on Sunday, driven by John Copeland's liveried man[222] *to Belfast, where he consulted a certain Barrister-at-law. And here there was a collapse. The said Barrister was too shrewd not to see the Chiel's blunder, and so, unlawer-like, he rejected the one-hundred-guinea fee and prospective Judge-ship which were certain to follow the caging of a chirping "Robin"!*

---

[222] John Copeland was a local businessman and long-standing Town Commissioner who served on the Newtownards Board contemporaneously with both WG and William Henry and lived on West Street. It seems he allowed his friend, Henry, the use of one of his business cars (a horse drawn vehicle) and his driver.

26 - A SETBACK

So WG was not sued after all. He was, however, advised to sue Henry for intimidating his agents—"a painful duty," the editorial concluded, "but in the interests of common justice we fear that these unpleasant steps must be taken." However, I think we can take this as written with tongue in cheek. It is followed by a news item headed, IMPORTANT NOTICE:

> *We are informed that a person calling himself the "Chiel," and described as of medium height, Aldermanish build, florid complexion, sandy hair and whiskers, the latter tinged with grey, pompous bearing and bumptious manner of speech, assaulted our newsboys on Friday and Saturday, last, and used language towards our Agents calculated to intimidate them from selling the North Down Herald and Bangor Gazette. Newsboys and Agents thus insulted will please communicate at once with our office. All persons who were refused papers will be supplied at the Bangor Office on application.*

New city, new technology, new destinations, a new church and a new edition of *Betsy Gray*

In 1888 WG would have been proud, I am sure, to be recording in his journal how Queen Victoria was granting city status to Belfast. He had seen it more than double in size in his own lifetime from around 50,000 people to well over 100,000. (By the turn of the century the population would exceed 300,000, briefly overtaking Dublin as the largest city in Ireland.) Belfast was fast becoming one of the world's leading industrial cities. WG would surely have admired the big firms like Harland and Wolff, shipbuilders, and the many advances in the linen industry and the rope works.

He was always one with an eye on the latest developments. Wasn't he, himself, the owner of the finest home printing press in County Down, complete with its gas engine. In June of '88 he was fascinated to report that the enterprising Bangor firm of Messrs E and W Pim had installed one of the new communication devices called a telephone in their Bangor office for use by the public. For the princely

THE STORYTELLER

sum of sixpence (a little under £3 in 2021) they could speak with people in the newly declared city of Belfast, Carrickfergus, Larne, Lisburn and Newtownards. This was a privately installed line; no exchange would be established in Bangor for a long time yet.

Anecdotal evidence in the family has always maintained that WG had the first telephone in Bangor; one of the few photographs of him that have survived shows him speaking on the phone.[223] However it would be 1891 before the *Gazette* introduced a column of (mostly spoof) interviews via telephone. The idea for these would undoubtedly have arisen soon after WG had his own private line installed. On this evidence, it would seem to have been three years after the Messrs Pim's installation of a public phone. It is likely, though, that WG's line *was* the first to a private house in Bangor.

Another story WG would surely have printed to entertain his readers was that of the development of a new device that could "listen" to speech or song and then reproduce the same, or a reasonable facsimile of the original sound. Its American inventor, Mr Thomas Edison, was calling it a Phonograph and WG's report would have explained that it recorded the sound on wax cylinders which could hold two or three minutes' worth of recording. The wax couldn't be too hard and so the "recording" soon wore off after about a dozen or so plays. It was just a novelty but fun for those who could afford it.

However, within only a few years, Edison had developed hard wax cylinders which were much more durable. Phonographs became popular, particularly with pre-recorded music on cylinders but also to make recordings of important speeches and the like, including humorous monologues. By 1894 or 5 it would have been perfectly possible for "Robin" to have been so recorded. Might he have been? Is there an ancient wax cylinder in its tubular cardboard box lying in someone's attic unwittingly holding the voice of WG as his alter-ego, "Robin Gordon of Ballycuddy"? What a wonderful find that would be.

Wednesday 17th July was the date for what had now become the Bangor Annual General Holiday—a daytrip out for crowds of local residents and summer visitors, alike. Many businesses and shops

---

[223] A photo of WG Lyttle on the telephone is at Appendix E, Figure 6

26 - A SETBACK

closed for the day to give their employees this holiday. Did the North Down Print Works close up shop, too? Most likely. Did some, or even all of the Lyttles join the holidaymakers? At least, WG would have had one of his reporters tag along and could well have chosen to go himself. If he did—with, or without his family—he would have been down at the pier by 6:30 in the morning to catch the paddle steamship, *Armagh*, sailing for Ayr in Scotland. He'd have spent some time looking round places of historical interest in that town before catching a special excursion train to pass a few fascinating hours at the Glasgow Exhibition. The train departed at 6:00 p.m. for its return journey to Ayr where the excursionists re-boarded the steamship which left for Bangor at 7:30 in the evening. Worn out but happy, they reached home in the small hours of Thursday morning. A few hours later, dawn would see most of them up again and preparing for another full day back at work.

August of 1888 also saw the opening of new premises on Main Street for 2nd Bangor Presbyterian Church. This was made possible by their recently appointed minister, Rev William Clarke, donating almost a third of the building costs. A competition had been run using the medium of the *Gazette* to come up with a suitable name for the Church which resulted in 117 entries. Unfortunately some of these, inspired by the close proximity of a private slaughter house, had to be disregarded. Nevertheless there was an eclectic variety of names suggested, from the more obvious, "Main Street Presbyterian" and the slightly optimistic, "Seaview Presbyterian" to the sectarian, "No Popery Church" and "No Surrender Church" and the more traditional, "Bethel" and "Ebenezer." The best entry was judged to be, "The Clarke Memorial Church", which won £4 for its originator. However, although it won the competition, the appellation was not adopted. The church stands to this day, known to all by the name it was eventually given—"Trinity Presbyterian Church".

Betsy Gray continued to be much in demand. A second edition was clearly needed. WG obtained the paper and all that was necessary for the covers and binding and got his printer to fit the work in between editions of the *Gazette*. He soon had a large stock of the novel to be sold at sixpence a copy—the 1888 edition. Several copies were destined to survive for well over 100 years and come to be regarded as "first editions," for none of the previous year's smaller print run, marked at one shilling, have apparently enjoyed the same longevity. (Unless someone reading this knows differently!)

Election time again

As that summer progressed, WG was being approached by a number of prominent Bangorians to see if he wouldn't consider standing at the elections in October for a seat on the Board of Town Commissioners to oust one of the Clique. He would always have answered in the same fashion, saying that ever since moving to Bangor he had felt he could best serve the people by remaining independent and holding the commissioners to account, if their conduct of municipal affairs was anything less than satisfactory. However, with polling day, Monday 14th October, drawing nearer and only one other potential new candidate in the offing—a friend of WG and a fellow-mason, solicitor Daniel M'Callum—WG yielded to the persuasion of his friends and allowed his name to go forward.

There were three seats being vacated and the sitting candidates, Bowman, Pollock and Cleland were all up for re-election. Closing date for nominations was the Thursday before polling and WG and M'Callum duly submitted their papers. These were scrutinised by Solicitor Dinnen, who had been employed by the commissioners, at the ratepayers' expense, to advise them on all matters to do with the nominations and polling. He declared the two new candidates' papers to be slightly informal and recommended they should be rejected. A commissioner warned, however, that if that were done "the editor of the *Gazette* would excite the indignation of the Ratepayers by giving them particulars of the affair." It was decided to allow the nominations to stand.

On Sunday, on the eve of the polls, in a blatant attempt to discredit one of the candidates and affect the voting, one of the commissioners let it be widely known that Mr M'Callum had telegrammed to say that he had not given any permission to have his name put forward for election. The claim was patently untrue as only the previous day, in the *Gazette,* M'Callum's election address had appeared along with WG's.

26 - A SETBACK

The main thrust of WG's statement was to say that if the people wanted open decision-making, transparency in how they were governed, a Board that held itself accountable to the people it was elected to serve, they should vote for Lyttle and M'Callum.

The polls opened at 8:00 am and voters came in dribs and drabs throughout the day—mostly with one or other of the sitting candidates who accompanied them right up to the voting booth. WG eventually objected to this, saying that, while candidates couldn't be stopped canvassing for votes outside the polling station, they really should not be allowed to influence how people cast their votes inside. The Presiding Officer agreed with him and said he would not allow it to continue. WG, himself, refused to seek to influence the voters, believing it was insulting their intelligence not to leave them to make up their own minds.

Perhaps, however, they didn't all have quite the intelligence he credited them with. Bowman came top of the poll once again with 120 votes; Pollock and Clelland polled 109 and 106, respectively. M'Callum, who had also refused to canvas, attracted 62 votes while 53 people voted for WG. A return to municipal leadership for the editor of the *North Down Herald and Bangor Gazette* was not to be.

What effect did his defeat have upon the man? Was his ego dented, his ambition thwarted? He allowed himself this statement in the next Saturday's *Gazette*:

BANGOR ELECTION
THANKS

I beg to return my sincere thanks to the fifty-three intelligent and independent electors who voted for me on Monday last. While I was willing to bring myself down to the level of the present Board I could not so far degrade myself as to resort to bribery, treachery and deception—therefore I was defeated. The voters' list must be properly prepared before an independent candidate can be elected. So long as that list is manipulated by a few ignorant and inflated residents, so long will Bangor be governed by a bigoted, intolerant, and bungling clique.

W. G. Lyttle

THE STORYTELLER

We must judge for ourselves how he was feeling.

But it was all soon water under the bridge and life returned, briefly, to its usual routine. It was, however, the first of a series of setbacks that, over the next twelve months, would rock WG's world to its very foundations.

Chapter 27 – THE STRANGLING ANGEL

1888, November – 1889, March

Henry gloats

The *Newtownards Chronicle* lost no opportunity to revel in the electoral defeat of its rival paper's editor. It must have felt like icing on the cake to William Henry, for less than two weeks earlier he had been honoured with a testimonial by many of his friends and colleagues from Newtownards and across the Province. He was presented with a gift of 200 guineas, from their subscriptions, for 40 years of service to journalism. The report of many tributes paid to him in speeches on that occasion showed him in a rather different light to the picture one might imagine through reading of him only in the columns of the *North Down Herald and Bangor Gazette*. He was, it would seem, (apart from any occasional errors of judgement which WG was always ready to point out) held in high esteem by his friends and regarded as a trustworthy and honest purveyor of the news. He was apparently considered by those present, who included some prominent dignitaries, to be of a fine and upright character whose contribution to the town, both personally and through his newspaper was highly regarded.

This, at least, is the conclusion that cannot be avoided from reading the *Chronicle's* own write-up of the event and the speeches. We shall learn later, though, that in addition to the many who contributed to William Henry's testimonial there were also prominent figures who refused to make a donation.

However, it was with such complimentary tributes still ringing in his ears that Henry sat down to compose his report on the Bangor elections. The Chiel wrote of WG in similar style to that used by the

THE STORYTELLER

Bangor man about the Town Commissioners. "The people of Bangor have shown their appreciation of the troublesome intermeddler in their business by putting him in his proper position at the bottom of the poll," he wrote. He accused him of "wallowing in the gutter, raking up all the vile charges he can gather against respectable people," and of "inventing malicious gossip." He referred to the "vile and contemptable slang written and uttered by him respecting ourselves," and how "he has vilified Mr James Bowman for years with a description of blackguardism which no decent man would take cognisance of." There was more in similar vein.

WG, I expect, filed away a copy for future reference—it would, no doubt, come in useful at some stage—and then forgot about it. He was looking forward to a rare evening out with a young lady. Nothing untoward, of course, the young lady in question being his eldest daughter, Agnes.

Family act

Soon after the election Wesley had been asked by the kirk session of Groomsport Presbyterian Church if he would contribute his talents to aid a concert they were arranging to raise much needed funds for building work. It wasn't due to take place until the middle of December but he was happy to oblige and when they told him they were still looking for other performers he must have mentioned that he knew a young singer who might be cajoled into taking part.

Agnes was the singer in the family and perhaps he hoped if he could persuade her to help aid this good cause by coming with him to the Groomsport concert it might be a means of improving their relationship; she still made it plain that she disapproved of his re-marrying. If he had ever asked her before, she must have always demurred, but now aged twenty, she allowed herself to be persuaded. She chose a risqué little piece about "Three young maids from Lee who had lovers three times three." It was called *A Bird in Hand* by the lyricist, Frederick E. Weatherly, set to music by Joseph Roeckel. She had probably bought the sheet music when it was first published three years earlier.

27 - THE STRANGLING ANGEL

Friday 14th December found father and daughter in their pony and trap, trotting down Groomsport's wide thoroughfare past a terrace of whitewashed, thatched cottages on the right shortly before turning into the grounds of the Presbyterian Church. Wesley was to perform twice, once as himself, reading *The Lifeboat* by GR Simms (in the event, he had to give an encore and chose *The Irish Hills* by Francis Davis.) Then it was off for a quick change to re-emerge as the elderly, bearded country farmer, "Robin." In this guise, his rendering of *Paddy M'Quillan's Twins* and *Wee Paddy's Bumps* "elicited the heartiest bursts of laughter and applause from start to finish," according to the write-up in the following Monday's *Belfast News-Letter*. The report also mentioned that "*A Bird in Hand* was charmingly sung by Miss Lyttle, whose first appearance in public was of a most promising character."

Agnes was, no doubt, impressed to see the large schoolroom adjacent to the Church filled to capacity. She may have overheard some of the audience when they remarked that the entertainment was "one of the best ever held in Groomsport." She could feel proud of her contribution to the success of the evening. Knowing that her father could be equally satisfied with his own, would still have been tempered by her feelings about his marrying the housekeeper. Nevertheless, the two must, surely, have enjoyed their evening together. Sadly, though, it did not achieve Wesley's secret hopes of a reconciliation.

If Agnes was uncommunicative on the journey home, at least it would have allowed WG some time to ponder a number of matters. Things like cash flow. These charity dos were all very well but he needed to be earning money. He had incurred considerable expense in the summer in order to print the large new stock of his novel, *Betsy Gray*. It was still proving to be extremely popular and these were selling but it would take time before he recovered his costs and started to make a profit. He was in dispute with W. &. G. Baird, his erstwhile printers, over amounts they were claiming he owed.[224] What he needed was a further boost to his newspaper circulation. How to achieve this, and all these other matters, could easily have occupied

---

[224] For about a year in 1884/5 the *North Down Herald and Bangor Gazette* had been printed by W. & G. Baird at their Telegraph Printing Works in Belfast.

his mind until they got home late that Friday, or early on Saturday morning, in fact. If Annie muttered something drowsily about Eva being off her food at teatime as he tumbled into bed, he was probably too tired to respond.

Lying, awaiting sleep, his mind would have been full of all that had been happening: of his night out with Agnes at the concert; of her beautiful singing and how well she had been received; of her coolness towards him and her downright rudeness to Annie; his debts, and Baird, the printers, threatening litigation; his *own* loss of appetite in recent months when he had been in indifferent health, himself, from time to time. Perhaps he found himself sympathising with young Eva as, exhausted, he drifted into unconsciousness.

Eva's Illness

From what we can determine from documentary evidence poor Eva's condition must have rather dominated family life at "Mount Herald" over the next few weeks. Let us join the Lyttle's for a while, as the Festive Season approaches

> Christmas wasn't such a joyous occasion at "Mount Herald" that year. Fourteen-year-old Eva could not enter into the celebrations. Having started off just feeling under the weather and not hungry, after a few days she developed a sore throat. Wesley sent Annie to buy some linctus that helped to ease the pain a little but by Christmas Day she was no better, in fact she was considerably worse and confined to her bed. Her breathing was becoming difficult. Annie spent a lot of time comforting her but Agnes stayed with her, too, and seemed to resent the times when her step-mother was there.
>
> The doctor was treating her for a bad case of laryngitis but the doses of medicine he prescribed were having little effect. Her throat remained painful and her breathing, laboured.

27 - THE STRANGLING ANGEL

Wesley had an important meeting of his Masonic Lodge to attend the night after Boxing Day but he was loath to leave his young daughter in such a poorly state. It was the installation ceremony of the officers-elect for the coming year, after which there would be a dinner with entertainment; Wesley was supposed to be doing a recitation. Annie told him he should go. He couldn't do anything to help Eva by staying at home.

Reluctantly, therefore, he set off to walk along Hamilton Road past his sister-in-law's home, and on until he reached the Lodge. He was in no mood for a jolly evening with his brother Masons but somehow he got through it. His recitation after dinner was "much admired" according to the report in Saturday's *News-Letter*. He even managed to reply with some suitable remarks when Lord Clanmoris proposed a toast to "The Press" with which he coupled the *Gazette* and named its editor. The hearty round of applause he received seemed a hollow echo somewhere beyond the reality of the anxious thoughts about his daughter that were flooding his mind.

Wesley hurried home as soon as he could get away and, late as the hour was, went straight to Eva's room. Agnes was there, sitting in a chair with an open book on her lap, her head falling forwards. She jerked up as her father entered. 'I must have just dozed for a moment. I don't think Eva's asleep; it's her breathing. Oh, Father, what are we to do?'

Wesley lifted Eva's clammy hand and held it. 'You go off to bed, Agnes. I'll sit with her. If she's no better in the morning we'll send for the doctor again.'

Eva had a bad night and the doctor duly arrived the next day. As soon as he saw her condition he began to fear she had contracted something much more serious.

THE STORYTELLER

It was painful for Eva to open her mouth wide but he examined her throat again and was alarmed to see the thick grey coating that had now built up on her soft palate and around her tonsils. It was this, he declared, that was restricting her windpipe and making breathing difficult.

The medical man recognised the symptoms. The covering of thick film at the back of the girl's throat was literally slowly strangling her. The disease had the horrific colloquial name of "The Strangling Angel of Children" but he couldn't say that to the child's despairing father.

When he left Eva's room he spoke to Wesley in a low voice. 'I fear strongly that she may have contracted something known as Diphtheria. It is a disease becoming increasingly prevalent with the growth of industrialisation. Little is yet known about it but I believe it is thought to be caused by a bacterial infection.

'Well, what can you do about it?' Wesley demanded. 'How should we be treating her?'

'There is no cure. I fear there is nothing we can do but hope that it will gradually start to subside, and go as mysteriously as it came. That does often happen,' the doctor added, in an effort to reassure Wesley. 'We will know one way or the other inside the next week.'

'A week! What—what are you saying, Doctor?'

It was the longest week of Wesley's life—the longest six days, in fact. The family took turns sitting with poor Eva as she struggled for each breath. Annie coaxed her to take a little nourishment. She made a delicious and nutritious vegetable soup to tempt the girl to drink—it was too difficult for her to swallow solids. But her condition continued to worsen.

27 - THE STRANGLING ANGEL

Each day they looked for signs that she might have turned the corner. Each day they saw only the poor child gasping harder to take in air. There were no New Year's Eve celebrations for the Lyttles, as Monday, 31st December rolled over into Tuesday, 1st January, 1889. New Year's Day passed quietly with the family always hovering not far from Eva's room, someone always with her, fearful she would not last another night.

Wednesday dawned. It was to be Eva's last day. "The Strangling Angel" had proved relentless. There was to be no reprieve. Agnes was with her when the struggle finally became too much. Eva had lost the battle.[225]

Five days later Wesley registered the death of his daughter—the second of his children to die before their time.[226] The certificate reads; "1889 Second January, Mount Herald Bangor. Evelyne Elisabeth Lyttle, female, spinster, 14 years. Daughter of Wesley G. Lyttle, newspaper proprietor. Diphtheria. Agnes Lyttle, sister, present at the death."

Plagiarism

There was to be little respite for WG following this private family tragedy. The very next month his business came under attack.

Volume 3 of *Robin's Readings* was being published by R Carswell & Son Ltd. It contained an advert saying a second edition of Volume 2 was "in preparation." Aware that he had mounting bills to be paid, WG was in the process of re-issuing *Robin's Readings, Volume 2—The Adventures of Robin Gordon* as an illustrated edition, printed on his own press. It would bring in more profit than he'd get in royalties from another publisher. So both volumes must have been

---

[225] Diphtheria infections, known then as "The Strangling Angel of Children", were common in WG's time. The disease was fatal in 5-10% of cases. Outbreaks are rare nowadays due to vaccination programmes. The life-saving treatments of antibiotics and tracheostomies were, of course, unknown in Victorian times.

[226] WG's second son, Robert had died in infancy in 1871 (see chapter 5).

released in the first half of 1889, with Volume 3 preceding the new, illustrated edition of Volume 2.

While undertaking this work he discovered that a Belfast printer was seeking advertisers, in his name, for a new edition of *Robin's Readings*. This flagrant act of potential plagiarism had to be stopped. WG placed a newspaper ad on 22nd February, 1889, which read:

> **IMPORTANT**
> **TO AGENTS, ADVERTISERS AND BOOKSELLERS**
>
> *I am informed that a Belfast printer is issuing an edition of my works known as "ROBIN'S READINGS"*
>
> *and that he is soliciting advertisements for the same in my name.*
>
> *I HEREBY GIVE NOTICE that I possess the sole right to publish the books referred to, and I desire Agents, Advertisers, and Booksellers to deal with me only both as regards to purchases of copies and the insertion of advertisements.*
>
> *My new edition, revised and illustrated, will shortly be ready. It will be the only authentic and authorised issue of the "READINGS" which are commanding so rapid a sale.*
>
> *W. G. LYTTLE*
> *NORTH DOWN PRINTING WORKS, BANGOR, CO. DOWN.*

Prison

WG's debt to W & G Baird was sizable, at £255. This is equivalent to almost £29,500 in 2021. He can't have been giving his business affairs the attention they needed during Lizzie's long illness. With the renewed family tragedy of losing Eva over Christmas and New Year, and the business with the rogue publisher, matters had deteriorated to a situation where he now had a court injunction granted against him.

27 - THE STRANGLING ANGEL

He had paid the Bairds £5 (about £550, in 2021) in a bid to keep them happy, but it wasn't enough. On 8th February the Dublin courts heard from Barrister Hume, on behalf of the plaintiff, W & G Baird, requesting an order that the defendant, WG Lyttle "should be directed to pay a sum of £250, with costs, by instalments of £7 a month, or that he be committed to prison in default of doing so."

The Judge made an order that WG should pay off the debt at £5 a month. This was going to be a considerable undertaking but he set about arranging how it could be done. He could expect extra income from the two volumes of *Robin's Readings* about to be released but what he needed was a new serial to run in his paper to give the circulation another boost and attract more advertising; it was well over a year since *Betsy Gray* had finished. The problem was he couldn't afford to pay a writer.

Daft Eddy

His thoughts turned to one of the stories that had been printed ten years previously in the *Newtownards Independent*—what was it? *The Merry Hearts of Down*, if he remembered correctly. It had been a good story about the eponymous band of smugglers, although rather poorly written, he seemed to recall, by the semi-anonymous "Rev. J. B." Some time ago, he had taken a good look at it and started to give it a thorough edit to make a better tale of it. He changed some clumsy phrasing, altered the occasional word that was repeated in close proximity; he put some chapter divisions in different places to increase the tension and even rearranged the order of some of the chapters to create a more coherent feel to the narrative. Also, not being convinced as to the original authorship of the story, he removed a few sentences where the Rev. J. B., or perhaps, an earlier, original author, had made one or two oblique references to themselves. But the biggest, and perhaps the best, improvement he made was to add fresh background material and relevant matters of current local interest to flesh out the basic tale as it had appeared in the earlier serialisation.

It was to these notes that he turned over the next few weeks.

As he further polished the manuscript he realised that, perhaps sub-consciously, but with the experienced ear of a storyteller, he had turned the tale into one, not primarily about a band of murderous smugglers but rather about the hapless young lad who brings about their downfall. What he ended up with was somewhere in the region of 25% his own writing and 75% someone else's, albeit considerably edited and improved by him.

He serialised the story in the *Gazette* from 22nd March, 1889 under the name of its hero, *Daft Eddy* with the sub-title, *The Smugglers of Strangford Lough—a Tale of Killinchy and the Ards*. The story was completely unattributed in the paper. It was, by then, an excellent yarn and served its purpose well, ensuring a healthy circulation and advertising revenue for WG's journal week by week.[227]

Henry rakes over the coals

As it happened, demand for the *Gazette* increased before March 22nd thanks to WG's long-standing rivalry with William Henry. The editor of the Newtownards paper spotted an item in the *Belfast News-Letter* that reported the facts of the Dublin court ruling on how WG must repay his large outstanding debt to W & G Baird. He gleefully pounced upon this and dedicated a full one-and-a-half columns of his next edition to disparaging WG.

By coincidence, the same court that ruled on WG's case was also hearing an entirely separate issue involving RS Allen, WG's co-defendant in the libel case that Henry brought against them some years back. The Chiel used this happenstance to introduce his article under the headline, "The Proprietor of the 'Chronicle' and his 'Libellers,' " and proceeded to broadcast to his local readership the full account of the size of WG's debt, the threat of imprisonment and the ruling made against him for the monthly repayments.

Then, having referred to the topic in his introduction, the rival editor went on to reiterate the circumstances of his five-year-old libel case against WG and his then printer. He wrote, "As there appears to be some confusion about the actual terms of Lyttle and Allen's apology, it may not be inopportune now to reproduce the report that appeared in the *Chronicle* of March 29th, 1884, and which, no doubt, will be exceedingly interesting reading at the present time."

---

[227] For a full analysis of the authorship of *Daft Eddy* see Appendix H.

27 - THE STRANGLING ANGEL

He seemed to relish the chance to publicise all over again how WG, in order to avoid a trial, as he put it, was forced to sign a statement withdrawing all the imputations Henry had complained of, regretting their publication and agreeing to pay Henry's costs in exchange for him withdrawing his charges of libel.

It might be questioned whether Henry was justified in reprinting the five-year-old account. Some might hold that this was gratuitous and even malicious, though others might contend that it was legitimate "background" to a current story about WG's debts.

Whatever WG's thoughts were on seeing his private financial situation plastered all over the *Chronicle,* he seized on Henry's eagerness to rake over the coals of the past to take the opportunity of letting his own, rather wider readership—which included Newtownards, of course—know the full truth behind the infamous libel case. For whatever might be thought of Henry's reprinting the article, now that he *had* raised the issue again, WG was perfectly justified in responding.

And this he was determined to do. He would print in his own columns the complete story that hitherto had not been publicised, since the matter never went to trial. He would complete what Henry had started.

Using almost the same headline as the one in the *Chronicle*, WG went with "The Chiel and his Libellers." He included a sub-heading, "Let Sleeping Dogs Lie", as a retrospective piece of advice for his neighbouring editor. WG planned to ensure the Chiel would regret raking up this case from the past.

THE STORYTELLER

Chapter 28 – RETRIBUTION

1889 – April to July

WG's article in the following Saturday's *Gazette*, "The Chiel and his Libellers,—Let Sleeping Dogs Lie" started by quoting "a popular County Down Magistrate speaking recently at a public board" who, it appears, was amongst those approached by William Henry's friends to contribute to his Testimonial. Not everyone was as eager to oblige as those mentioned in the *Chronicle's* write-up of the event. The magistrate claimed his failure to respond to the "dozen or twenty invitations, almost threats, demanding that I should subscribe" resulted in a *Chronicle* article about him headlined, "The Ballywalter Blusterer." Addressing the Board, he said:

> *I have been referred to once again by that animal known as the Chiel, who takes in gin, ale, Dunville, and Old Comber,[228] at other people's expense, and distils a portion into water, and the other into gas.*

WG wrote that "The pointed allusion to the alleged bibulous, spongy, and vindictive propensities of the Chiel elicited hearty laughter from those who heard it," inserting the word "alleged" in what would seem to have been a rare moment of journalistic caution. His article continued by saying that the Magistrate's words were reported in the *Gazette* without editorial comment. He went on:

> *The Chiel, emboldened by our silence—and possibly in other ways—has dragged the name of the North Down Herald into his greasy sheet of second-*

---

[228] Dunville's and Old Comber – popular brands of Irish whiskey

28 - RETRIBUTION

> *hand news... A garbled scrap from Dublin law reports, appearing in the Belfast News-Letter of 9th instant, headed "BAIRD V. LYTTLE" caught the eagle eye of the Chiel, putting him into such transports of delight that he narrowly escaped an apoplectic fit. Now it is perfectly right to criticise the public doings of a public individual, but only a coward will mock at a public man's misfortune. The proprietor of the North Down Herald freely admits that for years he was the victim of adverse circumstances. Ill-health[229] and unscrupulous printers will, in a very short time, ruin any literary man who does not happen to possess a gold mine or its equivalent, and it is to such circumstances that the Chiel is indebted for the delicate and savoury tid-bit which he is now in ecstasy rolling under his venomous tongue. The proprietor of the North Down Herald, it must be said, incurred his liabilities in all good faith, and he hopes to live to see them all honourably wiped out.*

Henry's transatlantic trip

WG then mentioned how his paper had remained sympathetically silent on many occasions to avoid embarrassing the Chiel. But not so any longer. In the guise of reminding the Newtownards editor of what he could have done, but didn't, he proceeded to detail a series of events in the Chiel's career for his readers' delectation. How, for example,

> *He went hat in hand to the Marquis of Londonderry's agent begging him to obtain from the Marquis sufficient money to take him to Canada. He should remember that the Marquis gave him £25 hoping to get rid of him. His efforts to get a free passage, his adventures across the herring pond, and*

---

[229] This is one of the very rare occasions when WG makes reference to the fact that he was not always in the best of health (see also Chapter 33)

THE STORYTELLER

> the manner of his return, we never touched upon, though urged by many of his so-called friends to do so. There was no congenial employment for him in Canada, no vacant governorship, not even an Indian tribe needing a white chief, and so he had a practical movement set on foot for the purposes of repairing his shattered fortunes. And here, again, he seems to forget our generosity. Despite the fact that the noble Marquis... refused to contribute even a shilling to the testimonial, and even although the parish priest, when asked to help the sinking Orangeman, returned the begging letter with the endorsement, 'I fail to see the merit;' despite this and much more that had better not be told, we wrote in advocacy of the scheme and were instrumental in sending cash to the Chiel's coffers. Unfortunately we appear not to have gone far enough, we refused either to act upon the presentation committee or to subscribe towards it, having no spare time for the one purpose and no spare cash for the other. And so, being on the Chiel's black list, the inevitable has happened—he pours out upon us the vials of his wrathful vituperations.

WG then turned to the fact that Henry had brought up the five-year-old libel case and said he was treading on dangerous ground.

> The public never heard all the TRUTH about the so-called libel case—"Henry versus Allen and Lyttle." Had it come to trial, as it would have come but for the wire pulling of the Chiel's followers and the cowardice of Allen, the public would have enjoyed a treat, indeed, and the Chiel would not now be referring to it. We are certainly not the aggressors in this matter, and though touching a lying slanderer and unprincipled braggart is an unsavoury task, still we feel constrained to lay this one across the knee. His dastardly conduct is our only excuse for the appearance of this article.

That's me!

It would seem that in the field of "wrathful vituperations" WG was well able to hold his own. He continued by mentioning other occasions when the Chiel had tried to claim libel against him. He reminded his readers how, at the very first issue of the *North Down Herald*, Henry claimed the announcement that the new paper was a re-issue of the *Newtownards Independent* was a libel. He made a big fuss but never brought any action.

WG went on to refer to the paragraph he wrote about a "gluttonous fellow" who so over-indulged on liquor at a free banquet on board a pleasure steamer that he managed to fall out of his car on his way home and get himself arrested. WG claimed that, "No sooner did the Chiel see this spicy item in the Herald than he at once exclaimed, 'THAT'S ME!' " But, again no action ensued.

Next, WG related the whole "Abner Byng" spoof about the blustering and drunken proprietor of the fictional "Ballycuddy Observer" (see Chapter 13) and how Henry took a copy of the offending poster to the *Gazette's* printers and said again, 'THAT'S ME!' threatening to sue if the promised article was printed. He was ignored and no legal action followed the appearance of the article. WG stated that, "the libel hunter was, in consequence, a good deal ridiculed upon all hands."

"Eventually," the article continued, "the Chiel did institute an action" over WG's "Count Rhinocera" fable. Denied the opportunity of having all the facts revealed in court at the time, as he had wished, WG was more than happy, five years later, to respond to Henry's re-raising the issue and explain to his readers the ludicrous nature of Henry's case when he pounced on the story of Count Rhinocera and yet again claimed, "THAT'S ME!"

He finished his column by promising another the following week, which—and he quoted Henry's own piece—"will, no doubt, be exceedingly interesting reading at the present time."

The truth revealed

Under the same heading, "The Chiel and his Libellers", the second article gave the *full* details of what really occurred in relation to the

THE STORYTELLER

libel case Henry brought. Its revelations about how WG had been denied the right to defend himself in court through the blackmailing efforts of his printer; of the true feelings of Henry's many subpoenaed witnesses; of how Henry had arranged his own victory parade upon his return to Newtownards—have all been documented previously in chapter 19. WG was able, for the first time, to make public all that had actually occurred. He concluded this second installment with reference to Henry's solicitor's fraudulent claim for exaggerated costs.

A thing called a newspaper

The final episode of "The Chiel and his Libellers" appeared the following week on the 8th March. Apart from whatever therapeutic benefit WG gained from writing them, they must have been popular with his readers, too, to warrant a trilogy. In this one WG responded to the Chiel's disparaging comments about the *North Down Herald* by using the Newtownards man's own words and referring to a "thing called a newspaper" [the Chronicle] that was printed each week by Henry's printers, mentioning their name.

> *The aforesaid "thing" is not very attractive either in content or appearance. Little can be said in praise of ink or paper; and less, far less in praise of the contents. The former are of the "shoddy" class; the latter—save a few columns—are the stale items that have already appeared in the columns of the Ulster Echo and to be found weekly in the Witness. That is how that particular "thing" is produced.*[230]

WG challenged Henry to substantiate his declared official circulation figures of 3,600 copies weekly in County Down alone, which the editor of the *Chronicle* had claimed in his tender to win the County Down Grand Jury advertising. "By which rule of arithmetic," WG asked, "can such a distribution be gained out of the quantity really printed, which may be put down at from five to six hundred copies?"

---

[230] The *Ulster Echo* and the *Witness* were sister publications from a respected Belfast Presbyterian stable

He went on to recount Henry's outrageous intimidation of the paperboys when WG had published the Chiel's attempts to defraud the Bangor Town Commissioners with his offer of 'free' advertising that he subsequently charged them for. WG reminded his readers how he had told them of this the following week and how Henry had tried to set up a criminal prosecution against the *Herald*. He had also told them of its ignominious abandonment.

Before concluding his trilogy of responses to Henry's disparaging article, WG threw in the advice that the Chiel would do well to consider his own position, recording that he had been sued by a Newtownards publican for four and sixpence worth of drinks supplied to him at the bar; or that he had been sued by Hanson, the clothier, for the price of a coat; or, indeed, about being told the 'evidence' he took it upon himself to offer in relation to a celebrated Belfast Insurance swindle was 'not worth the paper upon which it was written.

A further flurry of libel suits might have been expected to follow the publication of these three articles but there is no record of any such eventuality. In response to the Chiel's malicious sideswipe about his debts and the former libel case WG must have stuck close enough to the facts in his three articles that Henry decided keeping his head down was the wisest option.

Book promotion

In an effort to increase the sales of his books—or at least to sell them faster, for sales continued to accrue—WG approached Messrs. J Robb & Co. in Castle Place, Belfast. Robb's was a big department store[231] with a large and flourishing cut-price book department. With the newly-published third volume of *Robin's Readings* now out, they agreed to take this and Volume Two and promote them at a special price.

The following Wednesday, May 1, the *Belfast News-Letter* carried a large advertisement placed by J. Robb & Co. that read:

---

[231] J Robb & Co traded in Belfast until finally closing in 1973

THE STORYTELLER

> **READINGS BY "Robin".**
> **The most Humorous of Books.**
> **SECOND AND THIRD SERIES,**
> **Price 9d each; post free, 10½d (published at 1s).**

WG's delight at seeing it was turned to dismay when he turned the page and read under the heading, ROBIN'S READINGS:

> *As will be seen by an announcement in our advertising columns, that interesting and humorous collection of readings by "Robin" has become the property of Messrs. J. Robb & Co., Castle Place, and is now published in a very attractive form.*

The books had emphatically not "become the property" of Robb & Co. and to suggest that they had, reflected badly on the state of WG's finances. Weak as they were, he had no wish for this to be suggested to all and sundry through falsehoods. He was quick to dip his pen in his silver stag inkwell.

The first item in the *Belfast News-Letter's* Correspondence column the following Tuesday, May 7, 1889 was this:

> TO THE EDITOR OF THE BELFAST NEWS-LETTER
>
> *SIR—Your issue of the 1st inst. contained a paragraph to the effect that "Robin's Readings" had become the property of Messrs. John Robb & Co., Belfast. Permit me to contradict that statement, as it is erroneous, and calculated to place me in a wrong position before the public. Messrs. Robb & Co., like other booksellers, merely offer the "Readings" for sale, as they do their other stock. The copyright and the authority to publish are vested solely in me.— Yours truly,*
>
> *W. G. Lyttle*
> *Mount Herald, Bangor, County Down,*
> *4th May*

Robb & Co's subsequent advertisements dropped the promotional price of 9d and increased the post-free cost to 1s, the published price of the book. Whether this was in response to WG's terse letter we don't know but it still offered a good deal to readers ordering by post. The advert continued to appear all through May, June and July, so hopefully WG's royalty receipts were suitably enhanced because of it.

Smoking concert and a royal visit

The night before his letter of correction appeared in the *News-Letter* WG had been performing in Belfast as part of the line-up at a popular style of event known as a "Smoking Concert." For men only, these provided mainly musical entertainment for the patrons while they discussed politics and enjoyed their smokes. The same edition of the *News-Letter* that carried WG's correspondence also reported that the prosperous and expanding "Lyceum Club held its third Smoking Concert the previous evening, which included items by W. G. Lyttle." He chose to recite his poem of just a couple of years ago, "Bangor in 1907" and a very early story, one of the first to be printed in the *Newry Telegraph* called, "The Tipperary Policeman." This latter always seemed to be particularly well-received, perhaps because the policeman, although stationed in Belfast, had not lost his southern brogue, allowing WG to use a different stage voice. The general chatter in the Lyceum Club would soon have ceased as he started his tale:

> *Well, now it's a great honour intoirely to be invoited here amongst yez, fur it's moighty seldom that a poor polisman gets spakin' a word in public. Shure, if we're on our bates we darent spake a word unless to the disordherly fellows loafin' about the corners, an' it's only to tell them 'Move on! Move on, now, or I'll run ye in! Move on out ov that, or I'll take yez to the offis!' An' if we're in the Polis Coort shure it brakes my heart to hev to swer agin the poor craytures that's fined an' sint to jail for puttin' down*

THE STORYTELLER

their throats the very stuff that the magistrates give licences to sell.[232] [233]

When conversation resumed among the Lyceum Club members that evening it was sure to have included discussion of Queen Victoria's grandson, Prince Albert Victor, and his planned visit to Belfast on the 21st and 22nd May. WG may well have seen the preparations being made, particularly around the docks where the Royal Yacht would berth. He may have reflected upon how these big ships had been able to sail right into the heart of the city ever since the Victoria Channel had been dredged way back in 1839 and the mud piled up to form Queen's Island. Prince Albert would be officially opening the new Alexandra Dock on the Island, named after his mother, the Princess of Wales. WG would have seen that the whole area was being cleaned and spruced up and festooned with bunting in readiness for the royal visitor who would also be laying the foundation stone for the new Albert Bridge to replace the one that collapsed.

This imminent regal arrival gave WG an idea for a topical piece featuring "Robin." He'd have the ingenuous country farmer write a letter to "His Royal Highness" welcoming him to the country and offering him some homely advice on how he should proceed. The letter he wrote is preserved and appears in the third volume of *Robin's Readings, Life in Ballycuddy*. It is entitled, "THE ROYAL VISIT TO IRELAND—LETTER FROM 'ROBIN' TO H.R.H. PRINCE ALBERT VICTOR (AFTERWARDS DUKE OF CLARENCE)"

---

[232] Well, now it's a great honour entirely to be invited here amongst you, for it's mighty seldom that a poor policeman gets speaking a word in public. Sure, if we're on our beats we daren't speak a word unless to the disorderly fellows loafing about the corners, and it's only to tell them 'Move on! Move on, now, or I'll run you in! Move on out of that, or I'll take you to the office!' And if we're in the Police Court sure it breaks my heart to have to swear against the poor creatures that are fined and sent to jail for putting down their throats the very stuff that the magistrates give licences to sell.

[233] Quoted from "The Tipperary Policeman and his Sweetheart Biddy," that appeared in the first volume of *Humorous Readings by "Robin."* This story never made it into any of the three volumes of *"Robins" Readings* which survive to the present day but can now be read in the newly-published *Robin's Further Readings* published by AG Lyttle, 2021.

although the part in brackets could not have been added until a year later upon his being granted that title.

The letter was headed, "Ballycuddy, County Down, May the tenth, 18 and 89." That WG chose May 10th, which was a Friday, is a fairly clear indication that the piece appeared in that week's issue of the *North Down Herald and Bangor Gazette,* no doubt to the delight of all his readers as they enjoyed some of "Robin's" naïve well-wishes:

> *A hope ye'll hae a nice smooth passage whun yer crossin' frae Inglan'. They tell me yer comin' in a yott. A dinnae like them things, fur they're aye tummelin' ower the buddy, an' lyin' wi' their keels uppermaist. A'm shair Mister Moore Brothers wud a sent ower yin o' their steamboats that they rin tae Bangor, an' ye cud a cum ower in that as comfortable as if ye had been sittin' at yer ain fireside.*[234]

In spite of his own troubles, WG never lost his sense of humour, nor his delight in amusing his fans.

A New Bangor Attraction

That June, WG would have taken equal delight in reporting the opening of the UK's longest switchback ride on Bangor's seafront. The brainchild of John Moore, operator of the Bangor boat, as a further attraction to fill his boats with eager tourists, the ride gave thrills to hundreds each day throughout the summer season. The land on which it was erected was leased from R. E Ward, who was quoted in a June edition of the *Gazette* as remarking:

> *Going downhill has a marvellous effect, completely taking away your breath, but as you*

---

[234] I hope you'll have a nice smooth passage when you're crossing from England. They tell me you're coming in a yacht. I don't like those things for they're always tumbling over the body and lying with their keels uppermost. I'm sure Mister Moore Brothers would have sent over one of their steamboats that they run to Bangor, and you could have come over in that as comfortable as if you had been sitting at your own fireside.

ascend your breath returns with renewed vigour. This produces the most lovely blushes on the ladies' faces and makes them so attractive no gentleman could help proposing.

A Message from on high

One other bright spot, quite unexpected, in 1889—WG's *annus horribilis*—was to receive in July a private message by way of a letter from former Prime Minister and Leader of the Opposition, William Gladstone. It was addressed to W. G. Lyttle Esq., Printing Works, Bangor, Ireland and it read:

> *16, James Street, S.W.,*
> *July 4th, 1889*
> *Sir,*
> *Your 'Tale of Ninety-eight' was sent to me a few days ago and I have read the whole of it with extreme interest. I presume that copies of it can be had through the booksellers. But my special object in writing to you is to beg the favour of your directing me, if you are able, to the authorities on whom you rely as to the following portions of the work:-*
> *Page 36, case of Orr.*
> *Pages 33-35, case of Burns.*
> *Page 98, case of Dunn.*
> *   "   " of Heppenstall.*
> *Page 95, of Sloan.*
> *Page 141, of Jackson.*
> *Page 145, of the deaf man.*
> *   "   " of the imbecile.*
> *Page 157, slaughter of Betsy Gray.*
> *I have, myself, recently been engaged in exposing to the public eye the horrible policy and proceedings anterior to the Union. But most of the information known to me (except Teeling's Narrative) concerns Southern rebellion; and, as I may be called upon to go further into the subject, I should be greatly obliged if*

28 - RETRIBUTION

> *in the cases I have mentioned above you could supply me with such references to your authorities as would enable me to examine their sources, and in case of need to quote from them.*
>
> *I am sure you will excuse my giving you this trouble under the circumstances. Do I go too far in suggesting that it would even add to the value of your work, were you in any new edition of it, to supply references on the heads you deem most important.*
>
> *I take a further, but friendly liberty. In p. 37 Curran is called an attorney, and in p. 41 the name of Swift is inserted in error.– I remain, sir,*
> *Your faithful and obedient servant,*
> *W. E. Gladstone.*

Kenneth Robinson has written[235] that Gladstone was misusing WG's book in "asking for evidence of those cases where named individuals had been brutalised by the soldiery." He said WG would not have claimed his work as pure history; that "It was never meant to be a detailed and documented account of the events of 1798." Whether or not that is a fair commentary on WG's detailed research, certainly, much of the confirmation that Mr Gladstone was looking for would have been in the memories of the many people that WG spoke to about their family recollections. In any event, WG knew what his readership wanted and he never took Gladstone's advice about adding source references in subsequent editions.

With respect to his calling Curran an attorney, however, future editions show that he did change that reference. The sentence now reads, "Orr was defended by that able Irish lawyer, Curran..." In the 19th century there were two distinct levels of legal status: attorneys and solicitors were considered altogether more lowly than barristers and those who appeared in court. Gladstone obviously knew of Curran and that he was of a higher rank than a mere attorney and took the trouble of pointing this out to WG.

---

[235] in an article entitled "Betsy Gray Re-visited" for the *Journal of the Upper Ards Historical Society, No. 24* published in 2000

THE STORYTELLER

As to the last reference to the name of Swift appearing in error, that is impossible to trace as the name does not now occur at all in subsequent, extant editions. So, again, WG must have acted upon Gladstone's advice. It's not every writer who can claim a former Prime Minister as his proof-reader!

WG published the text of Mr Gladstone's letter in the *Gazette* on August 2nd, explaining that almost daily he received requests for copies of it ever since he had mentioned that such a letter had been received.

Sometime afterwards a paragraph appeared in *Jarvey*, a Dublin weekly, stating:

> Mr Gladstone has written to the prince of genial editors and "good fellows," Mr. W. G. Lyttle, of the Bangor Gazette—better known as "Robin." The letter is highly complimentary, and refers to "Betsy Gray," a story of '98, from "Robin's" facile and prolific pen. I understand that Gladstone means to quote from the book in a future speech

perhaps reading rather more into the letter than its writer intended.

Gladstone, himself, referred to the book in his diary entry of July 2nd, 1889, where he wrote, 'Read Lyttle's Tale of '98.'[236]

Summonsed

The reason WG did not print the letter for some weeks may be explained by the disastrous chain of events that befell him at that time.

Gladstone's letter was dated 4th July, 1889. WG would have received it late on Friday the 5th. We might imagine he would feel a certain excitement at opening a personally addressed letter to see that it came from the country's past Prime Minister. It is unlikely that he felt such elation, however. He could barely appreciate the honour being paid him for, in an earlier post the same day, he had received another letter; one that had left his mind in turmoil. It was a summons for non-payment of an outstanding debt of £8 (just under £870 in

---

[236] The entry is recorded in Volume 12 of "The Gladstone Diaries" edited by HCG Mathew, Oxford Clarendon Press, 1968.

2021.) This was on top of the £5 a month (£550 in 2021) that he was already now legally obligated to repay.

With his tragic family circumstances and his own indifferent health, he wasn't managing to keep on top of his financial commitments. He must have been aware that he could expect such a summons sooner or later, but knowing it now lay to one side on his desk as he read the words of William Gladstone would have cruelly blunted the impact of the "grand old man" having written to him. The debt could no longer go unpaid. As he finished perusing the politician's letter his eyes would inevitably have been drawn back to the summons sitting on his desk just by the silver stag ink stand with its willow-twig pen holder. He knew the legal document threatened not only the survival of his newspaper business but his whole life that he had built over the years for himself and his family. Was he about to lose it all and end up in the debtors' prison?

Chapter 29 – BANKRUPT

1889 – August to December

WG was a survivor. As a toddler, he had lived through the Great Hunger that had been responsible for the deaths of thousands of his contemporaries. He had endured the heart-breaking death of their second son, Robert, just after the child's first birthday. He had recovered from the loss of his beloved Lizzie following her protracted illness and, in time, he would get over the tragic passing of Eva, too, but he still mourned for his poor daughter. He must have been grateful to be able to take comfort from having Annie at his side to share his grief.

Annie was later to prove herself to be a competent business woman—able to run the newspaper after WG passed away—and, perhaps at this time, she was able not only to comfort her husband but to be an encouragement, too; a stimulus to help him face up to making difficult decisions about his finances.

It is hard to understand how a man who had run a successful accountancy firm in Belfast with a branch office in Downpatrick could have allowed the management of his newspaper business to reach such a sorry state. It can only have been the result of the crushing setbacks he had endured in recent times with his health and bereavements and the growing estrangement with his two eldest children over their attitude to Annie. All this was taking its toll and, with the day-to-day pressure of running the newspaper and all his other commitments, he had somehow allowed things to slip. He would have explained to Annie that the summons he had received—from James Pitchie, a paper-maker who traded as Macarthur & Co.—was not his sole debt. There was, of course, the large commitment to W & G Baird, proprietors of the *Evening Telegraph*, but there were a number of other creditors, too. It would seem that his total debts were in excess of £400 (in the region of £45,000 in 2021.) He had few assets. His home, "Mount Herald" was leased from its owner, James Skillen, now of Ballymaconnell, and all his printing equipment was hired from a firm in the North of England. He just couldn't see how he was going to be able to pay back what he owed.

In the end, it was from his early experience as an accountant that, together with Annie, probably, he began to formulate a possible way forward. He had helped others through similar situations. Loath as he must have been to go down the same path he had advised for some of the clients of his accountancy business, after much soul-searching he could see no alternative. An image of the unfortunate Archibald Thompson may have flashed through his mind as he told Annie of the decision he had reached. The next summons he received could well be to have him declared insolvent. Before that happened he would apply to the courts, himself. He would file for bankruptcy.

Bankrupt

Wednesday 28th August was the date set for the judge to hear WG's petition. He no longer retained John Dinnen as his solicitor but rather his masonic brother, Mr Daniel M'Callum who instructed a Dublin barrister, Ignatius O'Brien to represent him in court. The few intervening weeks left little enough time to prepare his case. He had to provide all the facts and figures about the state of his finances with proof of his income and assets.

On the Wednesday, WG would have left home early to catch the train to Belfast and make his way to the Courthouse in Crumlin Road. The hearing was protracted. WG's two main creditors, Messrs. Baird and Messrs MacArthur were represented by their own barristers and a third legal gentleman, who spoke for other, smaller creditors, was instructed by John Dinnen, so these other firms were probably local businesses to which WG owed various amounts. The creditors, at this stage, were reluctant to agree to an arranged settlement. By filing for bankruptcy, himself, WG had finessed any plans they may have had and forced the issue to be debated now. Ignatius O'Brien was eloquent in his persuasion that it would be in everyone's best interests for WG's petition to be granted but the other barristers produced strong arguments against such a decision. They preferred the hope of eventually receiving all that was owed to their clients, even if they had to wait some considerable time for the debts to be cleared, rather than to have to agree to accept repayment at a considerably reduced rate in the pound.

The daily newspapers had regular columns reporting from the Bankruptcy Court and, from these, we have been able to piece together WG's experience. The next day the *Belfast News-Letter* announced that the previous day Mr Henry Fitzgibbon, Q.C., County Court Judge, had held a sitting of the bankruptcy court in the Crown Court of the County Courthouse, Crumlin Road. Apparently, none of the other arrangements and bankruptcy matters disposed of possessed "any features of public interest." One, however, was "a petition by W. G. Lyttle, Bangor, *North Down Herald,* and," the newspaper declared, "after considerable argument, his Honour put the case into bankruptcy."

The die was cast. The official "First Meeting of Creditors" was set for Monday 16th September.

Belfast News-Letter, Monday, September 2, 1889.

> *IN THE BELFAST LOCAL BANKRUPTCY COURT.*
>
> *In the matter of Wesley Greenhill Lyttle, of Ballymagee Street, Bangor, in the County of Down, Printer and Publisher, a Bankrupt.*
>
> *NOTICE IS HEREBY GIVEN THAT A FIRST MEETING OF THE CREDITORS will be held in this Matter before the Court at the LOCAL BANKRUPTCY COURT, BELFAST, on MONDAY, the 16th day of September, 1889, at the hour of Eleven o'clock in the forenoon, for the Proof of Debts, and the purpose of considering the offer of Composition which will then be made by the Bankrupt or his friends, pursuant to the Statute.*
>
> *At which meeting, if three-fifths in number and value of the Creditors… shall agree to accept such an offer of Composition, or any modification thereof, a*

29 - BANKRUPT

second meeting of the Creditors will be appointed for the purpose of deciding upon such offer.
Dated this 31st day of August, 1889.
J. H. BURKE MURPHY, Deputy Registrar.

The offer of Composition to be made at the said Meeting is 2s 6d in the pound[237] on all his unsecured debts and Engagements, and all such portion of his secured debts as may not be covered by security, payable in three instalments at four, eight, and twelve months from the date of confirmation of this proposal by the Court, the last of such instalments to be secured by the joint and several promissory notes of the Bankrupt and a solvent party to be named at said Meeting.

The Statutory Notice was signed, JOHN GORDON SCOTT, Solicitor, for the said Bankrupt, 51, Lower Sackville Street, Dublin; and 102, Royal Avenue, Belfast; and 1, High Street, Antrim. It is interesting to note that this is a different solicitor than the one who instructed his Barrister three days earlier. At a subsequent court appearance, Mr Scott explained that, since the case was first brought to court, he had been instructed to act for the debtor. And he continued to represent him during the rest of the process.

In the meantime, Tuesday's edition of the *News-Letter* carried the official Court Notice of WG's bankruptcy. It included the information that there would be a second date, the 2nd of October to complete the proceeding of the "First Sitting." WG must attend these and provide "full disclosure of his Estate and Effects." The notice also required that, "All persons having in their possession any Property of the Bankrupt must deliver it, and all Debts due to the Bankrupt must be paid, to Edward Allworthy, Esq., Official Assignee."

---

[237] An initial suggestion of one shilling in the pound seems to have been withdrawn and substituted with this higher offer.

Can the *Gazette* continue?

Two questions would have been worrying WG. Would the Court agree a settlement of 2s 6d in the pound; would offering to pay one-eighth, 12½%, of what he owed in total, be sufficient to satisfy his creditors? Only time would tell. The other matter was more pressing. If he were to survive at all he could not afford to miss an edition of his newspaper. Where did he stand with the Court? Would he be in breach of his bankruptcy terms if he incurred expenditure in order to ensure his regular income continued? He instructed his solicitor to apply to the Courts for their official permission for him to carry on publishing the *North Down Herald and Bangor Gazette*.

On Thursday 5th September, it was the *News-Letter* again who reported this application, saying that Mr Scott had submitted the names of two sureties of £200 (over £22,000 each or almost £45,000 in 2021) in support of his client being allowed to continue his business. Sadly, the names of these two good friends are not recorded. They may well have been brother masons, who all swear an oath to support one another. The solicitor appearing for the principal creditors, Mr Coates, made no objection provided WG gave an undertaking not to bring the paper into litigation—perhaps, for him, the most difficult part of the whole proceedings! The Judge agreed and allowed the weekly publication to continue subject to that stipulation and the securities being received by the official assignee. The *News-Letter* ended its report with the sentence, "The other business transacted was not important." I expect it was of considerable importance to those involved but not to the *News-Letter's* readership, apparently. Anything relating to WG Lyttle, on the other hand, such was his celebrity status, clearly was.

Frustratingly, when WG and all involved in his hearing arrived at the Courthouse on 16th September, they discovered that, due to some informality, the case would be adjourned to 2nd October.

Before that, on Monday 30th September, WG enjoyed a little respite from his appearances in court when he attended a Complimentary Supper for Mr R Caughey, a prominent Newtownards businessman and former colleague of WG on the Board of Commissioners. The occasion was to wish Mr Caughey well as he took leave of the town that had been his home for many years to take up residence in Dublin. WG would have been pleased to see his old friend George Dickson there. Mr Caughey had been among the guests at a previous Complimentary Supper held for William Henry to which WG had not been invited. But that was a singular omission. As a prominent citizen of North Down his presence on such occasions was normally welcomed.

Settlement and a setback

When WG's First Sitting eventually did get under way there was much argument as to whether he could carry the sitting. His solicitor made it clear that the offer of settlement had been increased from 1s to 2s 6d in the pound. It was now up to WG's creditors to vote upon whether or not to accept this offer.

Awaiting their decision must have been nerve-wracking for WG. However, it seems that the required three-fifths of them agreed the settlement and WG was, at last, able to breathe a sigh of relief. Provided he could meet the three instalments, his debts would be cleared. The Second Sitting should be a formality in simply agreeing the amounts and dates of these payments. It was set for 23rd October. Life at "Mount Herald" began to return to normal.

And then the notice arrived from Robert S Allen.

He was filing a late creditor's claim that WG owed him £500 (£55,000 in 2021) more than doubling his total debt. Did WG have a moment of panic or throw up his hands in utter despair? Such a reaction would have been understandable. But once over the first shock and when he had calmed himself, he sat down to consider the claim. He became convinced it had no justification. In fact, he recalled, there was an outstanding sum still owed to *him* from his past dealings with Allen.

The meeting on the 23rd October that should have been the Second Sitting started off, indeed, as such, confirming the creditors' agreement to the settlement terms. Then the matter of the new claim for £500 was raised. Mr Scott, on behalf of WG, said he "was prepared to prove that the bankrupt did not owe Mr Allen one farthing, but that, on the contrary, that gentleman owed a sum to the bankrupt." The Judge said he could not go into the matter on this occasion and the Second Sitting had to be adjourned.

THE STORYTELLER

Life goes on

In the midst of all these Court appearances WG still had his paper to produce. Ads appeared in the *Belfast News-Letter* in October for a Compositor and in December for a Reporter and WG continued to write for the paper. In spite of his troubles, he never lost his sense of fun while doing it. The bane of all newspaper proprietors was the poor standard of letter-writing of their correspondents. Just two days after having his bankruptcy hearing adjourned yet again, WG chose to remind his readers of their obligations by writing the following for the *Gazette*:

> EXCUSE HASTE AND A BAD PEN
> There is a Man in our town, and he is wondrous wise
> Whenever he writes the printer-man, he dotteth all his i's:
> And when he's dotted all of them, with great "sang froid" and ease
> He punctuates each paragraph, and crosses all his t's.
> Upon one side alone he writes, and never rolls his leaves;
> And from the man of ink a smile, and mark "insert" receives.
> And when a question he doth ask (taught wisely he has been,)
> He doth the goodly penny stamp, for postage back, put in.

In November THE OLD TOWN CLOCK in Newtownards contributed another titbit concerning the editor of the *Newtownards Chronicle* who had apparently appeared recently in the columns of the *Gazette* with regard to his eating of some leeks!

> I have a good thing to tell you, wrote the Old Clock. A few days after the appearance of the famous

29 - BANKRUPT

report of the Chiel's leek-eating performance, that worthy met a gentleman who gave him a cordial handshaking.

"Do you know," said the gentleman, "that I have just been reading about you!"

"Ah, where, what?" queried the Chiel, his face beaming.

"In the North Down Herald," was the reply.

The glowing face darkened, and an apoplectic fit was imminent, as the Chiel exclaimed—

"Ah, that's Lyttle's paper! He's the greatest ruffian in the counties of Down and Antrim! He's a—! —!——!!———!!!———!!!!"

The gentleman smiled as he answered.

"I have another singular thing to tell you, and that is that Lyttle entertains precisely the same opinion regarding you."

The Chiel bolted.

More court hearings

The adjournment caused by the new claim for £500 was another setback, but hopefully only a delay—provided the Court would accept WG's evidence that he did not owe anything to Robert Allen. Allen hadn't requested a 'Sitting' but another "First Sitting" was arranged by the official assignee for the 12th of November at which Allen's claim would be considered. It was a big anti-climax. Allen was unprepared to go on with the proof. As a result, his claim was taken off the file altogether and a new date was set for the "Second Sitting" on the 23rd of November. WG was back where he was a month earlier, but having incurred yet more expense and trouble because of Allen's spurious claim.

At the hearing on the 23rd November his advocate asked for costs against Allen but the Judge ruled that he could not, reasonably, grant such in Allen's absence, so that matter had to be deferred. As to the main business, however, the Judge granted the application for a composition of 2s 6d in the pound and the "Second Sitting" was passed. WG was also ordered to pay the costs of the bankruptcy proceedings.

But at last his ordeal was over. His *annus horribilis* was drawing to a close. There is only one further reference to the bankruptcy in the newspapers and that is about a hearing "for costs" that took place in January, 1890—presumably to sort out what, if anything Allen should pay towards WG's Court bill.

I should imagine WG was determined now to put all the bad stuff that had happened in the past twelve months firmly behind him. On the positive side, the new volumes of his books were selling well and he (and "Robin") were much in demand for Readings. His 46th birthday was coming up in April; he was still a comparatively young man. Life was for living and, health permitting, he had it all ahead of him. With the relief, perhaps even euphoria, of having his terrible financial troubles finally resolved, WG must have been facing the future with considerable optimism. 1890 was starting well.

He was not to know he had just entered his final decade.

Chapter 30 – SIR WESLEY?

1890 – September 1891

As usual at "Mount Herald," the last few weeks of December would have been spent bustling around finalising and printing off the latest edition of Lyttle's Almanac. In the New Year a cheering letter arrived at the offices of the *Gazette*. It was addressed to "Robin", from a Belfast merchant:

> *I was lying during all the Christmas holidays, ill with quinsy, and suffering much discomfort. My wife handed me a copy of the North Down Almanac, in which I found your story of "The Ballycuddy Precentor." As I read I forgot my pain, and laughed so heartily that my wife thought I should choke. My dear old "Robin," that laughter cured me!*

Receiving such letters must have been very gratifying for WG.

As the days started to grow a little brighter in the early spring of 1890, he once more found himself seated upon the platform, amongst a plethora of other dignitaries in Glasgow. It was for the eighth annual Ulster Reunion and he was invited back after attending the sixth reunion in '88. His main contribution to the proceedings on this occasion was to read his own story, "Peggy, and How I Courted Her" in his County Down dialect, of course, which, according to the *Belfast News-Letter* on 14th March was "highly appreciated by the audience."

A cruise on the "Bangor Castle"

It was a couple of months after this that Messrs. Moore Brothers invited an illustrious group of gentlemen aboard their steamboat, the

THE STORYTELLER

"Bangor Castle." The occasion, on Saturday 24th May, was to mark the start of the Bangor Season. Her sister ship, the "Erin," made three packed journeys taking day-trippers from Belfast to Bangor during the day, while the guests, who included WG, sailing on the "Bangor Castle" enjoyed a leisurely cruise down the Lough to the accompaniment of the continuous churning and splashing of the great paddle wheels. The weather turned out to be perfect for such a trip and the *News-Letter* reporter waxed positively lyrical about the scene:

> *A bright sun, a clear sky, and a gentle breeze from the east were the prevailing conditions, and these served admirably to bring out the beauties of the sheet of water and a coastline which have few superiors... Belfast Lough, when witnessed in early summer, is one of the finest in these latitudes, and perhaps it has never appeared to greater advantage than it did on Saturday. Well wooded on either side, the sloping shores dotted with the mansions and villas of the opulent, the barer and more rugged scenery, the farther you proceed seawards, lends a charm which no judge of the beautiful in nature could fail to appreciate.*

WG must have so enjoyed the relaxing experience. With his cares and worries behind him, he could sit back and appreciate the cruise on the calm waters of the lough, bathed in beautiful sunshine. There were some speeches during the voyage, including one singing the praises of Belfast. It is pleasing to note that WG had been primed to be the one to respond in similar vein with a speech about Bangor even though, as he mentioned to his fellow passengers, he had only been living there for the past seven years. It seems that his brush with insolvency had not detracted from the esteem in which WG was held by his peers and fans, alike.

During his peaceful trip down the Lough he would have had time to think about future plans. Sales of *Robin's Readings* that he had printed on his own press the previous year had done well and he may have been wondering whether to reprint another volume of his works. It wasn't until the Summer Season in Bangor was almost over, however, that he was able to take the idea forward. He had decided to re-issue his debut collection of stories, *Humorous Readings by "Robin"—Vol I.*

On the 18th August an ad appeared in the *News-Letter* for

> *A competent, steady Compositor for news and jobbing; also smart Turnover Apprentice*—W. G. Lyttle, Gazette, Bangor.

Perhaps the successful applicants were responsible for setting the type for this third, 1890 "Author's Edition", a copy of which still exists in the National Library of Ireland.

Penny Post

In September, WG was praising the postal service in a brief item that appeared in the paper. It told how a postage stamp was handed in to the Portaferry Post Office Receiver. On the adhesive side were written the words "Gazette Office, Bangor, Down" and underneath was a communication in shorthand signed by the writer. The next day, after making his usual delivery at "Mount Herald," the Bangor postman opened his watch case and removed the postage stamp, safe and secure, and handed it over to its rightful recipient. Whilst the delivery method made the columns of the *Gazette,* we, unfortunately, do not have a record of the substance of the message.

The Chiel

WG would have been aware that his long-time sparring partner and fellow-newspaper editor, William Henry, had not been in his former vigorous health for some time, though such a sensitive matter would not have excited comment in the columns of the *Gazette*. It still, however, came as a shock to all when the proprietor of the *Newtownards Chronicle* passed away quite suddenly on the 5th November, 1890. A large funeral cortege including many Orange Lodge members and Town Commissioners marched with the heavy oak coffin from the Henry home on Francis Street, Newtownards to the family grave in Movilla cemetery.[238] There, a vast number of mourners gathered to pay their respects, including leading merchants and aristocracy of North Down and many clergymen of different denominations, no less than three of which officiated at the burial service.

The obituaries referred to him as "a man who was universally esteemed, and possessed the happy faculty of making friends." "His genial disposition, kindness of heart, and thorough regard for the feelings of others rendered him popular among all classes." "Mr Henry was a kind-hearted, hospitable gentleman, who had a very wide circle of friends." Of his strained relationship with the Bangor editor there was, perhaps wisely, not a mention.

It was decided that William Henry's wife, Sarah, should take up the reigns as proprietress of the *Newtownards Chronicle* (trading as "William Henry") and thus the newspaper overcame the loss of its founding editor to continue to grow and survive to become the flourishing journal that it is to this day.

It is a pity that no reference to William Henry's sad demise penned by WG remains—if, indeed, any such references ever existed. But his long-running feud with the late editor from Newtownards was finally at an end. The Chiel was no more.[239]

Rates protest

WG's other sparring partner, the Bangor Town Commission was still very much alive, however. For many years the Commission had placed annual ads in the Bangor paper to announce the rates set for the coming twelve months. They had a legal obligation to do so. But in

---

[238] Henry's grave can be seen in Appendix F, Figures 19 and 20

[239] As an interesting footnote, the *Newtownards Chronicle* would eventually be bought out and taken into the stable of the Spectator Group of newspapers while still retaining its own individuality. The Spectator Group is another family-owned business belonging to the Alexanders. The founder, David Edward Alexander was brought to Bangor by WG's widow to take over as editor of the *North Down Herald and Bangor Gazette* (see Under New Editorship, Ch 34) He fulfilled that role for seven years before leaving to set up his own newspaper, the County Down Spectator. How WG would have chuckled at the irony of the Chiel's newspaper being taken over by a Bangor Group that was founded by his own succeeding editor at the *Gazette*!

30 - SIR WESLEY?

1891, claiming they were not prepared to meet the price WG was charging for the ads, they had them published in the *Belfast News-Letter* instead—paying about half as much again over the price in the local paper.

In June, WG's friend, Bangor solicitor, Daniel M'Callum, who lived in a district that had only recently come within the town's newly-extended boundaries, refused to pay his rates. This was on the grounds that neither gas nor sewerage reached his property, yet he was being asked to pay for them, but principally on the grounds that he had not been legally notified of the rates. The Town Commissioners took him to court. WG appeared as a witness and we can't help but speculate as to just where the idea of withholding the payment of rates might have originated. In court there was some debate over whether the *News-Letter* had as big a circulation in Bangor as the *Gazette* and, even if it had, whether the Commissioners were justified in using it as an advertising medium when the town had its own local paper. However, it transpired that M'Callum had not lodged his appeal against the rates within the statutory 14 day period and the case was dismissed on this technicality.

Could the commissioners' decision to boycott their local paper have been a petulant reaction to something WG had printed back in March? In the *Gazette* that appeared on Friday 20th he questioned the legality of the Town Commissioners' planned arbitration sitting the following Friday, which was Good Friday. They didn't meet on a Sunday; were they allowed to determine the town's affairs on this, the holiest day in the Christian calendar?

The piece didn't go unnoticed. The legal status of any decisions reached, were the meeting to go ahead as scheduled, was argued over by the legal gentry who frequented the Belfast courts. As late as the following Wednesday enquirers were informed that the meeting would take place as planned. But in the event…

> *Why was the arbitrator's sitting postponed from Good Friday to Saturday? Surely not because the Bangor Gazette said a Good Friday sitting would be illegal. The subject was fully discussed in the bar-room of the County Antrim Courthouse the other day. Some lawyers said Editor Lyttle's law was faulty,*

others said it was sound. All the same there was a postponement.
Bangor Gazette, 3ʳᵈ April, 1891

The newspaper expands
It was just such gentle sniping at "authority" that made WG's paper so popular. Indeed, he had decided the time had come to increase the size of the journal to accommodate even more of what his readers demanded. He published this greeting in the first issue in January:

> *The Editor wishes to all his readers, at home and abroad, a very happy and a very prosperous New Year. He hopes they will be pleased with the enlargement of his paper, and he promises to cater for them to the best of his ability during 1891.*

When the paper started out in Newtownards in 1880, it was a single folded broadsheet—four pages of seven columns each, so 28 columns. With this enlargement, it now ran to 56 columns—two folded broadsheets, so eight pages. It had probably, previously, increased to 42 columns by adding a single extra sheet (two pages) inside the folded broadsheet. In 1894 it would again increase, by the addition of a single sheet, to ten pages, 70 columns. At the start of '91, it claimed a circulation "greater than that of any two other County Down newspapers combined."

Another "Tale of '98"
Early in the New Year WG received a letter from Thomas Fitzpatrick of Castlewellan, a gentleman he most probably knew, or certainly knew of. He was the author of a number of books, including a historical novel published just three years earlier under the pseudonym, Banna-borka[240] called, *Jabez Murdock, Poetaster and Adjint*. It was a story set in Drumgooland near Castlewellan about 50 years earlier and the eponymous character was of Ulster-Scots origin.

---

[240] Banna-borka is the anglicised version of the Gaelic for "Mourne Mountains".

30 - SIR WESLEY?

The book was written in the kailyard style that WG employed, using Ulster-Scots, as appropriate, for the speech of certain characters but standard English for others and for the narrative. Like *Sons of the Sod*, the novel included references to actual individuals who lived in the area at the time and, indeed, "Jabez", himself, is believed to be the weavers' poet, Hugh Porter—the Bard of Moneyslane.[241] It was just the sort of book that would have appealed to WG.

Fitzpatrick, a man of learning, was a regular contributor to newspapers on divers subjects, and WG would have been intrigued to learn why his fellow-author was writing to him.

The letter was dated 13th January, 1891. Fitzpatrick explained that he had just read *Betsy Gray* and it had reminded him of a story he had heard way back in 1865 from an old man called Michael Shaw, living near Banbridge. In his youth Shaw had spent some time in England as a "traveller in Irish linen" and he had once met an elderly gentleman in a cottage where he had called in the hope of interesting the lady of the home in his wares. Fitzpatrick claimed to have heard Michael Shaw tell the story on a number of occasions and felt confident that he could relate it accurately himself.

On hearing Shaw's accent, it seemed, the old man sitting in the corner of the cottage asked if he was from Ireland and if he had ever been in Ballynahinch.

'Often,' came the reply.

The letter went on:

'Well, I was once at Ballynahinch,' said the old man in the corner.
'Indeed!'
'Yes. I was there in Ninety-eight putting down the croppies.'[242]
'And what did you think of the croppies?'
'The best men I ever saw if they had been properly officered. I can give you an instance. When the fight was over, and the rebels began to fly they were pursued in all directions. Two comrades and myself pursued a number of men who ran across a potato field. We were well mounted. Yet we could not gain a yard upon them. When the rebels

---

[241] I have to thank Michael McCartan, of Newcastle (but formerly of Drumgooland parish) who, from his research into Thomas Fitzpatrick, has identified "Jabez" as Hugh Porter.

[242] Croppies, a nickname for the men fighting for Irish independence in 1798

had got quite across the field, they turned, stood, and fired. My two comrades fell dead beside me. It was high time for me to beat a retreat; and I did so.'

Thomas Fitzpatrick finished his letter by saying that he wasn't aware of the old trooper's tale ever being written down in the public record, but he felt it well illustrated the stout "Hearts of Down."[243]

It was also "living" confirmation of the sort of scenes WG had described in his novel. Of course, he printed the letter in the next issue of the *Gazette* and this gem has been preserved for us amongst the clippings held in the North Down Museum in Bangor.

A Masonic jewel

The frequent gatherings at the Masonic Temple in Hamilton Road were always good for filling columns in the paper. Of course, only the more public of these could be described in any detail. WG attended a regular meeting on Wednesday 11th March which included the bestowing of a Masonic jewel of considerable value upon Brother James Sibbett in appreciation of his tenure as Grand Master which had just ended. The piece in Friday's *Gazette* started:

> *There was a handsome muster of brethren in their fine temple last Wednesday evening. It must not be told what there transpired, much as we should like to gratify our lady readers. One item, however, there can be no harm in mentioning, and that is that there were five candidates seeking to know the mysteries. Later on they shall be enlightened.*
>
> *The curtain having been rung down upon the mysteries, the brethren adjourned to the refreshment room...*

The 'mysteries' thus preserved, the article then went on to report the various speeches in connection with the presentation. Bro

---

[243] I am indebted to Horace Reid, of Ballynahinch, for supplementing this tale with the information that the English trooper would have been from the 22nd Light Dragoons, who chased the rebels from Ballynahinch.

30 - SIR WESLEY?

Sibbett[244] concluded his speech of thanks by saying that he sincerely prayed that the Great Architect of the Universe would bless one and all, giving them length of days and increase of happiness in this world, and

> *"When the Master of All, from his star-studded dome,*
> *Shall issue His mandate to summon us home,*
> *May each brother be found to be duly prepared,*
> *In the Grand Lodge above us to meet his reward."*

He sat down to loud and prolonged applause.

During the evening some of the brethren provided entertainment with a number of songs and recitations. Those contributing included Bro Sibbett, himself and WG's friend, Solicitor M'Callum. WG gave a reading, too. These were followed by the usual toasts and it was Bro Sibbett who gave, 'The Press!' and coupled it with the name of WG— or, as he called him, "Robin"—who was, he said, known as a journalist and author, the wide world o'er. In drinking Bro Lyttle's health, he added, they were also to include his amiable and accomplished wife.

Wesley's own "jewel".

The church

It would seem that Annie's profile, as the new Mrs WG Lyttle was more public than Lizzie's had been. Amongst other things, she took an active part in the congregational activities of First Bangor Presbyterian Church, which she would have been attending with Wesley since their marriage. Wesley's church-going was later to be casually dismissed by the *Belfast News-Letter* when it eventually came to write his obituary. "Neither in politics nor in Church affairs," it said, "did he give himself much concern."

I believe this was an unjust and ill-founded judgement. It might, more accurately have stated, "He mostly chose to conceal his political and religious opinions," as was only prudent for an independent

---

[244] Whilst the IOGT, in their writings, tended to shorten Brother to Br, it seems to have been the practice of the Freemasons to use Bro.

newspaper editor. He was certainly concerned with local politics, perhaps less so with what the national politicians got up to. As to religion, throughout WG's story we see how he was involved in one way or another with various church activities. He felt sufficiently at home in the Presbyterian community to be able to poke fun at its inner workings or even at individual congregations—witness his stories about the attempts to introduce a harmonium to lead the singing at Newtownbreda Presbyterian Church and about the goings on at the General Assembly.

In that story he also demonstrated a familiarity with Presbyterian culture—enough to be able to satirise a particular religious publication known as the *Christian Banner* that was often causing controversy. It was during the debate in the General Assembly on Church Music and "Robin" is telling how the Newtownbreda minister, Mister Workman, pointed out that a number of other congregations were using musical instruments, too:

> *'A'm feared ye hae let yer min's be carried awa' wi' that abominable Banner,' sez he, but they stappit him then, an' a wheen o' them riz the maist tremenjus whulabaloo iver ye heered.*
>
> *A cudnae mak heid or tail o' it fur a bit, an' sez I till the man aside me—*
>
> *'Shair nane o' them pits up flags in their meetin'-hooses.'*
>
> *He lauched, an' sez he, 'Oh na; the Banner's no a flag; it's a wee bit o' a penny paper, a kin' o' squib that's no muckle thocht o' except by a wheen o' men that writes fur it.'*
>
> *Sez yin o' the meinisters, sez he, shuttin' his fist an' stampin his fit—*
>
> *'A'll no sit here an' alloo ony man or ony meinister till say a wurd agen that paper, an A call on Mister Wurkman till retract the wurd "abominable".'*
>
> *Mister Wurkman brocht his han' doon sich a slap on the back o' a sate, an' sez he–*
>
> *'A say it is abominable!'*

30 - SIR WESLEY?

> *There wuz a terble scene then, an' A cudnae hear my ain ears. Mister Herron stud up, an' sez he, 'It's nae peeryodical o' oors! It disnae raypresent the Presbyterians!' An' A wush ye had heered hoo that pleeses the fowk. At last Mister Wurkman said he wud withdraw it, but that he had got grate provokashin frae the Banner, fur it had charged him wi' a' soarts o' ekklesastyel offences, an' was aye breedin' quarrels atween meinister an' fowk.*[245] [246]

Mister Workman pointed out that he only used the harmonium in *extra* meetings, held in his spare time and asked—

> *'Hoo ir meinisters till okepy their spare time? Sum keep ferms, ithers mak elekshin speeches, an' ithers that can dae nae better write fur the Banner.'*[247]

---

[245] 'I'm afraid you have let your minds be carried away with that abominable *Banner*,' he said, but they stopped him then and a number of them raised the most tremendous hullaballoo you ever heard.

I couldn't make head or tail of it for a bit, and said I to the man beside me–
'Sure none of them puts up flags in their meetinghouses.'

He laughed, and he said, 'Oh no; the *Banner's* not a flag; it's a little bit of a penny paper, a kind of squib [short, carelessly written piece] that's not much thought of except by a number of men that write for it.'

Said one of the ministers, said he, clenching his fist and stamping his feet–
'I'll not sit here and allow any man or any minister to say a word against that paper, and I call on Mister Workman to retract the word, "abominable".'

Mister Workman brought his hand down such a slap on the back of a seat, and he said–
'I say it is abominable!'

There was a terrible scene then, and I couldn't hear my own ears. Mister Herron stood up, and he said, 'It's no periodical of ours! It doesn't represent the Presbyterians!' And I wish you had heard how that pleased the folk. At last Mister Workman said he would withdraw it, but that he had got great provocation from the *Banner*, for it had charged him with all sorts of ecclesiastical offences, and was always breeding quarrels between ministers and folk.

[246] From "The Newtownbreda Harmoneyum", *Readings by Robin, Vol 3*.

[247] 'How are ministers to occupy their spare time? Some keep farms, others make election speeches, and others that can do no better write for the *Banner*.'

THE STORYTELLER

But WG didn't just highlight the shortcomings of the Church. On a more positive note, he also reported most sympathetically on the efforts of local congregations to follow their calling. He was proud of First Bangor's—his own church's achievements to that end, which is obvious from his reporting of their annual social get-together towards the end of April that year.

> *On Wednesday night there was held in this church one of the most delightful social re-unions that has, for many years past, characterised its career of progress. The minister, session and committee of the church have made it their aim to render it the premiere in the district, and, judging by the remarks made last Wednesday night by the pastor, the Rev A. Patten MA, and Secretary, Mr S Cosgrove and several members, there can be no doubt that the most unqualified success has crowned their efforts, and that "First Bangor" stands out* facile princeps *over all other congregations here. This rivalry is not, however, of a jealous worldly character, it is activated solely with a desire to produce Christ's Kingdom here on earth...*

From this we can see that Wesley understood and supported both the social and spiritual aspects of the church.

The evening included a fine tea served by the ladies of the congregation, with Annie and Wesley's 12-year-old daughter, Robina, among them. There was also some splendid entertainment by the church choir. It fell to Wesley to thank Mr M'Auley, the precentor, and his excellent singers for their contributions and his brief speech was repeatedly applauded. To have had that responsibility suggests that WG was a member of the kirk session.

WG throws some further light on his congregational standing in an imaginary conversation with the Archbishop of Dublin that he reported in his paper, though typically, where truth ends and fiction begins is a line difficult to discern. Talking about his absence from a

30 - SIR WESLEY?

meeting of the General Assembly, he claimed to have said to the primate,

'I do not take a prominent part in church affairs—never did and never will, I fancy.'

'And yet, I'm told you are a ruling Elder,' replied the Archbishop.

'Have been for twenty years fully,' said WG before adding, 'in the Ballycuddy Presbyterian Church.'

Was he admitting here to being an Elder on his church's kirk session, who wasn't particularly interested in the wider politics of church government? It is improbable that he could have been an Elder for twenty years—since his time in Belfast, that would have been—that seems to be a reference to "Robin" of Ballycuddy. But was that just a light-hearted way of shrugging off his actual involvement in his local congregation? I believe, in one way or another, the Lyttles were well integrated into the life of First Bangor Presbyterian Church.

Having said all that, WG was also happy to print the following snippet:

> *Another constant reader of this paper writes to the Editor thusly:–*
>
> *I had a good laugh at your expense the other Friday evening. Returning from Belfast per rail, I placed a penny upon Olly's bookstall, at the city terminus and said to one of the young lady attendants, 'A Herald please.'*
>
> *'Is that the Christian Herald?' she politely enquired.*
>
> *'No,' I replied, smiling, 'it's the un-Christian Herald.'*
>
> *'Oh,' said she, smiling in turn, 'that is the Bangor paper!'*

Letter from America

Around the beginning of July, a letter arrived at the offices of the *North Down Herald and Bangor Gazette* from a Mrs Sanders in America asking for a copy of *Betsy Gray*. WG was used to receiving

THE STORYTELLER

such requests and sent one off, together with some other books, to the return address.

Mrs Sanders' maiden name was Macartney and she was descended from a George Macartney who married Mary Boyd. Mary was the niece of Hans Gray and so a cousin of Betsy. She came to keep house for Mr Gray after Betsy and her brother, George, were killed. In his will, Mr Gray left the cottage to Mary and his nephew-in-law, George Macartney, and it remained in the Macartney family until it was eventually bought by the Wardens of Newtownards who still owned it in 2021. After reading her newly delivered copy of *Betsy Gray*, Mrs Sanders wrote to her cousin, another George Macartney, who was then living in Hans Gray's (and Betsy's) old cottage.[248] Her letter was dated 20th July, 1891 and was written from Sandwich, Illinois. Part of it read as follows:

> *Yes, I had learned of the story of Betsy Gray, and had sent to the Author, Mr. Lyttle, for a copy, and it arrived a few days ago. Our mother had often told us all about her. I had also read about her in the "History of Ireland." Our grandmother, Mary Boyd Macartney, had the stockings and kerchief that was taken off her after she was dead. I saw them when I was at grandfather's when I was an infant. Mr. Lyttle sent me the "Sons of the Sod," his Almanac, and also 'Robin's Reaching" [sic] which we enjoyed reading, but I liked "Betsy Gray" the best. I did not remember until I had read the book that she was born in your home, but she was.*

A fine corroboration that WG was correct in his research that identified the cottage at Six-Road-Ends as the true birthplace of Betsy Gray.

---

[248] See Appendix F, Fig. 11 for a photo of Mr Macartney at Betsy Gray's cottage.

30 - SIR WESLEY?

Mrs Sanders' letter survived and in 1968 was in the safe keeping of Mr HJ Macartney of Groomsport Road, Bangor.[249]

Per Telephone

The new, enlarged *Gazette* needed to find ever more news to fill it. WG, happy to embrace New Technology, decided the time was right to have a private telephone line installed at "Mount Herald." Such a venture could not be achieved overnight but arrangements were put in hand and it was finally fitted and operating by July, 1891. This, as I have mentioned earlier, the family believe to be the first private telephone in Bangor.

The following month saw WG, the journalist, never one to miss an opportunity, introduce a new regular column which he called, "Per Telephone." It appeared weekly in the *Gazette* and was always headed with the explanation that

> *The Editor has found it absolutely necessary to establish telephonic communication between his Sanctum and the Great World outside its limits: special connections, by private wires, with Dublin, London, Edinburgh and New York. Subscribers and advertisers can have use of instrument, free of charge, provided they permit the Editor to publish such communications as tickle his fancy.*

The wording of this "explanation" hints at the whimsical nature of the content of the "Per Telephone" columns. While a few of the reported conversations were genuine and proved to be a popular and light-hearted way of purveying the latest snippets of gossip, many were spoof calls purporting to be from anyone from well-known local "celebrities" to dignitaries such as the Prince of Wales and his Holiness the Pope. One conversation with his Royal Highness about the successful American humour magazine, *Puck*, supposedly went like this:

---

[249] The story of Mrs Sanders' letter is recounted in an article entitled, "Where was Betsy Born?" in an Appendix to the 1968 edition of *Betsy Gray* published by the *Mourne Observer Ltd.*

THE STORYTELLER

"Hello!"
"Hello! Who be you?"
"Brother Wales, Greeting."
"Ah, How's Mamma?"
"Jolly well. She's taking dandelion and will live forever!"
"How's Kate?"
"Which Kate?"
"Abdi-cate!"
"Get along! Look here, Lyttle! You get Puck!"
"Rather."
"And I'm told you have stuck upon your dining room wall that nasty cartoon showing mother scolding me for playing baccarat."
"That's so."
"Take it down, like a good fellow, and I'll have you knighted. Ta, ta."

There were plenty more, week by week, in a similar satirical vein. But he also used "Per Telephone" for genuine news, though how much was the Gospel truth was not always easy to decipher. On the 18th September a news item in the *Gazette* informed its readers that the previous Wednesday the 16th September no magistrates turned up for the petty sessions court, causing much inconvenience to the public, witnesses and professional gentlemen. The paragraph ended by referring the reader to "our telephone intelligence" for further information.

The "Per Telephone" column reported the following conversation:
"Hello!"
"Hello!"
"I am John Mulhall, private secretary to the Lord Lieutenant of Ireland."
"What is your pleasure?"
"His Excellency presents his compliments and acknowledges receipt of your letter of the 16th inst. complaining of the inconvenience caused by the total

30 - SIR WESLEY?

absence of magistrates from Bangor courthouse that day."

"What action, then, will his Excellency take in this important matter?"

"He has expressed his intention of appointing a batch of fresh Justices, and begs of you to say, for his information, how many would, in your opinion, be sufficient."

"I would say fifty."

"Is not that a large number?"

"Not for a town such as Bangor."

"Very good. As you are on the spot you are the best judge of this, and his Excellency has implicit confidence in you. As a proof thereof, he desires you to nominate suitable persons. Can you do so now?"

"Certainly; but upon such short notice I may possibly overlook some worthy gentlemen."

"That won't signify. Your nominations at any time shall have immediate attention. Proceed, please."

WG reeled off about twenty names and addresses before being interrupted.

"Hello! Isn't that enough?"

"Not nearly."

"I can't undertake that all of these gentlemen will be appointed."

"That, of course, rests with his Excellency, but I give you the names of such as should be elevated to the bench."

"All right, proceed."

WG continued to supply Mr Mulhall with a further thirty or so names, including the notorious Archibald Thompson.[250]

---

[250] See Appendix G for the list of prominent Bangorians of the 1890s that WG proposed to the Lord Lieutenant as suitable to become JPs

THE STORYTELLER

"That's about all I can just now think of," he concluded.

"I observe that you have omitted your own name."

"I did so intentionally. I prefer a life of quiet retirement."

"I'm sorry for that, because his Excellency has for some time past contemplated offering you the Commission of the Peace."

"He is very good, but I respectfully decline the honour."

"Perhaps you may reconsider."

"Perhaps. Shall I ring off?"

"Thanks. Good bye."

"Good bye."

Was this the record of a genuine conversation? With its link to the news item and the reference to WG's letter to the Lord Lieutenant it seems that it was. Was he asked for nominations? As a prominent Bangor citizen, he could have been. Was he offered the position of magistrate, himself? Quite possibly. It would certainly have been a more likely proposition than a knighthood from the Prince of Wales!

Chapter 31 – THE BANQUET

1891 – October to 1892

Ratepayers' revolt

As often before, the town commissioners were failing to do an adequate job in running Bangor's municipal affairs—certainly in the eyes of WG and many of his friends. Their inefficiency, regularly reported in the *Gazette*, was causing rumblings of discontent amongst certain groups in the town. The 1891 election was due on the 15th October. WG decided to call a meeting of ratepayers.

Time was short with polling day just over a week away. He arranged to hire the Good Templar hall for the coming Friday, October 9th and was gratified when a large crowd turned up on the evening. There was only one item on the agenda: to select alternative candidates to stand for election to the board in place of the three retiring commissioners. The three had all put themselves up for re-election and two of them were James Bowman and Greer Cleland, members of the long-running clique.

The chair for the occasion drew the audience's attention to the purpose of the meeting and called on WG to speak to the motion. He started by citing the resolution, "That we, being ratepayers of the town of Bangor, in public meeting assembled, declare our dissatisfaction with the manner in which our municipal affairs are being conducted, and hereby pledge ourselves to vote for new candidates at the election to be held on the 15th inst."

The *Belfast News-Letter* reported his speech in the following Monday's edition. He continued:

> We are here tonight, however, to select three candidates to represent us at our local municipal

THE STORYTELLER

> *Board. Let me ask you, then, has the Board as present constituted given satisfaction to the ratepayers? I say no.*

And he proceeded to give his reasons, mentioning the times when documents were destroyed, when office locks were broken and papers mysteriously disappeared, and made reference to "a certain famous cheque."[251] He accused the present commissioners of being incompetent, negligent and wasteful and of conducting their affairs in secret. He scorned the new reservoir at Conlig that "cost thousands" but the supply had frequently to be cut off during the day and let run to waste at night. He derided the gasworks that were supposed to bring in rich profits so that the rates could be reduced. Instead the gas was so bad and so expensive that few used it. He continued:

> *Would competent men extend their boundary lines to Bryansburn House and to Bayparks, then refuse light or water to the residents, but make them pay for what they never got? How much of your money was spent in trying to recover from Messrs. M'Callum and Briggs a few shillings which they had no right to pay? [a reference to Daniel M'Callum's withholding of his rates.] I don't think we'll ever know that, but if you elect new blood we'll try and find it out for you.*

WG went on to ask wouldn't competent men provide a means of firefighting for the town? Wouldn't they send out the watering cart in dry weather[252] and give it a rest when it rained? Would they dig up the streets just as the summer season was starting? Would they light the gas lamps on moonlit nights and at other times leave us "in Egyptian darkness"? Would they oppose the construction of a pier that would bring thousands of visitors to spend their money in the town? Would they place on the voters' list the names of people who had died years ago?

---

[251] See "Commissioner Thompson upsets the Board" in Chapter 21
[252] To keep down the levels of dust rising from the un-metalled streets.

31 - THE BANQUET

WG decried the fact that often they don't have a quorum of five members when they meet and the town clerk has to be sent out to round up some more. Thanks to Mr M'Murray, "who was called upon to fill the chair of his late good father-in-law," the *Gazette* is informed of when the Board will be meeting, "but this is of little value as the real business, the business that vitally concerns the ratepayers, is transacted in committee and the Press is excluded."

He finished his speech by comparing Bangor's lack of progress with how other watering places such as Whitehead, Larne and Newcastle were forging ahead and warned if action wasn't taken they could find their golden opportunity had passed away forever.

The motion was vigorously seconded by Archibald Thompson and supported, too, by a speech from WG's solicitor and friend, Daniel M'Callum. It was passed unanimously and Mr Thomas Morgan, Mr Daniel M'Callum and Mr James M'Murray were adopted as candidates. After his previous attempt to gain office, WG had decided that he was better placed, as editor of the town's newspaper, to influence events from the outside—as his initiative in holding this meeting was to prove.

Much interest was taken in the election and heavy canvassing went on leading up to polling day. When the votes were counted James Bowman was returned, yet again. But Mr Cleland lost his seat to Daniel M'Callum and the co-opted James M'Murray had his place on the Board made secure by the electors' votes.

At the November meeting of the Town Commissioners, Daniel M'Callum gave notice of his intention to move, at the next meeting, that gas and water services be extended to the recently enlarged town limits. He was careful to do this before they adjourned to "secret" committee session and while the Press was still present. We can be quite sure that the ratepayers were kept informed through the columns of the *Gazette* as to how this progressed in the months ahead.

Rev Quartz

I think WG's New Year's resolution for 1892 was to sort out all his stories and get new editions of the various volumes printed on his own press—that way lay the largest profits. It was a long task, revising, updating and improving the older tales as well as writing the odd new one when inspiration came. He worked at it in any spare moments he could find all through the spring and into the summer before the time came for the press to start rolling out brand new copies.

In the meantime there were always other demands upon his time. Early in January, 1892, he would have had the sombre task of informing the readers of the *Gazette* of the tragic death of Prince Albert, only 28, who had developed pneumonia after succumbing to influenza during the pandemic that raged from 1889 to '92. As "Robin", WG had developed a distinct fondness for the young heir presumptive to the throne and as a family man he was able to empathise fully with the Queen on the sad loss of her grandson.

In March the Rev John Quartz of Ballygilbert Presbyterian Church completed his fortieth year of service to that congregation. To mark the occasion a sizeable gathering took place at the church embracing many dignitaries and other ministers and friends, including the Rev Patton from First Bangor. Wesley was there, too, and his old friend from Belfast, John Pyper. The Rev Quartz was given a purse of one hundred sovereigns and his wife was presented with a silver tea service. After a splendid supper served by the ladies of the congregation speeches were delivered praising the work and dedication of John Quartz. There were a few shorter speeches in addition to the main speakers and amongst these was one from Wesley. He, no doubt, would have mentioned that he and Annie had been married by Mr Quartz and probably referred again to certain other nuptials at which he was alleged to have officiated, recorded for all in *Sons of the Sod*.

Bazaar

A few weeks later WG was contacted by the Rev Latimer from Groomsport Presbyterian. He was planning a grand, three-day fund-raising bazaar to be held in Bangor in July and wanted what he referred to as a Guide Book printed for wide distribution to publicise all the details of the event. Always eager to oblige, WG accepted the printing job and also found himself promising to help in any way he could. Thus it was that from Thursday 7th July to Saturday 9th his ever-loving wife Annie was busy in Bangor's Good Templar Hall

31 - THE BANQUET

organising twelve ladies and girls and two men to run the refreshment stall at the event. A number of the ladies had their daughters helping and Robina was in attendance enjoying the prestige of her step-mother being the one in charge. Her father was there, too, as one of the pair of men helping out in this sea of womenfolk. He would have relished the family occasion. How much of his time was spent in serving guests, though, as opposed to talking to his many acquaintances as they strolled by the stall, is another matter.

Fourteen-year-old Roland may have attended the bazaar but, if so, he couldn't be persuaded to assist with the refreshments. Perhaps, though, he was needed back home to help in the print shop.

Spending this social time with Annie and Robina would have reminded Wesley of the estrangement of his two older children. At intervals during the three days of the bazaar he may have reflected on their decisions to leave the family home. When John's job with the railways had taken him to Larne he must have made it quite clear that this was preferable to living in the same house as the Byers woman. Sometime later Agnes had announced that her Aunt Isabella had said she was welcome to stay with her in Madrid Street in Belfast if she would like to "get away from Bangor."

We can imagine Wesley's thinking. He would always be grateful to Lizzie's sister for caring for his first wife through her long illness but he would have considered this offer to Agnes as interfering and not welcomed it. If he said so to Agnes it could only have served to help her make up her mind to leave home. He had lost two of his children to the Grim Reaper and now two more were gone through his own deed. But surely their reaction to his wanting to remarry was unfair. Wasn't he entitled to find some happiness in the affection of someone else? Apparently not in their eyes.

We can imagine him standing with his sleeves rolled up by a big washing-up bowl as Robina brought another stack of dirty dishes over to him from Annie—and how the pleasure he must have felt from helping with his family at the fund-raising bazaar was tainted with sadness and resentment.

But life goes on. In June he had placed an advert for another "smart Turnover Apprentice." He was gearing up for the extra work of printing new editions of his books which were almost ready. About this time, too, he took on a new Compositor by the name of Jack

Loughran. Jack was married to a young catholic girl called Mary Jane, or Jinny, from Cootehill in County Cavan. Jinny's father, Michael Keelan, also had two sons and another daughter, Margaret or Maggie and Maggie was destined to have a significant impact upon Wesley's family, as we shall see. Jack would stay with the paper, rising to become Print Shop Manager, and fathering three children with Jinny before doing what many a young Irish family did in those days and emigrating to Canada to find a better life. However, this would not be until some fifteen or so years later in the first decade of the new century.

Presbyterian follies
When Archibald Thompson fell out with his fellow members of First Bangor Presbyterian Church he transferred his allegiance across the road and down a bit to Second Bangor. It seems, however, that he found some of his new Christian brethren there just as disagreeable. He wrote to the *Gazette* in July to give vent to his indignation over the matter of the church's name. It was being referred to regularly now as Trinity Presbyterian Church but Thompson pointed out that, despite its "Naming Competition" when it opened four years ago, it has always been called "Second Bangor" and under Presbyterian law, "a name shall not be assumed by a congregation, or the name of a congregation be altered, without the leave of the General Assembly." He mentioned that about three years ago the names, " St James" and later "Christ Church" were submitted to the Assembly but were not sanctioned. Subsequently "Parathina" was favoured for a while before the leaders settled on "Trinity" and registered the name in Dublin without, Thompson declared, consulting either the congregation or the General Assembly. The name has still not been sanctioned, yet it is freely used by church officials, Thompson complained, branding some of them as "untrustworthy," "reprehensible" and "liars."

The following month another item in the paper was reporting that a schism had developed in Second Bangor congregation over the selection of a new minister. The *Gazette* claimed there was such antagonism, and the division of opinions so great, that a part of the members may take themselves off to worship in the old meeting-house on the hill and form themselves into Third Bangor.

31 - THE BANQUET

New road, new housing

Back in February the *Gazette* had run a big feature on a major rebuilding project that was going on in Bangor. A well-known Belfast builder, William Kerr, had taken an interest in the developing "little seaside village" as he referred to it and was investing much of his effort and money into helping it grow. Where Fisher's Hill ran up eastwards from Quay Street, he was building a new road, complete with fine terraced housing on both sides, where only shacks and hovels had existed before. He saw it as an investment opportunity. The *Gazette* and the people of Bangor saw it as a welcome and much needed improvement to a run-down part of town.

WG knew Mr Kerr, of Henryville, Lagan Village, Belfast, by reputation. He owned a large construction firm in the city, fulfilling civic contracts as well as private development works. Only the previous year, on the recommendation of the Commission Report following the Belfast riots of 1886[253], his firm had built the urgently-needed new police barracks for the RIC at the corner of Falls Road and Dover Road in a commendably short period of time. When WG interviewed the contractor for his article he was impressed with the builder's aspirations for the current project and his hope of further schemes in the future. The new thoroughfare, WG learned, was to be named in honour of the country's beloved sovereign—Victoria Road.[254] He gave Kerr a first-rate write-up, which would stand the developer in good stead with the Town Commissioners in obtaining agreement for any further work. He also suggested to Mr Kerr that he might do himself and the town a big favour if he would consider throwing a large celebration party for the official opening of the new road. The publicity, which his paper would be happy to assist with, could only be beneficial for the builder's future plans.

Mr Kerr thought this an excellent idea and agreed that WG should inform his readers that there would, indeed, be a Grand Opening Ceremony in the summer with a parade through the town, in which

---

[253] See "Riots" Chapter 22
[254] Today Victoria Road extends right back down to Quay Street incorporating the stretch that used to be called Fisher's Hill.

everyone was welcome to join. He would provide a banquet for some 500 invited guests and townspeople. Reading this announcement in the *Gazette* on a bleak weekend in February must have cheered the hearts of many a wintry soul as they anticipated the summer revelry.

Opening ceremony

The grand day arrived—Monday 22nd August, 1892 and a general holiday was observed from noon onwards. The weather co-operated, with warmth and sunshine and the town responded in their thousands to Kerr's generosity in arranging the celebration. The route of the procession was bedecked with bunting; crowds thronged the roadsides; hundreds more hung out of upstairs windows to wave and cheer as the vehicles and marchers passed by. Over 5000 joined the parade—one of the largest processions in Bangor since the laying of the foundation stone of the new Masonic Lodge back in 1876. The march was led by the combined bands of the Royal North Down Rifles and the Bangor Boys Brigade—at that time a fairly new organisation for adolescent youths that had been started by William Alexander Smith in Glasgow just nine years previously and was rapidly spreading through the land.

The cavalcade formed up along Brunswick Road in the early afternoon. It was due to start from the Boyne Bridge over the railway at two o'clock and on the stroke of the hour a small cannon was fired that had been brought up from the harbour and mounted on the bridge parapet. The driver of the leading car cracked his whip and its four splendid white horses moved off. They pulled a magnificent barouche in which sat the Lord Mayor of Belfast—the recently knighted Sir Daniel Dixon, with Mr and Mrs William Kerr and their elder daughter. Second to cross the bridge was an equally fine carriage containing Belfast's town clerk—Sir Samuel Black, and Mr and Mrs WG Lyttle together with Miss Kerr's younger sister. That Wesley and Annie should have been so honoured was down to his having suggested the event in the first place and no doubt, too, to the complimentary coverage Kerr received in the *Gazette*.

The day's event resulted in six full columns in the following Saturday's edition and WG must have taken great delight in recording that, third in line—*after* himself and Annie—came, "in a handsome

31 - THE BANQUET

drag, the Bangor town clerk and Banger town commissioners." There followed residents and visitors in their own, private conveyances—over 100 of them—and thousands more on foot and horseback, many of whom had come down from the city by train and boat, or in from the surrounding countryside, all to enjoy the splendour of this unique occasion. We know all this from WG's full description in his report.

Wesley and Annie must have been grateful to be in a horse-drawn carriage, for the crush of the throng walking behind along Abbey Street, squeezing between rows and rows of jostling onlookers was quite terrifying. It wasn't until they had passed the station that the marchers had strung out enough to make their progress easier. They continued along Castle Street, down Main street and Bridge Street to Quay Street where they turned right up Fisher's Hill to ever louder cheers from the crowds of bystanders.

As Wesley saw the barouche in front approaching the corner of Holborn Avenue he knew they had reached the start of the new development. The leading car stopped just past the junction and all the other vehicles pulled up behind; the parade stretched right back and round the corner onto Quay Street. The bands stopped playing and the Lord Mayor stood up in the leading barouche, an arm raised to hush the cheers of the crowds. He drew attention to the transformation they could all see—from "two rows of small, miserable, dilapidated houses few of which were fit for habitation" to the splendid edifices they now saw before them—"a credit to this beautiful watering place and a monument to the pluck, energy and enterprise of Mr William Kerr."

The fine houses on the new **Victoria Road** as they now look (Photo courtesy of Trevor Low, Bangor)

There was renewed cheering from the crowd which reached a crescendo as Sir Daniel called upon Miss Kerr to christen the new Victoria Road. Behind them, Annie helped the younger, Miss MJ

Kerr, to stand up on her seat so she could see her father hand a bottle of champagne to her sister. The cheering was so loud that, although she could see her sister's lips moving, neither she nor anyone outside the lead car could hear a word she said. They all saw the young girl's arm swing in a graceful curve launching the bottle forward to crash onto the ground ahead, saturating it in Geisler's golden champagne. A veritable roar erupted from the crowd as the procession moved off once more towards the recreation ground where a giant, gaily-decorated marquee awaited those who were to attend the grand banquet.

Celebration dinner

It proved to be a most memorable occasion for everyone present. After a magnificent meal came the toasts and speeches which WG reported in full. Their genial host, Mr William Kerr, started the proceedings with the customary toast to the Queen—to which Sergeant Kearney of the RIC responded—followed by one to the Prince and Princess of Wales—responded to by Sir Samuel Black. Then came "a most important" toast—Prosperity to Bangor. Mr Kerr linked with it the name of another generous benefactor of the town also in the building trade and the current Lord Mayor of Belfast, Sir Daniel Dixon, who stood to reply.

Such was the level of cheering that he had to wait "several minutes" before he could start his speech which continued to be interrupted by further bursts of applause throughout. He said, "A remarkable wave of prosperity is just now rolling over [Bangor]. Where once the sleepy cattle browsed we now gaze upon charming villas, and where wretched cabins stood stately buildings have been erected." This brought another huge outburst of cheering. He went on to compliment William Kerr on what he was achieving and promised to contribute what he could, himself, to Bangor's future growth.

Prosperity to Belfast was then proposed, and responded to by Sir Samuel Black who, as Belfast's Town Clerk, Kerr said, was largely responsible for Belfast's present enviable position. Sir Samuel concluded his response by mentioning that what he had managed to achieve for the city had not been done without having to "contend

31 - THE BANQUET

with carping critics and would-be reformers." Using this as a link, he continued:

> There is in the present company at least one gentleman who can sympathise with me in my efforts to discharge my manifold and arduous duties; one who fully appreciates what it is to deal with a tax-paying public;... one who knows how difficult a thing it is to make a multitude of masters believe you are serving them while all the time you are making them serve you—I refer to my accomplished and talented friend, Mr Francis Pollock, the Bangor town clerk.

Here, Sir Samuel paused as the banquet guests cheered the Bangor man, before concluding by proposing a toast to the Bangor town commissioners, coupled with the name of Francis Pollock. The toast was drunk to more tumultuous cheering.

The Town Clerk's speech

Up to this point the *Gazette's* description appears to be a full and accurate account of the afternoon's proceedings thanks to the presence of one of WG's shorthand reporters. We might just wonder, however, whether its "verbatim" report of Mr Pollock's speech also flowed *exclusively* from the reporter's pencil…

> Mr Pollock rose, visibly affected. His voice, at the outset, was hesitating and husky; but, as he gained confidence, his temporary nervousness passed away, and he spoke with his well-known fiery eloquence, pointed sarcasm, and side-splitting drollery. He said,
> My Lord Mayor, Mr Kerr, and gentlemen, I thank you from the bottom of my heart for this unexpected honour. It would, I think, have been more fitting for Sir Samuel to have coupled with this toast the name of the chairman of our board—("No, no!")—for whose absence I have to apologise. His soul is one above the vanity and pomp of displays such as this—(laughter)–

THE STORYTELLER

–and while we are here feasting to repletion he is, at one and the same time, making a calculation of the probable cost of our new waterworks—(laughter)—preparing instructions for our Belfast attorney re the approaching Local Government Board enquiry as to new loans, canvassing for votes for a minister for 2nd Bangor, and making arrangements for a Sunday school convention—(roars of laughter)

Sir Samuel Black has spoken of the difficulties that beset a town clerk. I can assure you, gentlemen, that the office is by no means a sinecure. In former years my duties were of the most primitive description; but, latterly, my path has been a thorny and tortuous one. It is astonishing how troublesome, how meddling, and how impertinently inquisitive a small company of taxpayers can be.—(laughter)—taken as a whole, I have nothing but praise for the ratepayers of Bangor. But there are individuals who, at one time or another, have made themselves exceedingly troublesome and obnoxious to our board. Our first trouble was Archie Thompson—(loud laughter and cheers) [Mr Archibald Thompson was among the guests present]––whose sharp exposure of numerous "leaks" caused a profound sensation amongst the public, and no small dismay to the board.—(Hear, hear)—Then came the local newspaper—the Bangor Gazette—(cheers)—Gentlemen, it is all very well for you to cheer, but if you had this newspaper sticking like a thorn perpetually in your side, if you were weekly in dread of its attacks and exposures, you would, I am sure, sympathise with us.—(Applause)—We tried "sugar" with the Editor but we couldn't sweeten him;—(laughter)—we tried salt but we couldn't cure him;—(laughter)—we bolted the doors against him, but he bought a telephone,—(laughter)—and now he can actually sit in his sanctum and hear every word that passes in our boardroom.—(Cheers, laughter and applause)—In October last we narrowly escaped

31 - THE BANQUET

being utterly smashed, but by judicious wire-pulling, and by keeping a sharp eye upon the voters' list, we lost only one man.—(Applause)—The new blood looked dangerous, being none other than that of the famous Dan M'Callum—(cheers)—the man over whom we had spent hundreds of pounds in order to recover a few shillings for water that he never drank, and for sewers to which he never contributed.—(Great laughter)—However, we took the bull by the horns; gave Daniel gas, water, and sewerage; and, would you believe it, there isn't a more easy-going-just-do-as-you-like member at our board.—(Cheers, laughter, and applause)—I do hear that trouble is brewing for next October, and that the malcontents mean to win two seats.—(A voice—"They'll win three!")

Mr Pollock (solemnly)—God forbid, gentlemen; God forbid!—(Loud laughter)—I assure you, gentlemen, it is no laughing matter. We have so long worked in harmony, and that, too, upon a very simple rule, which is that the chairman shall be the board, his word and his ruling being final in everything save that which concerns the interest of any one or more of the other commissioners.—(Loud laughter)—Without letting you into our secrets, I may tell you that we hope to be able to defeat our opponents when October comes round. Bangorians are with us, almost to a man; it is upon residents from Belfast that the malcontents—that is what our chairman calls them—rely for assistance, but I think we shall be able to secure even their votes should they manage to get their names on the registry.—(Applause)

It is hard, gentlemen, very hard, seeing all we have done for Bangor, that anyone should be dissatisfied.—(Hear, hear!)—I grant you that we have made mistakes and spent a lot of the rates unwisely; I admit that the reservoir at Conlig runs out and that our sewers are far too small. But, gentlemen, who could have foreseen the rapid growth of our township?—(Hear, hear)

I have spoken at too great length, I fear.—("Go on! Go on!")—Excuse me, gentlemen; I see by the looks of some of our commissioners that they don't wish me to say any more, but I would like to thank you—(a voice—"Give us a song, Sir Francis!" Tremendous cheers) [WG had taken to referring to the town clerk as "Sir Francis" in the columns of the Gazette]—Really, gentlemen—(loud cries of "A song!" "A song!" "The town clerk for a song.")

Mr Morrow—Go on, Francis: give them a verse.

Mr Pollock—Well, gentlemen, since you wish it, I will try.—(Cheers)

The town clerk, now in excellent voice, sang the following:-

The Town Clerk's song

    Oh, I'm the boss of Bangor, the boss of Bangor town;
    I'm not Lord Mayor, I'm not a knight, but I'm a Proper Noun;
    I hold the whip, I drive the team whichever way I please,
    And I soothe rebellious spirits with a rub of bullock's grease.
    Then when I want to do a job that no one else will touch
    Because it might be troublesome, or worry "such-and-such,"
    The card I play still takes the trick—well nearly always so –
    I write a wee "Memorial," and sign it, don't you know!

        Chorus
        It may not be in flowing phrase

31 - THE BANQUET

It may not be grammatical;
Yet suit the people and my craze,
Be terse or enigmatical.
It may be long, or even "square,"
Veracious and pictorial,
But, never mind, I'm always there,
To hand in my Memorial!

Should any builder want a sewer, and largely deal in bricks,
He should, of course, encouraged be, and never in a fix;
Should hobby-horses come to town and catch the people's pence,
Should certain people come to me to have them driven hence,
Should pleasure seekers from afar, who now and then come here,
Complain about our harbour small, and clamour for a pier;
Should rigid Presbyterians say—"We won't have so-and-so,"
I'll get a wee memorial and sign it, don't you know!

Chorus

The sewer fiasco, the board's attempt to close the fun-fair, their objection to a new pier and their involvement in the selection of a new minister for 2nd Bangor were all items that had been lampooned in recent editions of the Gazette.

A third verse and chorus concluded the song before,

The talented vocalist resumed his seat amid tempestuous enthusiasm, cheers, and cries of "Encore" that were absolutely deafening. He modestly bowed his acknowledgements.

THE STORYTELLER

So, was this, in its entirety, the speech delivered by the town clerk in jocular and flamboyant mood? Did he really make fun of his chairman, and de facto employer, in front of 500 witnesses? Or admit to wasting ratepayers' money and to mistakes the commissioners had made? And did he just happen to have some witty and satirical verses to hand on the off chance that someone should ask for a song? Of course, it's not impossible—just, maybe a little improbable.

Alternatively, could the speech, or parts of it, have originated at WG's desk and been inserted into the report of the event for the amusement of his readers? Mr Pollock, we're told, responded to the calls for a song, but no mention is made of what tune he sang it to, as might have been expected—unless these verses also flowed from the Editor's pen and were never meant to be sung but rather read in the columns of his newspaper.

I leave it to the reader to decide whether Bangor was blessed at that time, as it might have been, with a most witty, if incautious town clerk, or if it was WG's biting satire and reckless disregard for veracity that resulted in his readers being entertained in this fine style.

In the following week's edition of the *Gazette* the "Per Telephone" column included this:

> *Hello! Bangor Town Hall?*
> *Hello! Who's there?*
> *Editor Lyttle. Is the Town Clerk there?*
> *No, sir; he is not.*
> *Can you find him for me?*
> *No, sir; I can not. He hasn't been much seen ever since Mr William Kerr's big banquet.*

Was the report in the *Gazette* quite accurate and *this* was WG's quiet dig at the town clerk's indiscretions? Or was this, rather, WG dropping a broad hint that much of Mr Pollock's speech as reported was a spoof?

End of a wonderful occasion

Whether the revelling guests at the banquet were treated to Mr Pollock's "side-splitting drollery" that afternoon or whether they had

31 - THE BANQUET

to await the next edition of the *Gazette* to enjoy the jokes they, nevertheless, continued in gay mood in the beautifully decorated marquee, clapping and cheering each successive speaker who proposed or responded to a toast. Mr Kerr toasted the success of the Moors Brothers' "popular steamers, affording to thousands of people health-giving trips at nominal fares, and bringing golden harvests to the traders of Bangor," which evoked more cheers, as did Mr John Moor's reply. There followed a toast to the success of Bangor Harbour, coupled with the name of the harbour master, Captain Tregaskis who responded—all to further applause and cheering.

At this point, the new borough magistrate, Mr EW Pim, rose and asked his host's permission to propose a toast, which was readily granted. When he said that it was to be to Mr William Kerr there was tremendous cheering which was renewed again and again before Mr Pim could finally continue. He made an excellent speech extolling the virtues of Bangor's generous benefactor, punctuated by frequent bursts of applause as each new complimentary phrase was uttered. He finished singing William Kerr's praises by declaring, "Long may he live, and long may Bangor be one of the centres of his building operations. Drink, gentlemen, to the health of our friend and host!"

There followed "a perfect whirlwind of cheers. Hats, sticks, handkerchiefs, glasses, and bottles were waved in the air" in a scene of rapturous enthusiasm. The entire audience stood and sang, "For he's a jolly good fellow." This was followed by three ringing cheers for Mr Kerr, three more for Mrs Kerr and three for their two young daughters. When the cacophony eventually subsided, Mr Kerr rose to respond. With all modesty he protested he barely recognised the man Mr Pim had described in such glowing terms and that he would try to be worthy of all the nice things he had said. In the course of his speech he referred to "my friend, Lyttle, of the *Gazette*, who was the first to suggest this christening to me." A voice called out, "Three cheers for the *Bangor Gazette!*" and they were duly and rowdily forthcoming.

The festivities concluded with a few more toasts with their responses—to Bangor Visitors, to Bangor Merchants and finishing up, as usual, with The Press to which WG replied. A wonderful festive occasion ended with the entire company singing "Auld Lang Syne."

THE STORYTELLER

WG returned to "Mount Herald" with Annie. It had been a marvellous occasion, thoroughly enjoyed by all and his head was full of ideas as to how he might best present his report in the *Gazette*—not only to inform his eager readers but to entertain them as royally as he and his fellow-guests had been entertained at the reception. As he opened "Mount Herald's" front door and stepped back to allow Annie to precede him inside, did he have an impish germ of an idea relating to the Town Clerk's speech, as to how he might do just that?

Chapter 32 – THE *HERALD* UNDER FIRE BUT "ROBIN" EXCELS ON PAGE AND STAGE

1892

WG's newspaper 'empire' was growing. The local news coverage was no longer confined to the north of the county but had extended to include most of Down. In consequence, in addition to the branch office in Victoria Avenue in Newtownards he had opened a Downpatrick office, employing a Mr JW Gillmour to manage it. He decided that the name of the journal ought to better reflect the area it served. The 16th September, 1892 edition was the first to appear under its new banner, the *North Down Herald and County Down Independent*. Beneath this was added the words, *with which is incorporated the Newtownards Independent, established 1871*. It was just

> **NORTH DOWN HERALD.**
> "Live and Let Live."
>
> BANGOR, SEPTEMBER 16, 1892.
>
> TO OUR READERS.
>
> A SLIGHT change will be observed in the title of our present issue. Twelve years ago, the circulation of this paper was almost entirely confined to the Northern Division of the County of Down. It was not long, however, until it overstepped that boundary, and to-day the *Herald* is read in every part of the broad county. So much is it sought after in Downpatrick district, that the Proprietor has established a branch office there under competent management. Henceforth this journal will be known as *The North Down Herald and County Down Independent*. Prosperity, ever increasing, has necessitated this change of name. To a generous and appreciative public we are indebted for that prosperity, and to the public we offer our most grateful acknowledgments.

From a clipping of the *North Down Herald and Bangor Gazette* held in the "North Down Museum."

under two years since the untimely death of the old *Independent's* editor, William Henry. He could no longer bring legal action about WG's audacious claim to have incorporated the earlier newspaper into his own—as the Chiel surely would have done had WG printed such a statement while he was alive.

Home Rule coverage in the *Herald*

There was international news to report, too, of course, as well as from all over Ireland and Great Britain. After the first Home Rule Bill failed at the second reading back in 1886, the Liberals lost power in a General Election the same year. But the subject didn't go away. There remained a hard core of Parnellites still demanding Home Rule and Randolph Churchill, playing the Orange card, had ensured there was a large body of Orangemen and other unionists defiantly opposed to the idea. It was a subject that would have continued to be touched upon from time to time in journals such as the *North Down Herald and County Down Independent.*

As mentioned in an earlier chapter, commentators have said that the *Herald* was a Liberal and Home Rule newspaper. What little that remains to be read today, though, would suggest it maintained more of a neutral political stance with, perhaps a slight bias towards the ruling government of the day, which granted, for much of the time WG edited the paper, *was* Liberal. As to Home Rule, the impression we get from the clippings that have been preserved is that WG would be joking about it in his columns more often than politicising over it. In fact, back in May, 1892, he published a poem "by one of our lady readers" which began:

> *When we think of this fair Isle of ours,*
> *Of its beauty, its wealth and its trade,*
> *To Gladstone we say, Clear out of the way,*
> *And keep your Home Rule in the shade.*

32 - THE *HERALD* UNDER FIRE BUT "ROBIN" EXCELS ON PAGE AND STAGE

By then rumours were rife about an imminent General Election and Gladstone's intentions, were he to get back in power.[255] WG printed a spoof phone conversation with him in the "Per Telephone" column of the 13 May edition. It included this exchange with Gladstone asking for WG's support:

> *Can I rely upon the advocacy of the North Down Herald?*
> *That depends upon your attitude towards Ireland.*
> *Ah! You want Home Rule, don't you?*
> *Not the Archbishop Walsh kind.*[256]
> *Well, what would you say to the R. R. Kane stamp?*[257]
> *That would be infinitely worse. But I say, drop a hint as to your intentions.*
> *No, dear boy! That would not do. But I'm open to suggestions.*
> *I would suggest four Irish parliaments—one for each province.*
> *Ah! 'Pon my word's that's a capital idea. I'd prefer one, though...*

Three weeks later a serious report appeared in the *Herald* of a meeting in Bangor on June 3rd to select delegates to represent the North Down constituency at a planned Grand Unionist Convention which would be held on the 17th June in Belfast. The report named the Honourable Somerset Ward as presiding at the local meeting and quoted him as saying how he never would have thought it possible that Conservatives and Liberals could meet in the same hall as they did that evening on a great and political occasion. As a Conservative,

---

[255] The election was held in July and, although the Tories won the most seats, the Liberals improved their tally and, together with Parnell's Irish National Party, commanded a majority.

[256] The Roman catholic Archbishop William Walsh was openly sympathetic to Irish nationalism as well as a supporter of Home Rule.

[257] The Reverend Dr Richard Rutledge Kane of Christ Church in Belfast and Grand Master of the Belfast's Orange Order, advocated armed resistance in the North to any imposed government from Dublin.

he expressed his thankfulness "to those noble Liberals who had been associated with Mr Gladstone for so many years, and who when he separated himself from his former Liberal principles separated themselves from him."

Another speaker quoted Gladstone calling the people of Ulster who were opposed to his views, rogues and fools. The speaker wanted the Convention to stress that the struggle regarding Home Rule was not one between Protestants and Catholics, but rather between Unionists and non-Unionists. He believed this would have a great effect upon the English and Scottish constituencies.

James Bowman, the chairman of the Bangor Town Commissioners, said there was no class of the community that ought to oppose Home Rule with more firmness and determination than the working classes, who would lose employment as a result of the chasing of capital from the country under a Home Rule Parliament. Bowman, along with several other commissioners was among the 50 delegates selected, according to the report. The list included the Rev John Quartz and WG's friend, Daniel M'Callum as well.

On 17th June they joined with 12,000 other delegates from far and wide to declare publically their fiercest opposition to any attempt to impose Home Rule in Ireland. Apart from the defiant speeches and resolutions made, the Grand Unionist Convention was remarkable in a number of other ways. Anglicans and Presbyterians together buried their deep-seated denominational differences in defence of the Union. In spite of the importance of the Land Question at the time, landlords and tenant farmers sat side by side. As did representatives of Ulster's industrial and commercial elite, and their employees. All were united in their opposition to Home Rule.

Regretably, we have no record that this momentous event was reported in the *Herald*.[258] Instead we have another "Per Telephone" piece in June where WG is purportedly saying to the Church of Ireland Archbishop in Dublin:

---

[258] We are, of course, reliant upon the selectivity of the compiler of the scrapbook of clippings that cover this period. The absence of a clipping from the *Herald* does not necessarily mean that WG was silent upon any particular matter.

32 - THE *HERALD* UNDER FIRE BUT "ROBIN" EXCELS ON PAGE AND STAGE

>   [WG]...We won't come to that for a long time in this part of Ireland.
>   [CofI Archbishop of Dublin] Come to what?
>   [WG] To see clergy of various denominations upon friendly footing with one another.
>   [Archbishop] Indeed you will! And if you live ten years from now you will see one universal church prevailing.
>   [WG] Think you so?
>   [Archbishop] Nay, I am absolutely certain of it. Have you not observed the remarkable changes that have taken place in certain quarters during the past twenty years? Slowly, but surely, my church has been imitating or adopting the forms, rites, ceremonies and what not of the Church of Rome, while your church—the True Blue Presbyterian, as you call it—has been following and imitating mine. Is not that so?
>   [WG] I am unwilling to admit it, but I must grant you that some remarkable changes have lately taken place. May I ask your Grace what form of worship will be practiced in the "Universal Church" which your Grace mentioned?
>   [Archbishop] Like a chemist's prescription it will contain many ingredients, but all will be so blended, and in such quantities as to heal one of the greatest evils from which humanity has ever suffered—the holding of various creeds, resulting in unseemly wranglings, bitter jealousies, and fierce religious warfares. Many creeds will blend, out of which blendings will arise a mighty and noble brotherhood, who will strive for the glory of God, and the good of their fellow men. But I have kept you too long?
>   [WG] Not at all. It is delightful to converse with a man of your broad sympathies.

Was this WG trying to pour a little journalistic oil upon the fiercely troubled Home Rule waters, rather than giving the oxygen of

THE STORYTELLER

column inches to reporting the more extremist views of some of the delegates?

On regaining the premiership at the end of July, Gladstone announced his intention to introduce a second Home Rule Bill without specifying a timetable. In August, WG printed another "Per Telephone" conversion with the PM during which he asked:

> [WG] ...What about Home Rule?
> [Gladstone] *There you are again. Terribly inquisitive you are! By the way, you communicated to me some time ago your views on the Irish question, and I made a note of them. Do you still entertain those opinions?*
> [WG] *I do. Give each province a local parliament and every difficulty will vanish. Let the Ulster House sit in Belfast, and every opponent of your previous scheme will open their arms to embrace you...*

So here, in black and white, is WG's stated position on the question (though we must bear in mind it was "stated" during a spoof call with the Prime Minister.) However, combining all the "clues" in these reported conversations, he certainly wouldn't have supported armed resistance to Home Rule, but neither did he want it to result, as did the Nationalists, in independence from the Crown. He would be happy with a devolved form of government giving Ireland its own parliament—or, preferably more than one! so Belfast could determine how Ulster was governed. He probably never envisaged that actually happening but, nevertheless, WG had the idea, and published it in his journal, three decades before Northern Ireland was created by the Government of Ireland Act (1920)!

Gun attack

It would be February 1893 before Gladstone would be introducing his second Home Rule Bill. An uneasy state of political unrest existed in the months leading up to this. In spite of the *Herald's* easy-going stance of "Live and Let Live," there were elements amongst the more

32 - THE *HERALD* UNDER FIRE BUT "ROBIN" EXCELS ON PAGE AND STAGE

demonstrative of the Unionist fraternity in Newtownards who took exception to something that appeared in the paper at the beginning of September, 1892. On the evening of Saturday the 3rd, whatever had been printed that incensed them, a gang of ruffians proceeded up Victoria Avenue and made their way to the rear of the branch office of the *North Down Herald and County Down Independent*. According to a report in the nationalist, Dublin-based *Flag of Ireland* this was between nine and ten o'clock at night. They hurled stones at the building but did not attempt to break in.

They were back again on Sunday morning—or perhaps these were different agitators who had only just gotten around to reading their copy of the *Herald*. "A regular fusillade of stones were thrown into the yard," said the report and on this occasion a gunshot was fired which "providentially did not do any harm."

The story was picked up in a brief paragraph in the following week's *Yorkshire Gazette*; there had been no arrests. I have found no reference to the incidents in any Ulster papers and we know nothing more of the episodes. There were no reports of further incidents—nor any evidence that the *Herald* introduced any changes to its editorial policy. It continued to report and comment upon the news in its customary, laidback manner.

The violation of "Mount Herald"

Whilst WG always delighted in reporting on the sometimes misguided activities of the Bangor Board of Commissioners, their doings about the town did not usually involve him personally. An issue arose, however, a couple of weeks after the shooting incident in Newtownards with which he was directly involved.

Not long ago, the Board had moved their office from Ballymagee Street down and round the corner into Quay Street. Whether this had been the prompt to cause the commissioners to look at the signage of street names around the town, we do not know—people needed to be able to find their new office, after all—but a number of new street name boards began to appear, often mounted on buildings sited at strategic places near street corners.

The address of "Mount Herald" had been, variously, Number 110, Ballymagee Street, Number 113 and later 116, as other properties were constructed along the road. Now, however, in their wisdom, the town commissioners had decided Ballymagee Street should end at Clifton Lane and become Ballyholme Road from the other side of the lane onward. "Mount Herald" was therefore declared to be Number One, Ballyholme Road and an ugly road name board was affixed to the front of "Mount Herald".

WG contacted his landlord and owner of the house, James Skillen, who shared his indignation at the effrontery of the commissioners. On Saturday the 10th September he came round and took down the name. The Board hastily arranged to meet on Monday to consider what steps should be taken against Mr Skillen. However only three commissioners turned up along with a Sanitary Sub-officer and, lacking a quorum, the matter had to be adjourned. Of course, the *Herald* reported the whole story,:

> *[The commissioners']latest fad is to disfigure the walls of certain houses with what they call "name boards"—unsightly things costing probably sixpence each, less commission. The Editor of the Bangor Gazette objected to having his offices made repulsive by one of these hideous things, whereupon the boss commissioner said—"It must go up!" Well, it is not up yet. The "Board" was to come up in all its strength, to put up the board in broad daylight, last Monday afternoon. But they didn't. Monday passed, Tuesday also. On Wednesday...*
>
> *On Wednesday, when the sun had set,*
> *The chicken-hearted rulers met,*
>   *Saying, "Who will go?"*
> *Will you? Will you? Will you? Will you?*
> *All shook their heads—sad sight to view*
>   *And murmured "No."*
>
> *One ruler said, "I'll send a man*
> *To find out what is Lyttle's plan;*
>   *Bring him to court,*
> *And he will swear as he is told,*

32 - THE *HERALD* UNDER FIRE BUT "ROBIN" EXCELS ON PAGE AND STAGE

> *And teach this paper man so bold*
> *To stop his sport.*
>
> *And so at dark two labouring men,*
> *Procured a ladder, tall, and then*
>   *Walked up the hill;*
> *And why should they have any fear?*
> *Two constables were in their rere,*[259]
>   *The night was still!*
>
> *But soon they beat a swift retreat,*
> *The echoes of their flying feet*
>   *Reached James's ears!*
> *"Foiled once again!" he cried, full sore,*
> *"Foiled, not by blood, but legal lore,*
>   *Oh, boys-a-dears!"*

At the end of this merry ditty came the notice: "As we go to press, some labourers employed by the Town Commissioners have again placed one of their 'name boards' upon Mr James Skillen's house. The proceeding is both silly and illegal, and is likely to bring certain persons into court at next petty sessions."

A couple of weeks later there appeared the following:

> *Despite all their bounce and brag the Bangor town commissioners have decided not to prosecute Messrs James Skillen and W. G. Lyttle for their audacious and treasonable conduct in twice removing an unsightly name board from the front wall of the house known as Mount Herald. Of course, no one ever believed they would prosecute. Mr Skillen should sue the commissioners for trespass and damage. If he did so, those bunglers would be taught a lesson which might be of service to them in future.*

---

[259] rear

THE STORYTELLER

Name plaque

A happy outcome of all this was that Mr Skillen decided to have an attractive name plaque constructed for "Mount Herald" in a rustic wooden frame. It read MOUNT HERALD and underneath, BALLYHOLME ROAD in smaller print. He added the name of the road, he said, as a matter of courtesy to Bangor visitors, although WG told him he shouldn't have included the road name; it would be misconstrued as giving in to the "rulers." It was a handsome plaque, however, which Wesley was happy to have positioned prominently above his front door.[260]

And there the plaque was to remain for 90 years. Then, upon a decision made by the commissioners' successors, the Borough Council, the grand old house was demolished to make way for a soulless car park. At that time a far-thinking journalist named Robin Page had the presence of mind to ask the foreman in charge of the demolition work to remove the plaque first. Mr Page took charge of this historic piece and later presented it to the Mayor at Bangor Castle for preservation in their archives—now the North Down Museum. (Our picture of the plaque was taken at that presentation.) Sadly, over the years since 1982, the plaque was moved and the current museum archivist is no longer aware of its location. Should anyone reading this know of its whereabouts I should be most interested to hear from them.

In print once again

But back in September 1892, WG could not afford to be distracted by the commissioners' folly. His North Down Print Works had been busy printing books—lots of them. He was anxious now that they should be distributed to booksellers.

When he had been deciding which books to print and in what order, he bore in mind that his fist two anthologies—*Humorous Readings by "Robin," Vols 1 and 2* had each had two editions published by Belfast firms and he had already printed an Author's Edition of Vol 1 in 1890. The second edition of Vol 2, we must

---

[260] For an image of the "Mount Herald" name plaque that adorned the house for 90 years see Appendix F, Figure 8.

32 - THE *HERALD* UNDER FIRE BUT "ROBIN" EXCELS ON PAGE AND STAGE

assume, had been extensive and there were still plenty of copies available, because he chose now to release Author's Editions of *Readings by "Robin," Vol 3* and of *Robin's Readings, Vol 3*.

Since the book was ostensibly by the fictitious "Robin," he decided, on a whim, to dedicate it to "Robin's" fictitious wife. He wrote, "To Peggy, truest of friends, noblest of women, and best of wives, I affectionately dedicate this book," and signed it, "The Author," dated September, 1892. So, although a publication date was not included, as was so often the case with WG's books, we do know it was produced in September '92.[261]

But WG knew that printing was just a part of it; the books had to be distributed and made readily available to the reading public. He contacted a number of Belfast outlets, that had previously taken his books, to act as wholesale agents for him: Mullan of Donegall Place; Eason & Son, Donegall Street and their bookstalls; Olley on Royal Avenue. Not content with this, he looked further afield and roped in Porteous Brothers of West Nile Street in Glasgow and John Menzies & Co in Drury Street, Edinburgh and Hanover Street, Glasgow.

With distribution taken care of, the next item on the agenda was advertising. On the 28th September an ad appeared in the *Belfast News-Letter* announcing "Robin's Readings, Vol III now ready, at booksellers, price 6d or direct from Author, W. G. Lyttle, Bangor, Down." This would have been typical of others placed in all the larger papers.

Advertising worked two ways, of course. He could advertise to increase sales, but he could also sell advertising space in his books to increase revenue and this he never failed to do. Apart from his "product placement" references in the stories themselves, which have already been mentioned, he always included a number of pages of adverts at the beginning or end of his books, sometimes both. In addition, he realised that in each of his books he could place advertisements for his other titles, too.

---

[261] See Appendix B for a complete list of WG's publications.

THE STORYTELLER

The mystery of the "eight pamphlets"

In *Humorous Readings by "Robin," Vol 3* he decided to include, on the Contents page, the contents of Vol 1 and Vol 2, as well. He showed the price of all three of these octavo sized paperbacks as sixpence each, or about £2.10 in 2021. On another page he recorded all the wholesale outlets where copies could be obtained. He needed to tell everyone, too, about his planned re-release of his other series, *Robin's Readings*. He now had many more stories than had appeared in the earlier editions of the three volumes—certainly enough for a fourth or more. WG figured if he had four volumes worth of stories at the age of 48, all written over the past 20 years or so, he should be good for another four volumes in the years ahead. That is what he planned—an eight (or more) volume series of *Robin's Readings*. For now, though, he was confining himself to bringing out fresh editions of Vols 1, 2 and 3—*The Adventures of Paddy M'Quillan, The Adventures of Robin Gordon,* and *Life in Ballycuddy, County Down.*

Towards the end of *Humorous Readings,* therefore, he added a full page advert for the forthcoming *Robin's Readings*. It referred to "A NEW SERIES Consisting of Eight or more Volumes which will be issued from his own Printing Works with all possible expedition. All the old Readings have been carefully revised, and the books will contain many pieces entirely new. VOLUMES 1, 2, & 3 ARE NOW READY."

In his, *The Poets of Ireland,* 1912, David James O'Donoghue's entry on WG Lyttle said that "eight volumes of *Robin's Readings* ran through various editions." The late local historian, Aiken McClelland, picked up on this in his preface to the *Mourne Observer's* 1968 edition of *Betsy Gray*, maintaining that WG *did* produce "eight pamphlets under the title of *Robin's Readings.*" Over the decades, fans of his works have searched in vain for evidence of these "pamphlets." The truth is that, although as we've seen, it was his intention to produce further volumes of *Readings*, circumstances, including his declining health, decreed it was not to be. Apart from a further print run of the latest *Robin's Readings—Vol 3*[262], in 1893, he

---

[262] Evidence for this third edition of *Robin's Readings—Vol 3* comes from an advert in Lyttle's 1894 *North Down Directory and Almanac*, published in January, 1894. The adverts states: "Volume III of *Robin's Readings* IS NOW

32 - THE *HERALD* UNDER FIRE BUT "ROBIN" EXCELS ON PAGE AND STAGE

would only ever bring out one more reprint of any of his books. That was to be the 1894, third edition of his most famous and enduring novel, *Betsy Gray*.

"Robin's" success

While going through all his stories for re-release in their new editions, WG sat down one evening with his diary and accounts books. He wanted to work out just how widely distributed his stories had become. Even he must have been astonished at the figures he arrived at. So much so that he deemed them worthy of including on his self-promotion page in *Humorous Readings*. He wrote:

> *The demand for Robin's Readings has been phenomenal. The Author has given over 1000 Public Readings from them in the United Kingdom. During the past few years over 50,000 copies of these "Readings" have been sold, and they are to be found in almost every part of the world.*

He also inserted an ad seeking further bookings for his one-man show as "Robin"—TWO HOURS WITH "ROBIN." It said that he was "prepared to make arrangements with Secretaries of Associations, Clubs, Societies, or other social organisations" for giving public recitals of his writings.

It seems clear that WG believed, probably rightly at the time, that his main claim to fame lay in his humorous readings and stage performances. He doesn't even mention how many copies of his second novel, *Betsy Gray*, had been sold. This was two years before that book's growing popularity would encourage him to print "a very large" third edition. Although, nowadays, WG is primarily remembered as the author of *Betsy Gray*, within his own lifetime he probably believed that it was "Robin" who would be his lasting legacy. Even fifteen years after his death his son, Roland, believed the same (see chapter 34—WG's books). "Robin" has indeed endured, but more amongst academics and lovers of the Ulster-Scots language of

---

READY" implying that the previous year's print run had been sold out for some time and now a new edition was ready.

THE STORYTELLER

his writings that so well demonstrates its use in late 19th century North Down.

In searching through his records to establish the number of books sold, he came across press reviews written about his various appearances on stage and decided that these, too, could well be included to help boost his sales towards the next 50,000.

From these reviews it is clear that Wesley Greenhill Lyttle, or "Robin," was no mere amateur performer who enjoyed entertaining a few friends when the mood took him. By this time he had probably reached the pinnacle of his career, having earned the utmost respect and admiration from his peers as well as his thousands of eager readers and concert-goers. Wherever he appeared around the country it was always, it seems, to packed houses. Frequently, disappointed fans had to be turned away at the door of an overcrowded venue. The audience would break into applause as soon as "Robin" appeared on stage—or "was helped onto the stage" due to the advancing years of WG's alter-ego. His popularity as a storyteller was supreme.

And for good reason. He used the Ulster-Scots language of the common people that he had learned as a lad growing up in Newtownards. He captured the Northern dialect (as it was referred to at that time) "to perfection." It was obvious, from his performances, that he was a keen observer of human nature and people's idiosyncrasies. These he mimicked to wonderful effect as he recited his tales. But he did not just read them—although such was the perfection of his writing that many amateur and professional elocutionists would turn first to his "Readings" when selecting a piece for their own repertoire.

No, "Robin" did not just read, he performed. From the moment Wesley donned his wig and glued his greying beard around his chin, dressed in his loud checked trousers and blue swallowtail coat, he was no longer Editor Lyttle, nor even Annie's husband and father to his children; he *was* the well-to-do County Down farmer, ever-loving husband to Peggy and Elder of Ballycuddy Presbyterian Church (wherever that may be located.) He aged fifteen years as he took to the stage and the naive and friendly openness of this elderly gentleman immediately won over his audience and enabled him to develop a rapport with them. He was able to imitate their pet expressions and

32 - THE *HERALD* UNDER FIRE BUT "ROBIN" EXCELS ON PAGE AND STAGE

prejudices without ever causing offence but rather he brought the crowd along, laughing with him.

In the telling of his tales he would frequently gesticulate and match each gesture or facial expression to what the character was saying. One critic wrote, "There was no restraint in his histrionic actions." He could do pathos just as well as mirth, though mirth had the upper hand. The one theme that runs through all his reviews is laughter—roars of it, peals of it, from beginning to end. No one left a concert where "Robin" had performed wishing he hadn't bothered coming. "Robin" lit up the stage and lit up the lives of his audience.[263]

WG's press reviews enthused about the overall humour and flamboyance of his presentations while seldom dwelling upon the detail of his scripts. The fact that frequently his stories would include poems that he had written in the guise of one or other of his characters is not mentioned. Nor that, as we can see from the printed text, in some cases the poems were, in fact, songs that the characters would sing, perhaps to a well-known tune. For example:

> *An wid that I cleared my throat and rattled off to my favrit air ov 'My Luv Dan' the followin' illigant production*[264] *:-*

> *THE BOBBY'S HAT*
> *Oh come all ye people far and near,*
> *From town and coun-ter-ee;*
> *A doleful story you will hear*
> *If you listen unto me...*[265]

More verse is introduced in "Robin on Ice"[266] with these words:

---

[263] This authentic description of "Robin's" stage act has been derived from the many press reviews that have been preserved in the newspaper archives or quoted in WG's own writings. Some of the original reviews are reproduced in Appendix D

[264] And with that I cleared my throat and rattled off to my favourite air of 'My Love Dan' the following elegant production

[265] First verse of a song from "Mickey Mulrooney on the New Police Helmet", see *Readings by Robin, Volume III*

[266] See *Readings by Robin, Volume III*

THE STORYTELLER

> *Efter that they a' cried at the Meer fur a sang. He saw there wuz nae refusin' an' so he lauched an' stud up on the furm, and here wuz the sang he sung...*[267]

And in "Wee Paddy's Bumps"[268]:
> *"Oh, let him be," sez Wully, an' wi' that he begood an sung a verse o' a sang that I heered a man at a surree yin time singin'...*[269]

Whilst WG may have chosen, for his stage appearances, not to include any of his stories with songs, it is possible that WG's virtuoso performances as "Robin" included him singing the odd humorous verses on stage as well. Of course, having introduced a 'song' he could just have recited the words. Since I have been unable to find any direct reference in the reviews to WG singing, perhaps this is what he did, albeit with all the gusto of a singer.

As he would drive back in his gig, late from another successful concert with all of "Robin's" trappings in a valise by his side, Wesley would often be worn out from his exertions on stage. But he would be happy, the laughter and applause still ringing in his ears. Sometimes, he would even nod off for a while but the old mare trotted on; she knew her way home and would turn in at the yard behind "Mount Herald" with or without Wesley's touch on the reins.

With four new editions of his works now printed, published and distributed, WG was free to turn his mind to other matters. It was already October and the municipal elections were due imminently—another opportunity to unseat some of the old ruling clique. The concerned ratepayers had had a partial victory last year replacing one sitting member and re-electing the one (of the three) who had actually been doing a good job of representing them. Three more members

---

[267] After that they all called to the Mayor for a song. He saw there was no refusing it and so he laughed and stood up on the platform, and here was the song he sang...

[268] See *Robin's Readings, Volume III*

[269] "Oh, let him be," says Willy, and with that he began and sung a verse of a song that I heard a man at a soirée one time singing

32 - THE *HERALD* UNDER FIRE BUT "ROBIN" EXCELS ON PAGE AND STAGE

were up for re-election in a few weeks' time. WG's intention was to see them defeated.

THE STORYTELLER

Chapter 33 – ON THE MOVE AGAIN

October 1892 – 1896

Victory at the polls

Friday 14th October was the make or break night for the 1892 election of Bangor town commissioners. Three members of the Clique were up for re-election—James Neill, George Russell and Patrick Campbell. WG and his group of "concerned ratepayers" were determined to thwart their designs.

This year there were five new bloods to contest the three seats along with the sitting candidates, so eight in all. A pre-election rallying meeting was held on the Friday evening in support of the new candidates. It was well attended by an enthusiastic public. Ratepayers pledged themselves to go along the next day to cast their votes for the new men.

And vote they did, along with the rest of the townsfolk, despite the persistent rainfall throughout the day. The polling station at the commissioners' office on Quay Street saw a steady turnout of voters from eight o'clock in the morning until eight at night. It wasn't too long afterwards that the result was announced—two of the sitting candidates had lost their seats. Another victory for the "malcontents" as the chairman of the board called them.

James Neill retained his seat with 98 votes but the new men, Mr John Matthews and Captain William Johnston came 2nd and 3rd with 95 and 93 votes, respectively. Not one of the "old school" commissioners present at the count congratulated the newcomers on their victories.

Matthews and Johnston, however, both put letters in the *Herald* thanking the electorate for showing their confidence in them by voting them onto the board. They duly turned up at the commissioners' office

33 - ON THE MOVE AGAIN

at seven o'clock the next Monday evening for a scheduled board meeting only to find just three other commissioners present along with the town clerk. They were due to swear their declarations in order to take their seats on the board but the other commissioners thought this couldn't be done without a quorum. Francis Pollock, the town clerk assured them that any of the sitting commissioners could take the declarations but they were reluctant to do so without the chairman present.

There was other urgent business to be done which could not go ahead as they were inquorate. If they heard the declarations and the two new members took their seats they would then have a quorum and could proceed with business but caution prevailed and the meeting had to be abandoned. The newcomers said nothing but even the existing commissioners expressed their disgust with the chairman and others for failing to attend, which they interpreted as a slight to the new members.

Needless to say, the *Herald's* reporter had the whole sorry debate recorded in shorthand and it appeared, word for word in the next edition.

Party politics

WG had had enough of politics for the time being and besides, he was in need of a rest. He'd had a demanding time preparing and publishing the new editions of his books, and all that work had taken its toll.

'You're exhausted,' we can just hear Annie telling him and he couldn't disagree. Once he had the new edition of his Almanac put to bed, he was happy to take it easy over Christmas and plan a much more relaxed year in 1893.

But it was only a couple of weeks into January when politics was in the news once more. Not locally this time but over the water; WG had only to lift the story from the national news sources. It seemed an Independent MP at Westminster was dissatisfied with the Liberals' reluctance to endorse working class candidates representing the interests of the majority. He decided to form a new political party on the left. WG, along with many other editors of journals around the country, would have published the fact that Mr Keir Hardy had set up what he was calling the Independent Labour Party. He probably wondered what future, if any, a small independent political party could have in the well-established two-party system of British politics.

He may have spotted the name of Alexander Bowman amongst those involved in setting up the new party and remembered hearing of him previously, because he shared his surname with WG's nemesis, the chair of the Board of Commissioners, James Bowman, although the two were not related. Back in 1885, Alexander Bowman had become the first working-class man in Ireland to stand for Parliament. He was defeated, but, nevertheless, he had struck a blow for the developing labour movement that now had its own parliamentary party.[270]

In February, WG would have been reporting on yet more political manoeuvring, with Gladstone introducing his promised, revised Home Rule Bill. This time, as the *Herald* would have informed its readers, the Bill was passed by the House of Commons. By the autumn, however, it was to be thrown out by the Lords.

WG's health was such that late in the month of March until the third week in April he felt the need to have one of his senior reporters edit his newspaper in his stead. We know this from a passing comment in one of his *Per Telephone* conversations that appeared on the 21st April. In it, he took issue with another journal for something they had published back on the 1st April. When asked why WG was only mentioning it now he explained, "absence from the editorial chair,[271] alone, prevented me from sooner ringing you up."

Daytrip to Scotland

However, as the summer months came in, WG felt much better and quite up to taking a daytrip to Scotland when he received an invitation to do just that. A Scottish shipping company, Messrs G & J Burns were launching a new weekend daylight service between Belfast and

---

[270] Alexander Bowman went on to become the president of the Irish Trade Union Congress. His great-grandson, Terence Bowman, editor of the *Mourne Observer* until 2011 wrote his biography, "People's Champion", Ulster Historical Foundation, 1997.

[271] One of the rare references that WG made to the state of his health (see also Chapter 28)

Scotland. Along with many invited VIPs and dignitaries, several representatives of the press were offered the opportunity of sailing on the inaugural trip. Reporters or editors from the *Evening Telegraph*, the *Ulster Echo*, the *Belfast News-Letter*, the *Northern Whig*, the *Lisburn Standard*, and the *Lisburn Herald* were all on board as well as WG from the *North Down Herald*.

The boat, RMS Hound, was only recently launched and was finished "in an elegant and comfortable fashion" according to the Lisburn Herald's report in their edition of the 24 June, 1893. WG must have left home in Bangor at the scrake of dawn on Saturday, 24th June as the boat was due to steam away from its Belfast dock at 8:15 a.m. They had a misty start but were soon through the fogbank and into glorious sunshine for the rest of the trip. They were treated to a splendid view of the island of Ailsa Craig, or Paddy's Milestone as the Ulster folk call it, and of the Mull of Cantyre,[272] before starting the approach to Ardrossan. By this time, all on board were enjoying a fine four-course luncheon before disembarking.

The daytrippers were taken in two wagonettes on a pleasant circuitous drive inland to fill the hour-and-a-half before the return sailing. They docked in Belfast at 8:00 p.m. and WG still had to complete the journey back to Bangor. By the time he was able to flop into his favourite chair at "Mount Herald" he must have had that feeling of utter exhaustion again. But as he told his wife, it had been a grand day out. "Ay, a grand day, Annie."

Last will and testament

Did Wesley lie awake that night too tired to sleep? Did his mind ponder over how the delightful daytrip had left him so worn out? A couple of months ago he'd had his 49th birthday; 50, next year. Sure that's no age at all. He shouldn't be feeling like this. Did he worry long into the night before drifting off into a fitful sleep?

Whether that was so or not, and although by morning he was likely feeling much refreshed and ready to face another day, he awoke with a firm decision in his head. His state of health may or may not be a matter of concern—it was probably nothing—but, nevertheless, he

---

[272] Mull of Cantyre, known today as the Mull of Kintyre

THE STORYTELLER

knew he wasn't going to live forever. He ought to write his will—just to have everything in order when the inevitable time arrived. Perhaps there had been an earlier will, written when his children were much younger and Lizzie was still alive, but circumstances were now much changed.

He seldom met up with John—now making his own way in life—nor Agnes, though he had heard that she had been walking out with someone called Alexander; they attended the same Donegall Street Congregational Church in Belfast (similar in style to the Presbyterian Church of her youth but, perhaps, just sufficiently different to register her casting off her father's influence.) Apparently Agnes was to be married in October; no longer Wesley's responsibility.

Then there was Annie, too. Since Wesley had re-married, his new wife had to be taken care of. He gave the matter some considerable thought over the next week or so and then sat down to write.

> *I, W. G. Lyttle, of Bangor, in the County of Down, a journalist, make this my last will and testament, I give to my dear wife, Annie Bankhead Lyttle, all that I may die possessed of to be disposed of by her in manner following. She is to sell the copyright of all my published or written works, also of my newspaper, and to redeem [this word is unclear] all my printing plant, unless she may be able to carry on the printing business and publication of my works. Should she sell, I desire her to retain one half of the proceeds thereof to her own use absolutely, and to invest the remaining half for the benefit of my daughter Robina and my son Roland in equal shares. Should she, on the other hand, carry on the business, she is to retain one half profits and give to my said two children the other half in equal shares. In either case one half is to belong to my said wife absolutely. It is my wish that she shall not have any dealings, financially or otherwise, with any other relations who during my life treated her unkindly, and I appoint her sole executrix of this my will. I desire my said two children and my said wife to live together as long as possible on terms of goodwill*

33 - ON THE MOVE AGAIN

> *and affection. In witness whereof I have hereto subscribed my name this 9th day of July 1893.*

A friend or business associate, Alex Robertson, was over from Scotland, either staying with the Lyttles or at least visiting the Print Works. Having completed his will the previous evening, he called one of his senior reporters—it was Gillmour, in fact, who was now living in Bangor and no longer seemed to be running the Downpatrick office—to join him and Alex. He asked them both to witness his signature on the document which he proceeded to sign.

> *W.G. Lyttle*
> *Signed by the testator as and for his last will and testament in the presence of us, who at his request in his presence and in presence of each other, have hereto subscribed our names as witnesses,*
> *Alex Robertson 185 Crown Glasgow*
> *J.W. Gillmour Reporter Bangor Co Down.*

Sadly, such was the totality of his estrangement with his two elder children that they were to receive nothing from his estate. His wish that Annie should have no dealings with "any relations" who had treated her unkindly suggests more than just John and Agnes. Perhaps it included his sister-in-law, Isabella, too.

Agnes's young man, Alexander Holmes worked as a shirt cutter[273] and lived on Spamount Street, not far from York Road Station. He was 23, two years younger than Agnes, when they were married at their Congregational Church on Wednesday, the 4th October,1893. It can't have been fully the joyous occasion that Agnes would have dreamed of. We can only hope that Alexander's family—his father, James, was a carter like Agnes' grandfather, John Courtnay—we can only hope that they made up in love and affection for what must have been sadly lacking from his new in-laws.

---

[273] Might he have known Agnes' Aunt Isabella, a shirt maker, through his work and met Agnes when she moved into Isabella's Madrid Street house?

THE STORYTELLER

The pair took a house not very far from Isabella Courtnay's, at 26, Maymount Street where, a year-and-a-half later, Agnes gave birth to little Elizabeth (Lilly) Erskine Holmes—Wesley's first grandchild and the only one to be born within his lifetime. Sadly, I have found no records of whether he ever got to know Lilly; whether the child's parents allowed the proud Grandfather to visit and play with her and bounce her upon his knee. I hope they did.

Similarly, I have been unable to find any further references to Agnes' elder brother, John. Family anecdotes have it that he, too, married and moved to England, or possibly moved first and then married. Still working for the railways, he invented a new form of automatic coupling for railway carriages which, according to the story passed down the generations, was taken up only after his death. We know of no further contact with his family during Wesley's lifetime.

An evening with "Robin"

WG fulfilled another engagement three weeks after his eldest daughter's wedding when he was a guest speaker at the Rosetta National School annual meeting but it was still as his alter-ego that he was most in demand. Probably as a result of his advert in Humorous Readings, he had been invited back to Lisburn to perform in the Assembly Rooms the following January. The *Lisburn Herald and Antrim and Down Advertiser* carried an ad on Saturday 6th January, 1894 headed, AN ENTERTAINMENT consisting of READINGS BY "ROBIN," The Prince of Public Humourists.

On the 13th, two days before the event, they printed a fuller ad:

HUMOUR! MIRTH! FUN!
"ROBIN GORDON"
Of Ballycuddy
(The inimitable Humourist and mirth-provoking Mimic)
IN THE ASSEMBLY ROOMS,
On Monday evening, 15th inst.
At Eight o'clock,
Assisted by several distinguished Musical Amateurs.
DROLL STORIES, HUMOUROUS READINGS, LOCAL HITS, COMIC SONGS

---

33 - ON THE MOVE AGAIN

> **Chair—M.B. Mackenzie, Esq., M.D.**
> **Admission, Sixpence; Front Seats, One Shilling.**
> **Tickets at "The Globe," Gillespie's, "Herald" and "Standard"**
> **Offices, and at the door.**

While these adverts were appearing in Lisburn, Wesley was at home in Bangor fearing that he might have to cancel the event. He wasn't feeling at all well again and put it down to a bad dose of winter flu, though he wasn't sure what it was. However, he didn't want to let his fans down especially as he had added to his stories some comical local references to recent events around Lisburn. Feeling a bit better by the Monday 15th he wrapped up well and made the journey to the Antrim town.

The Assembly Rooms were packed to the doors. In introducing him, Mr Mackenzie, in the chair, said he was sorry to hear that "Robin" had been suffering from a severe attack of influenza, and had it been any audience other than a Lisburn one their friend would not have attempted to deliver his lectures. He went on to introduce some musical items but when it was time for "Robin Gordon" to make an entrance he was received with a storm of applause. His readings included *The Trip to Glasgow*; *Peggy, and how I courted her*; and *The Electric Light*. The audience were kept laughing throughout until many, as the *Lisburn Herald* said, "complained of pains in their sides. The many local hits he introduced into the various pieces," the report continued, "were greatly relished and provoked roars of laughter."

The adrenalin kept him going on stage and "Two Hours with 'Robin'," as the *Lisburn Herald* headed their write-up was another terrific success, even if it did leave Wesley drained. He took a few weeks to recover fully but by mid-February, '94, he was presenting yet another entertainment, this time together with his friend (but no relation), Joseph Lyttle and Mr W Abbotson Jnr. They showed a series of beautiful pictures of Irish scenery by limelight, along with a collection of comic views. For all of these WG provided the commentary to another delighted and satisfied audience.[274]

---

[274] This, according to the *Belfast News-Letter, 19th February, 1894*

THE STORYTELLER

"A very large third edition"

The new editions of his books were selling well and, although it had been hard work getting them all produced on his own printing press, Wesley wanted to publish another edition of his most successful book, too. He frequently received correspondence from people who could no longer get hold of a copy of *Betsy Gray*; he realised there was a need for a further issue. A significant number of readers, too, were enquiring whether they could contribute to a memorial to Betsy. He was in touch with a number of groups who were indeed planning to erect a suitable memorial by 1898, the centenary of the rebellion.

Working all through the early part of the summer, by August, WG had large stacks of the book printed, bound and ready for distribution. He wrote in the preface:

> *This story was originally written for and published in the columns of the North Down Herald. Its success was phenomenal, and the demand for its appearance in book form has been such as to warrant the issue of a very large third edition. The incidents have been collected from reliable sources; relatives of the sufferers of the '98 have been interviewed, and the places written of have all been visited by the author.*
>
> *The mournful fate of Betsy Gray has excited universal sympathy. Many letters have been received by the writer of these pages expressing a desire to subscribe towards a suitable monument to be erected at the lonely grave in the vale of Ballycreen, where the ashes of Betsy repose. A movement is on foot to have this object carried out in the year 1898.*
>
> W. G. Lyttle
> Mount Herald, Bangor, Ireland
> August, 1894

33 - ON THE MOVE AGAIN

The book carried the usual array of commercial ads, and in addition contained full-page adverts for *Sons of the Sod* ("only a few copies remaining"), *Life in Ballycuddy, Vol 3*—the latest book of *Robin's Readings*, and for the *North Down Herald* ("A file is kept on view at 52-54 New Oxford Street for the convenience of London advertisers"). A copy of this Third Edition of *Betsy Gray* is held at the British Library and at the Linen Hall Library in Belfast. These are two of the oldest known copies of the book in existence (unless, of course, a reader could inform me of the whereabouts of another 1888 or even an 1887 copy!)

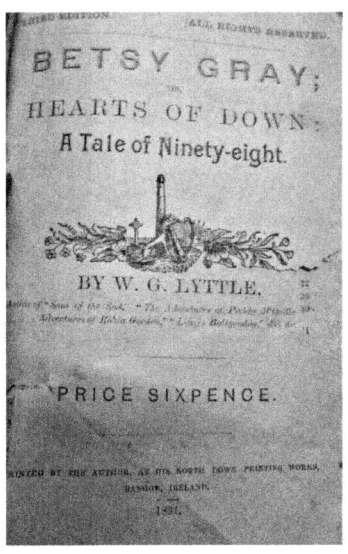

The title page of the **third edition of *Betsy Gray*** —one of the oldest extant copies, courtesy of the Linen Hall Library, Belfast (image, AG Lyttle)

The Tannaghmore Hole

The following month the papers were full of accounts of a breaking local government scandal, not in Bangor, but in Downpatrick. The *Gazette* would have covered the story, too, of course. WG was as incensed as his readers at the apparent negligence of those involved in providing a new reservoir to supply water to Downpatrick. The Tannaghmore Hole, the site chosen to flood, had been dug out of a bog which seems to have been an ancient dumping ground for carcases. As well as that, farmers were using nearby pools for steeping their flax and the polluted water was suspected to be leaching into the reservoir.

Needing some relaxation after the hectic activity of publishing the third edition of *Betsy Gray* WG decided to sit down and write a skit about the muddy water of Tannaghmore Hole. He wrote it in the cumulative style of *The House that Jack Built* and printed it in his newspaper. It turned out to be a lengthy tale that covered the whole sorry saga and the individuals involved. This is how it started:

THE STORYTELLER

This is the Tannaghmore Hole.
And this is M'Larnon, Contractor M'Larnon, who dug out the Tannaghmore Hole.
And this is Macassey, the clever Macassey, who instructed M'Larnon, Contractor M'Larnon to dig out the Tannaghmore Hole.
And this is the Bog, the wide-spreading Bog, the fathomless Bog, that was found by M'Larnon, Contractor M'Larnon, as he dug out the Tannaghmore Hole.
And these are the bones, the mouldering bones, of the horses and asses, the dogs and the cats, the puppies and kittens, that for centuries past have been flung in the Tannaghmore Hole.
And this is the water, the brown muddy water, that flows from the Tannaghmore Hole.[275]

Moving home

It may have been Annie who first suggested it. It would soon be seven years since she had been mistress of the big house at the top of Ballymagee Street—or rather, as it was now addressed, at the start of Ballyholme Road. With only her and Wesley and the two remaining children she was, perhaps, feeling that "Mount Herald" had more accommodation than they needed, even allowing for the business use of the top floor rooms. It was an old house, too, and probably not the easiest to keep looking spic and span.

After his brush with insolvency a few years earlier, an older and wiser Wesley may, too, have been looking to downsize their business premises for a lower rental outlay.

It so happened that the proprietor of the Imperial Hotel on Main Street, a Mr Matthews, was developing an adjacent plot and a number of properties, to be known collectively as Imperial Buildings, were soon to become available. Wesley and Annie made enquiries and

---

[275] No copies of the *Gazette* from this time still exist but by great good fortune I came across a re-print of the skit in a future paper. It is now included it in *Robin's Rhymes, Poems in Ulster-Scots and English* published by AG Lyttle, 2021. So now, for the very first time, this new piece by WG can be read by all.

33 - ON THE MOVE AGAIN

found that the accommodation to be offered by No. 1 Imperial Buildings would suit them perfectly. Behind the premises was a good-sized yard for a workshop to house the printing press and all the ancillary equipment, which could be accessed directly from Castle Street, a little side road off Main Street.

They thought hard about the pros and cons of moving. Wesley must have become very attached to "Mount Herald." It held many wonderful memories, though sad ones, too. Roland, 17, and his 15-year-old sister would have harboured mixed feelings about leaving the big house where they had grown up, although maybe Robina looked forward to living somewhere newer and less welcoming to the occasional mouse; she had developed a horror of the little visitors from the nearby fields. For Annie, this had been the first home that was truly her own—and yet… she would always have been aware that it had been Wesley and Lizzie's home first. So it might well have been Annie who tipped the balance in favour of moving.

Of course Wesley had checked that the new buildings would be supplied with gas that he needed for his printer, but Annie was more interested in having gas lighting in all the main rooms. When the deal was done and they were definitely moving, Annie asked Wesley, if he thought they could have one of the beautiful centrally-hung gasoliers in their sitting room—not just wall lights. Her husband consented.[276]

They were to move early in the New Year and Wesley was hoping it wouldn't be too early, as he was involved in a new venture planned for 25th January. As it turned out the completion of their new home was considerably delayed—by one of the most violent storms ever to hit Bangor. It struck in the December of 1894 and caused widespread destruction. Two large vessels in Belfast Lough were driven towards the Bangor coastline where they were dashed onto the rocks. Lives were lost. Dozens of small boats in the bay were smashed up at their mooring, such was the ferocity of the sea. Onshore, the winds wreaked more havoc. The seafront switchback railway that had been bringing delight to children and adults, alike, throughout the summer months for the last five years was completely wrecked. 25 houses

---

[276] We know this because there was some dispute as to whether or not the gasolier was a fixture when the house in Main Street came to be sold again (see Chapter 34 – WG's books).

throughout the town in the process of construction were blown down. Among those damaged were Imperial Buildings and the Lyttles had to wait several months before repairs could be completed and all was made ready for their move.

Burns Night

One of the snippets of information about WG that the potted biographies usually include is that he brought the first Burns Night celebration to Bangor. Well, it is true he was involved, along with JH Balfour, the artist. Which of them was the driving force behind it is hard to establish; perhaps it was a joint initiative. But it wasn't a traditional Burn's Night celebration as we would imagine it.

It was held in Bangor's new Guild Hall on Friday the 25th January. So the date, which was the 136th anniversary of the birth of Robby Burns, was certainly traditional. The entertainment commenced with a series of dissolving limelight views of the land of Burns, or more particularly, the Scottish lowlands, with Mr Balfour operating the "magic lantern." WG was the lecturer providing light-hearted commentary to describe the views in each painting. During the course of this he included a reading of *What the Wind Said in the Trees Above the Grave of Burns*.

But this first part of the evening concluded the Scottish element of the entertainment. There was no *Address to a Haggis*—there was no Haggis, nor, indeed, any food; no bagpipes and no singing of *Auld Lang Syne*. So although the *Belfast News-Letter* headlined its report of the event the following day with "BURNS ENTERTAINMENT IN BANGOR," this could hardly be called Bangor's first Burns Night celebration—not in the traditional sense.

It was, nevertheless, an enjoyable evening's entertainment "replete," as the write-up put it, "with mirth, music, and melody." It continued with a number of pianoforte and violin solos and songs, which were all well received.

While these were going on, WG was donning the regalia of "Robin" who emerged for the final part of the evening to tell all about Paddy M'Quillan's Courtship and Marriage. Uniquely, this time his recital was illustrated by limelight pictures especially prepared by Mr Balfour of Paddy and Maggie, his paramour. The programme

33 - ON THE MOVE AGAIN

concluded with a number of novelty views and pictures of Bangor, including some depicting scenes of the recent storm damage—anticipating Pathé News by some 15 years!

Some months later, the Lyttle family did manage to make the move from No. 1 Ballyholme Road to No. 1 Imperial Buildings, Main Street just south of the junction with Castle Street and Hamilton Road. The name, "Imperial Buildings," wasn't to last and the premises would come to be known as No. 85 Main Street—where the First Trust Bank is in 2021.[277] The Ulster Directory for 1896 lists Lyttle, W. G., Main Street, confirming that they moved in during '95. Workshops had been erected to the rear and all the plant was installed and made operational. The North Down Print Works had a new address—as had the *North Down Herald and County Down Independent*. And Annie had a new gasolier in her front room.

The Bangor Season

An updated edition of WG's travel booklet, *The Bangor Season*, was prepared and printed in time for the latest influx of visitors in 1895. We know this because this edition contains a reference to the *North Down Herald* in its chapter on Newtownards, which it describes, rather cheekily, as "the local newspaper" with not a mention of the *Newtownards Chronicle*! It records that, "The proprietor's offices are at 42 Arthur Street, Belfast and Main Street, Bangor."

This suggests that, since WG republished *The Bangor Season* in 1887, two years after it was first launched, he probably produced a biennial series, with new editions in 1889, '91 and '93, as well as this 1895 edition.

It also shows that The *Herald* now had a Belfast office, too. Ironically, at number 42 Arthur Street, it was right next door to the old publishing firm of Allen & Johnson, who had let WG down so badly in the libel case.

---

[277] On 17th December 2013, the Ulster History Circle unveiled a Blue Plaque mounted on the wall of the First Trust Bank at 85 Main Street, Bangor to commemorate the life of WG Lyttle. See photos in Appendix F, Figs 21, 22

THE STORYTELLER

Betsy Gray's memorial

Later in the year, WG would surely have been thrilled to be reporting that a small obelisk and surrounding wrought iron fence had been erected at Betsy Gray's grave near Ballycreen, about two miles from Ballynahinch. On the front face it read "Elizabeth Gray, George Gray, William Boal, 13th June, 1798," and on the opposite side were the words, "Erected by James Gray, grandnephew of Elizabeth and George Gray." WG knew that the immense popularity of his book about Betsy Gray was a big factor in bringing about this long overdue tribute.

A few years later, however, there was to be a sad corollary to this. Although Betsy Gray was a County Down protestant lass from the heart of what was now a staunchly loyalist area, increasingly, her name was being adopted as a figurehead by the catholic nationalists because of her strong association with the cause of the United Irishmen to expel the British from Ireland. As was only fitting, a ceremony to mark the centenary of the '98 rebellion was being arranged for June, 1898 and it would take place at Betsy Gray's graveside. But it was being arranged by Roman Catholic associations and Home Rulers.

Local loyalists were incensed and determined to prevent 'their' Betsy Gray being used to further the nationalists' cause. Out of no disrespect to their heroine, but purely to prevent her being the focus of a catholic commemoration, a few days before the ceremony was due to take place, a group of loyalists broke down the fence around her grave and smashed up the monument with sledgehammers. Pieces of the granite stone were removed as souvenirs and taken all over the world. The iron railings were fashioned into horseshoes by the local blacksmith and given to his friends.

So Betsy's only lasting memorial remains, to this day, the novel that inspired a generation and has continued to enthral readers down the decades ever since—WG Lyttle's *Betsy Gray or Hearts of Down*.

"Robin" plays to his largest ever audience

1895 seemed to be rushing by. In no time at all, it seemed to WG, another New Year had arrived. Belfast City YMCA Literary Society invited him to give a "Humorous Recital in the character of Robin Gordon of Ballycuddy" on Friday evening 17th January, 1896 in their brand new Wellington Hall.[278] The event went well. His friend and musician, Mr John Birrell provided musical interludes between his recounting of all Paddy M'Quillan's various adventures. This must surely have been the biggest venue he had played and it was to a "very large and appreciative audience" according to the write-up in the next day's *News-Letter*. Some 70 years later, his great-grandson, yours truly, would stand on the same stage with his guitar to sing one of his Gospel songs at a big Christian Rally—unaware, at the time, that WG had trod those self-same boards on what turned out to be a landmark occasion.

For WG it was just another concert, albeit probably his largest ever. Just another concert—but this one was to be the last "Robin" concert to be advertised in the papers or to receive subsequent write-ups full of critical acclaim. WG's health was to prevent him from ever again stepping into the limelight on an Ulster stage.

Declining health

WG turned 52 on 15th April. He was spending less and less time on the paper. His occasional periods of weakness had become times of exhaustion and were now more frequent. He lost his appetite and the girth of his portly figure reduced somewhat over the summer months.

In the middle of August the prominent Newtownards businessman, James Caughey, passed away. Mr Caughey had been one of the proprietors of the old *Newtownards Independent* so WG would likely have had dealings with him at the start of his newspaper career and probably since then as well; Mr Caughey, amongst other enterprises owned a print works in Newtownards. WG would have wished to attend his funeral and, hopefully, he was able to.

---

[278] See Appendix F, Figs 17,18 for photos of this big new venue now, sadly, demolished.

THE STORYTELLER

James Caughey's funeral procession in Conway Square, Newtownards (part of a "horslips5" image on Flickriver.com used under license—*creativecommons.org/licenses/by/4.0*)

However, towards the end of August he took a turn for the worse. By then the doctor, James M'Fee, could see a jaundiced complexion; the yellowing of his eyes was particularly noticeable. He didn't have to ask if Wesley often drank to excess; he knew his reputation of being a teetotaller throughout his adult life. Which made it all the more ironic that he felt sure he was looking at the symptoms of liver disease.

Wesley was quite poorly and in no state to consider the reasons for his illness but Annie, doubtless, wanted to know how he could possibly have developed liver disease when he didn't drink. Dr M'Fee would have explained to her that there is such a thing as non-alcoholic cirrhosis. It can develop from a number of causes. The bile ducts can become inflamed, the body's own immune system can go wrong and damage liver tissue or the liver can grow extra fat and become inflamed. All these conditions are fairly rare but each one can lead to cirrhosis. He really couldn't say how Wesley had contracted the disease but he could be reasonably confident that this is what was causing his symptoms. He likely prescribed complete rest and plenty of protein in his diet.

33 - ON THE MOVE AGAIN

Wesley would have hated being inactive but, for the time being, his body allowed him no alternative. His Senior Reporter, Gillmour, stepped up and, together with the rest of the newspaper staff, got the *Herald* out each week until the proprietor was back on his feet. WG felt sufficiently recovered by the latter half of September to take up the reins once more and, no doubt, his thousands of readers were as delighted as his friends and family to see his distinctive editorial prose once again.

In mid-October, however, the symptoms returned. He rapidly grew worse, worse than he had been a month earlier. He was confined to bed and each day he seemed to be sinking lower. Now aged 17 and 18, respectively, Robina and Roland were every bit as worried as their step-mother about their father's condition. As the 31st of the month came round, a Saturday, there were no thoughts of going off to Hallowe'en parties that year. In the early hours of All Saints Day Annie became very concerned for Wesley. Dr M'Fee was sent for. He came straightaway but there was little he could do for Wesley. The big-hearted man who gave so much of his early working life to helping individuals and families affected by the abuse of alcohol and a huge portion of his later life to bringing fun and laughter to thousands of his compatriots, could give no more.

The darkened windows of the bedroom were beginning to show hints of grey. Somewhere in the house a clock chimed out the hour of seven o'clock. In another twenty minutes or so the sun would rise on a new day. But for Wesley… for the loving husband and father… for the editor and proprietor of the *North Down Herald*… for the celebrated write and storyteller… the sun had set. There would be no more dawns. WG had breathed his last.

THE STORYTELLER

Chapter 34 – LEGACY

1896 – 1914

Obituaries

DEATH OF MR. W. G. LYTTLE, BANGOR
It is with regret we chronicle this morning the death of Mr. Wesley Guard [sic] Lyttle, proprietor of the "North Down Herald," which occurred at his residence, Main Street, Bangor, yesterday morning shortly after seven o'clock. The deceased for a long time past had been in very indifferent health, and a couple of months ago passed through a trying illness. A fortnight ago he again became ill, and soon afterwards was completely prostrated. He gradually sank until the end came.

Throughout Ulster especially the deceased was more popularly known as "Robin," the delineator of those inimitable readings which have brightened many a fireside, and charmed many an audience, and the many who thus knew him will today regret to learn that he has, while not an old man, passed into the ranks of the great majority. He was a man of ability and indomitable perseverance. A County Down man by birth, being born near Bangor, he was identified with the county, if not for all, at least for the most part of his life. His early business life commenced in a legal firm in Downpatrick, where he subsequently became connected with journalism, and at which time *he commenced to write those readings and parodies which have since made his name well known.*

From Downpatrick he came to Belfast, where he was a successful teacher of shorthand, and from thence he removed to Newtownards, where he established the "Newtownards Argos," afterwards removing himself and plant to the more progressive town of Bangor. Here he renamed his paper the "Bangor Gazette," but later he gave it the title by which it is at present known.

He was the author of "Betsy Gray: or Hearts of Down," a tale of '98—a little volume locally reminiscent of stirring scenes during the Irish Rebellion—and "Sons of the Sod." All his writings had local element and colour, which made him very popular throughout the county.

Mr. Lyttle was a Liberal in politics, and in religion a Presbyterian, but neither in politics nor in Church affairs did he give himself much concern. He was a member of the Masonic fraternity, being connected with Bangor 746. He was twice married, and is survived by his widow and the children of his first marriage, for whom there is much sympathy.

This is how the *Belfast News-Letter* recorded WG's passing in their Tuesday 2nd November edition. A pleasing tribute to a fellow-journalist but full of factual inaccuracies and part-truths, which unfortunately became enshrined through the annals of time as actualities.

The *News-Letter* is a protestant paper, while, on the other hand, the *Irish News* is catholic. It, too carried a fitting tribute to WG in its columns.

DEATH OF MR. W. G. LYTTLE. BANGOR
Bangor, Sunday
This morning the genial editor and proprietor of the "North Down Herald and Bangor Gazette" passed away at a comparatively early age. The news of his

death will be received with regret wherever he was known, but especially in North Down, by the people of which he was highly respected. He was a well-known figure in the Ards for upwards of thirty years, and his quaint and humorous portrayal of the local events of the period was a welcome feature of his editorship of the "Bangor Gazette".

Mr Lyttle, while a supporter of Unionism, was not ashamed to rise superior to party prejudices and give expression to his admiration for the humble heroes who struck a blow for Ireland during the stirring period of '98. In his history of "Betsy Gray," Mr Lyttle has left us a simple but very graphic account of the patriotic feelings that actuated the peasantry of County Down in those years. The recital of this pathetic story discloses a warm and generous nature in its author, and will keep his memory green at the firesides of the Irish peasantry for many a year.

Over the nom de plume of "Robin" he wrote several humorous sketches, which have found very favourable acceptance throughout the North of Ireland, and it may be said that through these sketches he was most generally and favourably known.

To his widow and family we tender our sincere condolence.

So, to the Catholics and Nationalists WG was seen as a Unionist, while to the protestant Unionists he was a Liberal and Home Ruler. It seems to me that this is the ultimate tribute to a journalist who, from the start, declared that his newspaper would be independent and free of party politics. In these two obituaries we can see that, for all his "quaintness" of style, he was a balanced reporter and commentator. While WG would have truly appreciated the accolades for his books and sketches, I believe the knowledge that he had remained true to his journalistic independence to the end would have given him the greater satisfaction.

Writing some forty years later in the columns of the *Herald* (by then called the *Northern Herald*) the then editor had occasion to mention WG. He wrote: "W. G. Lyttle was a remarkable man, far ahead of his day in both printing and journalistic spheres. His *North Down Herald, Bangor Gazette and County Down Independent* (now called the *Northern Herald*) of 50 years ago was a masterly production; indeed many of his features and methods are only now regarded as 'modern' in the bright national papers."

Annie placed a notice in Births, Marriages and Deaths in Monday's papers which said: "LYTTLE—November 1, at his residence, 1, Imperial Buildings, Bangor, County Down, W. G. Lyttle, proprietor of 'North Down Herald.' Interment in Bangor Churchyard tomorrow (Tuesday) afternoon, at half-past three o'clock. Friends will please accept this (the only) intimation."

Deciding the future

Annie had little time to mourn the loss of her dear husband of just nine years. That period must have seemed a lifetime to her; such a change from her youth spent as a farmer's daughter, one of nine siblings, and then in service as a housekeeper, before marrying a local celebrity and esteemed business personage in Bangor. She had blossomed as Wesley's wife and, although she had never managed to make friends with his two elder children, she had become a good and well-loved step-mother to Roland and Robina, who now stood by her in their grieving. But she had also been a staunch support to Wesley in his business ventures. She took an active interest in the running of the newspaper and the production of his books. Wesley, of course, would have discussed his Will with her and whether she would prefer to sell up or continue publishing. She would probably have been uncomfortable talking about such a morbid topic as what she would do in the event of Wesley's death, but I suspect, even if she did not actually mention it, she must at least have thought about William Henry's wife who, upon his demise, took over the running of the *Newtownards Chronicle*.

Now she told Roland and Robina that she intended to become the proprietor of her late husband's newspaper and she hoped Roland would play a big role in helping to keep the *Herald* running. And that is what happened.

THE STORYTELLER

On the day of Wesley's funeral Annie contacted the *Belfast News-Letter* to place a notice for the following day. It read:

> **NOTICE**
> **THE "NORTH DOWN HERALD" WILL,**
> As heretofore, be issued EVERY FRIDAY;
> and the business of the
> **NORTH DOWN PRINTING AND**
> **PUBLISHING WORKS**
> will be carried on as usual.
> **A. B. LYTTLE**
> **Bangor, 4th November, 1896**

Anne Bankhead Lyttle asked a seasoned reporter on the *Herald* staff named Robert Pollock[279] to edit the paper for the time being and the name A. B. Lyttle appeared as proprietress on the next edition, 6th November. Jack Loughran was in charge of the printing and Roland helped with day-to-day management on both the printing and the journalistic sides. However, over the next five or six issues Annie decided that Mr Pollock wasn't sufficiently up to the job and in January 1897 she appointed JW Gillmour as editor, at least in the short term. The paper continued to be published on time but as the year progressed Annie knew that it was lacking the flair that made it so popular when Wesley had been in control. The *Herald* needed new blood. She advertised for an experienced editor to head up her staff.

Under new editorship

One of the family stories about WG was that he was responsible for bringing David Alexander, the founder of the *County Down Spectator*, to Bangor. Well, as we have seen, he wasn't. At least, not directly. *Indirectly,* it could be argued that he was—by dying when he did and leaving a vacancy that Annie had to fill with a suitably experienced individual. She had a long list of applicants who answered her ad.

---

[279] Robert Pollock, not to be confused with Francis Pollock, the Town Clerk, nor indeed, James Pollock, Town Commissioner.

From that list, she chose a Scottish journalist who had been working in Ireland as an editor of the weekly journal, the *Leitrim Advertiser*. She offered him the post and in December, 1897, David Edward Alexander became the new permanent editor of the *North Down Herald and County Down Independent*.

Alexander was an excellent editor and soon the paper had picked up any of the prestige it may have lost since WG had left the helm. DE Alexander was too good, though. He gave it his all, as he did with everything he put his hand to, but he had ambitions to go further than running a newspaper for Anne Bankhead Lyttle. In 1904 he resigned and in June that year started his own paper, the *Spectator*, which has gone from strength to strength ever since and is still thriving in 2021. RD Montgomery[280] became the new and, as it would turn out, last editor of the *Herald*.

Three years later, Annie, now 66, was ready for retirement. Also, her step-children were anxious to have their share of their inheritance from Wesley. In May 1907, she sold her interest in the paper and plant, and the lease on the premises at 1, Imperial Buildings to Montgomery for £463 (£54,600 in 2021).

The new owner's first act was to change the name of the paper. *North Down Herald* had headed its banner since the very first issue in 1880, but no longer. The paper became the *Northern Herald* and the old name was denigrated to *"incorporating the North Down Herald and Newtownards Independent."* Montgomery continued to publish it for 32 years until 1939 when he went bankrupt. The business and premises sold for £1120 (£71,800 in 2021) and the last remnants of Bangor's first newspaper passed into history.

Probate

However, back in November, 1896, once the funeral was past and the immediate continuance of the *Herald* was assured Annie had to sort out probate as executrix of Wesley's will. When all WG's assets were valued his estate amounted to £799 6s 2d (about £104,000 in 2021.) This valuation is substantially higher than the sum raised eleven years

---

[280] RD Montgomery was a Unionist, the Secretary of Bangor District Loyal Orange Lodge 18 and a Methodist—quite a contrast to the newspaper's founding editor.

later when the business was sold, even allowing for the large quantity of unsold books that remained at that time with a face value of about £62, bringing the total sum realised up to about £525. Why there should be such a difference over a fairly short time-period is not clear. There was, of course, one other major item not part of that sale price––the value placed upon the copyright of all WG's writings.

One thing Annie was determined to do was to establish some sort of lasting memorial to her late husband—other than his written works, that is. Having given it some thought, she approached her minister at First Bangor Presbyterian Church and offered to pay for a stained glass window to be installed in Wesley's memory, if that would be allowed. The building has a number of such memorial windows and the suitability of having one for Wesley Greenhill Lyttle, a past member of the congregation and former Elder, was readily agreed. An attractive design was commissioned and the window was duly put in place. Its central feature is a robin standing on a closed, leather-bound book and the inscription at the bottom reads, "In loving memory of my husband W G Lyttle. Died November 1896."[281]

The window can still be seen in 2021; it is on the ground floor and is the first one on the right as you enter the sanctuary.

Some 30 or so years later the church would play host to another memorial, although this time, reluctantly. It was to someone who appeared regularly in the columns of the *Herald* when WG was editor and the last person the session of First Bangor might wish to honour. They had just added a new front vestibule, and stairs to the gallery, and a member of the congregation, Mr James Thompson, offered to bear the full cost provided he could have a plaque mounted in memory of his brother who had died four years previously.[282] The church did not wish it but they could ill-afford to turn down so generous an offer. On the wall of the vestibule, to this day, the plaque remains. It reads:

---

[281] See Appendix F, Figs 26 to 28
[282] Archibald Thompson's obituary in the *Bangor Spectator* included these carefully chosen words: "…outside the realm of church and civic procedure Mr Thompson was a genial and kindly man."

34 - LEGACY

**"To the Glory of God and in memory
of
ARCHIBALD THOMPSON of Bangor
Born 23rd March 1848—died 7th February 1924.**

**This vestibule and stairways
also the emergency exits were erected in 1928
by his brother Mr James M. Thompson of Bangor.**

Unlike WG's window, however, which is there for all to see and admire, many today do not even know of the existence of Archibald Thompson's plaque. It is still there, high on the vestibule wall, but discreetly hidden—with a certain irony—behind a hanging banner of a trumpeting herald angel![283] I am indebted to Mr Jim Wallace of First Bangor for telling me the details of this story.

Ongoing arrangements

Whilst still proprietress, Annie found the responsibility for producing the newspaper as well as running the household was becoming too much for her and she decided to employ a housekeeper. Jinny Laughhran, wife of her Print Manager, said that she had a sister back in Cootehill, County Cavan, who would love to come to Bangor and work for Mrs Lyttle and so this was arranged. Margaret Winifred Keelan, or Maggie, started work in the Lyttle home, probably in 1897. She was about 22.

The household at 1, Imperial Buildings (or 85 Main Street) settled down to a new routine. Roland, at 19 was working at the *Herald,* mostly as a printer under Jack Loughran. Robina, 18, had ambitions to be a journalist like her father. She had developed an independent spirit and decided she would prefer not just to work for her step-mother. She moved to lodgings in Belfast where she stayed with a Miss J M'Connell who ran a boarding house at 99 York Road.[284] Miss M'Connell was probably a close family friend as Robina called her

---

[283] See pictures in Appendix F, Figures 24 and 25.

[284] It is interesting to note that, unlike her elder sister, Agnes, she chose not to stay with her Aunt Isabella.

THE STORYTELLER

"Aunt."[285] Back in Bangor, Annie proved to be a capable proprietress of the newspaper and, with Maggie helping run the home, all was well.

Annie was becoming quite a prominent figure in her own right. Her name was frequently among the guests of civil and other official functions, which she often attended with her sister, Jane Byers. She was guest of honour at the school on Main Street where she spoke and presented the prizes. This was not just because she was Mrs WG Lyttle but in recognition of how she was handling her role as the proprietress of the town's newspaper.

Once she felt comfortable with how the *Herald* was functioning, she began to think about Wesley's books. Most were still in print and she was able to meet the steady continuing demand for copies. Except for *Betsy Gray*. As always, copies of WG's most popular novel were running low again. So in 1899 Annie organised the production of yet another, a fourth, edition at her own "North Down Print Works." She adapted WG's original preface and wrote:

> *PREFACE TO FOURTH EDITION*
>
> *The story was originally written for and published in the columns of the North Down Herald. Its success was phenomenal, and the demand for its appearance in book form has been such as to warrant the issue of a very large fourth edition. The incidents were collected from reliable sources; relatives of the sufferers in '98 were interviewed and the places written of were all visited by the author, who has, since the publication of the third edition, gone to his well-earned rest. The present edition has been issued by the widow of the late W. G. Lyttle whose works continue to be a valuable legacy to subscriber [sic] and the family of the late lamented author.*
>
> *The mournful tale of the beautiful Betsy Gray has excited universal sympathy. Many letters were received by my deceased husband expressing a desire*

---

[285] It's not impossible that she was an actual relation, a cousin of her mother, maybe.

> *to contribute towards a suitable monument to be erected at the lonely grave in the vale of Ballycreen, where the ashes of Betsy repose.*
> *A. B. LYTTLE*
> *Imperial Buildings, Bangor, Ireland*
> *June, 1899*

It is interesting that Annie retained the mention of correspondence about contributing to a memorial for Betsy but makes no reference to the recent, sad events at her graveside concerning her monument.

Twice blessed

In September of that same year, almost 20 years after it was first built on the corner of Hamilton Road, St Comgall's parish church finally had a peal of eight bells installed in its belfry. They rang out clearly across the town every Sunday morning and on a weekday evening, too, when the ringers were practicing. The tolls made a pleasant enough addition to the sounds penetrating the Lyttles' nearby home and busy newspaper office on Main Street.

Whether or not church bells had anything to do with the matter, some months later Roland made a decision. A young man with good prospects, he determined to act on feelings that had been developing ever since Maggie had come to work for his stepmother. He had become attracted to the Cavan girl and the attraction was mutual. Roland now realised he was in love with her and, although he was two-and-a-bit years younger than she was, Maggie accepted his proposal. They became engaged to be married.

But therein lay a problem. Mixed marriages were frowned upon. Maggie was catholic and Roland, a protestant Presbyterian. Maggie wanted to be married by a priest, but that was unlikely to happen if she was marrying a protestant. Roland wanted to be married in the church at Ballygilbert where his father had married Annie. What was to be done? The couple eventually came up with a solution of which I am sure WG, himself, would have been proud.

On Sunday, the 25th of November, 1900, he and Maggie, accompanied by family and friends presented themselves at the Roman Catholic Chapel of St Patrick in Belfast where Father JK

THE STORYTELLER

O'Neill baptised Roland as a convert to Catholicism. The priest then proceeded with a marriage ceremony joining Roland and Maggie as man and wife.

Although he was not quite 23 by then, Roland gave his age as 24 on the Marriage Certificate so that it wouldn't look too bad next to Maggie's 25, thus emulating what his father had done when *he* first married 36 years earlier. Under "Denomination" the certificate shows both of them as Roman Catholic. Four weeks later, on Saturday 22nd December the pair were married all over again at Ballygilbert Presbyterian Church. On the certificate, under "Denomination," both are shown as Presbyterian!

The wedding guests may well have included Roland's big sister, Agnes for, along with husband, Alexander, and five-year-old Lilly, she had recently moved back to Bangor where they were living at 33, Gray's Hill.[286] Agnes had returned to where she grew up, but only after her estranged father had passed away.

When Roland and Maggie's first child came along—my Aunt Eveline—she was christened in a Presbyterian church, Anne Bankhead Eveline. (This suggests that Roland gave his first daughter his stepmother's names out of the love and affection he held for the woman who had been a mother to him for most of his life. It was not after all, it seems, to perpetuate the memory of the "illustrious ancestor," Dr Charles Bankhead, Annie's great-uncle. And yet it was the physician's fame that was remembered tentatively by my aunt in her latter years, when the fact that her father was raised by a stepmother was forgotten. Lizzie and Annie somehow seemed to have merged into one in the collective memories of my father and aunt.)

When my father, Gerald Roland Lyttle, was born he was baptised into the Roman Catholic church. That was part of the deal in mixed marriages. Often the couple had to promise that all children would be given catholic baptisms but in this case they seem to have settled for just male children.

The 1911 Census shows the family living back on Ballymagee Street, listing them as:

---

[286] The 1901 Census shows the family at this address.

- Lyttle—Roland A, Head of Family, Presbyterian
- Lyttle—Maggie, Wife, Roman Catholic
- Lyttle—Eveline, Daughter, Protestant Pres.
- Lyttle—Gerald, Son, Roman Catholic

When my father was in his teens he had a conversion experience and gave his heart to the Lord Jesus. He was a keen evangelical Christian all the rest of his life, serving as an Elder in Trinity Presbyterian Church before moving away from Bangor. He would often be a guest speaker at protestant Christian events—even, occasionally, in church pulpits. I smile as I wonder what some staunch protestant loyalists in his congregations would have thought had they known he had been baptised as a Roman Catholic. His grandfather, WG, would have thought it a huge joke I'm quite sure.

Between the births of my Aunt and my father, five years later, Roland and Maggie had two more children, Veronica, who died within 24 hours of birth, and little Wessy, who tragically survived only two months. On Wessy's death certificate his name is given as Wesley G Lyttle. I could find no record of what the G stood for, but it seems likely that, had he lived, Roland's firstborn son would have become Wesley Greenhill Lyttle II.

Accident

Something WG had touched upon in his editorials over the years was the deplorable fact that Bangor did not have a regular Fire Brigade; the town's fire-fighting equipment comprised one, solitary fire hose. Under Annie's proprietorship the occasional campaign in the *Herald* to remedy the situation continued. A number of prominent citizens and officials were reported upon as having taken up the issue and eventually, in December, 1904, an ad appeared in the *Spectator* headed FORMATION OF A FIRE BRIGADE. It went on to say:

> *"THE BANGOR URBAN DISTRICT COUNCIL are prepared to receive application from suitable Men to be Members of the Bangor Fire Brigade at the following rate of remuneration: –*
>
> *One Second Officer at £2 per year, 15s per Fire and 4s per Practice.*

THE STORYTELLER

Six men at £1 per year, 10s per Fire and 3s 6d per Practice."

Bangor's first paid and properly equipped Fire Brigade commenced in January, 1905 and by June a steam-operated siren was erected at the Gasworks in Bingham Street for sounding the alarm to call out the members of the brigade when a fire was discovered. The "alarming" sound it emitted has been variously described in the local press as "a shrill hoot," "the warning shriek of the siren horn" and "a weird, unearthly shriek that rang through the town."

When it was first installed, the Council in its wisdom decided to carry out its inaugural test in conditions simulating a genuine emergency and so it was scheduled for 4:00 a.m. one morning in the first week of June. Until that moment no one in the town had heard the siren and only a handful of people even knew of its existence. The *Herald* recorded the event in its 9th June edition:

> *At the early hour of 4 o'clock some mornings ago many residents of this locality were aroused from their dreams by a series of unearthly shrieks that can better be imagined than described. A contemporary likens the hideous sound unto "the moans of a dog that had been run over."*

This "hideous sound" was heard, as it was designed to be, throughout the town and was still loud when it reached where Roland and Maggie were living with their two-year-old daughter, Evelyn. Roland awoke instantly at the discordant noise and jumped out of bed to investigate. As he rose, he caught his head a tremendous crack on the corner of the leaden mantelpiece next to his bed. He slumped, unconscious, to the floor.

As a result of his accident Roland became extremely ill. It is believed he developed meningitis and had to be confined to bed for an extended period. The couple were only just recovering from the tragic loss of their second daughter and Maggie had a two-year-old to look after, so Roland was taken to be cared for by his stepmother at 85 Main Street. He was gravely ill and at one stage his life hung in the balance but after a long time he slowly began to show signs of recovery.

While he was at his lowest, he found the sound of the church bells at St Comgall's, so close by and so loud, quite unbearable. The church was made aware of his condition and, possibly partly out of respect for his late father, they very kindly agreed to suspend all further ringing until he had improved.

Roland did recover to full health physically. His brain, however, had suffered some permanent damage which slowed his thinking processes. He was able to function fairly normally but within limits. He was no longer able to help oversee the whole of the newspaper business but he still managed to help to some extent in the print shop and Annie could also rely upon him to liaise with their advertisers. Then David Alexander, out of kindness to his former employer, offered Roland a job in the advertising department of the *Spectator*—a job which WG's son gratefully accepted. He was to remain in it throughout his lifetime.

John Lyttle's invention and his sister, Agnes

Back around the time of Roland and Maggie's marriage there was much controversy in Britain about the number of accidents amongst shunters on the railways. An average of 78 in every 1000 workers had accidents each year, some fatal. Developing and installing automatic coupling for carriages would go a long way towards alleviating this but the expense of this was stopping the railway owners from addressing the problem. However public outrage was demanding something should to be done. A Royal Commission was set up and later a nationwide competition was announced for civil engineers to come up with a coupling system suitable for British rolling stock.

It was against this background that WG's engineer son, John got to work and designed just such a system. When my aunt Eveline, was about four—it was definitely before my father was born when she was five, so about 1907—her uncle John and his wife came back to Bangor to visit Roland and his family. Eveline could remember only that John gave her a small violin but nothing else about the visit. She never saw him again. But it must have been on this occasion that John told his brother about his invention.

That it wasn't implemented until much later, after John had passed away, in fact, is down to the railway companies' procrastination and reluctance to invest money in something that was primarily designed as a safety feature and not as a way of increasing profits.

It's not clear whether Agnes was still living on Gray's Hill when John came back to visit. We do know, however, that she did not stay in Bangor more than a few years. Perhaps it was Alexander wanting to return to Belfast to be nearer his family but return they did. The 1911 Census shows the Holmes family living back in the same Ormeau district where their first home had been, this time at 17, Willowfield Drive. The census entry reads:

>   *Alexander Holmes, Head of family... 40...*
> *widower;*
>   *Elizabeth Holmes, Daughter, 15.*

What had happened? Not long after moving back to the city Agnes complained of a tiredness and muscle aches and pains; she developed a cough and often experienced shortness of breath. This must have gone on throughout much of 1908. By the spring of 1909 she was worse, with attacks of nausea and vomiting, frequent headaches and swollen feet and ankles. By Easter Sunday, 11th April, she had been experiencing severe pains in her chest, neck and arms for several weeks. Five days later her body could no longer withstand the strain Agnes' heart stopped beating on Friday 16th April 1909. Her death certificate gave the cause of death as Chronic Endocarditis, one year; Angina Pectoris, one month.

Yet another of Wesley's family tragically dying before her time; Agnes was still three-and-a-half months shy of her 40th birthday.

WG's books

In 1907, when Annie sold the newspaper business to RD Montgomery, she still had a large stock of WG's unsold books: around 2000 copies of *Betsy Gray* and some 500 volumes of *Robin's Readings*, along with other writings. Annie asked her solicitor, who was arranging the sale, if he could store them for her until she could

34 - LEGACY

have them herself. He was unable to do so but he arranged with Mr Montgomery that they could stay at Imperial Buildings until she was able to house them.

Having given up the printing business, Annie determined to make a clean break and "sell" the copyright of her husband's writings and all the unsold books to Roland for a nominal £20 (about £2,300 in 2021.) Roland could easily afford that out of his share of WG's legacy; the books, themselves were worth three times that amount quite apart from the copyright.

When Roland and Maggie got married they lived in two rented rooms in a house on Bangor's new Victoria Road, but by 1910 they had moved to premises on Ballymagee Street (they were certainly there in April 1911 according to that year's Census) and had sufficient space to store WG's unsold books. Roland told Montgomery that he could now take back his books but the new owner of the newspaper seemed to have had a lapse of memory in the intervening three years. He claimed not to recall any conversation about storing the books for the Lyttles; he said he bought the business and that included stock in trade. Annie was also in dispute with him over a portrait of Wesley[287], some window poles and the gasolier, none of which, she said, were included in the price he paid.

Roland had already widely distributed a leaflet advertising WG's books as available again. Montgomery responded by placing a full column add in his newspaper announcing that the books were on sale at the *Herald* office.

There was no alternative but to take the matter to the courts, both Roland's books and his mother's claim. In a hearing in June, 1910, the Judge ruled against Annie, saying that these were fixtures and fittings and were covered in the deed of sale. As for the books, he agreed that there was no mention of stock in trade in the sale document but that he thought the 2,500 books "weren't worth 2d," since many of them had been in storage for over ten years. He decreed that Montgomery should pay compensation of £1 (£117 in 2021) for depriving Roland of the books, reduced to 1s (£5.65) if he released the books within a fortnight.

---

[287] This was, most probably, the portrait presented to Wesley by his friend John Pyper many years previously (see Chapter 6, Social evenings.)

This was a rather ignominious endorsement of what remained of WG's life's work! Happily, however, the Judge was no literary expert and his valuation later proved to be somewhat on the conservative side.

After two weeks Montgomery had neither returned the books nor come up with the £1. On the contrary, he had republished his advert saying the books were available at the *Herald* office. Roland was forced to go back to the courts. He claimed that compensation of £1 was not nearly enough. The appeal court Judge decided in his favour and increased the compensation sum to 19 guineas (about £2,300 in 2021) unless all the books were returned within a week and Montgomery paid £4 4s 3d costs. The newspaper editor paid the costs and released the books.

Roland was delighted to have his father's books once more and a little later put his own series of ads in the *Mid-Ulster Mail* on four consecutive Saturdays for "*Robin's Readings* by W. G. Lyttle in three volumes, price sixpence each. 1- *The Adventures of Paddy M'Quillan.* 2—The *adventures of Robin Gordon.* 3—*Life in Ballycuddy, County Down.*"

He then set about arranging to have a new edition of *Sons of the Sod* produced as it had been out of print for some time. This, just the second edition, was duly published, "by the author's son, Bangor", in 1911. It was printed by his employer, DE Alexander at the Spectator.

In the meantime, sales of the remaining copies of *Robin's Readings* must have gone well for, also in 1911, he had an omnibus edition printed—all three anthologies bound in one blue hardback volume with gold lettering. He had learnt from his father and included a fair number of advertisements to offset the cost of production and it is through one of these that we can establish when the book was published, for there is no publisher's page or date. Subsequently, the omnibus edition was republished, this time in a green hardback with gold lettering, by R. Carswell and Son. This edition, also undated, carried no adverts.

The "Joseph Blair edition"

By 1918, Roland decided it was time to bring out yet another edition of his father's three volumes of *Robin's Readings*. As an advertising

34 - LEGACY

manager he was always looking for fresh ways of selling advertising space. To help finance these new editions he persuaded the manufacturer of "Ulster" Ranges, Joseph Blair, to pay for a series of one-sentence promotions for his cooking ranges that would appear at the foot of a dozen or so pages throughout each volume. As was often the case with these early books, Roland failed to include a title page showing himself as publisher. This omission was to lead to some confusion almost a century later when a Kansas University cataloguer, taking these adverts as a colophon, incorrectly attributed the copies they held of this edition of *Robin's Readings* to "Publisher: Joseph Blair."

Just as I have done, they also calculated the date of publication from an advert in the books –"Robert Watson & Co, established 1868" proclaiming their Jubilee Year. The cataloguer assumed a 25th anniversary and so recorded the publication date as c1893. However, as the books carry, on their back cover, "Printed at the 'Spectator' Office, Bangor, Co Down" and the *Spectator* wasn't founded until 1904, the Jubilee mentioned must have been the 50th anniversary, giving us the actual publication date of 1918.

In 2006, Loeber & Loeber, published their excellent, *A Guide to Irish Fiction 1650-1900*. In it, however they refer to a Belfast edition of *Robin's Readings* published by Joseph Blair, copies of which are held by Kansas University. Rowlinson, in his Introduction to the 2015, Books Ulster edition of *Robin's Readings* quotes Loeber & Loeber, thus perpetuating the error.

There is no Joseph Blair, 1893 edition. The copies held by Kansas University are the 1918 edition published by WG's son, RA Lyttle. Following my research the university has now corrected its catalogue entries.[288]

An undiscovered work?

Back in July, 1910 when Roland finally recovered WG's works from Montgomery, he must have been excited to find amongst the "other

---

[288] I am grateful for the helpful cooperation of Elspeth E Healey, Special Collections Librarian of the Kenneth Spencer Research Library at Kansas University in having the corrections made to their catalogue entries for Robin's Readings.

THE STORYTELLER

writings" that had been stored with the unsold books, a manuscript in his father's handwriting of an unpublished work. It was entitled *Daft Eddie or Smugglers of Strangford Lough*. He may or may not have vaguely remembered hearing of it, over twenty years ago, when he was just eleven and it was being serialised in the *North Down Herald*. He, no doubt, wondered why his father had never gotten around to publishing it in book form for it was clearly all written in WG's hand.

What Roland must have had before him was the complete amended and edited version of the original story; the version that appeared, unattributed, in the columns of the *Herald* back in 1889. There was nothing to say who had written it apart from the evidence of his own eyes that it was in his father's handwriting. There could be no doubt, Roland would have thought, that he had discovered a new novel by WG Lyttle. He had it published by R. Carswell and Son Ltd in 1914, erroneously attributed, posthumously, to my great-grandfather. It is possible Roland could have first produced an edition, himself, in 1911 or 12 but I have found no evidence of the existence of any such earlier copies.[289] So 1914 seems to be when *Daft Eddy* first appeared in book form—not "around 1890" as claimed by the Mourne Observer in their later edition of the book and by Loeber and Loeber in their *Guide to Irish Fiction*, 2006. (See Chapter 27 for more regarding the story's origins) Any future editions of *Daft Eddie* will need to have its authorship suitably amended:

DAFT EDDIE
or SMUGGLERS OF STRANGFORD LOUGH
Original story attributed to 'the Rev J. B.',
believed to be the grandson of Martha M'Fadden.[290]
Fully revised, edited and with extensive additional material, by
W G LYTTLE

---

[289] There just remains the curious fact that Stephen J Brown in *A Reader's Guide to Irish Fiction* (1910) makes reference to the story, as *Smugglers of Strangford Lough,* and attributes it to WG Lyttle, with no date. That entry could only have been referring to the serialised version of the story in the *Herald,* since, even if Roland *did* bring out a first edition earlier than 1914, it couldn't have been before 1910 as he didn't get hold of the manuscript until July of that year. Brown can only have assumed the author to be WG since the story appeared in his newspaper and was not otherwise attributed.

[290] See Appendix H, "Who Really Wrote *Daft Eddy*?

34 - LEGACY

As it happens, Roland's involvement in this piece of literary history-making might never have taken place, had it not been for the events of one fateful night, the catastrophic consequences of which were to affect many hundreds of lives both directly and indirectly. Included amongst those hundreds was the Lyttle family.

THE STORYTELLER

Chapter 35 – LIVES TAKEN

1907– 1927

Emigration

It seems to have started with Robina, although it is possible she was encouraged by conversations with Jinny Loughran. The Loughrans and the Lyttles had become good friends. By this time the printer and his wife had three young children, Jim, John and Ruby. Robina would certainly have been a willing baby-sitter for Jinny and Jack when she was in Bangor. After little Eveline came along to Roland and Maggie, all four cousins would have had playtimes together under Aunt Robina's watchful eye.

So whether it was Robina who first raised the idea, or whether it was Jinny, we don't know, but the possibility of joining the ever-growing numbers of Irish citizens who were deciding to emigrate to the New World did come up for discussion. Jinny said she and Jack were definitely considering it when the children were a little older. Big brother, John, had long since left Ireland's shores. The thought of a brand new life in a new country appealed to Robina's spirit of independence and hearing Jinny share her views perhaps spurred her into action.

She must have talked it over with her step-mother, who, loath as she would have been to be parted from Robina, didn't want to stand in her way. It was early in 1907 when Robina raised the topic with her. She was 28 and still single, so perhaps Annie thought emigration might be her best chance of finding a husband; going to live in Belfast didn't seem to have helped much. Her step-daughter wanted to know if she could have her share of the inheritance from her father.

This could well have been the main reason that Annie decided to sell up and retire when she did: to give Robina the wherewithal to start a new life across the pond. The newspaper was sold in May. Robina got her share of the proceeds and arrangements were made. A single ticket was purchased on the SS Haverford, sailing from Liverpool on the 23rd October, 1907 bound for Philadelphia. Her cabin trunk was packed.

It could well have been Jinny who, knowing how good Robina was with children, suggested that she could earn her keep as a Nanny, or Nursemaid as the position was called then. This would allow her time to become established as the journalist she wanted to be. Letters crossed the Atlantic as friends, probably earlier emigrants, were contacted. It was finally arranged that Robina would work as a nursemaid to the children of Mr FJ Porter who was now living in Philadelphia.

She would have crossed over to Liverpool on the night ferry from Belfast the day before the SS Haverford was due to sail. That night the moon was a day away from being full and it shone its silvery light upon the dark hair of WG's youngest daughter waving farewell to the land of her birth, the only land she had ever known. Did she recall stories her father had told her of how, as a young man, he had almost had the opportunity to travel to America with Dr Corry's Diorama, but how that hadn't worked out in the end? Was she proud that she was about to do what her father had never managed? She would have stood with the hundreds of other passengers lining the decks and waving; heard the long, deep-throated blast on its foghorn as the ferry inched out into the channel. The crowds on the quay waved back and cheered, but some were quietly weeping, wishing Godspeed to their nearest and dearest, knowing they would probably never see them again.

Alien

The SS Haverford's manifest lists all "alien passengers for the United States Immigration Officer" and Robina's entry makes interesting reading. She is down as a single female aged 25. Obviously, when starting a new life, she thought she might as well have a new—and younger—age, as well! For her "Calling or Occupation" she has put Journalist, so nursemaid was only to be temporary. She is declared to be able to read and write. In the column which asks for "the name and address of nearest relative or friend in country whence alien came" Robina put "Aunt, Miss McConnell, 99 York Street. Belfast." Why she chose not to put her brother, Roland, or even her step-mother remains a mystery.

Her final destination was shown as Philadelphia, it was acknowledged that her ticket had been paid for by herself and that she was in possession of £75 (about £8,800 in 2021.) It showed that she was going to join a friend, Mr FJ Porter of 1120 Foulkrod Street. Phila., declared that she was neither a polygamist nor an anarchist, and gave her description as being 5'3", of fair complexion with dark hair and brown eyes.

Thus was the diminutive, dark-haired and brown-eyed Robina Lyttle's arrival in Philadelphia recorded on the 4th November, 1907. Of her new life across the ocean we shall learn more anon.

The Loughrans emigrate

After Robina left for America Jinny and Jack Loughran grew more determined to make the break, uproot themselves from home and family and start afresh in a land of unbounded opportunities. Would it be America? Or Canada? Or Australia? Jinny must have talked a lot about it with her sister, Maggie. Indeed, both the Loughrans likely discussed the possibility of emigrating with Roland and Maggie. In the end, the two families decided that Canada was the place for them.

My father, Gerald, was born in October, 1908, so by 1910 he was not yet two and Eveline was about seven. The Loughran children were a little older and it was decided that they would leave first for a new life in Ontario. As soon as they were settled, Maggie and Roland would come out to join them when little Gerald was a bit older.

The Loughrans set off on their great adventure.

Disaster

In the spring of 1912 Roland and Maggie were busy putting all their affairs in order ready for their own departure. They had a big cabin trunk already mostly packed. They would have been following with excitement all the news about the maiden voyage of Belfast firm, Harland and Wolff's latest transatlantic vessel and been disappointed

35 – LIVES TAKEN

that it was sailing too soon for them. They wouldn't be ready to leave for another month or so.

Then, on the night of 14th/15th April, came the devastating news that rocked the world. The "unsinkable" new ship, the *Titanic*, had hit an iceberg—and sunk.

It had sailed from Southampton via Cherbourg and Queenstown in County Cork (present day Cobh) and left Ireland with 2,208 passengers and crew. 1,503 people died when the ship went down. A disaster of such a huge scale was almost impossible to take in. People were left reeling at the enormity of the loss.

All around the country countless families were hearing of the tragedy. The Lyttles read of it in their home on Main Street in Bangor, surrounded by suitcases, trunks and signs of their own imminent departure. Maggie's decision was instant.

'We're not going,' she said to Roland.

Whether or not there was much discussion or weighing up of the risks involved, we don't know, but the decision stood. Roland stayed in Bangor where, two years later, he published *Daft Eddie*. He and Maggie lived out the rest of their lives in the town Roland's father had adopted. And a small, four-year-old boy grew up with his elder sister in the seaside resort and eventually met a young lady from Whitehead who had recently moved to Bangor. They were married in 1937, a couple of years before war broke out. After the war ended, I was born to them in 1946.

Had the Titanic not suffered that terrible catastrophe, my father would have grown up in Canada and never met my mother. I would not exist. This biography, if written at all, would have been penned by a Canadian.

The Loughrans did well in their newly-adopted country. With their three children they had six grandchildren, 16 great-grandchildren and, at the last count, 18 great-great-grandchildren—43 Canadian cousins of one degree or another to relate to WG's grandchildren, Eveline and Gerald, and all their own offspring.

But what of Robina? How did she fare after arriving Stateside?

THE STORYTELLER

A new life

Robina's history can be pieced together mostly from newspaper clippings of the period. Once more, I am indebted to Terence Bowman for his invaluable help in tracing much of her story. We know that she started her American working career at the end of 1907 as a nursemaid in Philadelphia, Pennsylvania. She was still in Philadelphia in 1910, because she appears in the US Census of that year, but as a "head of household," so she must have moved out of the Porters and got rooms of her own.

At some stage Robina decided to head out of Philadelphia to see some more of the vast territory that was now her homeland. She went about a hundred miles southwest to Baltimore in Maryland where she looked after a Doctor's children. She had a photograph taken with them with her in her nurse's uniform.[291] By the time the 1920 census was taken, she had moved back north-east again, this time going another hundred miles or so beyond Philadelphia, to New York. She was living in Manhattan on 2nd Avenue as a Roomer in the home of Delia Walsh and her 23-year-old daughter, Eileen. She was still working as a nursemaid for another family. It seems that her hopes of becoming a journalist had never come to fruition.

It was most likely when she came to Manhattan, which was probably around 1918 or 19, that she joined the Central Club of Nurses whose headquarters were on East 45th Street. Evidence for this was a slip of paper in her Bible with the name Sarah Gunn of the Nurse's Club with its address. The flyleaf of the Bible bore a message that it was presented to Robina on Easter Sunday, 1919, by Sallie M Bardsley. So she did have a social life and some friends.

In 1922, she moved across the East River to work for a couple of years looking after the two children of George R Butts, a widower in Astoria. The elder child, who was ten at the time, was later to say that sometimes Robina would come back from her night off having been drinking. What, I wonder, caused her to abandon the teaching and example of her late father? Most probably it was the rapid growth of the number of speakeasies around New York—thousands of elicit drinking establishments that sprang up upon the introduction of

---

[291] See the photograph of Robina in Appendix E, Figure 11

35 – LIVES TAKEN

Prohibition a couple of years previously. Far from its intended outcome of reducing the consumption of alcohol it actually proliferated it with the added excitement of defying the killjoy enforcers.

More immigrants

About the time Robina moved to the Astoria area of New York, the SS Algeria set sail from Glasgow. Among its passengers was a 38-year-old Scottish couple called Patrick and Elizabeth McClafferty from Helensburgh, where Patrick had been president of the League of the Cross Temperance Society. Patrick, a baker and Elizabeth, a housewife, set off for a new life with £50 (£2,700 in 2021) between them. Their fair was paid by Elizabeth's father, John Kelly, who was the superintendent at the fashionable Sanford Arms apartments on Sanford Avenue in the Murray Hill area of Flushing, New York. Patrick was described as 5'7", of a fresh complexion with brown hair and grey eyes, while his wife was 5'2", fresh-complexioned, with brown hair and blue eyes.

After going through immigration on Ellis Island, Patrick lost no time in finding a job as a baker, still on the island. The couple settled and joined a chapel where "Paddy" sang in the choir. Tragically, after only two years, Elizabeth died of heart disease, leaving Paddy distraught. His father-in-law, John Kelly, suggested he come and occupy the basement apartment at Sanford Arms and work with him as assistant superintendent for the apartments.

A fateful meeting

Robina's time with the Butts family was about to come to an end and she would soon be moving to a new position she had found through her agency with a Mrs Moore who lived in West Somerville near Boston, Massachusetts—another journey north-eastwards of about 190 miles. Before she left New York she had occasion to catch the Rapid Transit train from the elevated station on 111th Street in the Corona district.

As she awaited its arrival, she found herself next to a mousy little man who looked a bit dejected. Perhaps she was wondering why, when, rather to her surprise, he spoke to her. His accent was Scottish;

it must have been like a voice from home. I imagine her heart gave a little leap at hearing those familiar intonations. Perhaps, into her mind flashed an image from long ago, of her father dressed as "Robin." But whatever the reason, she struck up a conversation with him.

Wherever Robina had been intending to go, she changed her mind and agreed to alight from the train, after only a few stations, at Flushing with her new friend, Paddy McClafferty. His apartment block looked really classy; Robina would have been impressed—until she discovered that his own apartment was in the basement next to the boiler room. It turned out he was the assistant janitor. But that didn't matter; Robina must have enjoyed his company. He poured her a glass of "hooch" as he told her how lonely he was; his wife had recently died. He probably didn't mention that he had been tee-total until then. Robina would have felt sorry for the little man. Perhaps she was feeling a bit homesick, listening to his blethers.[292] He was about her own age, 45, he told her. She, too, was 45 but since she'd knocked three years off when she emigrated, she would have told him, 42.

A Growing friendship

The two seemed to click and started seeing each other but, all too soon, Robina had to leave for Boston. Paddy stayed in touch and sent her weekly postcards. She stayed with Mrs Moore just one month before quitting and returning to New York. It seems the attraction of the little Scot had captured her heart and she didn't want to be separated from him by nearly 200 miles.

She became a frequent caller at the basement apartment of the Sanford Arms, where they would share a drink after work. Indeed, some of the snootier residents objected to the assistant superintendent entertaining a woman in his rooms. One day in February, 1926, John Kelly "found them together" in Paddy's room. No further details of that encounter are known but we can, perhaps, imagine the circumstance in which the couple were found, when Paddy's ex-father-in-law and now employer, told him repeatedly he was to get rid of his paramour.

---

[292] Blethers – inconsequential chatter

35 – LIVES TAKEN

Robina was now working as a domestic for Police Lieutenant Robert McCartney in Flushing. She often spoke to him of "her Paddy" in terms that made her infatuation clear, saying she intended to marry him. This, in spite of discovering that Patrick McClafferty had a darker side. Their relationship was not always harmonious. They would argue, particularly when he'd been drinking, and on occasions he would use his fists on her. But Robina must have thought this was a price she was willing to pay. Now at 47, she was unlikely to get another chance of matrimony. She probably thought if she could keep him off the bootleg whisky she'd be fine.

Her job with the Police Lieutenant ended in July and she found another position as a domestic over in Douglaston in Little Neck to the east of Flushing. By September she'd changed jobs again, this time to work for a Dr AS Lowaley back at an address in Flushing, and handy for meeting up with Paddy, which she did as often as she could. It was in September, though, that he told her he had to go to Philadelphia to visit his uncle. The few days he was away was one of the longest separations they had had since Robina had returned from West Somerville.

Concerned

Paddy was worried about how his relationship with the Ulster woman was progressing. He certainly must have enjoyed her company or he would have ended it long since. He must have been considering marrying her because he asked for the advice of his uncle, also called Patrick McClafferty. To the older man's mind, however, there was little to discuss. We can easily imagine the advice he gave.

> 'She's an Ulster protestant, you say? And you, a guid catholic all your born natural. Get rid o' her, laddie, she's no the yin fur you an' ye ken that richt weel, yersel'.'[293]

---

[293] 'She's an Ulster protestant, you say? And you, a good catholic all your born natural. Get rid of her, laddie, she's not the one for you and you know that right well, yourself.'

THE STORYTELLER

Returning from Philadelphia, Paddy was feeling, perhaps, as low as he had ever felt since Elizabeth died. He knew Robina wanted them to get married. But he just couldn't do that, could he? Not marry a protestant.

Strained relations

When he got back he said nothing. If anything, Robina was spending more time at his apartment but he had some relatives coming over to visit soon; she would have to be gone by then. Their relationship must have grown strained and Robina was finding it hard to keep her mind on her job. She quit the one with Dr Lowaley when a mouse was seen in the home; she used her dread of mice as an excuse. So by mid-September, she was working for a Mrs Guench, the wife of a former Astoria dentist, also living in Flushing, but spending, perhaps, more time round at Paddy's than she should. Her work as a domestic was considered unsatisfactory and she was asked to leave after only three weeks.

As she walked out, Robina must have taken perverse pleasure in telling Mrs Guench she was going to live at the prestigious Sanford Arms apartments. Which she did. She moved in with Patrick McClafferty in his basement apartment about the end of the first week in October, 1926. It was probably not what Paddy wanted but he didn't stop her. Instead he drank. He later said they both did—for three weeks. When the subject of making their relationship more permanent came up it would always end in an argument about their religious differences.

It seemed Paddy now saw Robina as an irritant he couldn't be freed of. In his own mind, she had done all the running from the start, none of it was down to him and with his relatives' visit imminent he needed to be rid of her. Rid of her for good. On a Thursday night towards the end of October—it was late on the 28th, maybe early on Friday 29th the two were having what Paddy later called a drinking party.

Religion came up again. They argued again.

Bitterly. Long and hard.

Paddy grabbed a hatchet and struck Robina behind her left ear.

35 – LIVES TAKEN

The argument ceased abruptly. Robina swayed and toppled. She was dead before her body hit the floor.

* * *

In the family anecdotes about WG and his offspring this tragic event has been 'remembered' as how one of my great-grandfather's daughters emigrated to Canada as a nurse where she was later shot dead. The mistaken destination can be put down to a mix-up with our 'cousins,' the Loughrans going to Canada. As a nurse? Well, again a simple confusion with the term nursemaid. As to her being shot, I can only assume my grandfather, Roland, decided to sanitise the story when he related it to my father and aunt, even though they were already 18 and 23 at the time.

Because, as I have now discovered, the actual story was much worse. So much worse.

* * *

Disposing of the body

All day Friday 29th October, 1926, Robina's body lay on the floor of McClafferty's apartment. It remained there throughout Saturday 30th. On Sunday, as the church bells of Flushing began to ring McClafferty stripped the body and hauled it into his bath tub. Using a carpenter's saw and a breadknife he performed a decapitation and then removed the two arms and both legs.

He carried the body parts the few yards to the boiler room where he proceeded to put the head, arms and legs through the iron fuel door into the furnace. When it came to the torso, try as he would, he couldn't fit it through the opening. He brought it back to his apartment and stored it in a closet just off his kitchen.

By the following Thursday 4th November he couldn't stand the smell of the decomposing torso. He put it in a burlap bag and took it back to the boiler room. There he buried it under a heap of coal. The smell continued, however, and tenants were complaining about the odour in the hallway. McClafferty "helped" search the premises for a possible cause. On Monday 8th November John Kelly told his son-in-law he planned to search the boiler room to try to find what was causing the smell. Patrick left the building.

It wasn't long before the location of the source of the smell became obvious. Police and some workmen dug out the coal from the bin and the torso in the bag was discovered.

Police and workmen searching beneath the coal heap in the boiler room of the Sanford Arms apartments (from the *Long Island Daily Press* Tuesday, November 9, 1926)

McClafferty was picked up by the police, later the same day, in a confused state wandering the nearby streets. According to the police he confessed at once to murdering Robina by hitting her on the head with the blunt end of a hatchet and burning her head and limbs in the furnace. But later he changed his story to say that they had both been drinking heavily and she had died of alcohol poisoning from the "hooch." Presumably he had realised that with the head incinerated there was no way the police could prove she had died from a hatchet blow to the skull—although an autopsy performed on the torso produced no evidence to support her dying from alcohol poisoning.

35 – LIVES TAKEN

The investigation

McClafferty lied about a number of things. He first claimed they met only three weeks previously, that he had only known her for the three weeks she was living in his apartment. But then he told reporters that every time he got a new job she kept following him around, but for the two years or so that they were a couple he was living at Sanford Arms apartments. Virtually nothing was known about the murder victim—only what McClafferty told the police, although her identity was eventually confirmed when her torso was identified by some marks on it that two ladies she had worked for recognised.

McClafferty was charged with first degree murder. He pleaded "Not guilty." However, he knew he would be convicted, so, in order to escape the electric chair, he tried to paint as black a picture of Robina as he could, as some form of mitigation. He claimed she ate nothing the whole of the last three weeks she shared his apartment but only drank continuously. With this and other such salacious statements, and no one to refute them, he managed to paint a scenario in which he claimed he had been driven to the drastic deed when he, himself, had been drunk and not fully responsible for his actions.

His tactics worked. Partway through the trial he asked to change his plea to guilty to murder in the second degree. The plea was accepted to save the court further expense and he was sentenced to twenty years to life hard labour in Sing Sing.

The horrifying truth discovered

The official New York City Municipal Records show Robina's death as occurring on 8th November, 1926—the day her torso was discovered, although, according to McClafferty's testimony, we know that she actually died over a week earlier on the night of the $28^{th}/29^{th}$ October.

News of such an horrendous crime, of course, made the national press and, indeed, with rumours that the victim had been Irish the story was picked up and copied in the British newspapers, too. Just as Christmas was approaching, Roland glanced at the morning paper before heading off to work at the *Spectator* office. It is impossible to imagine the horror he must have felt when he started to read of another gruesome murder in America, only to find he was reading about his own sister. We know this is what happened from a brief item in the *Long Island Daily Express* early in January, 1927. Under the heading: Brother in Ireland Learns of Murder of Sister in Flushing, it went on, "According to a letter that was forwarded to District Attorney, Richard S Newcombe, by the British consulate in Manhattan, Roland Lyttle of Bangor, Ireland, has just learned, through the newspapers of the death of his sister, Robina Lyttle. He asked for more details. This was mailed to him by the district attorney's office."

Like us, Roland would only have had McClafferty's testimony as to how poor Robina conducted herself throughout their two-year relationship and, heartbroken, he must have decided to keep the details from his children. Although we now know how Robina really died, we can never know the full truth about the tragedy of Wesley's youngest daughter and how she ended her days, thousands of miles from her childhood home in Bangor, the hapless victim of a New York axe murderer.

Chapter 36 – PASSING THE BATON

1914 – 2021

I imagine Roland would have withheld the gory details of Robina's death from his elderly step-mother, too. I hope he did. She would have been 85 when McClafferty was starting his incarceration in New York's notorious prison built on land purchased from a Native American tribe called the Sint Sinck, whence its name, Sing Sing. It was enough that she should know her step-daughter's killer was paying for his crime.

Annie

Annie lived for another nine years, passing away in 1935 shortly before her 95th birthday. Her obituary in the *Northern Herald*, as WG's newspaper was called by then, was headed, "Our Founder's Widow. Passing of Mrs. W. G. Lyttle."

> We regret to have to announce," it said, "the death of Mrs A. B. Lyttle, Bangor, widow of the famous W. G. Lyttle who founded this paper. Mrs Lyttle had reached the grand old age of 95. A native of Ballyboley, near Greyabbey, she was a Miss Byers before her marriage. The late Mr. Charles Byers, who was at one time proprietor of the Ava Hotel, Bangor, was her brother. She was a devoted member of First Bangor Presbyterian Church.

It went on to talk about her late husband, WG, and the early days of his paper, before mentioning the burial which took place at "the Old Abbey Churchyard," the same burial ground where her late husband was interred.[294] It was a wintry day in December, damp and overcast. But that did not deter a large number of friends, including some who had worked on the *Herald* in her husband's day, from joining her step-son, Roland, and his son, Gerald, my father, as the chief mourners, to bid their last farewells.

It seemed like closure; the end, indeed, of a regime in Bangor that would not soon be forgotten. A time when the son of a Newtownards cobbler, largely self-taught, had both informed and entertained the populace through his newspaper, and held municipal leaders to account. In so doing he helped to start the sleepy little resort of Bangor on its journey to become, by the time Annie died, Ulster's third most populated town that boasted a higher rateable value than any other. Bangor had come a long way since WG had first published the *North Down Herald and Bangor Gazette* from "Mount Herald" back in 1882.

Republications

And so WG's journey was over. The end of an era. But was it, really? Could it ever truly be over while hundreds of his books were still selling around the world?

After getting *Daft Eddie* published in 1914, Roland had all three volumes of *Humorous Readings by "Robin"* reprinted in 1916, followed in 1918 by the three volumes of *Robin's Readings* and a seventh edition of *Betsy Gray*. An eighth edition must have come out around 1922 because R. Carswell & Son Ltd published the ninth and last of the early editions of WG's most enduring novel in or around 1925.

In more recent times *Betsy Gray* was serialised in newspapers twice more: once in 1960 by the *Newtownards Chronicle* and again in 1968, by the Mourne Observer. Jim Hawthorne, the editor of that journal at the time, sought the advice of Easons booksellers in 1967 on the merits of reprinting *Betsy Gray* that had then been unavailable for

---

[294] My thanks are due to Sandra Millsopp who dicovered an old map of the Abbey Churchyard with "Mrs Lyttle" written in pencil in the corner where WG is burried. The implication being that Annie was burred in the same plot, although no indication of this has been subsequently added to the engraving on the obilisk.

many years. The view given was that it had been so long out of print that it was unlikely to sell many copies. Fortunately, Hawthorne was not put off by such pessimism. The *Mourne Observer's* 1968 hardback edition of *Betsy Gray* contained a preface by the late Aiken McClelland and "Other stories and pictures of '98" as contributed by readers during the story's serialisation. It was so popular that it eventually required a reprint in 1976 and another in October 1997 in time for the bicentenary of the '98 rebellion the following summer—a twelfth edition.

The same journal started serialising *Daft Eddie* in 1977 and followed that up with a serialisation of *Sons of the Sod* in 1978. They published a hardback edition of *Daft Eddie* with an appendix containing readers' recollections, in 1979.

Appletree Press produced their abridged, facsimile copy of WG's, *The Bangor Season* in 1977. In 1986, the Larne Folklore Society included one of WG's poems in an edition of their publication, *Corran*. They chose "My Brither Wully" from *Robin's Readings Vol 3—Life in Ballycuddy*.[295]

Sons of the Sod was re-published as a paperback in 2005 as part of the Ulster-Scots Classics series with an introduction by Philip Robinson, and a thirteenth edition of *Betsy Gray* was published in paperback by Ullan's Press in 2008.

In 2015, Derek Rowlinson, of Books Ulster, published a six-volume series of WG's works in print-on-demand paperback and e-books. These comprise *Sons of the Sod, Betsy Gray, Daft Eddie,* and *Robin's Readings Volume 1—The Adventures of Paddy M'Quillan; Volume 2—The Adventures of Robin Gordon; and Volume 3—Life in Ballycuddy, County Down.* These six volumes continue to be available on Amazon.

More recently, in 2018, the Ulster-Scots Education Project at Ulster University have put pdf files online of the first two volumes of *Robin's Readings,* along with *Sons of the Sod, Daft Eddie* and, of course, *Betsy Gray.*

Now, for the first time ever, an anthology of WG's verse has been complied and published as *Robin's Rhymes* (published by AG Lyttle,

---

[295] I am indebted to Angeline King, author of *Irish Dancing, Snugville Street* etc. for this information.

2021). It brings together all of WG's poetry, whether written as stand-alone poems or included within his stories. Some are written in standard English, others in Ulster-Scots. It has a foreword by Belfast poet, Gaynor Kane. Two other companion volumes have also just been released. The second of the three is an omnibus edition of *Robin's Readings* (published by AG Lyttle, 2021). comprising all three volumes of WG's Ulster-Scots yarns—"The Adventures of Paddy M'Quillan," "The Adventures of Robin Gordon" and "Life in Ballycuddy;" foreword by Books Ulster's Derek Rowlinson. The third includes all of WG's early stories that didn't make it into *Robin's Readings*. Called, *Robin's Further Readings* (published by AG Lyttle, 2021), it also includes seven new stories never before published in book form. Anne Smyth of the Ulster-Scots Society has provided the foreword.

All three of these companuion volumes include a handy Glossary of Ulster-Scots words for readers less familiar with the language.

Over the years there have been dramatisations of WG's works. Back in the 1940s, Kircubbin postmaster, Robert W Mateer and the Kircubbin Players staged versions of a number of his stories.[296] In the early part of the 21st century, BBC Radio Ulster broadcast some of *"Robin's" Readings* and, as recently as 2020, they produced Ian McElhinney reading an abridged version of *Sons of the Sod*.

Today, WG's works remain as some of the best written examples of Ulster-Scots as it was used in County Down at the end of the 19th century. As such, they still provide useful source material for linguistic scholars. Philip Robinson, in his *Ulster-Scots: A Grammar of the Traditional Written and Spoken Language,* drew for illustrations upon WG's accuracy of observation and recording of the peculiarities of Ulster-Scots grammar, sentence construction and idiom. WG's writing also provides social and cultural historians with a useful

---

[296] This, according to an unattributed article at the end of the *Mourne Observer's* 1979 edition of *Daft Eddie*, in which the drama group are referred to both as the Kircubbin Players and the Killinchy Players.

insight of rural folk-life and local history of the periods about which he wrote.

Family legacy

But WG's legacy is not only preserved in his books. He had six children but only two surviving grandchildren that are known to us. From these he had five great-grandchildren, seven great-great-grandchildren and 19 great-great-great-grandchildren so far. What, if anything, of WG can be seen in successive generations of his progeny?

Both his grandchildren—my father, Gerald and Aunt Eveline—were life-long teachers. It wasn't just a job for them, they were truly gifted and dedicated—something they were born with. Did they get that from WG, whose ability to teach shorthand spread that skill far and wide back in the 1870s?

Gerald also inherited WG's writing ability. At 16, he won the National Life-Boat Essay Competition for Elementary Schools, coming first in the whole of Great Britain and Ireland.[297] As he grew up he continued to write and had copious articles and short stories published in magazines and newspapers—including some in the kailyard style with Ulster-Scots dialogue. He wrote radio scripts as well, and had two scouting novels published. He had a flare for drawing, able to illustrate his articles with quick pen and ink sketches, just as WG did in his newspaper.[298]

One of my cousins, Evangeline, was a poet with several anthologies to her name. Her son, Ronan Paterson, performed as an actor at the Abbey Theatre in Dublin while studying at Trinity College and has continued to work as an actor, director and producer in

---

[297] We have, preserved, a photo of him with his headmaster, Mr Orr, holding the Life-Boat Shield. The photo appeared in the Glasgow paper, *The Bulletin and Scots Pictorial* on 24th September, 1925. Gerald also received a limited edition copy of *Britain's Life Boats* by Major AJ Dawson (Hodder & Stoughton, 1925) with an introduction by HRH, Prince of Wales, KG, who was president of the Royal National Life-Boat Institution. Gerald's copy was numbered, 19 out of 1,000 printed and was signed personally "Edward P," who later became, albeit briefly, King Edward VIII. (See photographs in Appendix E—Figures 14, 15 and 16)

[298] The adult Gerald Lyttle's photograph is in Appendix E, Figure 17.

theatre, film, radio and television. He is, in 2021, Head of Performing Arts at Teesside University. One of his adult children, David Paterson has also taken to the stage.

Ronan's brother, Michael Paterson is an accomplished artist and military historian with a string of non-fiction titles to his name and he is working on his first novel. He has also got WG's "gift of the gab," a born storyteller. In his spare time he has worked as a tour guide in London and at Eton College. His gift for describing the scenes and recounting the history behind the various sights in a most entertaining, as well as informative fashion must surely emulate exactly how his great-great-grandfather, WG, used to describe the paintings of Ireland's beauty spots when he was a lecturer with Dr Corry's Diorama.

Sister to Michael and Ronan, Carolyn Rowland-Jones is also an actor, drama practitioner and writer, who has had several of her plays produced under her professional name of Carolyn Fairlie. Her daughter, Eve's artistic talent has brought her joy as a children's book illustrator.

On my side of the family, my sister, Lorna Forrester, writes poetry and has published a novel; her daughter, Kathy Bushell, teaches.

Whilst Lorna's poetry is serious, I mainly entertain my friends and sometimes larger audiences with comic verse. It started with parties—just like WG. I would usually set my verse to music (as WG may have done sometimes)—a parody of an old Irish song or one of the latest "pops," provoking innocent laughter at the expense of the guest of honour and others present. I have also been, in an amateur way, a singer-songwriter—mostly of Gospel songs.

I write fiction, too. Just in time for the centenary of the 1916 Easter Rising, *Dillon's Rising* became my first published novel.[299] As a nod to the celebrated Storyteller, I claim that Dillon is descended from Jamie Dillon, a character in WG's famous novel, *Betsy Gray*.

---

[299] *Dillon's Rising* is a story of espionage, love and revenge, and Dillon's desperate struggle to survive six days of terror that changed Ireland forever. The book is available on Amazon. Use this shortcut if you wish to check it out: **viewbook.at/DillonsRising**

36 - PASSING THE BATON

My three children all have good singing voices and one, Jenny Lewry, also writes and sings gospel songs; this, in spite of inheriting a cleft palate from her great-grandfather, WG's son, Roland. Two of her own four children were born with similar conditions. When Jenny first left home, it was to become a nanny, just like poor Robina. My daughter's story, however, continues happily. She is currently a married mother of four, a primary schools worker and performs theatrical assemblies.

Her sister, Susan, showed early promise as a ten-year-old author of three short stories that her grandfather, Gerald, illustrated for her. Alas, her life as a busy farmer's wife leaves no time for such pursuits at the moment, although her hilarious accounts of life on the farm amongst all the animals would rival anything that ever came out of Ballycuddy and must, surely, one day find their way into print. Just one of her three children was born with a cleft palate, but, as with her cousins, modern surgical techniques have been wonderful in making everything as it should be with virtually no scarring, unlike Wesley's son who chose to wear a moustache all his life to hide his upper lip.

My son, Sean, in his spare time, is devoted to semi-pro and amateur dramatics. Apart from treading the boards himself in a variety of productions including popular musicals, he jointly runs a community theatre for adults and children. [300]

Of course, part of the inherited gifting within the members of our clan will have come from the many talented spouses' family lines, too, but it is good to think that at least some of it has been handed down the generations and is perpetuating the amazing skills and capabilities of a multi-talented, 19th century Ulster legend who is ancestor to each one of us—newspaper proprietor, writer, poet and storyteller, Wesley Greenhill Lyttle.

WG, we salute you.

---

[300] His "Lost for Words" Theatre Company, as well as running weekly tuition in all aspects of drama production for children and teenagers, also stages annual productions with adult actors in local theatres.

Epilogue

1897

Some 15 months had elapsed since the mortal remains of Wesley Lyttle were laid to rest in the Abbey Churchyard. The woodland beyond the graveyard had bloomed into full leaf and provided shade throughout the summer of '97 before autumn colours had begun to emerge once more. Leaves fluttered down to carpet the ground.

Now, around the secluded corner plot last autumn's fallen foliage had been blown clear by winter's winds. A small group of Wesley's family and friends had gathered once again at his graveside beneath the bare outstretched lime branches on a dank day in February, 1898.

The occasion was the dedication of a fine, Swedish granite obelisk that now graced the head of the grave. The memorial, exquisitely sculpted by Messrs. Purdy & Millard of Belfast,[301] was a gift to the family from some of WG's friends—possibly his brother masons. They wanted to honour the man who had brought so much to their town over the comparatively short period he had lived among them.

---

[301] Purdy and Millard advertised in the very first issue of WG's *North Down Herald*, 17 years earlier (see photo on next page.)

EPILOGUE

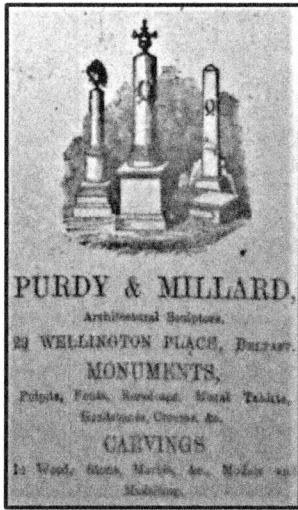

This advert is from the front page of the first edition of the ***North Down Herald*, July 1880** (by kind permission of the British Library – shelfmark MFM M14050, 1880)

With a double base and crowned with an elegantly finished capitol, the obelisk stands over six feet high.[302] Its polished granite surface bears this legend:

"Erected by a number of friends as a tribute to the memory of W. G. LYTTLE, Founder and Editor of the 𝔑orth 𝔇own 𝔥erald. Born at Newtownards 15th April, 1844. Died at Bangor 1st November, 1896. A man of rare natural gifts, he raised himself to a high position amongst the Journalists of Ireland. He was a brilliant and graceful writer, a true humourist and an accomplished poet. "Robin" was a kind friend, a genial companion and a true son of County Down."

In seeking the family's permission to pay this tribute to Wesley the friends had offered to add a dedication from them, too, on the side panel. In it, Annie quoted from one of her favourite poems by the poet laureate, Alfred Lord Tennyson, *Break, break, break, on thy cold grey stones, O sea!*

The inscription reads:

---

[302] A photo of the obelisk can be seen in Appendix F, Fig 30.

THE STORYTELLER

"Interred Nov. 3 1896. Deeply mourned by his sorrowing wife and children.

"Oh! For the touch of a vanished hand,
And the sound of a voice that's still!"

The sombre group around the grave lingered a while longer until Annie turned away. The others followed, with Roland last of all.

We might well imagine for a moment, as they left, that an elderly bearded gentleman in a blue swallowtail coat and loud checked trousers, who had hung back and not ventured to join them earlier, now ambled forward and stood facing the new monument at the head of his friend's grave. He read the inscription through, slowly, thoughtfully, and smiled.

'Thaim's splendid wurds his freens haes writ. A cudnae hae done muckle better masel. And thon's a bra' bit o' stane they hae gien him, but it's only richt. It's whut he deserves. Och, an' dae A no get a wee menshin, forbye? A wush Peggy cud hae bin here tae see it. She'd be that proud.'[303]

The old man continued to mutter to himself as he moved round to look at the inscription on the side. He read the quotation and thought for a moment.

'Och weel, the "soon may be still," richt eneuch, but A'm thinkin' no the tongue. Shair his voice wull last as lang as his buiks get prentit an' thair's oniebudie aboot ava tae read them. A ken Peggy is lairnin' wee Paddy his letters an' whun he's growed up, he'll lairn his ain weans. Thair'll aye be fowks wantin' tae ken what A hae

---

[303] 'Those are splendid words his friends have written; I couldn't have done much better myself. And that's a fine bit of stone they have given him, but it's only right. It's what he deserves. Oh, and do I not get a little mention, as well? I wish Peggy could have been here to see it. She'd be that proud.'

EPILOGUE

bin up to in Ballycuddy, an ma guid freen, the editor, wull aye be the yin tae tell thaim.[304]

At the gate, Roland turned and took a last glance over his shoulder towards the far corner of the churchyard. In the gathering dusk, he could just make out the dark shape of his father's fine new monument standing in the shade of the lime tree. He fancied for a moment he saw a figure peering at the inscription on the stone but it was probably just the shadow of a branch swaying in the breeze. WG's last resting place was quietly at peace in the deserted graveyard.

Roland followed the others out and the gate clicked shut behind him.

---

[304] 'Ah well, the "sound may be still," right enough, but I'm thinking not the tongue. Sure his voice will last as long as his books get printed and there's anybody about at all to read them. I know Peggy is teaching young Paddy his letters, and when he's grown, he'll teach his own children. There'll always be folks wanting to know what I have been up to in Ballycuddy, and my good friend, the editor, will always be the one to tell them.'

THE STORYTELLER

APPENDIX A – Lyttle Family Tree

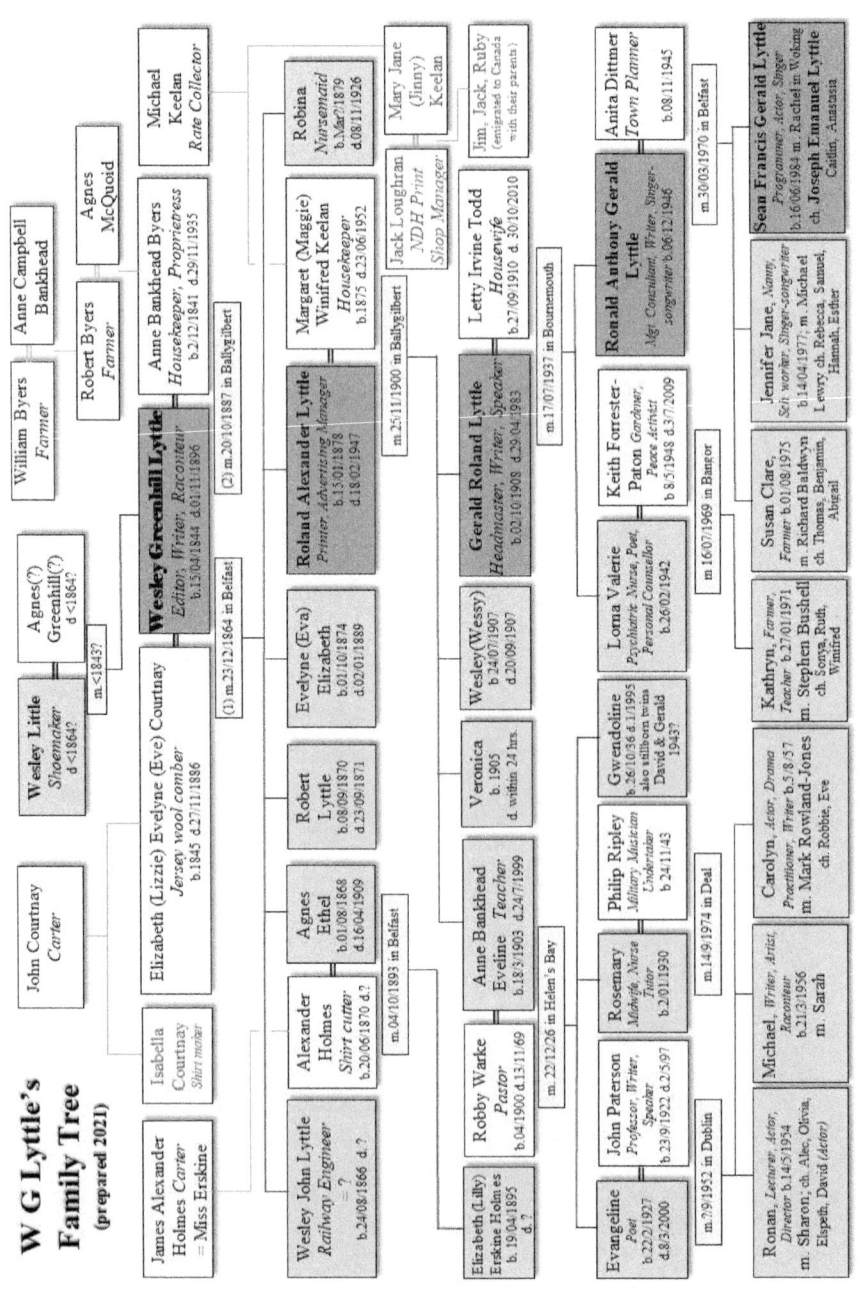

APPENDIX B
THE WORKS OF WG LYTTLE
(The lead numbers identify the edition;
dates in *italics* are approximate)

ANTHOLOGIES

Humorous Readings by Robin (1)
1. 1879, May—Allen & Johnston, book printers, 40, Upper Arthur St Belfast (brown cloth cover) When published "there were already enough stories for a second volume."
   Copy held at Belfast Library (re-bound in a hard cover)
- 1880—Reprinted
2. 1883—University Printing and Publishing House
   Copy held at Kansas University
3. 1890—Author's edition. Printed at the North Down Printing Works
   Copy held at National Library of Ireland
- 1916—Reprinted

Humorous Readings by Robin Vol 2
1. 1880, March—Allen & Johnston, book printers, 40, Upper Arthur St Belfast (green board cover)
   Copy held at Linen Hall Library, Belfast
2. 1886, July—Allen, Son & Allen, publishers, 40, Upper Arthur St Belfast.
   Title changed to Readings by Robin Vol 2
   Copy held at Kansas University and Linen Hall Library
- 1916—Reprinted

Readings by Robin Vol 3
1. 1886, May—University House, Allen, Son & Allen, 40 Arthur St Belfast (purple board cover) WG had said it would be ready by Christmas '85. *Copy held at Linen Hall Library, Belfast*
2. 1892, September—Author's edition (Readings by Robin, Author's edition Vol 3, Life in Ballycuddy) (pale brown board cover) *Copy held at Linen Hall Library, Belfast*
- 1916—Reprinted

THE STORYTELLER

Robin's Readings Vol 1, The Adventures of Paddy M'Quillan
1. *1884?*—R. Carswell & Son Limited, Queen St Belfast (pink cover)
   Copy held at Linen Hall Library, Belfast
2. 1885/6?—Self-published (pale green cover)
3. 1892, March—Printed at the North Down Printing Works
4. }
5. } up to 1898—Printed at the North Down Printing Works
6. }
7. }
8. 1899, Aug—Printed at the North Down Printing Works
9. *1913?*—R. Carswell & Son Limited, Queen St Belfast (illustrated cover) *Probably published together with their* Betsy Gray 6th edition *in 1913*
10. 1918—Re-printed by RA Lyttle at Spectator Office *Copy held at Kansas University* (where it was erroneously catalogued as the "Joseph Blair edition" due to the many adverts for Joseph Blair [cooking] ranges it contains. There is no such separate "Joseph Blair edition" and the Kansas University catalogue has now been amended.)
11. 2015—Books Ulster. Includes a glossary of Ulster-Scots words.
    Available as print-on-demand and eBook from Amazon
- 2018, August—Ulster-Scots Education Project, Ulster University.
    Available as a downloadable pdf file

Robin's Readings Vol 2, The Adventures of Robin Gordon
1. *1885/86?*—R. Carswell & Son Limited, Queen St Belfast
2. 1889—Self-published edition?
3. 1892, Apr/May—Printed at the North Down Printing Works
4. 1899, Aug—Printed at the North Down Printing Works
5. *1913?*—R. Carswell & Son Limited, Queen St Belfast (picture cover) *Probably published together with their* Betsy Gray 6th edition *in 1913*
6. 1918—Re-printed by RA Lyttle at Spectator Office (pale yellow paper cover) *Copy held at Kansas University* (where it

APPENDIX B

was erroneously catalogued as the "Joseph Blair edition" due to the many adverts for Joseph Blair [cooking] ranges it contains. There is no such separate "Joseph Blair edition" and the Kansas University catalogue has now been amended.)
7. 2015—Books Ulster. Includes a glossary of Ulster-Scots words.
Available as print-on-demand and eBook from Amazon
- 2018, August—Ulster-Scots Education Project, Ulster University.
Available as a downloadable pdf file

Robin's Readings Vol 3, Life in Ballycuddy, County Down
1. 1889—R. Carswell & Son Limited, Queen St Belfast
2. 1892—Printed at the North Down Printing Works
Copy held at the National Library of Ireland
3. 1893—Printed at the North Down Printing Works
4. 1902—Printed at the North Down Printing Works
5. *1913?*—R. Carswell & Son Limited, Queen St Belfast (illustrated cover) *Probably published together with their* Betsy Gray 6th edition *in 1913*
6. 1918—Republished by RA Lyttle at *Spectator* Office (pale green paper cover)
7. 2015—Books Ulster. Includes a glossary of Ulster-Scots words.
Available as print-on-demand and eBook from Amazon

Robin's Readings Volumes 1, 2 and 3 bound together
1. 1910, Oct—No publisher mentioned, almost certainly RA Lyttle
(dark blue cloth-covered hardback, gilt lettering, centred)
Copy owned by AG Lyttle
2. c1913?—published by R Carswell and Son Ltd, Belfast
(dark green cloth-covered hardback, gilt lettering, top left)
Copy owned by AG Lyttle
3. 2021, Nov—Robin's Readings Omnibus Edition, published by AG Lyttle, 2021
Available as print-on-demand and eBook from Amazon

THE STORYTELLER

Robin's Further Readings
1. 2021, November—published by AG Lyttle, 2021. Includes previously unpublished stories and others not contained in Robin's Readings. *Available as print-on-demand and eBook from Amazon*

Robin's Rhymes in Ulster-Scota and English
1. 2021, Nov—published by AG Lyttle, 2021. An anthology of WG's verse. *Available as print-on-demand and eBook from Amazon*

NOVELS
Sons of the Sod, a Tale of County Down
- *1885, early?*—Said to have been serialised in the North Down Herald. No evidence that it was. Betsy Gray was serialised from Nov '85, so if it was, it would have to have started early in the year.
1. 1886, November—Printed by Author at his North Down Printing Works
   Copy held at British Library, London
2. *1888?*} Two further editions were produced at the
3. *1892?*} North Down Printing Works between 1887 and 1894
- 1905, January to June—serialised in the North Down Herald
4. 1911—Re-published by author's son, Bangor
5. *1913?*—R. Carswell & Son Ltd, Queen St Belfast *Probably published at the same time as their* Betsy Gray 6th edition *in 1913.*
6. *1919?*—Re-published by author's son, Bangor (marked as "sixth edition") *Printed by DE Alexander,* Spectator, *probably the year after re-publishing* Betsy Gray.
- 1978, May to 1979, June—serialised in the *Mourne Observer*
7. 2005—Ulster-Scots Classics
8. 2015—Books Ulster, includes a glossary of Ulster-Scots words
   Available as print-on-demand and eBook from Amazon
- 2018, August—Ulster-Scots Education Project, Ulster University
   Available as a downloadable pdf file

APPENDIX B

Betsy Gray, or Hearts of Down, a Tale of '98
- 1885, November to 1886, September—Serialised in the North Down Herald
1. 1887—Self-published (Traditionally thought to be 1888 but 1st edit. was '87)
2. 1888—Self-published (Larger edition published in '88)
Copy owned by Mark Thompson of Portavogie
3. 1894, August—"A very large 3rd edition" printed by the author in his North Down Printing Works, Bangor, Ireland.
Copy held at Linen Hall Library and British Library
4. 1899, June—Printed at North Down Printing Works, Imperial Buildings, Bangor, Ireland by AB Lyttle (WG's widow) who wrote the preface.
Copy held at Linen Hall Library
5. 1904—Probably published by the author's son, RA Lyttle *(A "New edition" was advertised in the* North Down Herald *in December 1904.)*
6. 1913—R. Carswell & Son Ltd. Queen Street, Belfast (An illustrated edition)
Copy held at Linen Hall Library
7. 1915—R. Carswell & Son Ltd. Queen Street, Belfast *(Revised by Irish antiquarian Francis Joseph Bigger, Member of the Royal Irish Academy and Fellow of the Royal Society of Antiquaries of Ireland)*
8. 1918—RA Lyttle, printed at the Spectator Office (Paperback at 6d; cloth cover at 1/3)
Copy held at Linen Hall Library, Belfast
9. Undated, c.1922?—R. Carswell & Son Ltd. Queen Street, Belfast
- 1960, Aug to Dec—Serialised in the *Newtownards Chronicle*
- 1968—Serialised in the *Mourne Observer*
10. 1968—Mourne Observer Ltd, Printers and Publishers, Newcastle, Co. Down, Northern Ireland *Includes "other stories and pictures of '98"*
11. 1976—Republished by Mourne Observer Ltd, Printers and Publishers,

12. 1997, October—Republished by Mourne Observer Ltd, Printers and Publishers,
13. 2008—Ullans Press
14. 2015—Books Ulster. Includes a glossary of Ulster-Scots words
    Available as print-on-demand and eBook from Amazon
- 2018, August—Ulster-Scots Education Project, Ulster University
  Available as a downloadable pdf file

Daft Eddie, or Smugglers of Strangford Lough, a Tale of Killinchy (Original text attributed to "the Rev J. B." Revised, edited and additional material by WG Lyttle)
- 1889, March to October—Serialised in NDH (authorship unattributed)
- *1890?* "Published in book form", according to the *Mourne Observer* 1979 edition and the National Library of Ireland, but this has been stated in error; no evidence of such a publication has come to light and WG never claimed authorship during his lifetime.
- *1911?*—A possible first edition published by Roland Lyttle to coincide with his 1911 publication of *Sons of the Sod* but, again, no evidence of such an edition. More likely:
1. 1914—R. Carswell and Son, Ltd. Printers, Queen Street, Belfast. (I believe this was the first edition, erroneously attributed, posthumously, to WG Lyttle as author. See Chapter 34, "An undiscovered work?")
- 1977, November to 1978, May—Serialised in the *Mourne Observer*
2. 1979—Mourne Observer Press, Newcastle, Co Down, Northern Ireland. *Hardback with appendix incorporating readers' recollections.*
3. 2015—Books Ulster Includes a glossary of Ulster-Scots words
   Available as print-on-demand and eBook from Amazon
- 2018, August—Ulster-Scots Education Project, Ulster University
  Available as a downloadable pdf file

APPENDIX B

TOURIST GUIDE
The Bangor Season, What's to be Seen and How to See It.
1. 1885—Compiled and published by WG Lyttle, Bangor, Co Down
2. 1887—Compiled and published by WG Lyttle, Bangor, Co Down
3. *Probable subsequent editions biennially in 1889,*
4. *1891 and*
5. *1893, but no corroborating evidence*
6. 1895—Compiled and published by WG Lyttle, with a reference to the new Main Street office.
7. 1997—Appletree Press Ltd. 6, Dublin Road, Belfast (Abridged, facsimile copy)
(address in 2021: 164 Malone Road, Belfast BT9 5LL)

ALMANACS
Lyttle's North Down Directory and Almanac
1 to 5. 1881 to 1885—Allen & Johnson?, 40 Arthur Street, Belfast (As the printers of the Herald, they are most likely to have been used for the early almanacs, too)

6 to 16. 1886 to 1896—North Down Printing Press (published annually until WG's death)

Copies of 1888 and 1894 editions held by AG Lyttle

"Herald" Almanac and County Down Directory
17 to 33. 1897 to 1913—North Down Printing Press

Copy of 1913 edition held by AG Lyttle

34+? 1914 to ?—North Down Printing Press (Further editions were probably published)

NEWSPAPER
The North Down Herald, Newtownards
1880, July—Robert S Allen, Allen & Johnston, 40 Arthur St Belfast

THE STORYTELLER

The North Down Herald, Newtownards Argos and Bangor Gazette, Bangor
1882, June—Robert S Allen, Allen & Johnston, 40 Arthur St Belfast (The inclusion of the Argos title is recorded in the libel action brought by William Henry in 1883)

The North Down Herald and Bangor Gazette, Bangor
1884—W. & G. Baird, Telegraph Printing Works, 10 & 12 Arthur Street, Belfast *(Changed to Baird after Allen capitulated in the libel action.)*
1885—North Down Printing Works, "Mount Herald," Bangor *(WG set up his own printing press.)*

The North Down Herald and County Down Independent (with which is incorporated the Newtownards Independent, established 1871), Bangor
1892, September—North Down Printing Works, "Mount Herald," Ballymagee St, Bangor *(Name-change to reflect wider circulation.)*
1894—North Down Printing Works, Imperial Building, Bangor, Ireland
Published by the Proprietor, WG Lyttle

1896, November—North Down Printing Works, Imperial Building, Bangor, Ireland
Published by the Proprietress, AB Lyttle, for another 11 years, after 16 years under WG Lyttle.)

The Northern Herald, incorporating The North Down Herald and County Down Independent
1907—The *Herald* Print Works, Head Office, 85 Main Street, Bangor
Published by the Proprietor, RD Montgomery to whom AB Lyttle had sold the paper.
1926, November—Moved to new premises
Continued to be published by the Proprietor, RD Montgomery until 1939, when he went bankrupt.

APPENDIX C

APPENDIX C1
HUMOROUS READINGS BY "Robin"
by WG LYTTLE

Cloth-bound first edition, 1879 (image, AG Lyttle)

Board-covered second edition, 1883 (courtesy of Kansas University)

Contents
To my Friens (poem)
Paddy M'Quillan's Christmas
Paddy M'Quillan's Trip Tae Glesco
    Part First: Guid-bye Ma!
    Part Second: Scotch Fare
    Part Third: Sammy's Shoon
    Part Four: The Return Voyage
Paddy M'Quillan's Courtships
    No. I
    No. II
Paddy M'Quillan's Wedding
    Part First: Bespeaking the Licence
    Part Second: Stormy Scene
Paddy M'Quillan's Chris'nin' Perty
    Part First: Trials of Married Life
    Part Second: The Guests Arrive
The Tipperary Policeman and his Sweetheart Biddy
The Colorado Beetle
The Vegetarians
    Part First: Vegetarianism Extraordinary
    Part Second: Human Nature
    Part Third: Almost a Quarrel
Lecture on Light
The Londonderry Banquet
Hammy Kaig's Bedfellow
The Newtownerds Mileeshy
My Brither Wully (**poem**)
To Peggy (**poem**)

THE STORYTELLER

APPENDIX C2
HUMOROUS READINGS BY "Robin" Vol II
by WG LYTTLE

Cloth-bound first edition, 1880 (courtesy Mark Thompson)

Board-covered second edition, 1886 (courtesy of Mark Thompson)

Contents
My Brither Wully
Kirk Music
Betty Megimpsey
The General Assembly
The Ballycuddy Elders
Wee Paddy's Bumps
Paddy M'Quillan's Twins
Paddy M'Quillan's Tae Perty
    Part First: Paddy's Responsibilities
    Part Second: The American Auctioneer
    Part Third: A Spoilt Necktie
The Newtownerds Mileeshy
    Part Second: Expensive Necklace
Dipplemassy (Diplomacy)
Peggy, And How I Courted Her
    Part First: Peggy Meewbunyee
    Part Second: Tongue Tied
Wee Wully
The Newtownerds Flower Show
The Ballycuddy Cookin' Cless
Izek Neelson in Ballycuddy

APPENDIX C

APPENDIX C3
READINGS BY "Robin" Vol III
by WG LYTTLE

Board-covered first edition, 1886 (courtesy Linen Hall Library)

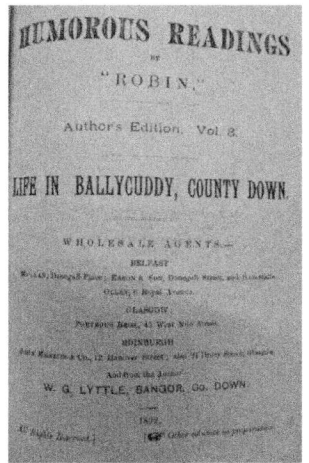

Title page of second edition, 1892 (courtesy Linen Hall Library; original cover missing)

Contents
Music Before Supper (filler)
A Crafty Butcher (filler)
Preface to Third Volume
A Crack Wi' Izek Neelson
The Newtownbreda Harmoneyum
The General Assembly of Echteen Hunner an' Echty
The Ballycuddy Precentor
The New Meer
Robin on Ice
Robin at Pickie Rock
A Crack Wi' Lord Dufferin
The Faugh-a-ballagh Pleeceman and his Baton
Mickey Mulrooney on the New Police Helmet
Mickey Mulrooney's Petition
A Crack Wi' the Prince o' Wales
The Ballycuddy Meinister
The Oyster Supper
The Farmer's Wife (Poem)
Maggie and the Roompaper (Poem)
Rabin's Auld Meer (Poem)
Mickey Mulrooney on Heather Dew Paddy (Poem)
Mickey Mulrooney and his Cruiskeen Lawn
Bangor Gossip (Poem)

THE STORYTELLER

APPENDIX C4
"Robin's" Readings Vol I—The Adventures of Paddy M'Quillan by WG LYTTLE

Illustrated, paper cover First edit., *1884?* (courtesy of Derek Rowlinson)

Contents
His Christmas Day
His Trip tae Glesco
    Part First
    Part Second
    Part Third
    Part Fourth
His Courtships
    Part Second
His Wedding
His Wee Paddy
The Chris'nin'
His Twins
His Tae Perty
    Part Second
    Part Third
M'Quillan Abroad

Paper-covered Tenth edit, 1918 (image, AG Lyttle)

Eleventh Edition, 2015 (image, AG Lyttle)

APPENDIX C

APPENDIX C5
"Robin's" Readings Vol II—The Adventures of Robin Gordon by WG LYTTLE

Illustrated, paper cover First edit., 1885 (courtesy of Mark Thompson)

Contents
Peggy, and How I Courted Her
    Part First
    Part second
Wee Wully
The Colorado Beetle
The Vegetarians
    Part First
    Part Second
    Part Third
The Meer's Proclamation
The Fechtin' Dugs
The Newton Flower Show
Robin on Ice
The Newtownerds Mileeshy
    My First Day's Drill
'Dipplemassy' (Diplomacy)

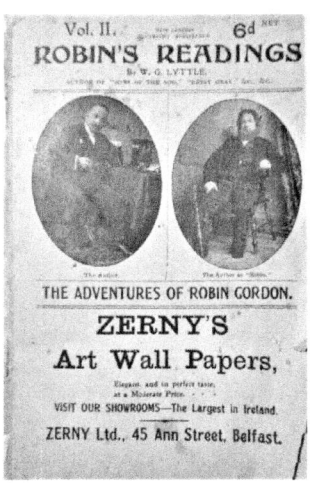

Sixth edition, 1918
(image, AG Lyttle)

Seventh edition, 2015
(image, AG Lyttle)

THE STORYTELLER

APPENDIX C6
"Robin's" Readings Vol III—Life in Ballycuddy
by WG LYTTLE

Illustrated, paper cover first edit., 1886 (courtesy Mark Thompson)

Contents
My Brither Wully
Kirk Music
The Ballycuddy Precentor
The General Assembly of 1879
The Ballycuddy Elders
The General Assembly of 1880
The Newtonbreda Harmoneyum
The Electric Light
The Ballycuddy Meinister
The Royal Visit to Ireland
Izek Neelson in Ballycuddy
Betty Megimpsey
A Story of General Jackson (filler)
General Gordon's Bravery (filler)
Wee Paddy's Bumps

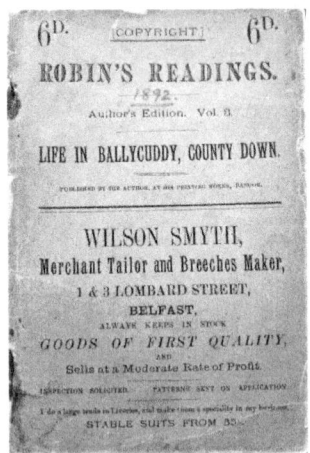

Second edition, 1892 (courtesy of Mark Thompson)

Seventh edition, 2015 (image, AG Lyttle)

APPENDIX C

APPENDIX C7
"Robin's" Readings Vols I, II and III—Omnibus by WG LYTTLE

First edition, blue hard cover, 1910
(image, AG Lyttle)

Second edition, green hard cover, *1913?*
(image, AG Lyttle)

Third edition, 2021
(image, AG Lyttle)

THE STORYTELLER

APPENDIX C8
Sons of the Sod—a Tale of County Down
by WG LYTTLE

First edition, 1886 (courtesy of British Museum - shelfmark YA2000.a.43197)

Fourth edition, 1911 (courtesy of Kansas University)

Fifth edition, *1913?* (image, AG Lyttle)

Sixth edition, *1919?* (courtesy of Mark Thompson)

Seventh edition, 2005 (image, AG Lyttle)

Eighth edition, 2015 (image, AG Lyttle)

APPENDIX C

APPENDIX C9
Betsy Gray, or Hearts of Down—a Tale of Ninety-eight by WG LYTTLE

Second edition, 1888 (courtesy of Mark Thompson)

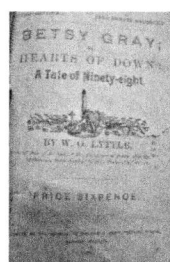

Third edition, 1894, Title page (courtesy of Linen Hall Library)

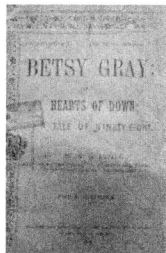

Fourth edition, 1899 (courtesy of Linen Hall Library)

Sixth edition, 1913 Title page (courtesy of Linen Hall Library)

Eighth edition, 1918 (courtesy of Linen Hall Library)

Ninth edition, *1922?* (image, AG Lyttle)

Eleventh edition, 1976 (image, AG Lyttle)

Thirteenth edition, 2008 (image, AG Lyttle)

Fourteenth edition, 2015 (image, AG Lyttle)

APPENDIX C10
Daft Eddy, or Smugglers of Strangford Lough
(Original story attributed to "the Rev J. B.", believed to be the grandson of Martha M'Fadden who was rescued by Eddie.)
Fully revised, edited and with extensive additional material by WG LYTTLE

First edition, 1914
(image, AG Lyttle)

Second edition, 1979
(image, AG Lyttle)

Third edition, 2015
(image, AG Lyttle)

APPENDIX C

APPENDIX C11
The Bangor Season—What's to be Seen and How to See It

Compiled and published
by WG LYTTLE

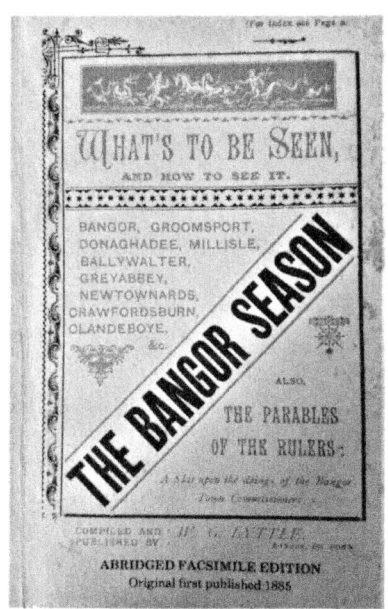

Seventh edition, 1977
(image, AG Lyttle)

THE STORYTELLER

APPENDIX C12

Robin's Further Readings
*
Robin's Rhymes

by WG LYTTLE

First edition, 2021
(image, AG Lyttle)

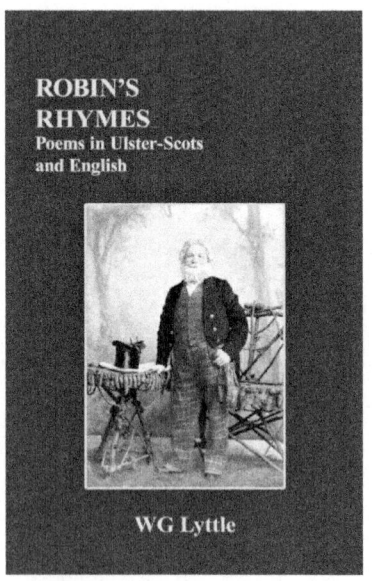

First edition, 2021
(image, AG Lyttle)

APPENDIX C

APPENDIX C13
Lyttle's North Down Directory and Almanac

Eighth edition, 1888
(image, AG Lyttle)

THE STORYTELLER

APPENDIX D
ROBIN AS A STAGE PERFORMER
A Few Opinions Of The Press

Robin's fame as a highly-talented writer, and most amusing humourist and reader, is so well established throughout Ulster that it is needless to utter any eulogistic comment regarding him, he is everywhere acknowledged to be not only one of the best readers in the North of Ireland, but a writer whose literary style and illimitable resources have elevated his genius far above most men of his time. His published works are accepted as standard models of "Humour, mirth, and fun" from which amateur and professional elocutionists invariably choose their best and most telling selections for the entertainment of public meetings. He is a gentleman whose "powers with pen and tongue" are unrivalled. Indeed it would be a needless task to attempt a criticism of his reading. It is perfection itself. There is no restraint in his histrionic action, nor dullness in his mode of expression. He gives a faithful representation of individualities and idiosyncrasies, and "holds the mirror up to nature" with a charming simplicity. On Wednesday night last he made a "palpable hit," and evoked shouts of laughter and applause from his crowded audience.—*Larne Reporter*

The room was crowded to excess, and many were unable to obtain admission. "Robin's" recitals drew forth peals of laughter. They were given in inimitable style, eliciting rounds of plaudits. The audience seemed as if they had inhaled laughing gas.—*Belfast News-Letter.*

The Adventures of Paddy M'Quillan fairly convulsed the audience, and the reader was frequently interrupted by loud peals of laughter and applause. Large numbers were unable to obtain admission.—*Northern Whig*

Created intense amusement.—*Morning News*

Carried everything before him. The trip to Glasgow is described with genuine dramatic power.—*North British Daily Mail*

APPENDIX D

Greeted with rapturous applause.—*Belfast Weekly News*

Robin has achieved fame as a humourist all over the North of Ireland.—*Midland News*

Robin's sketches are written in a strain which rivals our best Scottish authors.—*Ayrshire Weekly News*

Unmistakeable talent. Real humour.—*Witness*

Robin was received with great enthusiasm. Those who did not see and hear him missed a treat. Some of his touches are worthy of Dickens. Tears filled the eyes, or smiles lit up the faces of the audience, as the reader passed from grave to gay. The building was packed.—*Drew Memorial Parish Church Magazine*

Robin Gordon, of Ballycuddy, in his wonderful personation of the County Down farmer, delighted the audience by his venerable aspect, old-fashioned manners, quaint talk, and droll stories.—*Ulster Echo*

Robin's sketches are inimitable. The applause by the audience was hearty in the extreme.—*Coleraine Chronicle*

Robin related his stories in a manner that kept his audiences in roars of laughter.—*Coleraine Constitution*

Robin's recitals invoked enthusiastic applause from the audience.—*Newry Reporter*

The reception accorded to "Robin" by the large audience was of the most enthusiastic description. He kept the house in roars of laughter. His rendering of the Northern dialect is simply perfect.—*Irish Templar*

Completely captivated his audience and kept them in roars of laughter from beginning to end.—*Newtownards Chronicle*

THE STORYTELLER

On being assisted to the platform he received an ovation that proved his popularity with the crowded audience. As an amateur entertainer, "Robin" has no equal. He has marked out a line of his own, and his role is in every way unique. He personates the County Down farmer of the old school to perfection, every word and every movement being true to life. Indeed, simplicity and homeliness are the characteristics of "Robin's" recitals. But, in addition to these, he displays a wondrous knowledge of human nature, and touches the feelings of his audience with a master hand. As a mirth provoker he is *facile princeps,* and the woman or man who could not laugh at "Robin" is far gone in "green and yellow melancholy." We have been at public entertainments, and heard what might have been described as disjointed mirth. "Robin" does not call forth this sort of thing. He makes his hit, and, quick as a lightning flash, there is a peal of laughter, as simultaneous as the discharge of musketry at the order—"Fire!" Old and young were under the spell and not a few reminded us of Shakespeare's jolly god, "holding both his sides".—*Newry Telegraph*

Robin is the author of the most popular Ulster sketches of the period, and wherever he has appeared large audiences have listened with delight to his readings.—*Ballymoney Free Press*

In Ulster, across the Channel, in Canada and the United States—indeed wherever Ulstermen are to be found, "Robin" is highly appreciated. His "Readings" are replete with mirth-provoking sayings and scenes. To put our opinion in a sentence, we should say that Mr. W. G. Lyttle, in "Robin's Readings" has given to the world a series of sketches that will retain their great popularity as long as men and women relish fun and humour, and delight in a hearty peal of laughter.—*Evening Standard*

APPENDIX E
IMAGES OF WG LYTTLE and FAMILY

Fig 1. **A drawing of WG as "Robin,"** specially commissioned for the front cover of his first published collection of stories, *Humorous Readings by "Robin,"* 1879. It is reproduced here from a rather battered first edition copy of the book owned by AG Lyttle.

Fig 2. The second volume of *Humorous Readings by "Robin,"* published in 1880, had this drawing of **"Robin's wife, Peggy"**, reproduced, with permission, from a copy of the book owned by Mark Thompson of Portavogie.

Fig 3. This photo of WG dressed as "Robin" **appeared in the third volume of *Readings by Robin.***

THE STORYTELLER

Fig 4. One of the four original portrait photos I have of WG, here dressed as "Robin." (Photographer—**Balfour's Photographic Art Studio, Main Street, Bangor**, Ireland.) This photo is reproduced on the front covers of each volume of *Robin's Readings*.

Fig 5. The second of my four original portrait photos of WG, here again, dressed as "Robin." (Photographer—**Balfour's Photographic Art Studio, Main Street, Bangor**, Ireland.) From contemporary descriptions of "Robin's" attire, this photograph has been colourised for the front cover of *The Storyteller* by WG's great-great-grandson, Sean FG Lyttle.

APPENDIX E

Fig 6. From the third original portrait photo I have, showing WG, believed to be the **first in Bangor to have a telephone installed at a private residence**. (Photographer—Allison & Allison, Vienna Art Studios, 14 Queen's Arcade, Belfast.) A reversed image of this photo also appears on the front covers of *Robin's Readings*.

Fig 7. From the fourth and final original portrait photo I have. WG posed for this photograph **at a studio in Larne**. (Photographer—J Boyd, Main Street, Larne.)

Fig 8. This is the only '**family snap**' we have of WG but, unfortunately, no indication as to where or when it was taken. He looks to be, perhaps, in his 40's—so maybe the mid- to late-1880s.

THE STORYTELLER

Fig 9. Drawing of WG commissioned for **the front cover of *Lyttle's North Down Directory and Almanac.***

Fig 10. This photo of WG appeared in the **1894 edition of his *North Down Directory and Almanac***.

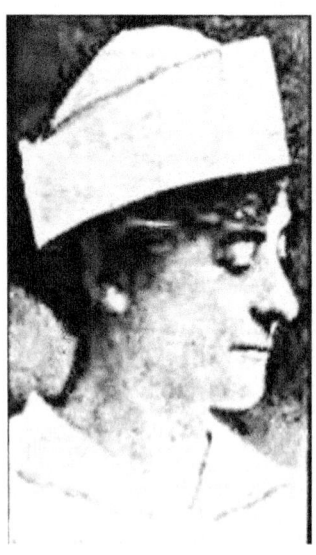

Fig 12. WG's son, **Roland**, as a young newly-married man, with his wife, **Maggie** (circa 1901).

Fig 11. WG's daughter, **Robina**, in her mid-thirties, from the *Long Island Daily Press*, November 16, 1926 who, it is believed, reproduced it, cropped from a photograph of her taken with some children of a Baltimore family where she was working as nursemaid (circa 1915).

APPENDIX E

Fig 13. **Roland with his wife, Maggie**, son, **Gerald** and daughter, **Eveline** (circa 1913).

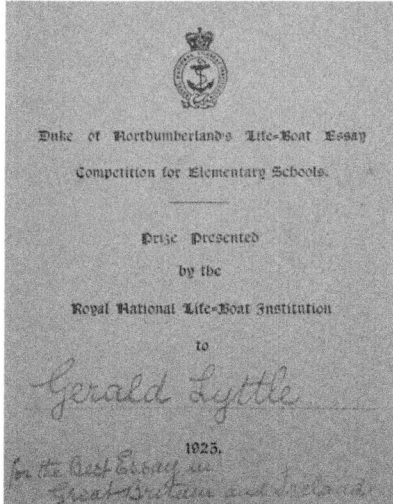

Figs 14, 15, 16. WG's **16-year-old grandson, Gerald**, who won first prize in the UK in the National Lifeboat Essay competition (1925), and the inscriptions in the limited edition book he received, "Britain's Life Boats" by Major AJ Dawson, signed by the Prince of Wales.

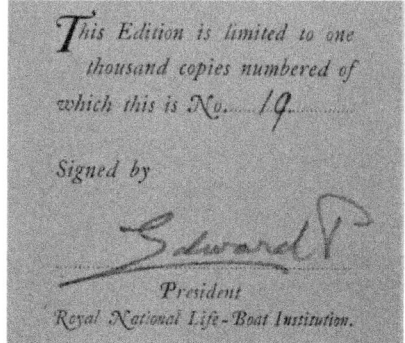

THE STORYTELLER

Fig 17 WG's grandson, **Gerald Lyttle**, headmaster, writer and broadcaster (circa 1975)

Fig 18. WG's great-grandson [left] **AG Lyttle**, retired Mgt Consultant, writer, and singer-songwriter; with [right] great-great-grandson **Sean Lyttle**, Senior Software Developer, actor and singer; along with [bottom] great-great-great-grandson **Joseph Lyttle** (photo, 2019)

APPENDIX F
PHOTOS OF LOCATIONS ASSOCIATED WITH WG LYTTLE

Fig 1. No. **16, Regent Street**, Newtownards (comprising in 2021, Ellison's Health and Wellbeing, Ards Dental Practice and The Man Cave) which was once the Ulster Hotel and before that a shop and dwelling where WG is believed to have been born in 1844. (photo, Michael Edgar, Newtownards)

Fig 2a. **St Anne's Cathedral**, Belfast (photo, AG Lyttle), built on the site of **St Anne's Church** (Fig 2b inset, photo provided by Archiseek) where WG and Elizabeth Courtney were married in 1864.

THE STORYTELLER

Fig 3. A row of modern terraced housing on **Denmark Street**, Belfast, replacing an older terrace where WG lived for a while after moving to the city. The spire of Carlisle Memorial Methodist Church can be seen in the background, a little way beyond which, WG worked as a teacher of shorthand at John Pyper's Belfast Mercantile Academy, while living here within easy walking distance. (photo, AG Lyttle)

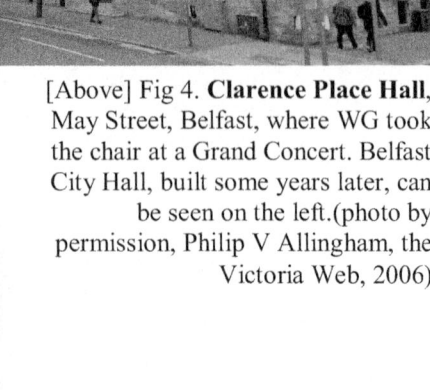

[Above] Fig 4. **Clarence Place Hall**, May Street, Belfast, where WG took the chair at a Grand Concert. Belfast City Hall, built some years later, can be seen on the left.(photo by permission, Philip V Allingham, the Victoria Web, 2006)

[Left] Fig 5.**No. 38 High St**, Newtownards (formerly No. 32) where WG launched the *North Down Herald* in 1880 (photo courtesy of local historian, Laura Spence)

APPENDIX F

Fig 6. **"Mount Herald"**, Ballymagee Street, Bangor (later, No 1, Ballyholme Road) where WG moved with his family and newspaper in 1882 and [inset] Fig 7. Workshops and garages behind "Mount Herald" where WG set up his print works in 1885. (photos, *County Down Spectator*, by permission)

[Left] Fig 8. **Name plaque from "Mount Herald"** rescued when the house was demolished in 1982 [photo by *County Down Spectator*] and [right] Fig 9. The **car park** which now occupies the plot at the corner of Clifton Road and Ballyholme Road where "Mount Herald" once stood. A solitary palm tree, one of two planted in the front garden after WG moved out, is all that now remains of one of Bangor's historic landmarks. (photo, AG Lyttle)

THE STORYTELLER

[Top] Fig 10. Author standing outside the ruined remains of **Betsy Gray's cottage** in 2017 (photo, AG Lyttle / Hugh Warden)
[Botom] Fig 11. **Betsy's Gray's cottage**, when it was still inhabited, circa 1900, with the late Mr George McCartney (from an old postcard held by Miss Jane Fletcher, great-granddaughter of Betsy's cousin.)

APPENDIX F

[Top] Fig 12 and inset. The modernised **"Grove Cottage" at Ballyboley** where the United Irishmen met. [Below Left] Fig 13. Rear of cottage showing the lean-to. [Below Right] Fig 14. Formerly there was no door in the lean-to. William Byers escaped from the pursuing Militiamen through the original window back in 1798. (photos, AG Lyttle)

[Top] Fig 15. **Ballygilbert Presbyterian Church** in 2017 and [inset] Fig 16. The interior with, its then minister, the Very Rev Roy Patton, who kindly allowed me to take these photos. This is the church where widower, WG, was married to Anne Byers in 1887 by the Rev John Quartz and where his grandson, GR Lyttle subsequently preached, one Sunday evening, circa 1960. These are believed to be the original pews in which WG's guests would have sat during his wedding. The present organ was not installed until 1949 (photo, AG Lyttle)

APPENDIX F

Fig 17. **YMCA, Wellington Place, Belfast** (demolished circa 1976)

Fig 18. **Wellington Hall**. The YMCA's capacious auditorium was "Robin's" largest ever venue—and his last. (photos privided by Archiseek)

THE STORYTELLER

Fig 19, 20. William Henry's grave in **Movilla Cemetery**. The inscription reads: "In memory of William Henry, founder of the *Newtownards Chronicle*. Died November 5th 1890 aged 54 years. Also his wife Sarah Singleton Henry who died Feby. 14th 1914 aged 75 years." (photos courtesy of local historian, Laura Spence,)

Fig 21. Yours truely at **85 Main Street, Bango**r, formerly, 1 Imperial Buildings, the address WG moved his family and newspaper to in 1895, and [Inset] Fig 22. The **Ulster History Circle Blue Plaque** commemorating WG's life, which was unveiled on 17 December, 2013 (photos, AG Lyttle / Anita Lyttle)

APPENDIX F

Fig 23. WG's Church, **First Bangor Presbyterian**, with its weeping ash tree that was planted in 1844, the year he was born (photo, AG Lyttle)

Fig 24. Plaque to the memory of **Archibald Thompson** (photo by AG Lyttle)

Fig 25. Jim Wallace, of First Bangor, shows how **Thompson's plaque is discreetly covered** by a hanging banner (photo by AG Lyttle)

THE STORYTELLER

[Top] Fig 26. The interior of **First Bangor Presbyterian Church**; WG's memorial stained glass window is the rightmost one on the ground floor.

[Inset] Fig 27. The **central detail** is of a robin standing on a leather-bound book.

[Right] Fig 28. **The stained glass window**, was donated by WG's widow, Annie, in his memory. It can still be seen today on the right as you enter the sanctuary. The inscription reads, "In loving memory of my husband W G Lyttle. Died November 1896." (photos, AG Lyttle)

APPENDIX F

Fig 29. In the background is the spire of **Bangor Abbey Church** of Ireland, from a contemporary photo of the period. The central lime tree is in the corner of the graveyard over-looking WG's last resting place. (archive photo)

Fig 30. **WG's grave**, with the monument erected to his memory by some friends. (photo, AG Lyttle)

The inscription reads: "Erected by a number of friends as a tribute to the memory of W. G. Lyttle, founder and editor of the *North Down Herald.* Born at Newtownards 15th April 1844. Died at Bangor 1st November 1896. A man of rare natural gifts, he raised himself to a high position amongst the journalists of Ireland. He was a brilliant and graceful writer, a true humourist and an accomplished poet. 'Robin' was a kind friend, a genial companion and a true Son of County Down."

Fig 31. **Bangor Abbey churchyard** where WG's remains lie buried in the far corner, under the spreading limbs of the lime tree. (photo, AG Lyttle)

APPENDIX G
PROMINENT BANGORIANS IN 1891

Following complaints that Bangor did not have enough magistrates, which came to a head one day when the Bangor Court House had a full schedule of cases but no magistrates turned up, the *Bangor Gazette,* 18 September, 1891, carried the story that claimed the Lord Lieutenant of Ireland's private secretary, John Mulhall, called WG for his advice on suitable Bangor citizens who should be appointed to the bench (see chapter 30). WG reeled off a list of over 50 suitable, prominent Bangorians which, for those readers who are interested, is reproduced below.

William Blessenden, Clanmorris Street
David Brown, Ormond Avenue
Hugh Blair, Clanmorris Street
Arthur Hall Coates, Seacliffe
Samuel Charles, Beaumont Terrace
Greer Cleland, Bridge Street
Mr J Campbell, Abercorn Hotel
Mr James Colville, Main Street
Samuel Cosgrove, Main street
James Crosbie, Ballymagee Street
William M'Cloy Currell, Stag's Head
Alexander Deans, Seacliffe Parade
Hu Furey, West End House
James Fletcher, Ballymagee Street
Thomas B Gorman, Bridge Street
Thomas Graham, St Agatha
Mr Hamilton, Glenlola
Thomas Hanna, Ballymagee Street
William Hanna, Main Street
John Henderson, Sandy Row
Thomas Henderson, Pickie Terrace
Paul D Hunter, Adrmore Cottages
William Kerr, Holborn Terrace
James Laughrey, Bridge Street
James Logan, Princetown Road
James Martin, Ballymagee Street
Thomas Matthews, Imperial Hotel

Aaron Minnis, Main Street
SG Montgomery, Main Street
Francis M Moore, Brunswick Road
John Moore, Mount Pleasant
Thomas Morgan, Main Street
David Morrow, Old House at Home
William Godfrey Murray, Oriel House
William MacDonnagh, Ruby Lodge
Dr Andrew M'Connell, Somerset Avenue
Samuel M'Cormick, Commercial Hotel
Joseph W M'Kee, Princetown Road
John M'Meekan, Clanmorris Street
James M'Murray, Glenlola
Robert M'Murray, The Baths
Charles Neill, Quay Place
Samuel Nelson, Main Street
John Peters, 70 Main Street
MJ Philipp, Main Street
WJ Salter, Pickie Terrace
James Sibbett, Martello
John Silcock, Main Street
John Smith, Main Street
T Smith, Mornington Park
Archibald Thompson, Princetown Road
John Tregaskis, Harbour Master

APPENDIX H

WHO REALLY WROTE *DAFT EDDIE*?

Derek Rowlinson, in his foreword to the 2015 Books Ulster edition of *Daft Eddie*, mentions that local historian, Kenneth Robinson, has pointed out "similarities" between *Daft Eddie* and a story that was serialised in the *Newtownards Independent* from February to May of 1872. That story was called *The Merry Hearts of Down—a Tale of Killinchy and the Ards* and claimed to be "compiled from authentic records of the county and written expressly for the *Newtownards Independent* by the Rev. J. B."

Upon comparing the text of this serialisation with that of *Daft Eddy,* I have found that it is not merely similar but possibly around 75% almost word for word the same! In fact, in a footnote to an article for the Upper Ards Historical Society in 2000, Kenneth Robinson mentions *The Merry Hearts of Down* and says, "This appears to be an early version of *Daft Eddie*, with Lyttle writing under a pseudonym."

It is, indeed, that similar. It is obviously the same story, which of course is to be expected, given that it is ostensibly a story based on records of true events. However two people can write accounts of the same events and end up with two quite different, if similar, tales. What we have with *The Merry Hearts of Down* and *Daft Eddie* are not just two accounts of the same events but essentially, in a large part, the same account.

Having said that, *Daft Eddie* is much the superior of the two written accounts. How can this be if they are virtually the same?

Well, the answer to that lies in the 25% or so that is different. If *The Merry Hearts of Down* was, in fact, Lyttle's first attempt at novel writing, his newness to the genre certainly shows. There are rookie writing mistakes such as instances of the repeated use of a word or phrase in close proximity and awkwardly phrased, or ambiguously written sentences—things that a copy editor, or, indeed, a more experienced writer, would easily pick up and correct. Was this Lyttle, finding his way as a writer, before he had begun in earnest to produce his much more polished short stories?

By the time the story appeared in the columns of the *North Down Herald* almost two decades later in 1889, Lyttle had published

THE STORYTELLER

numerous short stories and two other full novels that were much better written than *The Merry Hearts of Down*. Before printing *Daft Eddie* in the *Herald* WG set about editing the text to bring it up to what he considered an acceptable standard. He changed the repeated words, re-wrote the offending awkward sentences and generally improved the presentation by adding bits of extra background information and, from time to time, altering where the chapter breaks occurred to more dramatic effect. Perhaps most radically, where two strands of the story run in parallel, WG chose to rearrange the sequence of chapters in places, to realise what he believed would be a more exciting development of the tale. To a large extent I believe he achieved this and certainly, as I have said, the end result is that *Daft Eddie* is a better read than the original, *The Merry Hearts of Down*.

So who produced the original? A much younger and inexperienced WG Lyttle, accountant and teacher of shorthand, who might well have chosen to use a pen-name to preserve his professional anonymity? Or an actual clergyman with the initials J. B? There were a number of ministers around that time who might possibly have fulfilled the role. The Rev Mr Ball was at the Wesleyan Methodist Church on Regent Street in Newtownards; the Rev John Beatty was at Ballycopland, the Rev John Boyd led a church at Portaferry and there was the magistrate, the Rev Joseph Bradshaw of Milecross. I have no supporting evidence, however, as to which, if any, of these wrote the original story.

We have to ask, would WG really have plagiarised someone else's work even if it had been significantly edited by himself first? On the other hand, we must question whether the inferior style in which *The Merry Hearts of Down* is written could really have come from the pen of the renowned writer, WG Lyttle? What clues have we to the existence of an actual "Rev J. B."?

One compelling piece of evidence appeared in the *Newtownards Independent* on 14 September, 1872 when it announced the start of a new serial story, *Winds and Tides—a story of Comber and Ballygowan*, "written and compiled expressly for the *Newtownards Independent* by the author of *The Merry Hearts of Down*." There has never been any suggestion that this is another of WG's early efforts,

APPENDIX H

yet if it was not, then he could not have written *Merry Hearts* either. And there is more.

After the writing style of the period, the author of *Merry Hearts* makes reference to himself on a couple of occasions and these references are revealing. They both occur in Chapter XV of *The Merry Hearts of Down* and the first reads as follows:

> *The procession, as it moved on towards the town, received a perfect ovation from the loyal hearts that always lived in Newtown—aye, and live there still, as far as a country clergyman in this vicinity can know.*

The author clearly refers to himself as a minister living not far from Newtownards. The last phrase of the above quote is edited out in Lyttle's version of the story.

Here is the second quote:

> *...the house that M'Fadden built still stands overlooking the waters of the Lough under a new and happier name. And Martha M'Fadden, like the house, lived long afterward also under a new and happier name.*
>
> *Though removed a short distance from the home of her early days and living in a retired and quiet style in the midst of one of the most lovely paradises of Down, one of her grandchildren has lived to write this tale.*

So it seems clear that the Rev J. B was, in fact, the grandson of Martha M'Fadden, the daughter of the kidnapped magistrate—the girl whom Daft Eddie rescued from the smugglers. It is likely that this grandson first wrote down the story, learned from his grandmother, when he was much younger—circa 1830, and then adapted it for serialisation in the *Newtownards Independent* years later, in 1872. The author of *The Merry Hearts of Down* was, therefore, a distinct individual, a retired clergyman and *not* the writer and newspaper proprietor, WG Lyttle.

THE STORYTELLER

Interestingly, the second passage, quoted above, does not occur in Lyttle's edited version of Daft Eddy. Instead he states only that:

> *Mr M'Fadden died at a ripe old age, and not until grandchildren prattled upon his knees. Some of his remoter relatives are living in the Ards till the present day.*

Surely an oblique reference to the Rev J. B.

So, did Lyttle take the Rev J. B.'s story, considerably edit and improve it, and publish it under his own name? Why would such an established and acclaimed writer do such a thing—plagiarise the work of a fellow scribe? A number of possible explanations come to mind, though none that could readily be proved.

Lyttle's new *North Down Herald* claimed to be carrying on the tradition of the defunct *Newtownards Independent* and it is possible he may have acquired the rights to previously published material in that journal; possible, but maybe not very probable.

Another explanation could be that the work was actually out of copyright. Now if, as the *Newtownards Independent* stated, the story was "expressly written" for that newspaper, which only came into existence in 1871, then in 1889 the story must still have been well within the, then, copyrighted period of 42 years under the Copyright Act 1842. However the story contains a strange anomaly which suggests, as I have already surmised, that it was originally written at a much earlier date.

Referring to the smugglers' cave in the Tullynagardy Glen above Newtownards, destroyed by M'Fadden's rescuers, the quotation is again from Chapter XV of *The Merry Hearts of Down*:

> *To this day many of the inhabitants of Newtownards are ignorant of the position which the cavern formerly occupied. A little energy and perseverance, however, will easily enable them to find it, and the little knoll on the opposite side of the bank*

APPENDIX H

upon which poor Eddie sat when he received his wound is still to be discerned.

This presents us with a dilemma. If the above statement was written, along with the rest of the story, around 1871 or 2 "expressly for the *Newtownards Independent*" then it is patently false. The glen had long since been flooded by two dams that were built early in the 19th century to provide water for the mills that were constructed in that period. By the 1870s Eddie's cave had been drowned for decades beneath the waters of the High Dam. This passage is, in fact, one that WG 'corrected' in *Daft Eddie* where he writes, instead:

At the present day, the place may still be seen, but that ruthless scavenger Old Time has made many changes. Science and economy have destroyed the wildness of the scenery, by creating dams, the overfall of which now turns the busy mills. The tangled gorse and furze, and whins, and hazel are in a great part uprooted; a sheet of water flows over the spot where once the rabbit frisked.

The alternative explanation which must be entertained is that the statement made in *Merry Hearts* was true when it was written. I have been unable to discover exactly when the valley was flooded but an OS map as early as 1834 shows the dams and lakes already there so the dams must have been built around 1830 or even earlier. This would mean that the first draft of *The Merry Hearts of Down* could not have been written later than about 1830.

Could the Rev J. B., like WG Lyttle, have merely adapted an earlier text for publication in the newspaper columns. On the evidence of the quote about the cavern it seems quite probable (although, as I said earlier, he may have been adapting his own work.) When it appeared in the *Independent* in 1872 it would have been just out of copyright if the original was dated 1830 or earlier. It would certainly have been out of copyright eighteen years later when Lyttle published his edited version.

But why was no acknowledgement given to the original source of much of the text? When it first appeared in the columns of the *North*

THE STORYTELLER

Down Herald in March 1889 it was headed *Daft Eddie or Smugglers of Strangford Lough—a Tale of Killinchy and the Ards.* It was not attributed to any author. However, when it was published as a book, WG Lyttle was stated as the author with no other attribution.

Undeniably, the *Daft Eddie* that survives to this day owes much to Lyttle's skills as a writer, but huge chunks of it are not his own work. Why no recognition of its origins? To answer that question we must ask another. When was Daft Eddie first published in book form? It has previously been assumed that, as with *Betsy Gray,* the book first appeared soon after the newspaper serialisation finished; so that would have been in 1890, which is the date suggested in the Mourne Observer's 1979 republication of the book. Loeber and Loeber in their *Guide to Irish Fiction* (2006) put c1890 as it's original publication date, although they say they were unable to find a copy to confirm this. According to Derek Rowlinson in his Introduction to the 2015 Books Ulster edition of *Daft Eddie*, Stephen J Brown in *A Reader's Guide to Irish Fiction* (1910), says it was first published as *The Smugglers of Strangford Lough,* c1890.[305]

The National Library of Ireland's catalogue lists just three editions of *Daft Eddy*: Books Ulster, 2015; Mourne Observer, 1979 and R. Carswell and Son, 1914. I have been unable to trace any evidence of an edition prior to 1914—eighteen years after Lyttle's death.

Throughout his lifetime, whenever any of his work was published, whether in newspapers or in book form, following the title and his name there was always a list of a few of his other writings—for example "by W. G. Lyttle, author of *Betsy Gray, Sons of the Sod, Robin's Readings* &c. &c." But after 1890, when *Daft Eddie* was alleged to have been published, these lists of attributed titles never included that book. In 1894, the third edition of *Betsy Gray* was printed by Lyttle's own *North Down Printing Works*. It contained full-page adverts for *Sons of the Sod* and *Life in Ballycuddy—Vol 3 of Robin's Readings* and for his *North Down Herald* weekly newspaper. *Daft Eddie* is not mentioned.

---

[305] Actually, the entry for "*Smugglers of Strangford Lough* by WG Lyttle" in the original 1910 text of *A Reader's Guide to Irish Fiction* does not not show any publication date.

APPENDIX H

I am, therefore, convinced that Lyttle never did publish *Daft Eddy* in his own name, even though he could take much credit for its now being the fine tale that it is. But he did run the story, unattributed, in the *North Down Herald*. Why? I believe the answer to that involves three catastrophic events that occurred in his life during the year of 1889, any one of which would have been enough to dim a man's judgement. And how did his manuscript come to be put into print almost two decades after his death, erroneously attributing authorship to him? That, too, has a bizarre explanation that involves litigation to retrieve works of WG Lyttle being illegally withheld from his heirs.

The full facts are revealed and explained in Chapters 27 and 34 of this biography. That this eminent 19th century writer should have one less title to his credit does not diminish his brilliance in the slightest. The Storyteller, both on stage, and in print still preserved to this day, has eminently entertained many thousands in Ireland and around the world and continues to do so down the generations.

Publishing Note

Subsequent copies of Daft Eddy should have the Title Page changed to read:

DAFT EDDY
Or THE SMUGGLERS OF STRANGFORD LOUGH
A Tale of Killinchy and the Ards

Original story attributed to 'the Rev J. B.',
believed to be the grandson of Martha M'Fadden,
who was rescued by Eddie.

Fully revised, edited and extensive additional material,

by W G LYTTLE

(Lyttle's revised text first appeared in print,
serialised in the *North Down Herald,* in 1889)

BIBLIOGRAPHY

BRITISH NEWSPAPERS

Armagh Guardian
Ballymena Observer
Bangor Spectator
Belfast (Evening) Telegraph
Belfast Morning News
Belfast News-Letter
Belfast Weekly News
Caledonian Mercury
Daily Mail (Glasgow edition)
Daily News
Derry Journal
Downpatrick Recorder (Down Recorder)
Dublin Jarvey
Dublin Weekly Nation
Flag of Ireland
Freeman's Journal
Glasgow Bulletin and Scots Pictorial
Gloucestershire Chronicle
Irish News
Mourne Observer
Newry Telegraph
Newtownards Chronicle
Newtownards Independent
North Down Herald
North Down Herald and Bangor Gazette
North Down Herald and County Down Independent
Northern Herald
Northern Whig
South Wales Daily News
The Weekly Nation
Ulster Echo
United Ireland
Witness
Yorkshire Gazette

BIBLIOGRAPHY

AMERICAN NEWSPAPERS
Brooklyn Daily Eagle, New York
Daily Star, Queens Borough, New York City
Long Island Daily Press
New York Evening Post
Philadelphia Enquirer
The Standard Union, Brooklyn, New York City
The Sun, New York

JOURNALS, MAGAZINES etc
British Medical Journal, British Medical Association
Corran, Larne Folklore Society
County Down Portrait 1988-1989, Ulster Tatler
Distribution of Surnames/Householders, Ulster, mid-nineteenth century, Ulster Historical Foundation, c.1965 (online)
Ireland's History in Maps, 1845
Irish Templar W Erskine Maine, Belfast
Journal of the Upper Ards Historical Society, No. 24, 2000
Parish Church Magazine, Drew Memorial Church, Grosvenor Road, Belfast
The Shankill and the Falls: The Minority Experiences of Two Communities in West Belfast. Central Library, June 1, 1995, CAIN Web Service

BOOKS
Beiner, Guy, *Forgetful Remembrance,* Oxford University Press, Oxford, 2018

Bowman, Terrence, *People's Champion—the life of Alexander Bowman, Pioneer of Labour Politics in Ireland,* Ulster Historical Foundation, 1997

Brown, Stephen J, *A Reader's Guide to Irish Fiction* Longmans, Green and Co. 1910

Corry, Thomas Charles S, *Irish Lyrics, Songs and Poems,* D & J Allen, Belfast, 1879

Crossman, Virginia, *Poverty and the Poor Law in Ireland, 1850–1914,* Liverpool University Press

THE STORYTELLER

Dawson, Major AJ, *Britain's Life Boats,* Hodder & Stoughton, 1925

Dickson, Rev William Steele, *Narrative of his Confinement and Exile,* Dublin, 1812

Fenton, James, *The Hamely Tongue,* 1995, 4th edition, Ullans Press—Imprint of the Ulster-Scots Language Society, 2014

Lewis, Samuel, *A Topographical Dictionary of Ireland,* S. Lewis & Co. London, 1837

Lyttle AG, *Dillon's Rising,* AG Lyttle, 2016

Lyttle, Roland A, *"Herald" Almanac and County Down Directory, 1913,* North Down Printing Works, Bangor, 1913

Lyttle, Wesley G (editor), *Daft Eddy or The Smugglers of Strangford Lough—a Tale of Killinchy,* Books Ulster, 2015

Lyttle, Wesley G, *Betsy Gray or Hearts of Down—a Tale of Ninety-Eight,* Books Ulster, 2015

Lyttle, Wesley G, *Humorous Readings by "Robin,"* Allen & Johnston, 1879

Lyttle, Wesley G, *Humorous Readings by "Robin" Vol 2,* Allen & Johnston, 1880

Lyttle, Wesley G, *Readings by "Robin" Vol 3,* Allen, Son & Allen, 1886

Lyttle, Wesley G, *Lyttle's North Down Directory and Almanac, 1888,* North Down Printing Works, Bangor, 1888

Lyttle, Wesley G, *Lyttle's North Down Directory and Almanac, 1894,* North Down Printing Works, Bangor, 1894

Lyttle, Wesley G, *Robin's Readings—The Adventures of Paddy M'Quillan,* Books Ulster, 2015

Lyttle, Wesley G, *Robin's Readings—The Adventures of Robin Gordon,* Books Ulster, 2015

Lyttle, Wesley G, *Robin's Readings—Life in Ballycuddy,* Books Ulster, 2015

Lyttle, Wesley G, *Robin's Readings—Omnibus edition* Vols I, II and III, editor AG Lyttle, published by AG Lyttle, 2021

Lyttle, Wesley G, *Robin's Further Readings,* editor AG Lyttle, published by AG Lyttle, 2021

Lyttle, Wesley G, *Robin's Rhymes,* editor AG Lyttle, published by AG Lyttle, 2021

BIBLIOGRAPHY

Lyttle, Wesley G, *Sons of the Sod—a Tale of County Down*, Books Ulster, 2015

Lyttle, Wesley G, *The Bangor Season,* North Down Print Works, 1885

Mathew, HCG (editor), *The Gladstone Diaries Volume 12,* Oxford Clarendon Press, 1968

McComb, William, *Guide to Belfast,* M'Comb, 1861 (S. R. Publishers Ltd., 1970)

Mark-Fitzgerald, Emily, *Commemorating the Irish Famine: Memory and the Monument*, Liverpool University Press, 2013

O'Byrne, Cathal, *I Roved Out,* Irish News Ltd, Belfast, 1946

Robinson, Kenneth, *Indexes to the Newtownards Chronicle, 1873-1900 and the Newtownards Independent, 1871-1873*

Robinson, Philip, *Ulster-Scots—A Grammar of the Traditional Written & Spoken Language,* Ullans Press—Imprint of the Ulster-Scots Language Society, 1997

Teeling, Charles Hamilton, *Personal Narrative of the Irish Rebellion of 1798*, London, 1828

Three companion volumes have been released to coincide with the publication of *The Storyteller.* These are:

Robin's Readings Volumes I, II and III - omnibus edition*,* (AG Lyttle, 2021)—WG Lyttle's original "Robin's Readings"
Robin's Further Readings*,* (AG Lyttle, 2021) containing twenty-seven more of WG Lyttle's stories, including seven that have never previously been published in book form.
Robin's Rhymes*,* (AG Lyttle, 2021) an anthology of WG Lyttle's poetry.

All three are available as print-on-demand, from Amazon Viewbook.at/Readings; Viewbook.at/Further; Viewbook.at/Rhymes

Also by AG Lyttle:

Dillon's Rising
(AG Lyttle, 2016)
This historical thriller, set at the time of the Easter Rising in Dublin, is a tale of espionage, love and revenge and one man's desperate struggle to survive six days of slaughter and carnage on the streets of Dublin that would change Ireland forever.

Available as print-on-demand from Amazon.
See it at: *viewbook.at/DillonsRising*

Author's note:

I do hope you have enjoyed reading *The Storyteller*. If so, please consider leaving a review on Amazon

viewbook.at/AGLStoryteller

If you have any coments or questions, I should love to hear from you—particularly if you are the proud owner of an 1887 first edition copy of *Betsy Gray* or any copies at all of *Lyttle's North Down Directory and Almanac.* You can contact me here:

tonylyttle@ntlworld.com

With kind regards,
AG Lyttle

Printed in Great Britain
by Amazon